# Radicalism and Reputation

# Radicalism and Reputation

## The Career of Bronterre O'Brien

Michael J. Turner

MICHIGAN STATE UNIVERSITY PRESS · *East Lansing*

♾ The paper used in this publication meets the minimum requirements of ANSI/NISO Z39.48-1992 (R 1997) (Permanence of Paper).

Michigan State University Press
East Lansing, Michigan 48823-5245

Printed and bound in the United States of America.

26 25 24 23 22 21 20 19 18 17 1 2 3 4 5 6 7 8 9 10

Library of Congress Cataloging-in-Publication data is available.
cloth ISBN: 978-1-61186-229-4
PDF ISBN: 978-1-60917-514-6
ePub ISBN: 978-1-62895-285-8
Kindle ISBN: 978-1-62896-285-7

Book design by Charlie Sharp, Sharp Des!gns, East Lansing, Michigan
Cover design by Shaun Allshouse, www.shaunallshouse.com
Frontispiece: Bronterre O'Brien in 1839. Detail from a contemporary engraving.

Michigan State University Press is a member of the Green Press Initiative and is committed to developing and encouraging ecologically responsible publishing practices. For more information about the Green Press Initiative and the use of recycled paper in book publishing, please visit www.greenpressinitiative.org.

Visit Michigan State University Press at *www.msupress.org*

# Contents

# Preface

> Politics were seen as the way forward. . . . But I think we have to look at the other forms of Chartist culture . . . an alternative social basis, fraternal basis. This is something we can tend to miss when we look back if we see Chartism very much as a political movement. The question I think we want to ask is what are the things we might have missed by seeing politics much too prominently.
>
> —Dorothy Thompson, "The Chartists and Their Legacy," an address to the Bristol Radical History Group, 10 April 2010.

Based on a plan to democratize the system of government, Chartism was the largest and most impressive popular political mobilization in nineteenth-century Britain. It was a complex and diverse movement, with several important strands in terms of ideas and methods, and it had both an interesting prehistory and equally significant consequences. This book offers a detailed analysis of the career of Bronterre O'Brien, one of the most influential leaders of Chartism, and it relates his career—and the Chartist movement—to broader themes in the history of Britain and Ireland, Europe, and America during the nineteenth century. O'Brien (1804–64) came to be known as the "schoolmaster" of Chartism because of his efforts to express and clarify its intellectual foundations. The campaign for the People's Charter was a highpoint for him as writer and orator, but he was already well known before the campaign began, and during the 1840s he distanced himself from other Chartist leaders and from a number of Chartist initiatives. Why? This book will examine the personal, tactical, and ideological reasons and special attention will be paid to O'Brien's development of a social and economic agenda to accompany "constitutional" Chartism, in line with the evolution of radical thought before and after the Great Reform Act of 1832. In addition, it is necessary to evaluate O'Brien's reputation, among his contemporaries and among modern historians, in order better to understand his impact. His international perspectives and his legacy to later radicals will also be discussed.

Histories of Chartism began to appear while its roots and early flowering were still fresh in the memory. Over time the treatments have become more scholarly and more wide-ranging. Since the 1960s there have been many fine contributions to the relevant historiography as well as conferences and other academic events focusing on the Chartist movement. Students of Chartism have grown greatly in number. Clearly there is an abiding interest in the movement and in British radicalism more generally. This book is designed to contribute to a burgeoning of scholarly endeavor—to encourage further work on nineteenth-century British radicalism and, more immediately, to improve our understanding of it and fill some gaps in knowledge. It represents an up-to-date single-volume study of an important Chartist leader and contextualizes that leader's ideas and activities against the backdrop of political, social, and economic change. It explores his pre- and post-Chartist reform agitation and relates this activism to the ebb and flow of his influence and reputation. It is primarily intended to inform readers who have interests in modern British history, especially the history of nineteenth-century radicalism, and to complement other work in the field.

There has been no book-length study of O'Brien since Alfred Plummer's *Bronterre: A Political Biography of Bronterre O'Brien* of 1971; and Plummer's is in fact the only published biography. Much of his book was written before the Second World War, and therefore, despite its merits, it offers no engagement with the rich post-1960s historiography of Chartism. O'Brien features regularly in this historiography. There have been articles and chapters that focus on aspects of his ideology and conduct, and he gets at least a passing mention in most books about Chartism. O'Brien has also been the subject of several unpublished postgraduate dissertations. While building (gratefully) upon the researches of others, this book relies heavily on the writings and speeches of O'Brien himself and of those who knew and observed him.

The Introduction discusses the varying interpretations placed upon O'Brien's career by modern historians. Chapters 1 and 2 are mostly chronological in structure and provide a narrative framework for the rest of the book. They offer an account of O'Brien's career from the early 1830s through to the early 1860s. They describe and explain the making of the "schoolmaster," his activities as writer, speaker, motivator, and guide, his adoption of social and economic as well as political goals, his controversial abandonment of mainstream Chartism in 1841–42, and his subsequent campaigning for a specific and unique reform plan, mainly through the National Reform League that was formed during 1849–50.

Chapters 3, 4, 5, and 6 investigate the principal concerns and aims of O'Brien's career, grouped into the major subject areas about which he wrote and spoke. His priority remained manhood suffrage, but political reform was the means, not the end. Political changes—the democratization of government promised by the Charter—was to lead to fundamental social and economic transformation. For most of his career, and in his mature philosophy and the NRL manifesto issued by him at the end of the 1840s, social and economic issues were absolutely central. The O'Brienite creed rested on a combination of elements taken from his own experiences and ideas, from British political culture and the established tenets of political radicalism, from newer critiques of industrialization, class, capital, and labor, and from the values and aspirations professed in the early stages of the French Revolution. Chapter 3 elucidates O'Brien's concept of "revolution"—what it was, why it was necessary, how it should be accomplished, and what its outcomes would be. Chapter 4 explores "National Reform," O'Brien's radical program and its ideological underpinnings, which arose from the addition of seven propositions to the six points of the People's Charter. The six points had by this time become fixtures in the radical consciousness: manhood suffrage, annual parliaments, vote by ballot, equal electoral districts, no property qualifications for members of Parliament, and payment of salaries to MPs. The first three of O'Brien's seven propositions were meant to correct the errors committed by the "reformed" Parliament after 1832: the New Poor Law of 1834 to be drastically modified, sections of land to be purchased by the state and set aside for the unemployed, and the currency, debts, and taxation to be adjusted to lighten the burdens on the people. The remaining propositions would bring the permanent social and economic improvements that the people longed for (according to O'Brien) and without which a purely political reform would be totally unsatisfactory: nationalization of the land, conversion to a symbolic currency, establishment of a system of national credit, and the setting up of public marts for the exchange of goods and services. Chapters 5 and 6 demonstrate O'Brien's fascination with political, social, and economic relationships in the United States and in Ireland, his homeland, and they discuss the extent to which American and Irish circumstances might have shaped O'Brien's program. Certainly he believed that the United States and Ireland had need of the measures he was advocating, and that these measures could be implemented successfully there as in Britain and Europe.

Chapter 7 focuses on O'Brien's contemporary reputation and its personal and public dimensions. Without a positive reputation there could be no meaningful influence, and O'Brien was quick to defend himself whenever his proposals, integrity, conduct, or principles were queried or denounced by others. He saw himself as the people's servant, and he was determined to project this image, but as the years passed he complained that he had not been accorded the recognition and reward he merited. Though he had fame and influence, and some loyal disciples who preserved his reputation after his death, he also had detractors and enemies, and his place in the pantheon of radical heroes was not altogether assured.

This book, by examining O'Brien's career and placing it in context, offers a balanced portrayal. It highlights his talents and achievements while pointing also to errors and weaknesses, and it relates these to the opportunities and limitations of the times in which he lived. By exploring legacy and reputation, moreover, it will improve our understanding of the meaning, nature, and reception of the radical project to which he and others were honestly and deeply committed.

# Acknowledgments

I offer heartfelt thanks to my wife Catherine, our children Grace, Jill, and Ethan, and the rest of the family across Britain and the United States, for all the encouragement and good cheer that sustained me (more than they could possibly know) during the writing of this book. The kind interest of friends at Alliance Bible Fellowship in Boone, North Carolina, and in the Boone United O40s soccer team is also much appreciated.

I would like to thank Gabriel Dotto and everyone at Michigan State University Press who helped to see this book through to publication, and the anonymous referees who made many helpful suggestions after reading my original typescript. I have also benefited from questions about my work put to me at various times by colleagues and students at Appalachian State University and by participants at conferences and seminars in Honolulu, Hawaii (2012); Baton Rouge, Louisiana (2012); Mobile, Alabama (2012); the University of Oxford (2014); and Little Rock, Arkansas (2015). I am grateful to the Department of History and especially to the Dean's Office in the College of Arts and Sciences at Appalachian State for funding for research trips in 2011 and 2014.

Any errors or shortcomings in this book are entirely my own responsibility.

# Introduction

Problems of assessment must first be addressed in order to give an impression of the mixed opinions about Bronterre O'Brien that have been conveyed by modern historians. Disagreements about him and his legacy have persisted, in part because of the quality and content of the available sources, because of O'Brien's own volatile personality, and because his varying antiestablishment exploits are open to conflicting interpretations. These interpretations have of course been shaped by the increase in knowledge about events of the Chartist era, the influence over time of new research and intellectual fashions, and the political and other affiliations of the historians themselves. Some insist that O'Brien's importance has been exaggerated. Others suggest that he deserves more attention and respect than he has usually received. While it could be argued that there have been too many books and articles giving prominence to other radical leaders and underestimating O'Brien's role and importance, there is also the view that O'Brien was not as influential as he thought he was—or his admirers have claimed—and that the title "schoolmaster" of Chartism gives a misleading impression, in which case commentators have perhaps accorded to O'Brien a position to which he is not entitled. What follows is an inquiry into the range of opinions about O'Brien that historians have expressed. Some are more accurate and carry more weight than others.

O'Brien's rise can be traced quite clearly. He made his name with the *Poor Man's Guardian* (the most widely read of plebeian radical periodicals) between 1832 and 1835, and by the late 1830s he was well known in reform circles, and one of the celebrities of early Chartism, before breaking with the mainstream movement in the early 1840s. He continued to write and speak into the 1860s, but his reputation and support base were not what they had been. For immediate purposes it should be noted that O'Brien was generally overlooked in the memoirs of other Chartists, probably because he quarreled with them and because, in their experience, his importance had declined. Yet he was regarded by later observers as central to Chartism, especially by writers on the political Left. R. G. Gammage, admittedly, was a friend and supporter of O'Brien, but this is not the only reason why there were many more references to him than to other leaders in Gammage's *History of the Chartist Movement*, for the book can be read as a statement about the nature of British radicalism and about what radicals should think, be, and do. First published in 1854, Gammage's book was reissued some forty years later, rekindling interest in O'Brien's career and helping to make his ideas more familiar to a new generation of radicals. (In the late Victorian period, many radicals drew inspiration from Chartism and expressed admiration for O'Brien.)[1] In 1929 the Russian Communist politician and writer Theodore Rothstein, who had spent thirty years in England as a journalist and member of such bodies as the Social Democratic Federation and the Communist Party of Great Britain, published *From Chartism to Labourism: Historical Sketches of the English Working-Class Movement*. O'Brien featured in Rothstein's book as the most sophisticated and radical figure among the Chartist leadership. G. D. H. Cole, the journalist, historian, and university professor of social and political theory who was prominent in the Fabian Society and cooperative movement, included an essay on O'Brien in his *Chartist Portraits*, originally published in 1941. On the one hand, these treatments of O'Brien indicate that he remained a significant figure for the political Left. On the other, O'Brien has no entry in the thirteen volumes (so far) of the *Dictionary of Labour Biography*, which began to appear in 1972 and has come to be recognized as one of the most important sources for British radical and labor politics. This typifies the mixed opinions about O'Brien among modern historians.

In fairness to those responsible for commencing the *Dictionary*, however, it is possible that the absence of an entry on O'Brien is less an indication that he has been held in low esteem than a result of the policy of the founding editor, radical historian John Saville, who may have wished to hold important figures back for later volumes. In this case, one might wonder how long O'Brien will have to wait before he gets his due! Saville himself was convinced of O'Brien's importance, as he made clear in several of his own works and in his introduction to a reissue of Rothstein's *From Chartism to Labourism*, which appeared in 1983. Saville accepted Rothstein's positive appraisal of O'Brien's contribution.

To Saville, Rothstein was an intelligent commentator on the development of British working-class politics, "a creative scholar" for whom O'Brien, "understandably," was an "especial hero." This common admiration of O'Brien was not unmitigated, it should be noted. Although (in Saville's words) O'Brien was "a superb political analyst" who wrote "brilliant polemical articles" in the 1830s and promoted a necessary understanding of class struggle in British history, his ideology was inadequate. Based on Saville's reading of Rothstein, the main weakness was "the emphasis upon the *moral* condemnation of labour under capitalism; the failure to see labour, or more accurately, labour power as a commodity, and the inability to develop a coherent theory of exploitation which could take account of temporary, or long term, improvement in living standards."[2] As Rothstein put it, the crux of the matter was this: since the capitalist order was not fully formed when O'Brien wrote, it was not possible to discard "subjective" thinking and make "scientific" judgments upon it. There was more to it than merely "knavery and plunder which could be stopped by legislation." In time, O'Brien "saw the need of socialization of the land and of the means of production," but "the English proletariat . . . could not have followed O'Brien because it was just then emerging as a class, and its eyes were turned to the past rather than to the future. The component elements of the future were not yet visible." Even with mass support O'Brien could not have done more, because he was incapable of advancing beyond his early "discoveries." He was gifted, but limited.

> It was as yet impossible to separate the objective effect of economic laws from the subjective psychology of the individuals operating them, in other words, to distinguish between the mechanism of the exploitation of labour-power, inherent in capitalist production, and the excesses of individual employers of labour. . . . The thinkers of those days on the whole lacked a true perception of the objective nature of social and economic laws.

Offering evidence that O'Brien, if only intermittently, did arrive at this "true perception," Rothstein speculated that "the subjective mode was not really his way of thinking, but rather his method of expression." Nevertheless, O'Brien ultimately fell short: "Though we may admire the high level attained by his genius, we are bound to recognize a certain crudity in his ideas." O'Brien ended his career devoted to land and currency reform, and the economic theory behind these "pet schemes" remained defective.[3]

Apart from this, however, Rothstein was full of praise. Though different sections of his book were written at different times, before being collected and published together in 1929, the heavy reliance on O'Brien's writings was accompanied throughout with tributes. O'Brien had "breadth" and "originality" and "keen historical insight." In his prime he was "sharp," "profound," "far-seeing," and "brilliant." He was erudite, philosophical, and way ahead of his contemporaries, and he realized that social and economic change could only follow "the conquest of political power." Above all, he understood class antagonism.[4] Malcolm Chase is cautious about the Saville-Rothstein agenda because he thinks that O'Brien became a marginal figure; but Chase agrees that O'Brien was significant for taking up and recasting the emerging anticapitalist political economy of the 1820s and passing it on to later radicals in the 1850s and 1860s. As for Rothstein's use of O'Brien's writings, Chase points out that Rothstein had no choice but to push O'Brien to the fore: he wanted to stress Chartism's "revolutionary potential," and no other leader fit the bill like O'Brien (but it required some "sleight of hand" to turn O'Brien into the principal figure in the movement; and Chase also states that Rothstein's work was not widely read or discussed until the 1950s).[5]

Interest in O'Brien has been kept alive by many books, articles, and reviews, and by reprints of older works that were thought to be of use to later scholars. In 1916, for example, a series of studies of Chartism appeared under the auspices of Columbia University in New York. They included Frank Rosenblatt's *The Chartist Movement in Its Social and Economic Aspects*, which focused on the late 1830s and made extensive use of O'Brien's writings (though Rosenblatt thought that O'Brien had been overrated by other commentators). It was stated at the time that publications about Chartism were thin on the ground and might remain so because of the Great War:

> With the havoc that the war is making among the younger generation of students of history in England, it is unfortunately not probable that any book on Chartism by an English student can be forthcoming for a long time. Under these circumstances students of history all over the English-speaking world are under an indebtedness to [the authors] and to the department of history at Columbia University, for these distinctly serviceable studies of the Chartist movement.

Rosenblatt's volume was republished in 1967 (by Frank Cass of London), a result of and a contribution to the surge of attention given to radicalism, class, and "history from below" in that decade. F. C. Mather thought that the book, though "dated," retained its importance because it contained so many excerpts from O'Brien. Since the 1960s the book has often been cited, by Gregory Claeys among others, while its limitations have also been acknowledged.[6]

Numerous studies of nineteenth-century British reform movements have relied on the large body of sources now in the British Library collected and commented upon by Francis Place. An enemy of O'Brien, Place presented a picture of radicalism that reflected the goals and disappointments, the likes and dislikes, of nobody but himself. G. D. H. Cole used the Place Papers, which probably shaped his negative view of O'Brien's career. The same is true of Graham Wallas, cofounder of the London School of Economics and subsequently a professor of politics, and Fabian socialist in outlook, who published a life of Place in 1898. The original *Dictionary of National Biography* entry for O'Brien, dating from 1895, was written by Wallas. In this account, by 1837, when O'Brien wrote his "eulogistic" volume on Maximilian Robespierre, "his own opinions were strongly revolutionary and socialistic, although he never adopted the name of socialist." O'Brien soon proved to be "the best-informed man among the Chartists," but at the convention of 1848 he was "completely out of touch with the other delegates." According to Wallas, O'Brien achieved very little after the early years of Chartism, and, taking his career as a whole, he was a failure. Though he was "the only prominent Chartist who showed himself in any way an original thinker," and despite his "great power of attracting and preserving the affection of his personal followers, several of whom, though poor themselves, used to contribute regularly to his support in his later years," O'Brien inevitably sank into obscurity: "His literary work, though sometimes eloquent, was always rambling and inaccurate, and he was a rancorous and impracticable politician."[7]

The Place Papers were also used by Max Beer, a left-wing journalist and historian of British and international socialism who had for a brief time been a student at the LSE. Beer contacted Wallas in 1911 when he was working on his *A History of British Socialism* (published in two volumes in 1912, originally in German). He informed Wallas about his research and asked for advice. "I should very much like to have a chat with you on Chartism—also on the veracity of Place. I began reading his collection with a great deal of prejudice against him, but now my attitude has become more impartial." Beer added that "O'Brien interests me greatly." He remarked upon the limited availability of biographical information about O'Brien, and gave a summary of what his sources had so far revealed. "In my opinion O'Brien was a very able eclectic and an impressionable mind, easily susceptible to new and original ideas and essentially a rhetorician." He was a "scholar," but not an original thinker. "My assumption that Bronterre O'Brien was not the originator of the Class War Theory appears to me to be all but certain."[8]

In early histories of Chartism by Mark Hovell (1918), Julius West (1920), and Reg Groves (1938), O'Brien received several compliments but was more commonly subjected to negative, simplistic, and inaccurate judgments. Hovell described him as "clever" and possessed of "intellectual genius." If some of his writings were "educative" and showed "good sense," though, others were vague and difficult to understand. Above all, he was "somewhat cranky" and "uncertain-tempered." His career was ruined by "instability of will and conduct" and "very irregular" personal habits. He was dominated by "pique." Hovell considered him inconsistent. During 1839 he shifted from an aggressive stance to an abandonment of "violence and precipitancy"—having been "one of the stalwarts of the physical force revolutionaries," he decided that Chartists should draw back from militancy and confrontation. (Hovell seems to think that this reflects badly on O'Brien, but there was no dramatic shift. O'Brien knew from the outset that tactics had to suit the condition of the movement and that illegal methods would not work; and he realized in the summer of 1839 that most Chartists had no liking for violence. He also believed strongly in democratic accountability: the Chartist leadership should consult widely before making important and binding decisions on the movement's behalf.) During the 1840s O'Brien moved away—largely by choice—from mainstream Chartism. He "began to hedge." He was "drifting" and "clearly wobbling." By the end of the 1840s he was "virtually lost" to the movement, and, now a much less important figure, his program was merely one of several advanced by "Radical-minded Chartist seceders." Hovell's portrait is one of inconsistency and instability, of a man prone to bellicosity. As journalist and orator O'Brien was "virulent." Notwithstanding the supposed shift in 1839, he was a "demagogue" who went in for "vehemence" and "insurrectionary suggestion." Then he was a "socialist." His proposals were "communistic." His ideas were also those of "doctrinaire Jacobinism," and he was a "revolutionary" of the "downright" and "frank" sort.[9]

Apparently, Hovell was not quite able to make up his mind about O'Brien. Julius West had the same problem, though he was adamant about one thing: O'Brien's intellectual legacy was more important than what he actually did while alive. West noted O'Brien's democratic instincts and his "intellectual power," which was an asset to the Chartist movement; but West thought of him in the late 1830s as an "uncertain figure" who veered around the different radical factions of the time. He was an "effective" speaker, "but not overwhelmingly so," and in his journalism he "anathematized vigorously." His writing in the later 1830s was poor, "a curious, spluttering mixture of statistics and socialism, diluted with abuse of the government, with occasional excursions into the merely topical." As he broke with Feargus O'Connor and other Chartist leaders in the 1840s, his remarks about them were false and self-serving. His ideas were "revolutionary," but in the excitement of 1848 he advocated exclusively legal methods. He was both an "out-and-out" Chartist and a "socialist" and "Marxian." According to West, O'Brien had a lasting influence on radical thought. He helped to shape a practical democratic socialism that came to fruition in the twentieth century—not the utopian and philosophical type of the Owenites and communists, but a relatively benign state socialism (O'Brien was "the first preacher of socialism in the modern sense").[10]

Sympathetic to the political Left though they both were, Hovell and West did not see O'Brien in the same way—he was too "revolutionary" for Hovell, and the type of benign state socialism imagined by West reveals as much about that author's own preferences as it does about O'Brien. To Reg Groves, a communist writer and activist who was also for a time a member of the British Labour Party, and who—like Hovell and West—wrote history with an eye on the present, O'Brien was a disappointment. Groves recognized his "keen insight": O'Brien understood class conflict and realized that the workers needed their own independent movement and that political reform would be useless if it did not bring social change. But Groves was struck most by what he took to be O'Brien's moderation. The mature O'Brienite program for new laws on the land, money, credit, and exchange did not involve the abolition of private property.

> He was not a socialist or communist. . . . No doubt his writing could be quoted to give a more Marxian appearance, but his appreciation of the role of the classes and of the state-machine arose solely from his own experiences, though aided by the keen insight he possessed into the class relationships of his time. His was a reformist program, a number of palliatives rather than a socialist transformation, and, since it was reforms, not revolution, he wanted, he jibbed . . . at following the logical path of revolutionary struggle indicated by the Chartist demands.

Groves complained that O'Brien's radical stance of 1839 had been abandoned by 1842 when he openly cooperated with middle-class reformers; and after 1848, like other Chartist leaders, he was distracted by varying priorities that "failed to win the support of the Chartist workers."[11]

Observers who take the view that in recent decades O'Brien has been neglected might point out that although he usually gets a mention in books and articles about Chartism, there is little in-depth treatment. This is understandable: personal papers for him are scarce; his was not a particularly attractive personality; and historians have placed their focus elsewhere on the grounds that his involvement with the movement was more limited in time and, they think, influence than that of other leaders.

A great deal about O'Brien's life remains unknown. There exists only a small amount of scattered, unpublished personal material, which necessitates reliance on his publications, yet he completed few of his major writing projects, and important shorter pieces from the early part of his career were not revised or expanded later. The one modern biography of O'Brien, Alfred Plummer's, is detailed, and not lacking in insight, but it offers little discussion of the work of other historians before 1971 and of course no engagement with the massive Chartist historiography that has come into existence since the 1960s. Plummer appears to have completed the bulk of his writing during the 1920s and 1930s (he submitted the thesis "The Life of James Bronterre O'Brien" at Ruskin College, Oxford, in 1928, and published an article on O'Brien in 1929 in the *Economic History Review*; G. D. H. Cole knew his work, and, in the preface to the *Chartist Studies* of 1941, thanked Plummer, "who allowed me to make very full use of his, so far, unpublished biography of Bronterre O'Brien, of whom no other study exists"). The biography leaves gaps. Among the items not consulted by Plummer is the correspondence that Ray Faherty analyzed in 1975, which confirms that O'Brien could be crotchety and difficult, his personal disappointments, failed newspapers, and quarrels with other radicals having created quite a persecution complex.[12]

If some scholars of British radicalism have paid insufficient attention to O'Brien, others have made excellent use of the available sources to evaluate his career and to place his ideas and activities into a meaningful context. The publication of David Stack's edited collection of documents in 2007 indicates that interest in O'Brien remains strong and that there is awareness of his political and intellectual role, even if it is confined to historians who work in a rather specialized field. Younger scholars are contributing too, notably Ben Maw, whose PhD thesis "Bronterre

O'Brien, Class, and the Advent of Democratic Anti-Capitalism" (University of Swansea, 2005) has been followed by several published articles. Maw has built upon the research of, among others, Gregory Claeys and Noel Thompson, who elucidated the development of social and economic theories in the first half of the nineteenth century and drew attention to O'Brien's participation in that development.[13] Nevertheless, it remains true that while historians who wrote in the Victorian period and early twentieth century recognized O'Brien's importance, he was often overlooked thereafter; and though he is mentioned in books and articles that have been published since Plummer, he continues to be somewhat elusive. One might go further and suggest that the lack of an up-to-date, in-depth, book-length study of O'Brien's career is a glaring omission in the otherwise impressive (and rapidly expanding) modern historiography of Chartism.

Marginalized by some he may have been, but he has not been ignored. Among modern historians, Asa Briggs—whose edited volume *Chartist Studies* of 1959 opened the way for many subsequent researches—has appreciated O'Brien as one of the few Chartist leaders who developed a social theory and analysis, which included class rhetoric and the tracing to a political source of the workers' social and economic problems. Regarding "physical force," Briggs usefully stresses the difference between believing in it as the people's right and unequivocally encouraging the people to use violence. Some of O'Brien's more unguarded comments were taken at the time to be insurrectionary and seditious. Prison in 1840–41 taught him to promote radical change without taking personal risks—though also without sacrificing his principles and his forthright style. Violent upheaval was not a core part of Britain's history and political culture, and O'Brien knew that it was unlikely to occur. More likely and, for Britain, appropriate was a gradual, orderly, and nonviolent "revolution." Insurrection would not be needed because political and social change had happened, and could happen again, without it. Briggs sees this in O'Brien's philosophy and concludes that (prison or no prison) his methods were bound to vary, for Chartism was flexible and fluctuating: "The movement itself provided an education in political action. There were 'lessons' to learn or to avoid."[14]

Writing at about the same time as Briggs, F. C. Mather stresses O'Brien's impact as a platform orator and as a contributor to the *Northern Star* who—for large audiences and a mass readership—inculcated democratic ideas and explained the system of government, class relationships, and economic conditions.[15] Mather calls O'Brien "the most potent intellectual force in the movement and the writer of a fine polemical style," a comment prompted by the publication of Chartist material edited by Yuri Kovalev, a literature professor at Leningrad University. In line with a tendency noted above, O'Brien was overlooked in Kovalev's selection of sources! Like Briggs and Mather, John Saville has no doubts about O'Brien's contribution to Chartism and to subsequent social and political thought. According to Saville, O'Brien showed that the people could gain no satisfaction in the social sphere while their oppressors held political power, and that political rights were a means, not an end. The people had to understand how society functioned if they were to solve problems (those associated with land and money, for instance). Noting that O'Brien's ideas and proposals featured in wider debates about "progress," Saville thinks him remarkable for trying to reconcile the existence of private property with the rights of labor.[16] O'Brien's oratory, his ability to *instruct* and not merely to rouse an audience, and his effectiveness as an educator and a communicator of ideas, are highlighted by W. H. Maehl (who presents Chartism as planned, rational action, and its best leaders as men who could politicize the people through public speaking).[17]

Dorothy Thompson is more sparing in her praise. She argues that O'Brien was an important figure in the 1830s—and "at his best, the ablest of all the radical journalists of this period"—but much less so thereafter. While his writing for the *Poor Man's Guardian* and later for the *Northern Star* was especially powerful, "his main positive contribution to Chartism was made in its early years," and in the 1840s most of his writing consisted of mean and unedifying attacks on others. Having regarded himself as the Chartist movement's potential chief, his failings and foibles made him sensitive, unbalanced, and quarrelsome. In Thompson's opinion, the allegations O'Brien made against others were unfair and untrue, and though he claimed that he was standing on principle, in reality his clashes with O'Connor and the rest of the leadership were personal. Thompson's view is that O'Brien became unstable and paranoid. He could not hold down a job; his newspapers and other ventures collapsed; his friends gave him money and raised funds on his behalf, but he was constantly in need; and he repeatedly blamed others for his financial problems and loss of popularity, as if they had deliberately plotted against him. The real reasons why O'Brien sank in the estimation of most Chartists, insists Thompson, were his decision to combine with middle-class reformers and his rivalry with O'Connor. He chose to withdraw from mainstream Chartism: "Had he remained in its central councils, he might well have influenced its later development, but his personality and his delusions made that impossible." Thompson rejects O'Brien's criticism of the Land Plan, regarding it as a practical and useful endeavor, and doubts that O'Brien knew much about working-class life or understood the nature and potential of Chartism. Perhaps there is something to this. O'Brien preferred structured, rational, orderly forms of protest, but it is not clear how these could be reconciled with other styles and phases of Chartism—confrontational, enthusiastic, spontaneous, inclusive, and exciting. In the spring of 1847 O'Brien denounced the torch-lit assemblies, banners, triumphal processions, and other "trumpery" favored by O'Connor. Bluster and noise and excitement, O'Brien believed, were not in line with "true Chartism" (at any rate, this is Thompson's interpretation).[18] Thompson attributes O'Brien's eccentricities, at least in part, to excessive drinking. Other historians, including Stephen Roberts, Miles Taylor, W. H. Maehl, and G. D. H. Cole, have also made this charge.[19]

Thompson's opinion of O'Brien can be questioned on key points. That he was sensitive and could sometimes appear unbalanced and quarrelsome is indisputable, but it is not the case that his writings after the 1830s consisted primarily of personal attacks on other public figures. There were plenty of these, to be sure, but there were many more constructive reform proposals. Thompson's treatment of O'Brien probably owes a lot to her fondness and respect for O'Connor; after their divergence in the early 1840s the two leaders were never reconciled. She describes O'Brien as a "perfectionist" who refused to compromise *and* as flexible—"someone with a less intransigent attitude than the main body of the Chartists"—which raises the question of how he can have been both. He was probably not an alcoholic, and on major issues like the Land Plan there was at least as much merit in O'Brien's arguments as there was in the opposing rationale. Nor was he against all spontaneity and excitement in radical politics. O'Brien valued the social and participatory aspects of the Chartist movement. He just advised that circumstances mattered and that, as the occasion warranted, some forms of interaction were more appropriate than others (and by promoting a *thoughtful* radicalism he was purposefully distancing himself from bombast and the cult of O'Connor). Rather than public-house dinners, there were times when he commended tea parties and soirées because these were less expensive and enabled workingmen to bring their wives, daughters, and sisters. Another of the social and cultural underpinnings that helped to sustain the movement was the naming of children after Chartist leaders ("Feargus" was the most popular choice, but there were "Bronterres" as well). This can be related to O'Brien's call for established norms and institutions to be challenged.[20]

O'Brien's vision of an alternative culture was partly based on the high importance he attached to literacy and mutuality. He was a champion of working-class self-education.[21] But he was also willing to concede that formal educational bodies, despite their sectarianism or other flaws, should not be discounted. In 1843 he described Sunday schools in this manner, for they had taught thousands to read who would otherwise not have learned. At the same time, it was essential that the workers read only what was *useful* to them.[22] O'Brien made much of this in the *Poor Man's Guardian* and subsequently. Trashy ephemera that improved neither mind nor character was highly popular in O'Brien's day, but he was confident that "the gloomy mists of mystery and fiction will shortly dissolve before the rising sun of political and moral science."[23] O'Brien argued repeatedly that unless the people had control over education, it would remain a form of indoctrination. Knowledge should mean power, he asserted, and the most important knowledge to be gained was that concerning individual rights and the nature of government and legislation. People had to understand the causes of exploitation, poverty, and oppression. This, among other reasons, was why a free press was so vital. If the truth could be more easily communicated and explained, nobody could hide or deny it. Through knowledge would come unity, and through unity strength. All three were needed if fundamental reforms were to be secured. O'Brien railed against so-called improving bodies, especially the Society for Promoting Christian Knowledge (founded in 1698) and the Society for the Diffusion of Useful Knowledge (founded in 1826). These pumped out cheap publications that were supposed to inform and enlighten, but the real purpose was to mislead. The SPCK and SDUK competed with the radical press, preyed on the weak-minded, and tried to make the poor content with their station. Such organizations were part of a gigantic apparatus of subservience, fashioned in the interests of the landed and moneyed elites.[24]

What was at stake here was the ability to shape and direct opinion. O'Brien endeavored to form opinion from the outset of his career, when he first began writing for the unstamped in London. Patricia Hollis suggests that he helped to give the unstamped an "intellectual function"—the creation and coordination of the working-class mind.[25] O'Brien was in no doubt about the power of opinion, or the role of the press in making it effective. He told Robert Owen in May 1832 that most governments, whether monarchical or republican, rested on public opinion: "It is therefore of vital importance to gather up this Public Opinion—concentrate it on the Social System, and make it bear irresistibly on the Government, by the weight, unity of direction, and simultaneous action of all its parts."[26] The way to form opinion, O'Brien believed, was to use immediate and local complaints to open people's eyes to the bigger picture. Attention could thereby be focused on chosen targets. Instead of stopping at the new police, the national debt, the standing army, heavy taxes, factory conditions, misgovernment in Ireland, tyranny in Europe, or indeed any other specific issue, they could all be discussed together and combined in a general interpretive framework, one that taught the people about property ownership, class relations, political exclusion, economic exploitation, and social injustice. O'Brien comes across in Hollis's account as a writer who "always tried to turn isolated issues into a coherent public opinion, not just by broadening the basis of their class or regional support but also by meshing them into a wider ideological analysis."[27]

To Paul Pickering, O'Brien's importance was limited to a brief period—the early years of Chartism, when he was "the foremost literary figure in the movement."[28] Edward Royle and James Walvin share Dorothy Thompson's notion that O'Brien was at his most effective when he wrote for and edited the *Poor Man's Guardian*: he "brought to the paper a sharp intellectual critique of capitalism which went beyond the staple anti-clerical radicalism of the day."[29] This is in keeping with Hollis's remarks about the didacticism of the radical unstamped of the 1830s and O'Brien's role in the development of "a systematic critique of the established order and its magic circle of law, property, and economic power, which deliberately confronted many of the premises of the middle-class political economists."[30] Such statements tend to reinforce the impression that his career after the 1830s was disappointing and anticlimactic, but this ignores the impact of his ideas and activities in the 1840s and 1850s. Of course it would be wrong to exaggerate his importance after the 1830s. Equally, it would be wrong not to acknowledge his achievements alongside his shortcomings.

Ray Faherty's study of some of O'Brien's correspondence does reveal a bitter, disappointed, almost "hysterical" individual who blamed others for his misfortunes. Even his friends thought him unreasonable. Faherty has no doubt that O'Brien descended into a state of "near paranoia," especially around the time of his return to London in 1847 after a failed publishing venture on the Isle of Man. His irritability was hardly assuaged by the fact that O'Connor was at the height of his success and popularity. O'Connor was elected MP for Nottingham in July 1847 (he served until 1852), which made O'Brien all the more jealous.[31] Thomas Kemnitz's view of O'Brien as the most important Chartist newspaperman *after* O'Connor was exactly the type of judgment O'Brien wished to preclude![32]

To J. T. Ward, O'Brien was a "splenetic and changeable journalist-philosopher." He was passionate and intelligent; he was the only leader who understood the social and economic causes behind the people's suffering; he developed a Chartist philosophy and explained concepts such as class antagonism and the labor theory of value in a clear and accessible way; but he was a "militant" and "bitter, temperamental man" whose career after 1841 evinced one overwhelming feature: "His Chartism was evaporating." From the end of the 1840s, in Ward's account, O'Brien was long past his peak and did little more than rehash "old campaigns" and restate "his individualistic socialist views." His was just one of many contributions to the large and diverse array of "Chartist and pseudo-Chartist literary efforts" and the "ever-increasing variation of views among the diminishing Chartist ranks." The tone of Ward's observations is pessimistic. Still, it cannot be denied that "in adversity, Chartism was ever more splintered over largely personal issues."[33] Ward generally follows earlier historians of Chartism who were sympathetic to "moral force," condemned "physical force," and regarded O'Connor as a dishonest egomaniac. Another study of Chartism, by A. R. Schoyen, is slanted in a different way. Schoyen dislikes the middle-class reformers of the early Victorian age and thinks that O'Brien, among others, was wrong to propose an alliance with them. Schoyen alleges "inconsistency" and "ambivalence" on O'Brien's part, especially on Chartist tactics in 1839 and 1842; and, though willing to praise O'Brien's writings of the 1830s (he wrote with "ease and logic" and had "one of the finest polemical styles of the period," his invective "could be both bludgeon and rapier," and he was "the dominant intellectual force in shaping the radical ideas of the working classes"), Schoyen contends that O'Brien ceased to be important in Chartism after 1842.[34]

Ward is certain that O'Brien was no longer a genuine Chartist after his spell in prison (which "cleared his head") because he veered more toward socialism and advocated a coalition with middle-class reformers.[35] Not only does this interpretation overlook O'Brien's continuing and unquestionable commitment to the six points of the People's Charter after 1841, but it is also problematic in terms of how his socialist ideas fit with the desired coalition. Ward contends that the Complete Suffrage Union prioritized free trade and had no social program. This was not O'Brien's position, and though he joined the CSU he did not compromise his own beliefs and take up what Ward regards as the CSU agenda. Ward describes O'Brien as "changeable." What is more striking, however, is the degree of consistency in his ideology, notwithstanding the impact of events and circumstances, broken relationships, and personal resentments.

Another historian who exaggerates the effect of prison upon O'Brien's ideas and activity is Gary Entz, who draws a clear line between the years before and after 1841. Entz goes so far as to claim that O'Brien switched from "physical force" to "moral force," and, wishing to foster an alliance with middle-class groups, combined with Richard Cobden and John Bright and the Anti–Corn Law League as well as Joseph Sturge and the CSU. Entz interprets O'Brien's separation from O'Connor as the result of tension between militancy and moderation: most Chartists were militant, O'Brien left prison a moderate, and thereafter he abandoned the mainstream movement to go his own way. His radical social program, especially land nationalization, made him a "cult hero" and gave him an "intellectual renaissance" during 1848, after which the National Reform League propositions on the land, currency, credit, and exchange had growing appeal; but "O'Brien no longer possessed the nerve, and lacked the widespread popular support, to assume any sort of meaningful leadership position."[36] These statements about O'Brien emphasize a discontinuity that did not occur. There was no abrupt and blatant change of direction after 1841, and O'Brien did not relinquish a leadership role after 1848. There was more consistency than Entz seems to realize.

O'Brien's consistency has also been questioned by Ben Maw, who thinks that his radicalism "lost its bite" over time, with shifts occurring before 1841 that rendered him less popular and less important. Maw argues that there was an "agrarian turn" as O'Brien came to accept possessive individualism and prioritize family-based, small-farm production. This was followed by a more obvious abandonment of core parts of O'Brien's former democratic and anticapitalist political economy. He became a more temperate critic of the established order. Maw explains the shifts by pointing to personal circumstances that had ideological consequences, especially O'Brien's prison term, his job insecurity and poverty, his alliances with other reformers, his need to attract an audience, and the information he gathered about the kind of society that audience wanted.[37] Maw concludes that O'Brien's thought became fragmentary, but perhaps this is to confuse what was temporary (or tactical) and what was permanent. As the following chapters will show, there was continuity and consistency in O'Brien's career, not least in his concept of revolution, his vision of political change leading to social and economic transformation, and the whole range of commitments in his manifesto for "National Reform." After his time in prison he argued even more forcefully for many of the measures he had advocated previously.

Focusing on his role in "international democratic socialism," Gwynne Lewis contends that O'Brien's influence *increased* after the mid-1840s, the time when Chartist internationalism was boosted by George Julian Harney, Ernest Jones, and bodies such as the Fraternal Democrats, and when closer ties were established between British and European activists. O'Brien assisted in these developments, and his interpretation of Robespierre and Gracchus Babeuf and the first French Revolution, and the revolutions of 1830 and 1848, shaped the thinking of many of his fellow radicals. This, as Lewis suggests, makes plain one of the essential consistencies in O'Brien's career.

> Few, if any, British Chartists were more profoundly influenced by the example of French revolutions or learned more from the history of the defeats of the French working class than Bronterre O'Brien. . . . This detailed and continuing study of revolutionary movements in France represents the determining influence upon his actions as a leading figure in British radical and socialist movements, distinguishing him from both the British Owenite socialists and the sometime admirers of Marx and Engels like Harney and Jones.

Lewis points to this "element of consistency" and to "an honesty, a remarkable consistency" in O'Brien's ideas and activity. He stayed true to principles that allowed him to combine with middle-class reformers *and* attack the social and economic injustices he associated with capitalism. By "continuing to plough his own particular Franco-British furrow," he made an important contribution to post-1848 politics, and "no leading reform figure in Britain did more to lay the intellectual foundations for the bridge which links Chartism and twentieth-century English democratic socialism."[38] The French Revolution became an interpretive and political tool—as C. C. Barfoot and Theo D'haen put it, "not only the creator of rhetoric but the creation of rhetoric"—and O'Brien was among the first to grasp this and to employ the Revolution as a pliable and indeed indispensable device. His inculcation of a positive definition of "democracy," linked with his rehabilitation of Robespierre and his emphasis upon the salutary libertarian aspects of the Revolution, has been noted by other historians, and in Henry Weisser's study of Chartist internationalism O'Brien is referred to as the conduit—leading to the Fraternal Democrats—for radical ideas from the British and French traditions (whatever the skepticism of Marx and Engels).[39]

According to David Jones, O'Brien had exceptional "ideological integrity." Jones considers him a "brilliant" man of ideas who carefully explored social and economic problems, offered solutions, and engaged also with wider questions about democracy. He wanted a government that was truly responsible to the people. He spread knowledge and encouraged debate in order to help the working class to educate itself, and he kept alive an important tendency within popular radicalism, favoring the tactics "of the French Jacobin and not the Owenite communitarian." This last point needs qualification. French examples were very important to O'Brien, but he stood for nonviolent change, and his mature program was largely based on a communitarian ethos he respected all through his career, one he learned about early on through his association with Owen, even if he also decided that not all forms of property should be held in common. Another suggestion made by Jones is that O'Brien tended toward condescension, in that he harbored doubts about the inclusivity and excitement of Chartism and wanted a movement in which an enlightened few instructed and mobilized the many. Victor Kiernan has made similar arguments—the masses did not want the changes that radicals advocated for them; leaders were often from non-working-class backgrounds and tended to talk down to their followers; and these leaders considered the workers incapable of helping themselves and therefore in need of guidance—and Delbert Schafer thinks that, after the early 1840s, there was a disparity between O'Brien's radicalism and popular aspirations ("Perhaps his worst mistake was that he taught but never learned from the working classes. As time progressed, his ideas no longer fit the wishes of the workers"). Jones surmises that O'Brien's perspective provided "intellectual guarantees against disappointment": leaders should not promise immediate success, and radical politics should be "an exercise in discipline and hard work." Yet Chartism probably owed less to this type of approach than to noise, display, ritual, and charisma, especially in the Midlands and the North. O'Connor liked to think that his provincial speaking tours did more to create Chartism than did local mutual improvement societies and self-instruction classes, and among historians there is sympathy for his claim. If O'Brien was a little blinkered in this respect, however, in another he made a lasting contribution. As Jones points out, it was O'Brien who added the "capital versus labour" paradigm to the familiar radical critique of "aristocratic corruption," and who explained how and why social and economic emancipation was to be accomplished through political action.[40]

These remarks resemble those of other historians, including Thompson and Briggs, and can be linked with O'Brien's role in the international aspects of Chartism and with the place he has frequently been given in Chartist historiography. In the latter regard, one trend has been to distinguish between rationality and violence—between the moderate Chartism of respectable London artisans and the "hunger Chartism" of the more militant North—and (looking at his career as a whole, and remembering that "moral force" and "physical force" were not mutually exclusive categories) O'Brien was usually more comfortable with moderates than with militants.[41]

Some historians have demonstrated a bias along these lines. The books of Hovell and West published in 1918 and 1920 reflect both the increasing amount of information about Chartism that had become available by the early twentieth century and these authors' partiality toward unhurried, reasonable, nonviolent constitutional change (Hovell in particular was led by his reading of Francis Place and William Lovett to pronounce a negative verdict against O'Connor's radicalism, and while he recognized O'Brien as a man of ideas, he doubted his capacity for leadership). It was partly in reaction to this approach that Theodore Rothstein published *From Chartism to Labourism*. Rothstein, influenced by the Russian revolutions of 1905 and 1917 and by the rise of the Labour Party in early twentieth-century Britain (the party was able to form minority governments in 1924 and 1929), wrote with a message for the working classes: that compromise would get them nowhere, that "physical force" was necessary, and that they were being let down by leaders who were too moderate and accommodationist, both in the trade unions and in the Labour Party.[42] Given his agenda, it is not surprising that Rothstein made heavy use of O'Brien's writings. He selected those that best suited his purpose.

G. D. H. Cole's *Chartist Portraits* reflect his affinity with late nineteenth- and early twentieth-century British socialists who believed in a nonrevolutionary, unspectacular, gradual permeation through state and society of their collectivist principles. Cole's political leanings affected his treatment of documentary evidence and his opinion of O'Brien. In Cole's account, O'Brien's influence and popularity waned rapidly after 1841. By 1848 he had nothing to offer but "a curious mixture of agrarian democracy and protest against the developing abuses of capitalist monopoly." Since agrarian democracy was "out of date," and it was "too soon" to rouse the people against monopoly capitalism, O'Brien "fell between two stools." No movement was available in his lifetime to help him develop his theories, and "he floundered." Cole sees O'Brien not as a socialist, but as an antimonopolistic radical social reformer. Prison rendered him "much less revolutionary" (most notably in his attitude toward private property). Cole also speculates, as others have done, about the reasons why O'Brien did not set his ideas down systematically in one major book. O'Brien explained on several occasions that his poverty was the main cause, along with his friends' inability or unwillingness to help, and, more seriously, the denial of publishing outlets by malevolent factions that controlled most of the press. But Cole suggests a serious character defect: O'Brien was "never able to pull his thoughts together into coherence." He could not finish projects. Personal disappointments brought on depression and disillusionment, and after his term of imprisonment he was capable of no "sustained creative effort." He felt rejected. He was angry about the path Chartism was taking and resented the fact that his talents had not been more widely recognized. An original thinker and proficient speaker and writer, he enjoyed success with the *Poor Man's Guardian* in the 1830s, but then "his abilities ran largely to waste." All he produced in the 1850s was "the work of a man whose day was over." His essays in *The Rise, Progress, and Phases of Human Slavery*, published after his death, were interesting, concedes Cole, "but, like much of his work, they break off abruptly with the task less than half done."[43]

Cole's strictures seem excessive.[44] O'Brien's career was far from over in 1841, and prison might have affected his methods but did nothing to blunt his radicalism. His mature program was thoroughgoing, uncompromising, and built upon the experiences gained and principles explored in earlier years, and it attracted a highly articulate and committed (though limited in numbers) following. Cole's low opinion of O'Brien's character need not be accepted unreservedly. As for O'Brien's postprison writings, it can be clearly demonstrated (a primary purpose of the chapters that follow) that they were not without merit or authority.

That there was more to O'Brien than theory and intellect is the view of Patricia Hollis, who finds in his activism in the 1830s a "sense of the concrete." Though he was a man of ideas, he also knew and cared about the real condition of the workers and "the here-and-now of radical struggles." Yet it is mainly for his ideas that O'Brien was and is known. Hollis echoes the point about O'Brien's merging of older and newer styles of radicalism, especially the attaching of class claims and economic analyses to the established case against the exclusive aristocratic state and "Old Corruption." Hollis thinks that the older rhetoric remained the dominant one and that O'Brien and his fellow agitators of the "socialist" persuasion were in the minority. Their enemies possibly exaggerated their influence in order to galvanize opposition or to discredit plebeian political mobilization as a whole. The implication from Hollis is that O'Brien was a failure in at least one respect: he was one of those who tried without success to displace the older radicalism so that the newer form would hold sway. An "innovator" who sought to elucidate class conflict, economic exploitation, and the labor theory of value, all of which seemed so relevant to the politics and society of the 1830s, O'Brien had to accept that the traditional approach (targeting political corruption, aristocratic rule, monopolies, and heavy taxation) retained its wide appeal.[45]

Hollis overstates the difference between old and new concepts. The role and function of labor, for example, had been under consideration for many years and radicals were debating it long before O'Brien's day, although there was a novelty in that, previously, the value of labor was linked with the workers' spending capacity. The newer practice, associated with the class exploitation motif, was to compare labor's reward with that of the employers and to define profit as the part of the product of labor that "capitalists" seized for themselves. As Hollis shows, O'Brien was among those who made advances in describing all this: "Their technique was to collapse the newer analysis on the old, using terms that could be translated from one level to the other." Words were interchangeable. The task was to demonstrate the dichotomy between groups and interests—between the parasitical and useful, the unproductive and productive, oppressors and the oppressed, landowners and the dispossessed, capital and labor. The unjust burden of taxes, tithes, rents, and pensions was still condemned, but as a symptom, not a cause, and the mixing of ideas and vocabulary was easy because they were so flexible. Despite ingenious theorizing and writing, however, Hollis maintains that O'Brien and the others did not manage to supplant the older style of radicalism. Can it be assumed that this was their goal? Might they not have wanted to combine old and new concepts and terms, rather than remove older arguments entirely from the radical canon? Hollis pushes her thesis too far. A merging of old and new was not unreasonable or inappropriate, and "innovators" like O'Brien could be influential without having to replace one with the other. Hollis argues that in the Chartist period, as in earlier times, the traditional radical analysis was still dominant, but she also admits to some degree of integration, as elements of the new analysis became "an accepted and important part of working-class radicalism." Although O'Brien's creed was adopted by only a small number, many more expressed gratitude to him for making them aware of problems and ideas they had not thought about before, and by the 1850s popular politics were not what they had been fifty or sixty years earlier. Nevertheless, Hollis contends, the O'Brienite and "socialist" impact is easily exaggerated: "The socialist authors . . . did not create or manipulate a working-class radical public. They were one group among many clamoring for hearers."[46]

This has been reiterated by Noel Thompson, who regards the noticeably less thorough and less confrontational tone in radical politics between the 1840s and 1880s as a sign of changing attitudes toward Britain's economic development. Though some were still suspicious of free markets, others were not, and there were proposals to integrate different approaches (competition *and* control, whether communitarian or statist). O'Brien remains noteworthy because he kept up a scrutiny of social and economic arrangements that both rested on older theories and anticipated arguments taken up later, and he was ideologically consistent. One of his achievements was in shoring up the popular attachment to and facilitating further discussion of the "moral economy." Following up on E. P. Thompson's study of this web of mutual rights and obligations, community bonds, and traditional face-to-face fair dealing, Sharon Bolton and Knut Laaser have identified O'Brien as one of the defenders of a stable moral order against a self-regulating, market-based system. Concerned about the plight of the worker, O'Brien highlighted the social costs of "progress" (with its increased production and cheaper commodities). In doing so, with others, he helped to prolong the relevance of older notions about an economy that met human needs—or what Bolton and Laaser call "a moral architecture which framed economic practices with shared values of subsistence rights, redistribution, reciprocity, and mutuality." O'Brien was no small-minded decrier of the Industrial Revolution. Rather, he thought that "progress" could and should be guided along just and beneficial paths, and he stood with those who opposed "primitive accumulation" and the commodification of labor, land, and money. He would not be out of place today with those who deny that, in the words of Bolton and Laaser, "a disembedded and self-regulated market can exist without destroying the human character of labour and the natural resources of the environment." Thanks partly to O'Brien, the meaning of "moral economy" was extended, and Peter Linebaugh notes that scholars since E. P. Thompson have also used the phrase in an expansive way. From a term describing the eighteenth-century crowd's repertoire of responses to the market, it has come to include "customary practices of production," and "entitlement to necessities of life," and "values other than accumulation in economic planning."[47]

O'Brien features in a small way in E. P. Thompson's *The Making of the English Working Class*, originally published in 1963. Though Thompson's coverage does not extend much into the years after 1832, he has no doubts about O'Brien's significance (which might or might not tally with his wife Dorothy's assertion that O'Brien ceased to be important after the 1830s). E. P. Thompson is impressed most by O'Brien's role in the "war of the unstamped" (during which he "consciously sought to develop working-class Radical theory") and by his commitment to an alternative social and economic order, shaped primarily by Owenite communitarian impulses (and Thompson rightly declares: "It is easy, in retrospect, to see this spirit as naïve or 'utopian' but there is nothing in it which entitles us to regard it with academic superiority"). In E. P. Thompson's view, O'Brien was "an authentic voice of his times," and his writings "are a central thread through the abundant agitations of the early 1830s, providing a nexus for the old democratic claims, the social agitations (against the New Poor Law and for Factory Reform), the Owenite communitarian experiments, and the syndicalist struggles of the trade unions." O'Brien *did* bring together and carry forward these campaigns—and if Thompson's assessment of him as the "theorist of stature" who *defined* "the working-class predicament" is a little overblown, it is undeniable that O'Brien "was very far from being an eccentric at the edges of the movement."[48] E. P. Thompson's respect for O'Brien offers another reminder of the latter's status in and relevance to the British Left.

O'Brien's biographer Alfred Plummer regards him as "zealous" and "persistent," one of the "pioneers of the British working-class movement," and a pivotal figure who created a sense of continuity between past struggles and a future "promised land." He "spent a lifetime on the frontier of politics and did much to pioneer the way to the welfare state." Though he finished few of the large-scale literary projects he began, he was, among other things, "the chief channel through which the influence of the French Revolution reached the working people of his day." He was one of the few radicals who turned ideas into practical programs, and he longed to improve the condition of the workers. One should look to O'Brien not for meticulous socialist theory, Plummer argues, but for a series of reforms that were meant to alter state and society and establish a government that would respond to the problems posed by industrial and commercial development. O'Brien influenced and was influenced by other radicals, and Plummer thinks that his main legacy was his contribution to criticism of nineteenth-century capitalism.[49]

Plummer's O'Brien had his flaws. He was naive and overoptimistic. He expected victorious reform mobilizations once political, social, and economic problems were properly exposed and explained. When setting up his newspapers he was "over-sanguine as always." At one stage he thought that *Bronterre's National Reformer* might sell fifty thousand copies a week, but it never approached anything like this, and when it folded its sales amounted to about four thousand a week. Later, he wanted the *Southern Star* to have the same impact in the southern counties that the *Northern Star* was having in the industrial North, a wildly unrealistic fancy. In fairness to O'Brien, though, it should be remembered that many radical papers failed, for this was an overcrowded field. O'Brien's lack of success as a newspaper proprietor had multiple causes. It cannot be assumed that failure was entirely his fault. In other respects, Plummer is ready to give credit where it is due. He compliments O'Brien for his intellectual caliber and command of language. He thinks he was a visionary, ahead of his time, and argues that for all his temperamental defects he would have made a better member of Parliament than O'Connor.[50]

Confinement in Lancaster Castle from April 1840 to September 1841 is regarded by many historians as a turning point in O'Brien's career (though it was less important than the breach with O'Connor that followed). Plummer emphasizes O'Brien's role before prison, especially in the "war of the unstamped" and in early Chartism. He was recognized as a bold theorist and a highly effective communicator. While the campaign against newspaper taxes was exciting and satisfying for O'Brien, however, Chartism was dogged by obstacles and divisions, and Plummer contends that he made a mistake by siding initially with the militant wing when his skills were more appropriate for peaceful agitation utilizing press and platform. After his release from prison he was determined never to return there, and though he remained committed to radical reform, he knew that it would not come quickly. He became more cautious, Plummer thinks. Yet he was also a divisive figure, turning against former allies for a range of offenses, personal and public. For his sharp intellect and literary talents he earned the title "schoolmaster," but Plummer suggests that here, again, O'Brien made mistakes, overestimating the reasoning capabilities of the working class and failing to adapt his message to suit his audience. Having made his reputation with short, clear, hard-hitting essays and editorials, he put many people off with his longer and more densely packed publications. Even so, and despite the lack of a definitive treatise covering all of the political, social, and economic issues that concerned him, he did provide ideas and arguments that shaped later debates. He influenced the evolution of socialism (Marx knew of him and adopted some of his ideas and terminology). Later commentators on Owenism, Chartism, knowledge, welfare, class, the state, and indeed any of the other subjects tackled by O'Brien were in his debt. Plummer pays tribute to the "range and penetration of his mind" and calls him "an outstanding political pioneer" who opened the way for a range of reforms. He was an activist of "outstanding insight, originality, and courage, coupled with a passion for social and political progress." Long after his death, O'Brienites were still pressing for land nationalization and their Eclectic Institution continued to provide adult education in London.[51]

These O'Brienites were involved in several organizations and political campaigns. As Mark Bevir points out, in some cases they built upon the democratic ideas and strategy of O'Brien by bringing in other components, including elements taken from Marxist and other forms of socialism. This marked not an abandonment of the popular radicalism of the Chartists but a process of adaptation that created something new. Bevir shows that while the O'Brienites upheld their hero and his program and were not converted wholesale to alternative proposals, they were affected by the circumstances and debates of the late nineteenth century, and they added to their earlier beliefs (there was a "subtle shift," Bevir explains, not a "sudden conversion").[52] Some stayed closer to O'Brien's teachings than others, and those who proposed, set up, and went to live in the O'Brienite colony in Kansas in the late 1860s and early 1870s were among the most devoted. They were certain that the National Reform League's program could work in practice, and they wanted to prove that it could. For them, nothing else would do. Gary Entz suggests that their dogmatism and inflexibility ("uncompromising O'Brienite rigor") contributed to the breakdown of the Kansas experiment.[53] In their single-mindedness they were much like O'Brien himself, for he also pursued the NRL program relentlessly, ruled out compromise, and disparaged alternative reform strategies.

Historians' verdicts on the extent to which O'Brien had continuing appeal and relevance depend in part on the changes they think occurred in British radicalism. After 1848, according to Miles Taylor, O'Brien was "passed over" by more successful radical journalists who enjoyed mass circulation, and former Chartists became less autonomous as they joined with other reform movements in a "drift" back to the coalition-building that Taylor sees as typical of pre-Chartist popular politics. Socialist and republican preferences were subsumed in an older political analysis prioritizing "Old Corruption." Agitation against the Crimean War in the 1850s brought together groups that had been rivals just a decade before, and O'Brien, though at first he condemned the "drift," was soon a participant. Taylor argues that "the Chartist leadership responded to the defeat of the movement, and the loss of its mass following, by rejoining and becoming reconciled to the mainstream of radical and liberal politics." The militancy and polarization of the early 1840s was gone. Goals and tactics became more explicitly constitutionalist, as in former times, and there was more talk of combined working- and middle-class pressure on the government for "retrenchment and reform," with an effort to unite with pro-reform MPs in the House of Commons and less emphasis on manhood suffrage. Although some newer ideas were embraced on the land question, Taylor writes, most British radicals eschewed socialism, and when they argued for a fairer distribution of wealth and opportunity, they still had in mind individual rather than collective ownership of the land.[54] Growing respect for the constitution has also been noted by Robert Saunders, who links it with Britain's comparative stability and prosperity in the 1850s and 1860s. There was a post-Chartist "reimagining of the working man." No longer dangerous and subversive, the worker was encouraged, and widely reckoned, to be sober and sensible and devoted to savings banks, respectability, and self-improvement. It was on this basis that a case was made for an extension of political rights.[55]

The changing course of British radicalism has been explained in a similar way by Bernard Moss. While admitting that economic growth and a more flexible, conciliatory approach by the government had major effects, Moss accords most importance to the fall of Chartism—due to its own divisions and the use of coercive power by the state—and the tendency of organized labor, especially the skilled, to seek limited sectional goals within the established order (they accepted market capitalism, Moss explains). By the end of the 1850s radicalism was tamed: "Incorporation into the state and industry was made possible by the defeat of working-class radicalism and the capital export boom. . . . This involved the concession, by employers and the government, of bargaining rights and limited suffrage in return for an acknowledgement of property rights, managerial prerogatives, and the British constitution."[56]

O'Brien consciously and intentionally stood apart from and condemned most of these developments. His relevance was not lost. For those who continued to feel alienated and aggrieved by prevalent economic relationships and the system of government, O'Brien was a principal spokesman (and, as Janet McCalman has argued, social "embourgeoisement" did not necessarily lead to political moderation).[57] O'Brien went on agitating for collective, not individual, ownership of the land, as part of the NRL program announced in 1849–50, and he was not in favor of the "drift" posited by Miles Taylor beyond a temporary tactical juncture with other groups on specific issues. Any idea that O'Brien was no longer willing or able to follow his own path is incorrect.

Mention has often been made by historians and political scientists of the debt owed by Marx and late nineteenth-century socialists to earlier thinkers such as O'Brien. On some matters there was disagreement. Marx defined class in economic terms, and for him class did not exist unless there was an awareness of itself and its interests as opposed to the interests of other classes. This is a more rigid version of class than that elaborated in O'Brien's heyday, when political as well as economic definitions were used, and class was not necessarily understood as a homogeneous entity. O'Brien was acutely aware of the gap between classes. It gave them coherence and identity, and one of its most obvious indicators was possession and nonpossession of the vote. The vote was so important to O'Brien's perspective that he could assume a class consciousness without having to adopt a definition of class that accorded with the later definition established by Marx. Another difference was that O'Brien posited gradual and peaceful change in state and society, whereas Marx advocated upheaval and discontinuity. In addition, Marx's idea of revolution as the outcome of mass consciousness conflicts with Babeuf's notion of revolution as the work of minorities, transmitted to later generations by O'Brien's translation of *Buonarroti's History of Babeuf's Conspiracy*, published in 1836. O'Brien's association with Philippe Buonarroti helped to ensure continuity in revolutionary, patriotic, and egalitarian philosophies that were international in their nature and appeal. If the dichotomy between enlightened minority and mass movement had a debilitating effect in the long term, by adding common ownership to elements of Jacobin democracy O'Brien and his fellow travelers enriched the revolutionary thread and facilitated its longevity. Samuel Bernstein has made this plain in a series of articles (Bernstein's affiliations were with the political Left). As well as regarding O'Brien's as the most important and influential translation of Buonarroti, Bernstein described O'Brien as the main representative of Jacobinism in Britain in this period and "perhaps the best mind Chartism brought forth."[58]

O'Brien's research and writing about Babouvism was not without risk, which testifies to his courage (one of the precautions taken by him and Buonarroti when they became acquainted in the mid-1830s was the use of anagrams to identify surviving followers of Babeuf). As David Thomson puts it, Babouvism "would have remained a tragic and picturesque historical incident . . . had there not been this timely reminder of the story in Buonarroti's book." Babouvism's survival also impressed Ulysses Weatherly, who, in the early twentieth century, opined that Marxism owed more to French than to British sources, and in the same period the Russian-born economic historian Vladimir Simkhovitch made use of O'Brien's translation of Buonarroti in a piece linking Babouvism with class struggle. Non-French as well as French contributions to nineteenth-century socialism, and the mixed effects of Buonarroti's book, have received attention in several more recent works.[59]

O'Brien's translation of Buonarroti was reissued in 1965 (by New York publisher Augustus M. Kelley). One reviewer welcomed the reprint on the grounds that the original English edition of 1836 had become almost impossible to find. Furthermore:

> This classic study, first published in 1828 by a leading figure in the movement which is its subject, is the definitive history of Babouvism, despite the fact that it was written three decades after the event largely from memory, a consequence of the fact that the bulk of the relevant documents had been seized by the police following the arrest of Babeuf. Those documents which, fortunately, survived are reproduced in the second half of the present volume. The doctrines of Babeuf were less important as operative principles than as a seminal source upon which later socialists drew.[60]

Again, O'Brien's determination to pass this "seminal source" on to future radical movements should not be underestimated; and when a French historian of Chartism, Edouard Dolléans, used many of O'Brien's writings for volumes he published in 1913, he showed thereby that some of the language and concepts generally regarded as "Marxist" were absorbed into British radicalism by the 1830s.[61] More recently, Joel Wiener and Richard Ashcraft have named O'Brien as one of the figures who linked different generations of radicals. O'Brien helped to connect the essentially eighteenth-century "undifferentiated appeal to 'the People,'" as seen in Thomas Paine's writing, with the more sophisticated approach of the "socialist precursors of Marx," who raised the demand for "democracy" in industry as well as politics and pitted the "rights of labour" against the "tyranny of capital."[62] In a similar fashion, Desmond Morton associates O'Brien with an "English School" from which Marx and other European socialists adopted many ideas, and Christiane Eisenberg has outlined some lasting differences between British and German popular politics. "The pervasive myth that the British are pragmatic moderates even in their radicalism," Morton argues, "has obscured the contribution of the so-called English School to the development of socialist thought in the nineteenth century." While French and German socialists tended to focus on the natural right to subsistence, in Britain there was more individualism and voluntarism in radical politics and more interest in the workers' right to the whole product of their labor: "Oppression could be explained by the unearned surplus extracted by capitalists, landlords, and aristocrats, to say nothing of government tax collectors." This was an ideology that O'Brien did much to develop.[63]

Other writers on the political Left have named O'Brien among the precursors and inspirers of movements to which they adhered, at least in a minor way. In some cases this can only be because they have chosen to see in O'Brien what they wanted to see; but equally, there are concerns that they shared with him and theirs was a comparable search for solutions. In a centenary edition of the English translation of the *Communist Manifesto*, published in 1948, a new introduction was added by Harold Laski, the socialist intellectual and university professor, apologist for the Soviet Union, and erstwhile chairman of the Labour Party. Laski, not unlike Rothstein had done in *From Chartism to Labourism*, treated O'Brien as an early British forerunner of international socialism. This impression was given new life in 1999 when Laski's piece was reprinted (to mark the 150th anniversary of the *Communist Manifesto*). Another left-winger, Max Morris, a pupil of Laski who went on to be a teacher, trade unionist, communist leader, and—much later—local councilor (for the Labour Party, in London), argued that nobody did more than O'Brien to show the need for a broad working-class political movement. O'Brien uncovered both the class nature of the British state and the economic basis of class rule. He helped to create "a coherent proletarian outlook," a "popular heritage," and "a working-class political philosophy," and he made these available to later thinkers and activists.[64] When Morris published a collection of documents to illustrate the development of radicalism between 1815 and 1848, O'Brien featured prominently; and in Morris's editorial comments there was the now familiar praise for "the outstanding thinker and most effective writer of the Chartist movement."[65]

O'Brien was a talisman for the political Left during the 1980s and 1990s, a time when the Left in Britain was weak and in need of revival. To Joan Maynard, who served on the National Executive of the Labour Party and was MP for Sheffield Brightside (1974–83), O'Brien was a paragon. She learned her politics from British history and culture, from domestic rather than external sources (she was "a very English socialist").[66] In June 1996 an address was delivered over O'Brien's grave at Abney Park Cemetery, in Stoke Newington, London, by Arthur Scargill, a leader of the recently founded Socialist Labour Party and former president of the National Union of Mineworkers. Scargill had risen to national prominence during the Miners' Strike of 1984–85. An ardent and controversial class warrior, he argued in his address that O'Brien had much to teach the workers of the late twentieth century.

> I understand what Chartism has meant in the long development of the working class—my class. . . . The struggles of the Chartist movement, and the work of Bronterre O'Brien, are part of our heritage, and in examining that heritage I am reminded of the past and inspired for the future. . . . It is clear, from the days of

> O'Brien to the present, that there is no way to ameliorate the attacks the capitalist system will make on the working class. It has become clear that massive political change is essential if workers and their families are to defend themselves.[67]

Left-wingers in British politics and the labor movement have retained an abiding sense of affinity with O'Brien and his ideology. O'Brien was a central figure in the development of non-Marxist and Marxist forms of socialism.

While describing Marx's thought as more sophisticated than O'Brien's, Paul Sweezy has also suggested that some components of Marxism were based upon O'Brienite foundations. "In later life," according to Sweezy, "O'Brien became rather a commonplace currency crank," but "this has unfortunately tended to obscure the fact that in his prime during the 1830s he was one of the most vigorous and original thinkers yet produced by the British working class movement." Marx coalesced for a time with the O'Brienites of the National Reform League. Though he disliked some of their ideas, he thought they could be useful in helping him to gain a popular following, and they were, he wrote in 1871, "more revolutionary" than trade union leaders, "firmer on the land question, less nationalistic, and not susceptible to bourgeois bribery." The admiration soon dwindled, and Marx alienated "the sect of the late Bronterre O'Brien." There were philosophical and tactical disagreements. NRL leaders preferred O'Brien's ideas to those of Marx and found Marx to be obstinate and domineering.[68]

Did Marx learn much from O'Brien? Ralph Fox thinks not. To Fox, O'Brien's influence was limited because he did not fully understand "class struggle," but Mark Bevir warns against dividing British styles of socialism too starkly from other styles, preferring to use the paradigm of "encounter" rather than "exceptionalism." In the late nineteenth century, Bevir explains, different groups learned from each other. Even if specific concepts were not accepted, they were discussed, and this discussion brought forth intellectual and political collaborations involving radicals, socialists, labor leaders, positivists, liberals, and others, and also shaped the practical programs upon which they based their campaigns. There were disagreements, but some distinctions were blurred through interaction. Ben Maw argues that O'Brien and Marx both regarded ownership of resources as a fundamental cause of division in society, that languages of "class" could be used in more than one way, and that O'Brien saw himself as moving away from older approaches and priorities to the extent that class relations could be treated as a global problem and as the focal point of history. Later writers who were interested in these matters *must* have owed something to O'Brien, judging by Maw's findings. "While the prioritization of economic power, and the division of society into two hostile, economically defined groups, did not begin with O'Brien, class analysis worthy of the name certainly did." This verdict echoes that of Joel Wiener, who, as mentioned earlier, sees in the development of British radicalism a displacement of eighteenth-century thought about "the People" by the more refined propositions of O'Brien and his contemporaries.[69] Wiener highlights the "nascent socialism" in O'Brien's pieces for the *Poor Man's Guardian* during 1832–35, and describes him as "the most articulate working-class publicist" and "most challenging thinker" to emerge at that time.[70] It was to Theodore Rothstein a "great injustice" that Marx eventually dismissed O'Brien as a "crank."[71]

O'Brien was both an originator and a transmitter of ideas. He ensured that arguments about government, democracy, the land, money, and labor that had intensified during the 1780s and 1790s were still influencing debates a hundred years later. Noel Thompson regards O'Brienite "Chartist socialism" as one of the links in this chain and discerns an underlying continuity. Accordingly, 1848 marks neither an end nor a beginning because "an integration of Chartist political objectives with an anti-capitalist political economy was, in some measure, already available prior to 1848 in the writing of O'Brien." Gregory Claeys identifies O'Brien's position in the 1830s—on land and money, Owenism and labor, and the variety of social arrangements that would allow for equal opportunities and justice—as unique for the time, and Noel Thompson shows how O'Brien altered Chartism *and* socialist political economy. O'Brien saw the interconnectedness of political and economic power; he explained why true reform could not be accomplished by solely political or solely economic means; and this was a decidedly *British* creed that had little need of European input (though it was present). O'Brien was consistent: government had to be democratized and then used to socialize those spheres of economic activity in which exploitation was most pronounced.[72]

To Claeys, O'Brien was "one of the principal teachers of many of those around him" and "the most intellectually active of the major Chartist leaders." As "the first important radical journalist of this period to break decisively from the tenets of liberal political economy," he adapted and expanded upon what he had learned from William Cobbett, Owen, Babeuf, and his other sources, formulating a program of radical measures to improve the condition of the people. Carefully dissecting British society and political culture, he developed his own version of Chartism, Owenite socialism, land nationalization, revolution, and class-based politics, and he proposed a middle way between competition and communitarianism. Claeys nonetheless sees him as a peripheral figure after the early 1840s, and, overall, not as influential in promoting change as Owen's movement ("far less successful as a publicist by comparison with the cumulative, collective efforts of organized socialism").[73] Delbert Schafer also tends toward the view that O'Brien's career was over by 1842. Thereafter, his best years were behind him and "success eluded him to death." Robert Iverson similarly underlines O'Brien's loss of influence after the early 1840s, but contends that he had hitherto been "the intellectual leader of Chartism" and "the intellectual mentor of the movement."[74]

One of the first detailed modern studies of socialism in late Victorian Britain—Henry Pelling's *The Origins of the Labour Party, 1880–1900*, published in 1954—does not pay much attention to earlier thinkers.[75] Yet H. M. Hyndman, who founded the Social Democratic Federation in London in the early 1880s, and later the British Socialist Party, greatly admired O'Brien's theories, as did some of the Fabians, and in the United States a number of O'Brienites took an active role in late nineteenth-century reform politics. Hyndman argued that the SDF was in part a revival of Chartism. He thought of Chartism as "practical socialism" and "the first really important and organized upheaval of the proletariat in modern Europe against the bourgeoisie, for the attainment of definite class objectives." Hyndman was struck by the fact that O'Brien discussed "social democracy" as early as the 1830s. His writings were "far in advance of the rubbish written by so-called Radicals today."[76] Laura Mayhall suggests that O'Brien appealed more to the "strong" democrats of the late Victorian period (including the SDF) who favored popular government and participatory citizenship, to be accomplished through universal suffrage, proportional representation, the referendum and initiative, and industrial self-management, and much less to the "weak" democrats, who were willing to operate within the existing constitutional system.[77] There seems to have been a keen awareness of O'Brien's legacy and more than a few friendly judgments about him.

Nevertheless, there were late Victorian commentators who, if they knew of O'Brien at all, did not rate him highly. In one instance it was stated that even if O'Brien gave British radicalism "a social character," it was all to no avail, for radicals remained ignorant and unrealistic and achieved very little.[78] The appearance of Cole's *Chartist Portraits* some fifty years later prompted a similarly dismissive comment from Charles Fay. In Fay's estimation, Chartists suffered from a narrowness of vision.

> They had little sense of the sweep of capitalistic development in Western Europe. None of them, not even their schoolmaster Bronterre O'Brien, had it in him to produce anything of the stature of Karl Marx's *Capital.* Their emotions took charge of their intellect; and though they might hate, they hated individual persons and things, not the system itself.[79]

This comment indicates a misunderstanding on Fay's part. Chartists did not neglect the international situation, and O'Brien's approach was nothing if not intellectual and directed toward the systematic political, economic, and social reconstruction of Britain. Admittedly, though, it is easy to exaggerate the influence that O'Brien and other radical theorists of his era had on late nineteenth- and early twentieth-century developments. Max Morris has been criticized for assuming that "social revolutionary" sentiment was at the core of popular protest and trade unionism in Britain by the 1830s. The strength of this sentiment can be questioned. Even within Chartism it competed for acceptance with other preferences and theories. Some Chartists were idealistic and doctrinaire, while others were pragmatic and moderate. Some looked back to a golden age they wanted to re-create. Others held that the better society lay in the future.[80]

To those historians who think that O'Brien pointed the way forward to a socialist upsurge in late Victorian Britain, the appearance of the second edition of Gammage's *History of the Chartist Movement* in 1894 is important because it created a stronger sense of his ongoing relevance. Gammage's favorable assessment of O'Brien in the 1854 version was repeated in the second edition. Gammage also wrote a series of "reminiscences" about the Chartist period, published first in the *Newcastle Weekly Chronicle* in 1883–85. He expressed confidence that a democratic suffrage would soon be enjoyed in Britain, and pride in the part that Chartists had played in ensuring "steady progress" in political reform (two of the six points, he enthused, had already been secured—the ballot and the ending of property qualifications for MPs). Gammage insisted that O'Brien, a "brilliant political instructor" and "my late lamented friend," was not only the most important of all the Chartists but was continuing to teach from the grave: "In all the efforts politicians of this day are making to understand the land question, the principle O'Brien laid down is cropping up day by day—must and will crop up, even if aristocrats frown and millionaires wince." Gammage stressed that O'Brien had changed people's minds about, among other things, the democratic legacy of Robespierre and the correct balance between individual and social duties: "Whatever others may have done since that time, he was the first man in England boldly to set forth that Maximilian Robespierre was the great man of his age, and, accordingly, acted on his principles. But O'Brien was no system monger. He was no communist. He believed in individual responsibility, and taught it."[81] No less important than the Gammage material was the publication in 1885 of O'Brien's *The Rise, Progress, and Phases of Human Slavery*—an effort by his followers to maintain his reputation and guide debates about reform at precisely the time when American campaigner Henry George's best-selling *Progress and Poverty* was stirring up radical energies and George himself was visiting Britain for speaking tours.[82]

While O'Brien's treatment of class relations has become a prominent theme in the historiography, Gareth Stedman Jones presents Chartism as a movement of the politically excluded rather than the working class, and though he accepts that O'Brien was a key figure, he denies that class consciousness and class-based analyses were essential to Chartism. This casts doubt on O'Brien's contribution to later socialism. Many commentators disagree with Stedman Jones, however, and some will continue to regard O'Brien as significant primarily because of the socialistic and class-based elements of his thought. A few might focus more on his contributions elsewhere, to revolutionary internationalism for example.[83]

The labels applied to O'Brien have prompted and will go on causing disagreement. Whether or not he should be regarded as a "utopian" or a "socialist," or any number of other things, depends on how these terms are being used, for rarely are there single agreed definitions. Gary Entz believes that "O'Brien's philosophy evolved out of the utopian socialist traditions of the early nineteenth century," but he does not explain how or why, and Entz's evaluation is also complicated by his view that O'Brien was an opponent of model communities and cooperative colonization schemes.[84] All of this needs qualification. O'Brien's ideas were shaped mainly by British radical traditions, the social and economic doctrines of Owen and other contemporary thinkers, and the principles and events of the French Revolution. How far any of these were "utopian" is open to debate.[85] There were communitarian elements in O'Brien's thought and he did advertise and endorse efforts to set up model communities, even if he did not consider them to be pressing priorities. Some of his ideas clearly had Owenite roots. As for the "utopian socialist" description, O'Brien did have in mind an ideal society, but he was not overly idealistic. He advocated practical measures in pursuit of realizable goals, given the situation at the time and the information available to him. Furthermore, he did favor the socialization of resources, relationships, and institutions, but he was also a zealous democrat who wished to maximize individual rights and opportunities. He hoped for a mix of social and economic arrangements and the balancing of private and public interests.

According to Eldon Barry, it was O'Brien who *permanently changed* British radicalism by advancing an alternative to private ownership of the land. The ramifications were many, and Barry insists that "to Bronterre O'Brien . . . can be attributed the earliest demand for true nationalization of the land." This is a big claim; and while underlining O'Brien's commitment to nationalization Barry also notes his noncollectivist preferences, as with the coexistence of individual and cooperative modes of production.[86]

Whichever specific ideas or activities are emphasized, it is necessary to approach O'Brien's weaknesses and faults—the reasons why he did not achieve all that he wanted—with a sense of proportion. Opinions differ as to O'Brien's role and legacy, but the positive and the negative must be weighed up properly in order for the picture not to be distorted. In his entry on O'Brien for the *Oxford Dictionary of National Biography* published in 2004, Miles Taylor comments that O'Brien wasted time and energy on "bitter personal quarrels" that fueled much of his writing, especially after his release from prison. Later, there was a rapid decline in his influence and importance in years of "poverty and alcohol-related illness," but even before this he could be unpleasant, sullen, acrimonious, and difficult to work with. As Taylor supposes, his financial situation and personal and political disappointments magnified the less agreeable sides of his nature. Despite all this, Taylor also reinforces the general impression that O'Brien was "one of the few Chartists whose radicalism was the product of an original mind," and although his modern reputation is far from glowing, O'Brien can be regarded as an outstanding nonutopian socialist who worked for an alternative Britain—one based on a practical radical program (especially nationalization of the land and monetary system). "For all his failings and idiosyncrasies," Taylor concludes, "O'Brien was a powerful character." Thomas Horne also acknowledges O'Brien's originality ("Though O'Brien drew on all parts of the radical tradition, he criticized much of it to create his own political perspective"), and Malcolm Chase agrees that O'Brien made a major contribution to Chartism and left an ideological legacy, especially on the land question. In addition, though his National Reform League was perhaps "only incidentally Chartist" and "its reach did not extend much beyond Soho," it remained in existence after O'Brien's death to become one of the most enduring institutional expressions of Chartism.[87]

Others have tried to evaluate O'Brien's career in this balanced way. Some add a sympathetic note, admitting that O'Brien had shortcomings and made mistakes but suggesting that he achieved as much as he could in the circumstances. Joseph D'Oronzio thinks that he probably deserved more popular appreciation:

> There is a sad contrast between O'Brien's high level of theoretical discourse and the rudimentary context of his practical political activism. . . . His advanced ideas on state socialism, wage slavery and the labour theory of value, and land nationalization could hardly get a proper hearing in the context of political repression and a barely liberated press.

D'Oronzio accepts that much of O'Brien's energy was "drawn off" by quarrels. Even so, he was "articulate and far-sighted" and an "advocate for the unrepresented" who espoused "remarkably original social and economic ideas." His career also serves as a reminder that tactical disputes within Chartism can be exaggerated and that the distinction between "physical force" and "moral force" was not rigid but fluid and contingent. Certainly it is too simplistic to treat O'Brien as a "physical force" Chartist who turned moderate after a spell in prison. In his case the purported abandonment of "physical force," if it really happened, might be deemed a matter of discretion ("personal survival," as D'Oronzio would have it), not of discontinuity in principles or methods. W. H. Maehl sees continuity, especially in connection with the personnel and principles of working-class radicalism. Maehl recognizes that O'Brien had an impact before, during, and after Chartism. He was the movement's "outstanding social and political analyst," and though his posthumous influence was small, Chartism would not have been the same without him. Maehl points in particular to its international dimensions, which were boosted by O'Brien's interest in the French Revolution. Other Chartist leaders lacked his knowledge of and fascination with that phenomenon. Patricia Hollis presents O'Brien as the most eloquent writer and most powerful theorist in Chartism, but adds that, just as the movement was itself highly complex, so O'Brien was "a less than straightforward figure." He demonstrated the interdependence of political and economic power and of political and economic strategies, and, "with perhaps more sophistication than subsequent historians, could run together a decidedly socialist programme for land and currency reform with a conciliatory attitude to middle-class radicalism."[88]

We cannot know everything about O'Brien, of course. While some of his eminent contemporaries have been assessed in full biographies and other studies,

O'Brien has not been the subject of comprehensive and thorough personal investigation because the available sources have not permitted this. The lack of other evidence has led commentators to attach too much weight to apparent character flaws—hence the portraits of O'Brien as petulant and difficult, someone to avoid rather than to like. According to one writer, this was the "overwhelming defect in his personal make-up. . . . It is certainly remarkable that favourable references in Chartist reminiscences and correspondence tend to be limited to an admiration of his intellectual ability and rarely contain any personal warmth or affection." It might be argued, also, that O'Brien tried to achieve too much.

> In the period of the "unstamped" agitation he was, successfully, a radical journalist, political agitator, and organizer of a campaign for a limited political objective. But the very successes of the campaign and the heightened consciousness which it helped to arouse forced him into the bigger arena of total social and political change. Here he could no longer offer both political and intellectual leadership. In the end, perhaps inevitably, perhaps because of the fatal flaws in his personal make-up, he did neither successfully.

In this rendering of O'Brien's career, he lacked the talent for organization that O'Connor and others possessed, and he could not combine theory and action without getting sidetracked by rivalries within "day-to-day mass radical politics." Despite his "many acute insights into industrial capitalist society," he did not have "the sensitivity to opinion or the ability to simplify issues which are essential to the politician, nor yet the time and the application which are needed for the development of intellectual work," all of which makes O'Brien a "shadow-figure" in the history of radicalism.[89]

Some of these remarks are unduly negative. If there is cause to reproach O'Brien on both personal and political grounds, there are also numerous compliments paid to him, during his career and afterward, that should be taken into account. Another matter to consider here is that O'Brien cared about his reputation enormously, and it is unlikely that he would have jeopardized it through lack of attention or effort. He enjoyed the title of "schoolmaster." To his adherents he was a man of integrity and generosity; and, as David Stack has remarked, there were figures (Italian revolutionary and sometime London resident Giuseppe Mazzini was among them) who objected to O'Brien's ideas but still considered him worthy of respect. Stack contends that many historians, especially those sympathizing with the political

Left, have underestimated character as a force in history (it has been dismissed as uninteresting, or as a "bourgeois" preoccupation). But character was important in O'Brien's day and featured in debates about reform and capitalism as well as manners and virtue. O'Brien spoke and wrote a great deal about this, and one of the reasons why he so admired Robespierre was the latter's wish to create citizens of good character. As for the accusations about O'Brien's alcoholism and querulous temperament, Stack points out that some of the most unflattering portrayals were written a long time afterward and might not be trustworthy. Moreover, drinking was perfectly normal at political meetings during the period, and if people had to pay to get in, they would surely not have done so only to hear the ramblings of a drunkard. It is also worth noting that the men with whom O'Brien quarreled most fiercely did not refer to his drinking. Had it been a problem, they would have used it against him. In 1841, during his imprisonment, a doctor spoke of his sobriety. Stack suspects that a later illness created symptoms like alcoholism, and adds that, had he been a heavy drinker, O'Brien would not have inspired such emerging radical leaders as Charles Bradlaugh, the secularist and republican, who was teetotal. (Admittedly, alcoholism might help to explain O'Brien's volatility and the difficulties with his newspapers and other projects; and one can be a heavy drinker without engaging in incessantly destructive behavior. But the evidence that he had a drink problem is hardly overwhelming.) Other assumptions—about O'Brien's paranoia, for instance, and his vendetta against O'Connor—might also be questioned. After 1848 there were times when O'Brien flourished, while O'Connor and the *Northern Star* declined, meaning that O'Brien's anger and jealousy could abate.[90]

Indeed, 1848 brought a new opportunity for O'Brien because he could become more influential in a different kind of radical movement. Stack refers to his "rehabilitation" and "renaissance." After the end of "the mass activism of monster meetings and large-scale petitions," Chartism became a smaller and more intellectual campaign, which suited O'Brien. The pamphlets and poetry of his later career show that he was still at the cutting edge of political theory and expression: "It is possible to see O'Brien as part of the broader convergence of literary romanticism and democratic protest that occurred after the abortive revolutions of 1848."[91]

With regard to O'Brien's alleged alcoholism some consideration ought to be given to the remarks of his friend Gammage, who was involved with the temperance movement, and, though he drank occasionally while an itinerant Chartist lecturer, also abstained for long periods (not least, he later confirmed, because he needed to be physically fit for his speaking tours, on which he walked several hundred miles).

On Gammage's first meeting with O'Brien, in 1842, they shared a glass of wine; but there is no other mention of O'Brien's drinking in any of Gammage's recollections. While acknowledging that many Chartists enjoyed a drink, Gammage suggested that excessive drinking was much more common among their opponents—it often led to rowdyism and violence *against* Chartists. Perhaps O'Brien did have a drink problem and Gammage hushed it up; but this seems unlikely, for if there was any such gossip Gammage would have responded, as he did with regard to another of his Chartist friends, Dr. Peter Murray McDouall.

> I can only say that, if the doctor and others in the Chartist movement fell into that error, they did no more than thousands of men of other parties without a tithe of their excuse. Men who are buffeted about in every direction, who have left their usual walk in life to engage themselves in a popular movement, when they cannot expect to gain, deserve some amount of sympathy even in their errors. I can say for myself that although I have been frequently in the company of McDouall I never saw him in anything approaching a state of intoxication.

There was also an unkind story about McDouall's plan to settle in Australia. Money was raised for his journey and he made ready to go, but he spent all he had on drink and died in poverty in or near Manchester. Had this been true, Gammage would have heard of it when visiting Manchester, and he had not. "I set it down, as I have been compelled to do many other statements, as having no foundation in fact."[92] Since he felt obliged to respond to allegations about McDouall, Gammage would probably have done the same for O'Brien—of whom he was genuinely fond—had such allegations been made; and O'Brien himself must have realized that excessive drinking would have ruined the reputation and influence he was striving to maintain.

In Stack's account, O'Brien saw himself as a romantic hero. The surviving private papers do offer a basis on which to understand more fully O'Brien's self-perception, and the romantic hero motif is helpful. By appending it to the other assessments made by modern historians, and to what may be gleaned from the recorded speeches and many published items by O'Brien and the small amount of personal material, a clearer picture can be seen. It exhibits a long career of honest endeavor, and influence that rises and falls several times. There is talent, ambition, calling, service, sacrifice, and strength, but also, unmistakably, obstacles, struggles, disappointments, and defeats.

Historians have been both kind and unkind in their statements about O'Brien, and most mix positive with negative remarks. A good deal of comment relates to his personality, but for all the focus on his flaws—whether verified or merely imputed—he was able to command the affection and respect of friends and followers and he was well regarded long after his death (and continues to be so in some circles down to the present day). Few of the surviving sources offer insights into O'Brien's private and family life. Detail is lacking. Some historians have nevertheless made judgments about him personally that rest on guesswork or bias. Evidence is more plentiful in connection with O'Brien in a public capacity. Much can be learned about his activity and influence and his career can be placed in its proper context. His goals, beliefs, and methods have been much discussed by scholars (even if other radical celebrities of the nineteenth century have received greater attention). O'Brien was many things: writer, orator, organizer, campaigner; a democrat, a revolutionary, an individualist; workers' champion; "schoolmaster" of Chartism; promoter of and envoy for a bold variant of socialist political economy; communitarian, internationalist, visionary. His principles and strategies were taken from Paine and Cobbett and British radical traditions, from Thomas Spence and Owen and contemporary critiques of emergent social and economic relationships, and from Robespierre, Babeuf, and the French Revolution. O'Brien's own ideas, experiences, and observations enabled him to fuse these many components together in an original reform plan that could be presented and vindicated as the plan that Britain (and other countries) most needed. O'Brien and his program remain worthy of attention. Radicalism—the tracing of political, social, and economic problems to their *roots*—had various strands, and the O'Brienite strand was one of the most fascinating of the mid-nineteenth century and held its appeal long afterwards.

CHAPTER 1

# Rise of the "Schoolmaster"

James O'Brien was born in 1804 in Granard, county Longford, Ireland. His father, a failed wine and spirits dealer, died when he was young, but O'Brien had the good fortune to be noticed by the educator and reformer Richard Lovell Edgeworth, who offered him a place at the experimental school in Edgeworthstown. Here, the focus was on developing the ability to reason. O'Brien thrived in this environment and in 1822 proceeded to Trinity College, Dublin, where he won several prizes for his academic accomplishments. He began training for a legal career, and in 1830 moved to London to complete his qualifications. Gripped at this time by popular agitation for parliamentary reform, London was the place where the talented and ambitious O'Brien devoted himself to politics rather than the legal profession (although for a time he kept rooms at the Inns of Court and was listed as "an Attorney's assistant"). He mixed with prominent reformers, notably Henry Hunt, William Cobbett, and Henry Hetherington. He also met political exiles from the continent. He joined several radical associations, addressed meetings, and wrote for the reform press. O'Brien quickly attracted attention as a forthright champion of the workers' demand for political, social, and economic rights. From early 1831 he used "Bronterre" as a nom de plume, and this would become the name by which he was generally known. In Gaelic, *brón* means "sorrow" or "mourning" and *tír* means "land" or "country." The French form of the latter is *terre*. David Stack has suggested that O'Brien's adoption of the name "sorrow of the land" was both "a powerful affirmation of his self-perception as a spokesman for the poor and dispossessed" and a signifier of the "amalgamation of Irish and French radicalism" upon which his politics were based.[1] Certainly his Irish background and his fascination with the French Revolution would be of central importance as his career progressed.

O'Brien wrote initially for the *Political Letters and Pamphlets*, published by William Carpenter, a pioneer of the radical unstamped press whose interests included religious inquiry, cooperation, and the rights of labor. As his reputation began to grow O'Brien edited a radical weekly in Birmingham in 1831–32. Then he returned to London, where he was installed as editor of one of the most influential of all unstamped radical publications, Hetherington's *Poor Man's Guardian*. He played a prominent role in the campaign against "taxes on knowledge" and restrictions on the press, and the tone of stubborn defiance in his writing helped to expand his readership and influence. (The agitation for press freedoms was blessed with some success in 1836, when stamp duty was reduced from 4d. to 1d. per copy, but the penalties for producing or possessing unstamped papers became more stringent.) O'Brien denounced government policies, attacked the middle class, and defended trade unions. He discussed class antagonism, Owenism, the poor laws, and factory conditions, and pushed for the ballot and an extension of the suffrage. His writing for the *Poor Man's Guardian* was bold and uncompromising, and O'Brien developed an analytical approach that he hoped—in league with other writers—would give the case for radical reform a convincing intellectual basis. He appealed to the minds as well as the hearts of his readers and in time would be dubbed "schoolmaster," the title given to him by Feargus O'Connor, who was the closest thing that Chartism would have to a national leader.[2]

O'Brien's attempts to set up his own newspapers were not blessed with much success. He appears not to have had sound business sense, and the number of readers who were willing to persevere with his often lengthy and complex essays proved not to be as large as he expected. He could be difficult and quarrelsome, too, which did not endear him to fellow radical leaders and journalists who might otherwise have given help and advice. The newspaper taxes also meant that he could not easily lower his price per issue in an effort to boost sales, and at times he had to exclude material in order for his publications not to come under the relevant legislation. For much of his career O'Brien was in debt. Still, he had remarkable reserves of resilience and optimism. When Hetherington ceased publication of the *Poor Man's Guardian* at the end of 1835, O'Brien devoted himself to book projects (mainly concerning the French Revolution), wrote a series of "Bronterre's Letters" that appeared in several publications during 1836, and planned for the launch of his own paper. *Bronterre's National Reformer* only lasted for three months in 1837, however, before it folded. He was briefly involved with the *London Mercury* and then edited a new collective concern, the *Operative*, in 1838–39. As the Chartist movement gathered momentum, O'Brien was the most respected contributor to its main organ, O'Connor's *Northern Star*. He yearned for his own paper nonetheless. With William Carpenter he secured backers for the *Southern Star*, which commenced publication in January 1840, but within months he was in prison. A plan of late 1841, to establish a Chartist newspaper for Scotland with O'Brien as editor, fell through. From July 1842 he was the editor and part owner of the *British Statesman*, another short-lived venture. It ceased publication in January 1843, "beaten down," according to one source, by O'Brien's enemies within the Chartist movement, which was a change from the earlier allegation that his newspaper difficulties were caused by official persecution (as when the Stamp Office refused his sureties in 1840 and he was unable to organize regular printing and distribution for the *Southern Star*). O'Brien continually tried to make his papers pay. None of them did, despite such initiatives as the inclusion of illustrations and portraits. Many Chartist periodicals developed this "graphic dimension" in an effort to attract subscribers, especially the *Northern Star*. O'Brien himself featured in a series of portraits in the *Northern Star* in 1838–39. Then he used the same ploy with his own papers, though without much effect.[3]

O'Brien's political goals in the late 1830s were made plain in the mission statements he issued with his newspapers. In the first number of *Bronterre's National Reformer* he explained its purpose:

> To promote a radical reformation in GOVERNMENT, LAW, PROPERTY, RELIGION, and MORALS. The reformation to be in favour of the great mass of the community—to be effected in the shortest possible time, consistently with inflicting the least avoidable injury on existing interests—to be operated without bloodshed or violence of any kind, by the sole force of a new public opinion—and to be (if possible) conducted and consummated by the constituted authorities of the realm, in obedience to, and protected by, the moral and (if necessary) the physical force of the great majority of the community, in whose interests the reformation will be.[4]

The *Operative* continued in this vein, though O'Brien had to share control with others (there was a management committee of twelve: three trade union secretaries, two printers, two smiths, two tobacconists, a compositor, a joiner, and a currier). Established "by the working classes, to defend the rights of labour from the aggressions of capital," the *Operative* was funded by shareholders. The plan was to issue four thousand shares, at five shillings each. Manhood suffrage and vote by ballot were chief among the paper's objectives, along with a list of related aims:

> A fair day's wages for a fair day's work. The total abolition of the Corn Laws. The annihilation of all Church Rates. An improved system of taxation—that the rich may be assessed according to their wealth, and the poor in proportion to their poverty. Cheap and honest government. An equal administration of the laws—justice for the employed as well as employers.[5]

O'Brien championed these goals throughout his career, and as the "schoolmaster" of Chartism he did his utmost to explain and justify them in an intelligible way.

O'Brien's first piece for the *Northern Star* was published in January 1838 to great fanfare and congratulation: "We have much pleasure in announcing to our readers that we have at length succeeded in adding the valuable services of the glorious BRONTERRE to that phalanx of talent already attached to the *Northern Star*."[6] O'Brien enjoyed the adulation, though he also wished for independence and expected before long to do well in his own right as an owner-editor. Dorothy Thompson contends that Chartism would not have been a viable movement without a national organ like the *Northern Star*, and that O'Brien's papers were inadequate. Though this is true, O'Brien's efforts ought not to be dismissed too readily, not least because his involvement with the *Northern Star* helped it to become a success. In addition, he made an important contribution to the broader development of a politicized popular press shaped by working-class consciousness and a break from established literary fashions and opinions. Here was an alternative culture, a will to construct new sites of literary and intellectual power.[7] O'Brien's role in the development of Chartist communication and language went beyond the written word. Indeed, Chartist communication was multifaceted. Verbal, visual, symbolic, and ritualistic forms were all used to get the message across, and O'Brien's appearances on the public platform were not without impact.[8]

At the end of the 1830s it was primarily the *Northern Star* that gave O'Brien the exposure he wanted. He was a celebrity. The paper's circulation increased and he gained access to a much wider readership than he would otherwise have had, which (albeit temporarily) added to his status and reputation. He had already made his name as a writer before he joined the *Northern Star*, and the paper did make frequent reference to his pre-Chartist activity, but in this period success for the *Northern Star* was also good for O'Brien and it was in his personal interest to maximize the paper's influence.

When he launched the *Southern Star* he was not intending to diminish the *Northern Star* but to complement it. A speaking tour in the South of England led O'Brien to think that a new Chartist paper ought to target the region, and O'Connor publicly approved (although it is not impossible that the title of O'Brien's paper was "indicative of rivalry with O'Connor").[9]

Within popular radicalism there was an ongoing debate about tactics. Insurgency and bloodshed were expected and even recommended by some, but the majority of leaders and activists preferred constitutional methods. During the 1830s O'Brien characterized violence and illegality as foolish. The state had the means to put down any uprising, he reasoned, and it would be better to try other options—those offered by the existing electoral system, for instance, including exclusive dealing. Pressure could also be exerted by mobilizing large numbers for meetings, processions, and demonstrations. These activities could win respect for the cause, gather new adherents, and demonstrate unity, strength, and discipline in radical politics. People could abstain from commodities like alcohol, tea, coffee, and tobacco, all of which were taxed. The government would lose revenue, and participants in this form of protest would save money and improve their own health. They might go further, and simply refuse to pay direct taxes until their grievances were addressed. An older idea—the "run on gold"—still had support too: people could simultaneously withdraw all their savings, plunging the banks into crisis. Britain's credit and debt arrangements would not stand, piling greater difficulties upon the government.[10]

Another suggestion was to organize the workers in their capacity as producers, but not everyone agreed with O'Brien on this. While he pointed to the connections between political and economic power, some leaders thought of the two as separate and argued that economic problems could only be solved through economic means and that political action was unnecessary. This disagreement affected discussion of trade unionism, cooperation, and proposals involving labor exchanges and a general strike (or "national holiday"). O'Brien did not reject nonpolitical methods. He favored almost anything that might serve to boost the workers' boldness, influence, vision, and self-consciousness. But he maintained that the supreme goal was the vote. Before the advent of the People's Charter, O'Brien had pulled together different strands of protest and activism in his articles for the *Poor Man's Guardian*. As he put it in November 1833:

> Let us deal with no middleman who refuses to vote or petition for Universal Suffrage. Let us deal with no villain who is opposed to Trades' Unions, or in any other way hostile to our rights and privileges. Let us resist every attempt of the shopocrats to cut down the workman's wages, and uphold every effort of the men to obtain equitable advances. Let us support one another in all struggles against the mercenary combinations of slave drivers, and encourage exclusive dealing with the people's friends in all lines of business. Let us as far as possible promote mutual exchanges of labour for labour, on the cooperative principle, so as to intercept the profits of trade in addition to the wages of labour. . . . But meanwhile, neglect no opportunity of seeking Universal Suffrage, which is the grand panacea for all our evils.

In O'Brien's view, manhood suffrage was the only way to make advances and to protect any gains that were made[11]

All this was shaped by O'Brien's negative opinion of the Reform Act of 1832. It had been passed in response to popular pressure, but to many radicals it was a disappointment. Among its main provisions was the uniform £10 borough franchise. Although this seemed like a progressive measure, in practice it excluded large numbers of urban workers. The size of the British parliamentary electorate rose from about five hundred thousand to about eight hundred thousand, a large increase, but as a proportion of the total population the electorate was small: only one in five adult males could vote in England and Wales, one in eight in Scotland, and one in twenty in Ireland.

O'Brien complained that the 1832 Reform Act delivered the nation over to "Mammon" and facilitated exclusion, plunder, and tyranny. It "united all property against all poverty." He regarded the Reform Act as a trick, designed to deny workers the vote and keep them in subjection to political parties drawn from the landed aristocracy and wealthy middle-class employers. The key to everything was a democratic suffrage, and the lesson of 1832 was that workers should carry on campaigning, assisted by a cheap press that could educate and guide: "We have our battle still to gain." O'Brien wrote that the Reform Act could only be accepted as an installment, "part payment" of what was due, and that liberty of the press would help to secure further installments: "The emancipation of the press in this country will be tantamount to a quiet, orderly, constitutional, irresistible revolution." In his musings about the best way to generate a large, disciplined, united popular movement, O'Brien initially advised that use must be made of the talent and strength in the trade unions. He reached out to them in the belief that no effective mass campaign was possible without them. He subsequently called upon them to join in the campaign for the Charter. The alliance between Chartism and the trades proved to be stronger in some places than in others. In London and Glasgow it was an important and enduring feature of early Victorian popular politics. But all too often O'Brien was left complaining that trade union leaders did not appreciate the interconnectedness of economic and political power. They preferred not to commit themselves and their members to explicitly political agitation.[12]

To O'Brien, 1832 marked a victory for the propertied middle classes. Their incorporation into the political system greatly enhanced their influence, he thought, and after 1832 he continued to make plentiful use of class rhetoric. The national debt, for instance, was a middle-class creation. He told an audience in Manchester in 1839 that the debt, which imposed such heavy burdens on the laboring population, was a blessing for bankers and speculators. The national debt "arose with the middle classes of society." Similarly, he drew attention to what the "reformed" Parliament actually did during the 1830s. In Irish policy, in the punishment of trade unionists, and in the New Poor Law of 1834 (a "Starvation Law") he saw class oppression. Everywhere, it seemed, the rights of the workers were under attack, and instead of extending liberty the post-1832 Parliament was abridging it.[13]

> The "Reform Act"! It is a monstrous perversion of language. It was neither more nor less than a foul and felonious conspiracy between our land-usurpers and money-jobbers to perpetuate their own power of plundering and enslaving the nation with impunity. A reform act! It was an act of treason towards the sovereign people, for which its authors and instigators deserved to suffer death on the scaffold a thousand times more than ever did a wretched pauper deserve to die of water-gruel and a broken heart in a *liberal* workhouse.[14]

In June 1842, with trade slack and distress increasing, a move to suspend the operation of the New Poor Law was heavily defeated in the House of Commons. It gained only twenty-nine votes. This small number of MPs, thundered O'Brien, spoke for "four-fifths of the people—all but those who feed and fatten upon the plunder of the industrious millions."[15] O'Brien's discussion of the social and economic factors that were behind the formation of the middle class, and determined its status, power, and activities, tells against the hypothesis that "middle class" was an imagined construction—not a material reality but a political and linguistic device that was used to describe and represent British society in these years.[16]

O'Brien's attacks on the middle class did not go down well with some of those who read his works and heard his speeches. One Oldham radical was prompted to write to the *Northern Star* in October 1838 to protest that the middle and working classes had some interests in common. Oldham was a notable radical stronghold in the North of England, but D. S. Gadian argues that radical strength there was based not on class conflict but on an alliance of working- and middle-class groups, and that the rise of an independent working-class consciousness *undermined* local radicalism. This has been questioned by R. A. Sykes, who stresses O'Brien's role in "popularizing an anti-middle-class form of radicalism."[17]

Most radicals would have concurred with O'Brien's diatribes against the financial operations of the British state. Resentment about the national debt was entwined with continuing outrage against the heavy taxes imposed by what was deemed to be a corrupt government. The debt was regarded as a cynical device to subsidize the selfish and unproductive. It had nothing to do with the workers: they were not responsible for it and should not have to pay it. In contemplating the workers' lot, O'Brien identified heavy taxation as more symptom than cause, but he still campaigned for tax reform. Indirect taxes, mainly on food and drink, had raised £35 million in 1832, when the total revenue of the state was £50 million. O'Brien pointed out that more than half of all public spending went to service the national debt, and about a quarter was for the armed forces, which meant that the main beneficiaries of over 75 percent of expenditure were fundholders and property owners. The tax system was not only regressive but also redistributed wealth upward. Tax cuts would not be a sufficient remedy. O'Brien argued that indirect taxation should be abolished and replaced with a direct tax on property ("property not industry should bear the burden of taxation"). It was not a great leap from this to the belief that "land monopoly" was at the root of most contemporary problems. O'Brien was convinced that general prosperity could be secured "by the adoption of correct principles in the mode of raising the public revenue," and the prime targets for reform were the national debt and the tax code.[18]

As O'Brien focused on the need for thorough social and economic reorganization, he attacked liberal political economy and tried to promote a better understanding of "capitalist warfare" and the growth and nature of industrial society. One of his catchphrases was "Knowledge and Union," and he urged workers to join together in pursuit of the political rights without which they could not secure the primary goals, social equality and economic justice. He explained that political reform was the necessary precursor. O'Brien enthusiastically embraced the People's Charter issued in 1837, and at once set about giving Chartists a philosophy as well as a program. Most of them agreed with him about the legislation passed since 1832, especially the New Poor Law. O'Brien was and remained adamantly opposed to the Malthusian prescriptions behind the New Poor Law. He set aside the ideas about government intervention in the social sphere and the balance between population and resources that had been advanced by political economist Thomas Malthus. According to James Huzel, opponents of Malthus regarded him as an enemy of the laboring poor but ignored aspects of his thought that might have mitigated their denigration of it. In addition to this, they never formed a cohesive body. O'Brien, for instance, was committed to a general assault on liberal political economy, not just Malthusianism. Disunity hampered the resistance to a powerful consensus that developed in favor of measures that many radicals disliked, including the New Poor Law. Even so, there were numerous districts of the country in which opposition to the New Poor Law merged with agitation for the Charter.[19]

O'Brien condemned the "pauper bastilles" and the "liberal" tenets that brought them into being. At the local level, he admitted, there were Tories who were more "humane" than Whigs. Whatever the party complexion of the national government, though, greater assistance for the poor would only be granted in return for their submission, and the New Poor Law proved conclusively that the working classes were not respected. As well as lambasting "false friends" who claimed otherwise (notably Francis Place, the veteran "radical tailor of Charing Cross"), O'Brien argued that restoring the Elizabethan "compulsory relief" statute would be less harmful than the continuance of the new system:

> I defend the system of compulsory relief awarded by the famous Act of Elizabeth, which made the old poor law system of England. That Act was, *abstractedly considered*, unjust and tyrannical towards the whole body of ratepayers. But these ratepayers being themselves the authors and abettors of a much greater injustice towards and at the expense of the paupers, I defend the Act and detest the Whigs for repealing it.

Promoters of the New Poor Law had justified it with lies (for example, that the old system of relief was destroying "agricultural capital," when the truth was that rents, taxes, and tithes were to blame). O'Brien considered the administration of the new rules to be too harsh and rigid, not least because of the composition of local elected boards—"people of property have always the least sympathy with poverty"—but the system itself could not be redeemed, even if different men were chosen. O'Brien kept up a damning assault on the New Poor Law over many years, often reporting in detail on the situation in specific parts of the country when he could use this information to bolster his position. The landed and moneyed elites, he maintained, had gained in the New Poor Law an added power to plunder the people, along with all their other opportunities for doing so. They limited relief in order to lower poor rates, and they also benefited because the higher incidence of pauperism kept wages down. O'Brien attributed crime and immorality not to flawed human nature but to unbearable poverty.[20]

If O'Brien was disappointed with the failure of trade unions to combine with political radicals, he was even more dismayed by the attitude of Robert Owen and the Owenites. O'Brien had enormous respect for Owen's ideas about social and moral improvement, but the two disagreed on a fundamental point. O'Brien advocated manhood suffrage, the means by which Parliament could be made more representative and the ability to make laws transferred to the people. Owen eschewed political action, keeping faith with cooperative practices. In his address *To the Chartists of the British Isles* of 1842, Owen insisted that to expect anything from political action was to fly in the face of reason and experience. Even if the Charter were enacted, he thought, nobody would be more disappointed with the outcome than the Chartists themselves. O'Brien disagreed, on the grounds that social and economic change could only follow political reform and that Owen's methods would take too long.[21] O'Brien's wish for a redistribution of power and wealth shaped his comments about other matters, including those concerning personal ethics. Entering the fray against advocates of birth control, for example, he saw contraception as a tool of the dominant elites, designed to diminish the working classes, inhibit their pleasures, and divert attention from the existence of remediable social and economic inequality.[22]

While disagreeing with aspects of Owen's thought, O'Brien embraced much of it and would continue to associate and debate with Owenites throughout his career. This interaction began in London at the beginning of the 1830s, and by the time he became editor of the *Poor Man's Guardian* in September 1832 O'Brien was no less interested in communitarian and cooperative solutions than he was in the claims of political radicals like Hunt and Cobbett. He made the acquaintance of Owen himself, as well as prominent associates of the latter such as John Finch, a Liverpool iron merchant, James Rigby, a publisher (and Owen's principal agent and supporter) in London, and William Pare, a Birmingham shopkeeper who went on—as did Finch—to govern one of the Owenite communities and write several works on cooperation. Another of O'Brien's Owenite contacts was Alexander Campbell, who promoted cooperative societies, trade unions, land and education reform, and anticapitalism first in Glasgow and then elsewhere.[23] O'Brien and Owen had a number of mutual allies and correspondents over the years. They included James Bernard, the eccentric Cambridgeshire farmer who promoted land, currency, and other reforms through the Central National Association during 1837 and was owner of the *London Mercury* when O'Brien was its coeditor with the radical newspaperman John Bell. In May 1837, when Bernard, Bell, and O'Brien were due to address meetings in the West Riding, Bernard urged Owen to join them on their trip, which he promised would have "important consequences."[24]

During the 1830s O'Brien praised Owen's principles and pointed to the many people in Britain and the United States who lived peacefully and happily under Owenite guidelines, in "communities founded on the equal distribution of enjoyments and of labours."[25] He was still making such comments in the 1850s, though he could also be dismissive of individual Owenites. After one meeting in London in 1855, at which a number of them spoke, O'Brien noted that the sentiments they had expressed bore little resemblance to cooperative values as he understood them.[26]

The tension between Chartists and Owenites frequently prompted comment in their respective newspapers. Owen was accused of autocratic tendencies, as in the summer of 1843 when the *Northern Star* featured a dispute about his Rational Society. Originally called the Universal Community Society of Rational Religionists, and established in 1835, the Rational Society had more than sixty branches of self-styled "socialists" by 1840, concentrated in the manufacturing districts, with perhaps fifty thousand attending weekly lectures. The society's paper, the *New Moral World*, ran for eleven years (1834–45) and achieved a weekly circulation of about forty thousand at its peak in 1839–41. Owen's teachings against competition and for cooperation were gaining ground, but Chartist observers focused on the control he wanted to exercise as leader of the Rational Society. No matter how intelligent and talented he might be, it was argued, there was danger when a leader went too far with his schemes and aspired to absolute command over a movement or organization.[27]

O'Brien occasionally corresponded with Owen, and one of their earliest exchanges concerned the Birmingham Political Union, which played a significant role in the reform agitation of 1831 and 1832, as O'Brien saw at first hand while resident in the city. The BPU was a large and influential body and a model for political unions elsewhere, though it was quite distinctive in the cross-class nature of its support. There was more contact and less conflict between employers and workers in Birmingham than in other growing urban centers, owing to the nature of local economic development. O'Brien, while not complimentary about the BPU's middle-class leadership, recognized its success in convincing "Brumagem operatives" that the Reform Bill was worthy of their backing, and he admitted that the BPU conducted an impressive campaign: "To this body, more than any other, is confessedly due the triumph (such as it was) of the Reform Bill. Its well-ordered proceedings, extended organization, and immense assemblages of people, at critical periods of its progress, rendered the measure irresistible."[28]

In May 1832 O'Brien suggested to Owen that the cooperative movement ought to imitate the BPU's organization and methods. William Pare agreed. O'Brien thought that the time was right to implement the plan. He cited social and political circumstances and the "energy and zeal I have recently witnessed on the part of my brother Cooperators," and declared that "nothing is wanting to fix public attention on our cause and thereby create a new public opinion but some such popular and judicious plan of organization as that so successfully exemplified in the constitution of the Birmingham Union." O'Brien stressed the need to "gather up" public opinion and direct it against the existing social order. To this end, the Owenites' National Equitable Labour Exchange in Gray's Inn Road, London, "should be made of a more popular character," and the BPU model was suitable "so far as organization is concerned." O'Brien thought that once the Reform Bill was passed, and excitement about it faded and people realized it would not solve their problems, the Owenites should lay down clear purposes and rules and draw in "great numbers of the working classes" with low subscription rates and equal access to lectures, a library, and other facilities. He envisaged an elected council that would prepare petitions to Parliament and gain maximum publicity (the reason Owen and his colleagues had hitherto received hardly any press attention, according to O'Brien, was that they were "weak, inactive, and disorganized"). Owenite societies across the country would back the council, and there would be full meetings of a representative "congress" at least twice a year. O'Brien was confident that by such means the movement would become ever stronger—for "the suffering and deluded people are fast recovering their senses"—but he warned that Owen's more unconventional ideas (especially those on "religion and responsibility") should be kept in the background as much as possible. It was not that O'Brien himself found these ideas objectionable. He was thinking only of the sensitivities of the people, and he advised Owen that some tact was required if popular support was to be built up.[29]

Owen appears to have decided that he had nothing to learn from the Birmingham Political Union. In November 1832 he delivered a series of lectures in Birmingham and reported to his friend and supporter Thomas Allsop, a London stockbroker who would also become a close friend of O'Brien, "I have been much pleased with my reception here; it exceeds my most sanguine expectations." Invited to a meeting of the BPU, Owen was astonished to be introduced formally "in the strongest terms of approbation, both of myself and plans." Though he wanted his followers to make use of this breakthrough, he made it plain that he had little in common with the BPU.[30]

O'Brien's earlier letter to Owen also described plans for a new weekly paper in London—"a powerful engine for the dissemination of cooperative principles" to be conducted by O'Brien and Pare. O'Brien wrote:

> I have been promised considerable support. A great number of persons in various ranks of life have volunteered their services and promised to become subscribers. . . . The trading community are very bitter against us, but I am not without hope that they will before long find it expedient to join us or at least to let us alone.[31]

Although this project was abandoned, and O'Brien would soon join the *Poor Man's Guardian*, his willingness to promote some of Owen's core ideas remained strong.

Utopian elements in O'Brien's creed were less important than the practical program he developed for social and economic change, but he did express respect for utopian schemes, notably the setting up of model communities. His newspapers and other publications gave coverage to Owenite efforts of this kind. He also reported on the activities of German-born utopian John Adolphus Etzler, approving of the latter's commitment to social equality and the common ownership of property while rejecting Etzler's notion that people could change their circumstances irrespective of the form of government under which they lived.[32] Another utopian arrangement that interested O'Brien was the settlement of "Rappists," or the

"Harmony Society," set up by followers of German Pietist Johan George Rapp in Economy, Pennsylvania, on the Ohio River near Pittsburgh.[33]

At no point in his career could O'Brien bring himself to sympathize with the refusal of Owenites and trade unionists to engage in political activity. In December 1833 he wrote:

> In viewing the struggle which is now in progress between labour and capital, or between the trade unions and the master manufacturers . . . there is one circumstance which fills us with astonishment and regret—we mean the disposition of the chief leaders of the workmen to disconnect their cause altogether from politics.

O'Brien described collusion among employers, the harassment of trade unionists, and the use of troops in strike-affected districts, and lamented over the number of women as well as men who had been "turned out to starve." None of this could happen, he declared, if Parliament, the magistracy, and the forces of law and order were made accountable to the people, which was why a democratic suffrage was essential. "The present objects of the trade unions can never be obtained under the existing Government, and for this reason—because they are incompatible with the present form of society, which it is the design of that Government to maintain."[34] The crux of all this was, of course, legislative power. O'Brien's wish for a properly representative legislature was no doubt intensified by his experiences as a victim of the law. Arrests, convictions, and imprisonment would deal a huge blow to the Chartist movement. Its adherents complained about unfair treatment and claimed that the law was a class tool. Their rhetoric was more nuanced than it might at first appear, though, for they knew that the law was more than simply the instrument of malevolent elites. Historically, the law was also the bulwark of liberty. Chartists themselves wanted to be part of the lawmaking process and tended to reproach the administrators of the law rather than the law itself or the rules of trial procedure.[35]

Chartism was a potent expression of political and social grievances. Dissatisfaction with the 1832 Reform Act and a determination to win the vote combined with protests about the hardship and dislocation associated with the Industrial Revolution. The six points of the Charter had been core radical goals since the late eighteenth century. Now they were brought together in one document, stated with boldness and clarity and backed by a mass mobilization.

One of the largest meetings to take place in the early stages of the Chartist movement was in Birmingham in August 1838, under the aegis of the BPU. Delegates attended from London, the North of England, and Scotland, and the main address was delivered by the BPU's leader, Thomas Attwood, a banker and iron merchant, who spoke of nonviolent agitation for popular rights. The meeting attracted considerable press attention, and there was a dispute about what speakers had said and how many people attended. Antireform newspapers tried to portray Attwood as an extremist and claimed that only about ten thousand were present, while other estimates suggested two hundred thousand. O'Brien wrote to the *Northern Star* to remind Chartists of the BPU's past errors, especially its support for the 1832 Reform Act and its willingness to give the government more time to implement necessary measures. He hoped that the recent meeting, which had reportedly approved all six points of the Charter, marked a change in BPU policy; but while he was willing to acknowledge that Attwood had "an excellent heart and genuine sympathy with the working classes," O'Brien did not think that the BPU should be allowed to set the course for the whole movement. He advised that Chartists should seek guarantees. Would BPU leaders promise to accept nothing before or instead of manhood suffrage? O'Brien was less than impressed by some of the remarks attributed to Attwood, and he offered to debate reform questions with *any* public person in order to clarify and inform. All he asked was one month's notice, a venue that could hold five thousand people, and an agreement to make no charge for admission.[36]

O'Brien saw Chartism as an excellent opportunity for "honest reformers" (whom he habitually distinguished from "dishonest" and "sham" pretenders) to rise up and lead the people. Grievances were to be removed, needs satisfied, and rights secured. In 1838 he wrote of the psychology of reform. "Reformers," he suggested, "are the creatures of circumstances." Antireformers among the aristocracy and propertied middle classes stigmatized reformers as morose and contentious oddities who, not having the good life, wanted to deny it to others. This was false, O'Brien insisted. Any reformer who had "comforts" enjoyed them as much as anyone else would. But a person who knew only poverty and oppression was bound to seek redress. Such an experience was what *made* a man a reformer—being deprived of happiness and security through no fault of his own, and seeing the wealth he created taken by others so that they could enjoy its blessings to his disadvantage. An "honest reformer," O'Brien declared, was necessarily angry and assertive. The "dishonest" ones had a different bearing.

> The honest reformer asks no enjoyments but what he is willing to earn, and he will go without enjoyments rather than get them at other people's expense; whereas

> the dishonest reformer cares not by what means or at whose expense he gets them, provided he *does* get them, being equally regardless as the anti-reformer himself of the rights and enjoyments of others. The honest reformer is at all times consistent with himself, because he is always governed by principle and conscience. If he be rich, he enjoys himself and wishes to enable others to do the same, never taking into account whether justice to them may or may not lead to a diminution of his own comforts. If he be poor, he seeks the enjoyments he wants, but he seeks them through equitable means. He asks no exclusive advantages—he demands nothing for himself that he does not equally claim for all others similarly conditioned, and neither for himself or them does he require pleasures which would deprive others of their legitimate proportion. His motto is: *do unto others as you would that others should do unto you.* The dishonest reformer, on the contrary, is never consistent a moment longer than suits his purposes, because his only governing motive is self-interest or convenience. Accordingly, let some exclusive advantage only present itself, and farewell, for him, the general advantage! Such men are reformers only from the *accident of position*, for the instant they can better their own condition they become anti-reformers, and persecute the very parties with whom they acted before. In short, the dishonest reformer and the anti-reformer are the same person under opposite circumstances—for let them only interchange conditions and forthwith they will exchange characters.[37]

Though he was to find many "dishonest" reformers in the Chartist movement, he hoped that it could be guided in the right direction, and in his publications of the 1840s he gave extensive coverage under such headings as "Progress of the Movement."[38] Developing a clear program of social and economic measures that he thought the Charter would make possible, he adopted as one of his slogans at the end of the decade "The Charter as the Means and the Social Rights of Man as the End."[39]

O'Brien was still campaigning for the six points of the Charter in the late 1850s. He dismissed other proposals for political reform as limited and piecemeal. These included a Reform Bill of 1859, which would have brought a small increase in the number of borough and county electors and a modest redistribution of parliamentary seats. The bill was defeated in the House of Commons, and among its critics were the enemies of Chartism and former leaders of the Anti–Corn Law League Richard Cobden, John Bright, and the "Manchester School." While O'Brien welcomed the defeat of the Reform Bill, he wrote that an alternative scheme favored by the Cobden-Bright faction was no better. It would increase middle-class influence and offer nothing to the working classes. It would leave social evils untouched. O'Brien condemned Cobden and especially Bright ("the most belauded, be-slobbered, of our great public men, our loudest reformer") for wasting time on "ridiculous stock-grievances" concerning church rates, game laws, inheritance duties, primogeniture, and the House of Lords. Their idea of making Parliament more representative was to increase the preponderance within the British electorate of the middle classes. They advocated voting by ballot, more seats for large towns, and property qualifications for the vote (based on assessment to local rates), "a concoction of fraud and injustice which would not seat one honest man in parliament in a century." O'Brien argued that the Cobden-Bright reform plan could not release the voteless masses from the yoke of landlords and capitalists. In fact, it had the opposite tendency.

> No man will be allowed a vote but the man who least wants it—the householder rated to the poor for three years in the town he resides in—the man well enough conditioned to be able to keep others besides himself and family (which is not the condition of one working man in seven or ten), and as the house he lives in is sure to belong to some landlord or profit-monger, and as the work he lives by depends on the same classes (to give or withhold), it is obvious the landlord and profit-monger will have an ultimate controlling power over every poor-rated inhabitant in the borough. Besides, the few working-class votes possible under such conditions would be perfectly useless to the voters, as they would in every borough be swamped by the vastly larger number of voters the aristocracy, clergy, and middle classes, with their dependants, could bring to bear against them. In short, the working classes would not be able to return even one representative of their order throughout the whole kingdom. A bill that would enable them to return only a dozen representatives for the twelve largest towns, to be chosen exclusively by non-electors, would be infinitely better for them than the hocus-pocus bill projected by the Manchester School. Through twelve able and conscientious men so chosen, their real wants, grievances, and sentiments could be made known to the world through parliament and so force a real reform; but under the Bright and Cobden concoction they would not be suffered to return one such member as would be of any use to them.

By this time the Charter had been available for more than twenty years. It offered the only route to the political democracy that would make possible social and economic transformation.[40]

According to Gareth Stedman Jones, Chartism was a political movement characterized by the language and ideology of the politically excluded, not a class movement shaped by the workers' experience of the Industrial Revolution. Many scholars have criticized this position. One objection is that no distinction was made between the "political" and the "social" in the era of Chartism, that people did not separate their problems into different categories but addressed them all as part of a "lived reality." O'Brien has been used to exemplify the "multiplicity of beliefs" in Chartism and to show that there was more behind the movement than a sense of political exclusion.[41] O'Brien did prioritize the vote, but as the means to other ends (and this was a constant as his detailed reform program evolved during the 1830s, 1840s, and 1850s).

O'Brien believed fervently in the democratic ethos of early Chartism. He expected the movement's leaders to consult and respect the wishes of the rank and file. Chartists should be democratic in practice as well as in aspiration, he thought, and he used headings such as "Chartism and Equality" and referred to "the democratic party" in particular localities when reporting on the movement in his newspapers. The nature of "democracy" was also one of the themes he repeatedly took up in his lectures and speeches. In 1838 he defined it as "universal equality of rights and duties." There might still be rich and poor in a democracy, but all would be treated the same. Unearned privileges would not exist, and everybody would be rewarded according to their services and talents. Individuals would be "perfect arbiters of their own destiny." O'Brien contrasted "democratic virtue" with "aristocratic wiles and wickedness." In 1842, pointing to the movement's loss of unity and direction, he called upon Chartists to follow the right leaders ("true friends of democracy should value men on account of principles and not principles on account of men"). In 1843 his *Poor Man's Guardian and Repealer's Friend* adopted the banner heading "Equal Rights and Equal Laws for All," and when the *London Chartist Monthly Magazine* advocated a "democracy" that allowed for a concentration of power, O'Brien warned that liberty would be in jeopardy unless legislative authority was devolved and divided. Leaders should be under the control of their followers, not the other way round.[42]

For O'Brien, as Alfred Plummer puts it, the Charter meant "the achievement of political freedom and social justice through universal suffrage and a socially-conscious legislature." This was the way to counter the "cannibals" who preyed on labor, including the middle-class leaders of the Anti–Corn Law League. O'Brien was sure that they wanted to divert the workers from the Charter and only sought cheaper food so that they could cut wages. They were not democrats. O'Brien agreed that the Corn Laws should be abolished, but maintained that this would not benefit the workers unless other changes were also made (especially the extension of the suffrage and reform of the currency). His ally Gammage summarized O'Brien's stance as follows:

> He had no objection to the principles of free trade as such; but he contended, that in order to make free trade honest for all classes, there ought at the same time to be an equitable adjustment between the public and private debtor and creditor, as otherwise the non-producing class would rob the producers to exactly the amount of difference in the prices of all that they consumed.

O'Brien evinced the democrat's concern for the people's welfare. Shortly before his release from prison in September 1841, he objected when the *Northern Star* proposed that a fund be collected for him and a triumphal procession arranged. He did not want to take the workers' pennies, he declared. Many of them appreciated his services and sacrifices. At the height of his popularity during the late 1830s and early 1840s he featured on banners and in other Chartist iconography. The Chartists of Manchester commissioned a painting of him from a local artist.[43]

One of the clearest statements of his philosophy in the early years of Chartism was O'Brien's address "To the Electors and Non-Electors of the Borough of Newcastle-upon-Tyne" of June 1841 (Newcastle radicals had asked him to stand as a candidate in the upcoming general election). He explained that he stood for "peace founded upon liberty," "law founded upon justice," and "order founded upon contentment for all."

> I am for unqualified obedience to the laws (even where they are bad and vicious) so long as any hope or chance remains of altering or amending them; but I am for giving to the people every facility of altering and improving them in conformity with the will of the majority. I am for conserving all that is sound and valuable in our institutions, and for radically reforming all that is unsound. . . . I am for unbounded liberty of opinion above and before everything else.

O'Brien regarded all property, private as well as public, as inviolable. Public property, he insisted, should be used only for public purposes, and "only the voice of the entire public (constitutionally expressed by the vote of the majority) can justly or honestly appropriate or dispose of the property of the public." Moreover,

> I consider the public has no more right to invade or appropriate the property of individuals (without their consent) than individuals or fractions of the people have to invade the property of the public . . . At the same time, I hold it to be perfectly just and competent for the legislature to interfere with any and every species of private property where such interference is required by the public interest, provided always that the parties interfered with be fully indemnified by compensation.

He opposed all monopolies of wealth, power, and knowledge, and wished to eliminate any laws or institutions that gave these benefits to some while denying them to others. He identified the monopoly of the Bank of England as a great evil, for "the prerogative of making and issuing money . . . cannot be delegated or parceled out to individuals without danger to the commonwealth." He called for the establishment of a "National Bank . . . which shall afford equal facilities to all classes alike," and the abolition of all existing banks of issue. Restrictions on trade and industry also had to be removed, especially those that enriched special interests. O'Brien favored the total and immediate repeal of the Corn Laws, but added that this should be accompanied by measures to reduce the national debt and other public burdens "in proportion to the fall of prices" that repeal would cause.

> Otherwise the repeal . . . would benefit only fund-holders, mortgagees, usurers, and men of fixed income (not immediately derived from the land) . . . but to the millions of workpeople, who have only their daily labour to live by, to the numerous body of shopkeepers dependent upon their custom, and to the industrious classes generally, it would yield no benefit at all, while it would augment the burden of all.

O'Brien wanted a fundamental change in the system of taxation. First, taxes should be drastically reduced, and second (in line with the need to free industry and trade) customs and excise should be replaced by direct taxes "to be raised from landed funds and other property." Other major problems discussed in the address included the connection between church and state, the presence of "placemen" in the House of Commons, and "restrictions on the liberty of the press, whether by bonds, stamp duties, or censorship"—to all of which O'Brien was opposed.[44]

The Newcastle manifesto has been accurately described by Alfred Plummer as "an advanced radical programme designed to win the support not only of convinced Chartists, but all others holding genuinely progressive opinions."[45] O'Brien's advanced position was also reflected in his commitment to what he called "genuine democracy," or "whole hog" Chartism, the slogan he used in his *British Statesman* in 1842–43.

Early Chartism was marked by enthusiasm but also by quarreling and division. For someone who often preached unity and restraint, O'Brien was not reluctant to engage in disputes, notably those among London radicals over tactics and ideas. He broke with Hetherington during 1836–37. O'Brien doubted Hetherington's principles and attacked him for siding with "sham-Radicals," but there were additional reasons for the split. Hetherington tended not to pay his journalists regularly and O'Brien resented this, calculating that Hetherington made a good income from his publications. O'Brien complained that he should have received more from his association with Hetherington. There may also have been tension between them because O'Brien wanted to branch out on his own rather than work for someone else. After the split the two men publicly condemned each other and tried to damage each other's papers. In the Chartist period there were rivalries in most large towns, and O'Brien's followers formed one of the competing groups. Yet he continually called for unity and emphasized the one common objective: manhood suffrage. If radicals could combine on that, O'Brien thought, disagreement on other matters might not be problematic.[46] The division in London, though, had lasting ramifications, as when it came to the election of delegates to speak for London in regional and national bodies. Questions were raised about the suitability of persons known to be "democrats" and "Jacobins." They were put in nomination, it was alleged, by militant cliques that invaded meetings and hijacked the selection process.[47]

O'Brien explained to his friend and benefactor Thomas Allsop that the conflict with Hetherington rested on two simple matters: Hetherington would not pay him the money he owed, and O'Brien wished to write independently of particular persons and parties. In November 1836 O'Brien laid out his situation to Allsop and asked for money. This pattern would prevail throughout their long friendship. Allsop, it appears, was well placed to help. He was affluent and connected. He moved in literary and reform circles (and was a close friend of the poet and philosopher Samuel Taylor Coleridge). He knew Cobbett, Owen, and O'Connor, as well as O'Brien, and frequently dispensed financial and other assistance to his radical friends.

O'Brien informed Allsop that he had been "cruelly and shamefully used" by Hetherington, who had swindled him out of several hundred pounds over the preceding years (O'Brien claimed that Hetherington had stopped his profits and cheated him out of part-proprietorship of the *London Dispatch*). Now O'Brien needed money to start a new paper.

> A few friends to whom I have stated my case have generously proffered me their aid in the bringing out of an unstamped two-penny paper, and I have a publisher willing and eager to give effect to their and my wishes, but I have no funds, and the friends alluded to are too poor to advance any beyond a small trifle, which it would not be worth my while to compromise my independence for, the more especially as I shall be at their services in other ways not pecuniary but more valuable towards the ends I have in view.

O'Brien stressed that he did not want Hetherington or anyone associated with him to know where the money was coming from, and that in order for the new venture to succeed O'Brien had to be "absolutely master from the beginning" and not "under a variety of obligations to different parties of conflicting views and opinions." O'Brien asked Allsop to provide the necessary funds, or to persuade others to do so, and promised to pay back the full amount, with interest if required. He was also ready to provide security (he did not specify what this was). "I have a vast number of friends throughout the country who, I am convinced, will do their utmost to promote my success from the moment I start, so that if I am only properly backed in the beginning I have no fears whatever for the result." O'Brien wrote that he was reluctant to seek help in this way. "But if you knew how I've been treated and the circumstances in which I have in consequence been placed, I am sure you would excuse this act for the cause, and even approve it, however you might wish the application to be made elsewhere." O'Brien thanked Allsop for his friendship and declared that Hetherington could "go to the devil."[48]

A popular figure who devoted himself fully to the movement in its early stages, O'Brien wrote numerous items for the Chartist press and went on speaking tours. He attended the first Chartist Convention, which opened in February 1839, as a delegate for at least six localities, having been selected by the radicals of London, Leigh, Bristol, Norwich, Stockport, and Newport on the Isle of Wight. Nobody at the convention represented more places than O'Brien. This was a mark of their faith in him, no doubt, but it was also practical: owing to the costs and distances involved, and the legal restriction that kept the total number of delegates below fifty, it made sense for individuals to represent more than one place. At the convention, too, O'Brien could be disputatious. His comments were more pleasing to the "physical force" minority than the supporters of "moral force," and he tried unsuccessfully to deny the post of convention secretary to London moderate William Lovett. O'Brien disagreed with some of the proposals presented at the convention—including that for a "general strike"—and repeatedly urged that the sense of the people should be taken before final decisions were made, to ensure maximum unity in the movement and to give the leadership a clear mandate. He also tried to create the impression that the convention was holding back the masses—that the government should make concessions in order to prevent violence—and he took up the older ideas of "anti-Parliament" and "legislative attorney," arguing that if the government refused to negotiate, the convention, rather than acting simply as a petitioning body, would make itself a permanent assembly of the real representatives of the people. O'Brien addressed several of the "monster meetings" that took place in the summer of 1839 (the convention's proceedings were adjourned between 26 July and 26 August). Sometimes he issued statements in order to clarify his position, because he was accused of expressing extreme and incendiary opinions. He wanted land reform, he explained, as a matter of social justice, not because he hoped for the spoliation and murder of the rich, and he did not want Chartists to engage in illegal acts, only to defend themselves and their rights when treated improperly by the authorities. Government repression got the better of O'Brien, however, and he was convicted of political offenses in March 1840 and imprisoned for eighteen months in Lancaster Castle.[49]

He had been a marked man for some time,[50] and as far as antireformers were concerned, his (bad) reputation went before him. In the spring of 1839, for example, when it was announced in Chichester, Sussex, that O'Brien would be addressing a meeting in the town's council chamber, there was an immediate protest by "inhabitant householders" who placarded the walls and induced the mayor of Chichester, George Irving, to call the meeting off. These protesters claimed that permission to hold the meeting had been obtained under false pretenses, and in order to leave the municipality in no doubt of the danger posed by O'Brien's impending arrival, garbled versions of statements he had made (mainly in the *Operative*) were circulated. Attention was drawn in particular to O'Brien's opinion that "landlords, capitalists, and farmers" were "willful robbers, traitors, and murderers of the people" who "deserve to be driven with fire and sword out of every community on the earth." To allow the meeting to go ahead, O'Brien's local opponents insisted, "must be productive of present evil, and will leave an indelible stain upon the character of our City and its Municipality." It could not be "right and fitting" that a "Public Room hitherto dedicated to the administration of the Laws and the preservation of Peace and Order" should be used for "the propagation of doctrines hostile to all these great interests, endangering property and life and leading to the subversion of the civil and social institutions of the Country."[51] As well as demonstrating the fear and loathing that O'Brien could inspire in those of a contrary political persuasion, the Chichester controversy also shows that the struggle for the Charter often merged with preexisting local conflicts. The meeting in Chichester had been arranged by men in the "Liberal Interest" who had recently contested municipal elections and had links with the Radical Association in Brighton, thirty miles away. Among those who wanted the meeting canceled was businessman William Mason, a candidate for election in Friary Ward. Mason and his colleagues prepared a petition against O'Brien, which was placed in Mason's office for signing.

An official backlash against Chartism was partly prompted, and greatly facilitated, by the Bull Ring Riots of July 1839 and the Newport Rising of November 1839. It is possible that these disorders were linked with insurrectionary intentions in other Chartist regions. O'Brien later implied that the Newport insurgents had been encouraged by promises of support from extremists in Manchester.[52] The growth of the "physical force" wing of the movement disappointed many Chartists. In Leicester, for example, the preference was very much for nonviolence, and O'Brien's opposition to the "general strike" met with approval. Yet O'Brien also shared responsibility for the rise in militancy elsewhere, as when he told the crowds on Peep Green, near Leeds, on 21 May 1839, that the people were determined to secure the Charter and would abandon peaceful methods if these failed. When he went to Scotland, where "moral force" sentiment was strong, some of his remarks were not well received. Having been eulogized at a dinner in Glasgow in June 1838, he was criticized a year later for "frequent recourse to oaths and blasphemy" in a series of lectures in Edinburgh. On this speaking tour he rather stood out, because other radical celebrities at the time were more careful with their language so as not to alienate the moderates among Scottish Chartists.[53] But even in "moral force" areas like Scotland, Chartism was not uniform or unvarying. Many could imagine a resort to violence *if necessary* and gave it a tacit acceptance.[54]

Gammage later recalled that in all his writings and speeches of 1839, O'Brien implored people to support the national Chartist petition; "but he plainly told them that if they were not prepared to back their signatures with something still more powerful, they would never produce the slightest effect." The threat of violence was just that, a threat, and O'Brien meant only to frighten the government into making concessions. Emphasizing the availability and legitimacy of "physical force" was not the same thing as directly recommending its use. As Malcolm Chase observes, O'Brien liked to address audiences in London rather than in the Midlands and the

North of England because he was not committed to violence and was embarrassed by the disturbances breaking out in the provinces. O'Brien's importance to London Chartism has been queried, however, by Iorwerth Prothero, who emphasizes the grassroots elements of "artisan radicalism" in the capital and suggests that Chartists there were not reliant on high-profile leaders or on these leaders' ideas.[55] As for Scotland, O'Brien retained a following there in later years despite the reproaches of 1839 (Gammage met with O'Brienites in Galashiels and Lasswade, for instance, in August 1843).[56]

At the convention, and at the mass meetings of 1839, O'Brien talked of calm and sober protest while giving cues toward more decisive action. Everything was conditional. Chartists should stay within the law, provided "our oppressors" behaved in the same spirit. If they did not, Chartists would have a "duty" to "meet force with force." While "premature and partial outbreaks" must be avoided, tyranny was not to be borne and "all men who wrung a fortune from the sweat of the people" would be held accountable "in life and property." If radical reform was delayed, arrangements should be made to elect a "people's parliament" to rival the corrupt and unrepresentative body at Westminster. O'Brien's speeches exposed an array of hate figures: "our oppressors in the middle and upper ranks" included "monopolists," "fellows who live by profits, who live by usury," "a rascally crew of attorneys, bishops and parsons, pawnbrokers and stockjobbers," and "military officers." In the spring of 1839 O'Brien told a rally in London that the national petition had 1.2 million signatures, but he also mentioned an equal number of pikes. Then in May, when the convention moved from London to Birmingham, it was O'Brien who toned down the wording of a proposed address to the people. Yet he still declared that arming was appropriate, even while urging Chartists to go to their meetings unarmed and in good order.[57]

O'Brien was sending out mixed messages. If this was intentional, it also reflected confusion within Chartism itself. Most importantly, perhaps, there was no clear sense of the role and responsibilities of the convention. Was it a temporary body that would disband once the national petition had been presented to Parliament? Or should it carry on and serve as the movement's decision-making council? Many of the Chartists who had chosen delegates and collected money locally to pay its expenses wanted the convention to remain in place. O'Brien did not trust some of its members and measures, but he also wondered if it could usefully develop into an alternative parliament, which the Chartists might need if they had to coerce legislators at Westminster. O'Brien did not favor violence, though, and counseled against hasty or illegal measures. On one occasion, when lecturing in Bury, he even had the doors of the meeting room locked so that the Chartists in attendance could not join in an antipolice riot that had flared up outside. Mass mobilization was certainly a Chartist intention, but the weight of numbers had to be employed shrewdly. O'Brien wanted discipline and organization.[58]

The unstable mixing of confrontation and restraint can also be seen in Chartist notions of petitioning. O'Brien was convinced of the need for something more than ordinary petitioning. The people's pleas were routinely disregarded, he complained early in 1837, and therefore a way had to be found to bring more pressure to bear. One possibility was to include in petitioning activity the demand that the people should be heard at the bar of the House of Commons: "A petition of this sort, accompanied to the House by 200,000 people and headed by all the popular leaders of good repute throughout the country, would be worth ten thousand of the ordinary kind." Here was a picture of mass, coordinated, nationwide action generating a petition that would be backed by the physical presence of leaders and petitioners—a demonstration of power that could not be ignored.[59] Or could it? John Plotz has used O'Brien's concept of the mass petition as the basis for a discussion of the "representative" nature of the crowd and of the crowd as a form of language. Some contemporaries were unimpressed by O'Brien's proposal because they did not accept that the crowd was a representative entity. O'Brien's priority was not the petition but how it would be used. The main task was not to request something from Parliament, Plotz concludes, but to change the attitude of Parliament.

> This is a significant innovation in petition-making because it demands that the assembly of massed people themselves be construed as representative of a desire to be represented. O'Brien wants parliament to acknowledge that political discourse must be expanded so that two hundred thousand people peaceably assembled in the streets of London can be counted as a speech act as comprehensible as any written petition—and ten thousand times as effective. He is demanding that a movement that makes its supporters physically present in the streets be granted proxy authority to speak for the larger body that its crowds are meant to represent.

With the rise of the Chartist mass platform, crowd action served as collective speech. Chartist meetings and other events were evocative of something bigger, but this became a matter of contention. Many responded negatively. They disliked the hint of danger carried by what Plotz calls "the bodily presence of the crowd behind its peaceable speech," which explains their hostility and their determination to deny the crowd any representative quality.[60]

O'Brien's efforts to find a way forward for Chartism were affected by his time in prison. As the Chartist challenge to the government mounted, and was punctuated by outbreaks of violence, the government hoped to quell unrest through the arrest and trial of prominent spokesmen. O'Brien defended himself and was acquitted when tried for seditious conspiracy and unlawful assembly in Newcastle-upon-Tyne in February 1840. Acquittal enhanced his reputation, and there was much rejoicing in the radical press. But only weeks later he was found guilty of sedition in Liverpool (in this case, the offenses related not to a specific meeting or speech but to O'Brien's activity throughout Lancashire in the previous year, making a legal defense more difficult to put together). His prison experience was disturbing and damaging to him on several levels. Other imprisoned Chartist leaders also suffered greatly. For intelligent, active, and politically literate individuals, as Stephen Roberts points out, prison conditions at this time were "appalling" and "particularly punitive."[61]

The lawyer, writer, and former editor of the Tory *Quarterly Review* (and nephew of the aforementioned Samuel Taylor Coleridge) John Taylor Coleridge, who was present at O'Brien's trial in Newcastle, recorded that the many miners who sat in the gallery had been an intimidating presence (they seemed "not to want the will for an outbreak"). O'Brien

> made a very eloquent, very amusing, very exciting and mischievous speech in his defence. He had, however, a very unfavourable jury; for the Chartists had contrived to frighten those who had anything to lose, and none, in general, were more opposed to them than the shopkeepers, tradesmen, and small farmers. But I thought him, on the evidence, entitled to an acquittal, and acquitted he was.

Coleridge believed the Chartists to be "honest and misled enthusiasts." Though most of them sought "only to vindicate to themselves what they thought their labour entitled them to," their agitation became dangerous, and Coleridge approved of the government's clampdown as the only way to prevent "plunder and havoc." At the same time, he was impressed by the way the leaders conducted themselves in court. They proved themselves to be well read, courageous, and highly skilled in speechmaking. After the conviction of O'Brien and others, the authorities became more lenient: "It is usual in such cases, when the Government has succeeded in convicting the ringleaders, and a sufficient number to produce the effect of example, to deal gently with the remainder."[62]

Owenite John Finch wrote of O'Brien's Liverpool trial to Owen in April 1840. There was a suggestion that O'Brien felt let down by the Chartist body. "Bronterre O'Brien is entirely with us," Finch commented, "and I know he is sick both of politics and his party." Finch thought that O'Brien's eighteen-month sentence might be a watershed. The authorities had taken their vengeance and should now be satisfied. The wise course would be to cease the prosecutions and release political offenders on condition that they give up "physical force," for this "would do more to put down Chartism than all the penal laws ever passed in Parliament." Owen should call for mercy, Finch recommended, and if he did he would win more popularity and influence. Finch hoped that the government would not opt for further repression in case this laid up "a store of wrath" for the future.[63]

Three letters from O'Brien to Thomas Allsop, smuggled out from Lancaster Castle, attest to the "degrading," "loathsome," "melancholy" situation in which O'Brien found himself. He was "poor and broken down," he wrote. Prison rules were oppressive, and though the governor was kind, his discretion was limited. O'Brien was frequently unwell. He was plagued by "intense mental suffering." On one occasion he became so sick that his fellow prisoners demanded that a doctor be called in. An appeal was made to the local magistrates for better conditions, and O'Brien thought of extending this effort to the radical press and even Parliament. A group of Liverpool reformers had donated a small sum to allow him to meet his basic needs, but he really wanted to write and thought that he could thereby earn a few pounds a week—"as to public support, not only is it too precarious to depend on, but, what is worse, it always tends to degrade and injure a public man in the eyes of those he desires to serve." O'Brien was not asking for an easy time. He understood that he must submit to the daily routines.

> I am not above doing for myself what somebody must do. I make my own bed, brush my own room, empty my own slops, clean my own knives, forks, plates, cook my own food, clean my own boots, etc.—and find the occupation rather pleasant than otherwise. Indeed, without something to do the place would be intolerable. We should have to cut out throats for want of other occupation.

Above all, O'Brien longed to have books and paper and a place to write. Without these things, he told Allsop, he could not maintain himself or his family while he was incarcerated: "I am quite useless to myself, as well as to the public."[64]

Even in this sorry state, however, O'Brien had energy enough to begin another feud with former colleagues. Without O'Brien's knowledge or approval, William Carpenter had asked Allsop and others for financial backing for the *Southern Star*. O'Brien denounced this "villainy" in the prison letters and wanted it to be known that he was not responsible. He feared that Carpenter had presented these requests as if they came from O'Brien himself—"I never in my life felt such indignation"—and he was all the more embarrassed because Carpenter had approached individuals to whom O'Brien already owed money ("heavy obligations" that he was unlikely to make good for some time). O'Brien assured Allsop that he would never solicit money in this manner for a newspaper that had little chance of success; and he would be reluctant to apply to Allsop in particular because of the latter's past generosity: to ask for more would be the height of ingratitude. The one thing that had made O'Brien unhappy "for years," he avowed, was placing burdens on his friends.[65]

His misery was soon compounded. O'Brien learned that allegations had been made by Thomas Smith, of the Strand, London, who, with Allsop, had helped O'Brien and Carpenter to set up the *Southern Star* (by standing security) early in 1840. It appears that Smith was offended by Carpenter's request for more money and blamed O'Brien. Smith declared publicly that he had been urged to conduct the paper for O'Brien's benefit while the latter was in prison and that he had documentary proof that O'Brien had made the request to him personally. O'Brien denounced this "infamous fabrication" and again questioned Carpenter's conduct.

> To him mainly I attribute Smith's conspiracy to degrade and destroy my poor family and to blast my reputation with the public, though I can never acquit Smith himself for the part he has taken. All I had left after nine years' devotion to the people's cause, and after unexampled private persecutions and sufferings, was *my character*, and this Smith has endeavoured to destroy.

O'Brien insisted that he had not approached Smith and that, since he was no longer associated with the *Southern Star*, he expected no remuneration from that source. When he was sent to prison, he left the paper entirely in the hands of Smith and

Carpenter. Now, knowing that O'Brien could not defend himself, Smith had attacked him and driven his wife Sophia to despair with his "cold-blooded perfidy." Smith and Carpenter, a "monster of infamy," were ruining O'Brien's chances of supporting himself and his family through journalism, and their conspiracy "has nearly cost me my life and made poor Mrs. O'Brien so miserable that she has often wished to be dead. . . . When I suffered them quietly to appropriate the *Southern Star* and do what they liked with it, why could not the assassins let me alone?" O'Brien hoped that Allsop and others would accept *his* version of events, not that of his enemies.[66]

Efforts were made to raise money for O'Brien's family while he was in prison. In view of what would happen subsequently, it is important to note that Feargus O'Connor was among the participants. He knew that Allsop would help and expected others to join in (he mentioned Smith, but this was before O'Brien and Smith turned against each other). As O'Connor informed Allsop late in April 1840:

> In compliance with a request from poor O'Brien I called upon Mrs. O'Brien on Friday night last and promised to converse with you and others who wished for my cooperation in anything that has to be done for her. Use my name in your undertakings as you shall think fit, as the nature of the case demands and as circumstances require. I will give double per week what any other person gives and between us I think we may make up £2 per week, which would make the poor thing comfortable. . . . No time should be lost, as she has literally no means of support beyond that volunteered by her friends.[67]

It is likely that O'Brien's mental condition and physical health were already declining before his incarceration in 1840–41. He was depressed and tired. Then the length of his sentence shook him deeply, as did the restrictions placed upon his reading and writing in prison. His spirits improved when these restrictions were lifted, but his experience of the retributive capacity of the state made him think more critically about the ends and means of radicalism. Another significant development in this period was O'Brien's rift with O'Connor. They had disagreed on a number of matters in the past but had continued to work together. In 1841, when O'Connor urged Chartists to back Tory candidates at the upcoming general election in order to punish the Whig government for its crimes against the people, O'Brien dissented. Neither the Whigs nor the Tories cared about reform, he argued, and neither was deserving of support. Since they were just as bad as each other, the Chartist movement ought to put up its own candidates. O'Brien's relationship with O'Connor began to deteriorate from this time. Meanwhile, the meetings in Liverpool, Lancaster, Edinburgh, Manchester, Newcastle, and other towns that were held to celebrate O'Brien's release from prison gave an indication that he still had a personal support base.[68]

The meeting at Liverpool generated a two-penny pamphlet given over to the speech of local Chartist leader William Jones.[69] Describing O'Brien and O'Connor as victims of "Whig persecution," Jones gave voice to the promise in which all true Chartists believed:

> As surely as class-legislation has produced the present state of things, so would the People's Charter give to the bulk of the population the power of adopting that system of society which they believe would be best calculated to promote the interests of the whole community, and to secure the real object of human existence, the practice of virtue and the enjoyment of happiness.

This might have been taken straight from one of O'Brien's writings. Jones paid tribute to his "gigantic intellect" and declared that with O'Brien to instruct them, and O'Connor to direct, the Chartists could be confident of victory.[70] The remarks of Jones were echoed by other speakers in other towns at this time.[71] O'Brien continued to attract followers. Soon he would have his first meeting with Robert Gammage, who called at his home in Holborn in 1842, and, already familiar with his ideas, would go on to advocate them energetically in later years.[72]

Although he remained influential in print and on the platform, his breach with O'Connor, whose popularity with the rank and file he could not match, and his willingness to join with middle-class reformers, castigated by him previously as enemies of the working class, meant that a gap began to open up between O'Brien and mainstream Chartism. His time in prison prompted him to reflect on the movement's prospects, and he concluded that other methods had to be tried if radical objectives were to be accomplished and that (especially for him personally) it would be better to avoid conduct that might provoke official retaliation. This is not to suggest that his ideology was any less radical after prison than it had been before. He considered emigration but decided against it in order to continue campaigning, only to become increasingly irritated by O'Connor's imperious manner. O'Connor condemned his ideas and vetoed proposals for a cross-class reform effort. He responded with a *Vindication*, urging Chartists to change with the times. In the 1830s, O'Brien explained, it had been appropriate to combat middle-class power, but now circumstances were different. Some of the middle classes were prepared to agitate for goals that they shared with the Chartists. To accept them as allies would be to strengthen the movement and widen its appeal. In any case, O'Brien asserted, the honest radical committed to democracy had a perfect right to join whatever groups and associations he wanted. He was not to be dictated to, and if he remained steadfast to principle, nobody should presume to deprive him of independence. O'Connor and his followers rejected all this. Chartism was already splintering, and the quarrel between O'Connorites and O'Brienites added to the confusion. Historians have various notions about what was really going on. Dorothy Thompson suggests that O'Brien was reaching for a program that would attract the widest possible support and give him the popularity and status that O'Connor enjoyed; David Jones and J. T. Ward think that O'Connor was seeking more control over Chartism for his own sake but also in order to keep the movement united; Malcolm Chase contends that the breach between O'Brien and O'Connor was less damaging than the waning of support among local grassroots activists. There is truth in all these statements. For his part, O'Brien realized that disunity would be fatal. During 1842 he often called for an end to internal battles and for perseverance in the face of adversity, though this did not stop him from continuing to criticize O'Connor and others.[73]

The first part of O'Brien's career was over. He would remain active for upwards of twenty more years, however, and he was certain that he still had plenty to do. Private considerations took second place to his public responsibility, as he saw it, and indeed this had been the basis on which he had operated since 1830. He had become a radical celebrity, his status and influence established at the *Poor Man's Guardian* and preserved through his own newspapers and books but mainly as a leader of early Chartism and a contributor to the *Northern Star*. After 1841–42 the attributes, options, and supports available to him were not so plentiful. But there was no question of him giving up. He was determined to succeed in the newspaper business and to sustain his reputation as writer and orator; to guide Chartists along the path that he thought they should take; and to develop a comprehensive reform plan that would make clear the social and economic benefits to be made possible by the shift to a democratic form of government.

CHAPTER 2

# Radical and Outsider

O'Brien's departure from the highest echelons of the Chartist movement, following his clash with O'Connor, caused him some uneasiness and regret, but he believed himself to be in the right, and, at least initially, his new situation might have given cause for self-congratulation and a sense of release. Now he could be truly independent. O'Brien looked forward to developing and promoting more radical and far-reaching ideas. He could dedicate himself to his own program rather than schemes and policies devised by others. Though he was still loyal to the Charter, he had evidently lost sympathy with certain styles of Chartism (especially O'Connor's); and while he had previously had some inhibitions—perhaps not wishing to undermine Chartist unity—these inhibitions receded, not least because unity was patently impossible. Nevertheless, whatever personal and political gains were made by O'Brien in 1841–42, they came at a high cost. He faced isolation and marginalization such as he had not known before, and with so many Chartists turning away from him he lost potential readers for his newspapers, which in turn affected his livelihood. His ideas and proposals still attracted interest and approval, but O'Brien's ability to support himself and his family was seriously impaired.

O'Brien gave his backing to the middle-class Complete Suffrage Union of 1842, led by the Birmingham radical, pacifist, and antislavery campaigner Joseph Sturge.[1] This body endorsed most of the Charter but would not use the name "Chartist," and it embraced free trade and repeal of the Corn Laws while excluding the social demands to which many Chartists were attached. O'Connor and his followers eventually infiltrated the union and broke it up. O'Brien had warned that their involvement would be "without influence for any purposes but those of mischief."[2] Sturge and his friends were willing to combine with O'Brien and his followers, and even more so the "moderate Chartists" surrounding William Lovett, but O'Connor blocked the move (and Sturge also found that the closer his relations with Chartist groups, the more he was chided by members of the Anti–Corn Law League). The union collapsed in December 1842.[3]

In his *Vindication*, O'Brien positioned himself between O'Connor, who refused at this time to work with middle-class reformers and reproached anyone who did, and Lovett, whose wish for cross-class collaboration would soon lead him to turn his back on Chartism.

> While I differ essentially from Mr. Lovett and his friends, as regards the practicability of a union with the middle classes generally, I differ still more from those heartless and factious politicians, who would not only confound the honest middle-class man that would give me my rights, with the knave who would not, but show themselves on all occasions a thousand times more intolerant and hostile to the objects of their own personal jealousy (however friendly to our principles) than they have ever done to our merciless oppressors—the would-be exterminators of the Chartist body.[4]

This was to be O'Brien's stance for the rest of his career.

The *Vindication* emphasized the following points. O'Brien's formal association with the Complete Suffrage Union arose from his selection as a delegate of the Chartists of Wooton-under-Edge (a market town near Stroud in Gloucestershire), and he was not alone, for other Chartists also involved themselves. Together, they persuaded the union's first conference to adopt the People's Charter. Most members of the union were "well disposed towards our cause," and this facilitated an agreement to hold a further conference, "to be elected on democratic principles," at which the whole Chartist strategy could be discussed, "details, name, and all." Instead of building upon a useful accord, the *Northern Star* attacked the union and "grossly and shamefully misrepresented" O'Brien's conduct. Rather than have the workers think him a traitor, O'Brien demanded a public meeting at which he could answer his accusers in person. This was refused. Then he wrote to the *Northern Star*, laying out his motives and actions, but his letter was not published. Others wrote letters in his defense and sent them for inclusion in the *Northern Star*. They were ignored. Denied an opportunity to explain himself, O'Brien issued the *Vindication*. It included his own statements along with material from other sources that supported his position. There was an address from the Chartists of Wooton-under-Edge, for instance, in which they thanked him for representing them, denounced those in the movement who sowed division, and insisted that O'Brien retained their complete confidence. The *Vindication* cost only a penny, "as the object is merely to cover the expense of printing and publishing." O'Brien stated that his wish was not to besmirch individuals but to set himself right with his fellow Chartists.[5]

Unfortunately for him, his standing in the movement was damaged by his breach with O'Connor. As well as falling out on public grounds—primarily electoral strategy in 1841 and the Complete Suffrage Union in 1842—the two engaged in bitter personal disputes. Accusations and counteraccusations multiplied. O'Connor thought O'Brien ungrateful and disloyal, while O'Brien maintained that he was not accountable to O'Connor for his words and deeds. By September 1842 there was no holding back. The *Northern Star* claimed that O'Brien, the "starved viper," was trying to raise himself up by putting O'Connor down and had admitted as much to a reliable witness. Many Chartists decided that O'Brien had gone beyond the pale.[6]

In a long letter published in the *Northern Star*, O'Connor called O'Brien "rash," "insolent," and "irascible," and declared that he would not have responded to O'Brien's lies had his honor not been impugned. He took particular exception to O'Brien's description of the circumstances surrounding the gift of a small weekly sum that O'Connor had contributed toward the upkeep of O'Brien's wife and children while O'Brien was in prison. Instead of being thankful, O'Brien asserted that the donation had been made in order to prevent his family from receiving a greater sum through an open appeal to the Chartist body. This O'Connor denied. Since they became colleagues in 1837, he went on, he had treated the impecunious O'Brien with unusual generosity, making loans and gifts, finding benefactors for him, and paying him well for his pieces for the *Northern Star* (even though they were "very slovenly and hastily written . . . low-spirited and pointless"). O'Connor revealed that O'Brien had also been considered for the post of editor of the *Northern Star*—during 1839 when it was expected to fall vacant—but that when this was put to O'Brien he made difficulties. There were other examples of O'Connor's kind consideration for O'Brien and his family. Meanwhile, O'Brien tried and failed to make a success of his various newspapers. He blamed others for his own shortcomings. In his anger he now claimed that O'Connor's generosity was a ploy, an effort to control him and destroy his reputation. O'Connor found this bizarre. Had he really been so cruel, O'Connor asked, why—when he heard that O'Brien had become ill in prison—did he immediately offer to cover the cost of whatever treatment and supplies were needed? If anyone was malicious it was O'Brien, whose allegations, demands, and schemes during his imprisonment and after indicated that he wished to undermine every other Chartist leader and break up the movement. His conversation and his correspondence were "low, base, scurrilous, false, and ungentlemanlike."

O'Brien held O'Connor partly responsible for his arrest and conviction (pointing to the *Northern Star*'s manner of reporting his speeches and the nonattendance of witnesses at his trial), but O'Connor's version was rather different: he had done what he could to help. As for their disagreement about the Complete Suffrage Union, O'Connor presented his own conduct as consistent, honest, and open, and O'Brien's as the opposite; and he maintained that O'Brien had not been denied opportunities to explain himself. Indeed, it was O'Brien, a "base and perfidious wretch," who tried to suppress statements that might cast him in a negative light. O'Connor and the *Northern Star* did not do this, for they welcomed disclosure and debate. O'Connor told O'Brien categorically that he had done nothing to offend or injure him "until you deserted the cause of the people," whereas O'Brien had, since his release from prison, attacked O'Connor in the most brazen and despicable manner. In addition,

> You did more to cause strife, confusion, and dissension than all the mischief-makers that ever went before you. You preached abstract notions upon subjects that you do not understand. You denounced everyone but J. Bronterre O'Brien. You did not make a single Chartist, but on the contrary, weakened the faith of many. . . . You intrigued and defamed with private letters, and made secret charges against every man whom you think to stand in your way.

O'Connor ridiculed O'Brien for his failed newspapers and counted on the people, before whom O'Brien was now "uncovered and unmasked," to make a distinction between a "miserable self-tormenter" and a man who "never assumed other character than that which I have and ever shall maintain, that of an honest, uncompromising, and resolute advocate of the people's rights." If O'Connor was "coward and traitor," what was O'Brien?

> You have neither constitution, head, or stomach for the position to which you would vainly aspire. You have neither knowledge, brains, nor temper to retain the position if fate had assigned it to you; and so from your masked battery you would aim your missiles at those whose knowledge, courage, and prudence but serve as a contrast to your lack of all those attributes which distinguish a good and honest man. You would be a pensioner upon any man's bounty, rather than lead a life of industry.... You have lived well upon the performance of those tricks with which your audience have become disgusted. You have well supported your position. You have succeeded in fomenting and perpetuating discord from the moment you entered upon public life. I trust that, in the retirement to which sound public opinion has now consigned you, you will have time for reflection and repentance.[7]

All this was quite a turnaround from previous years, when the two Chartist leaders had shared platforms around the country and complimented each other in their publications. During 1837 *Bronterre's National Reformer* had included items written by O'Connor.[8] But in 1842 the *British Statesman* became his severest foe, drawing attention to Chartist meetings at which O'Brien received votes of confidence, carrying letters that praised him and disapproved of O'Connor and the "knavery" of the *Northern Star*, and featuring O'Brien's direct exculpatory appeals to the radical reformers of Britain: "As a servant of the Chartist body, I hold myself responsible to them for my every public act. But I will not be responsible to any particular clique or faction, or to any dictator or knot of dictators, who may pretend to act in their name, without their authority." O'Brien warned repeatedly that O'Connor was not to be trusted. He published accounts of O'Connor's quarrels with a number of prominent radicals, all of which amounted to the same thing: O'Connor wanted to control them, and when they objected, he turned against them and tried to ruin them. O'Brien argued that Chartism could not prosper while O'Connor was in charge; and when his own remarks were challenged by correspondents, he insisted that they were not aware of everything going on "beneath the surface of Chartist politics" and that he wrote to serve not personal ends but the public interest.[9]

A pattern was established. O'Connor's friends and supporters assailed O'Brien in the radical press. Frequently, when meetings were held at which O'Brien was to be a speaker, they turned up in numbers to shout him down. O'Brien called upon O'Connor to meet him face to face at a public debate, but O'Connor refused. According to Gammage, as more Chartists came to share O'Brien's opinions about the movement and about O'Connor, the fact was hushed up or denied.[10] In Manchester,

Birmingham, Glasgow, and elsewhere, feuding continued for some time between the followers of O'Connor and those of O'Brien.[11]

After the candid and fiery altercations of 1842, O'Brien continued to condemn O'Connor and his accomplices. They were "base hypocrites" worshipped by "dupes." Proposals to reorganize the National Charter Association led O'Brien to repeat his claims about dictation. The NCA had been established in 1840 and soon boasted fifty thousand members and hundreds of local branches (O'Brien had for a time served on its executive, before O'Connor had him removed). O'Brien argued that strong local leadership would be better than a top-down structure dominated by a small central committee.

> Chartism has been wrecked—frittered away—all but annihilated by the attempt to force the whole Chartist body into one association. We said it would be so, before the experiment was tried. We now repeat our former prophecy. We predict that a still more fatal failure will be the result of the new projected organization supposing it to take place. . . . It will throw us back many years. It is an attempt to concentrate the whole strength and resources of Chartism in a few individuals, to whose ambition, venality, selfishness, and ignorance we shall be exposed, upon every emergency that may either result from the state of the country or be concocted by the government for the sake of breaking us up.

O'Brien was appalled by O'Connor's ascendancy and his policies. He also attributed the failure of his newspapers largely to O'Connorite opposition and spite. In 1846 there was another diatribe against the National Charter Association:

> It is neither national nor Chartist. It does not include one in a thousand of the Chartists who signed the National Petition, nor ever will. It is a mere coterie of O'Connor's partisans, and its object is not the Charter, but the bolstering up of that demagogue and the hunting down of every man of worth and spirit who will not submit to his dictation.

In 1849, in his *Social Reformer*, O'Brien was still urging readers not to be misled by O'Connor.[12]

The two came into personal contact, albeit briefly, at Chartist meetings in 1848, but there was no reconciliation. Their mutual friend Thomas Allsop tried to bring them together during 1847 and formed the impression that O'Brien was too inflexible. Allsop wanted O'Brien to forget personal differences and join forces with O'Connor for the public good. O'Brien insisted that the problem was on O'Connor's side, not his, and that if the three of them could meet privately—just Allsop, O'Connor, and O'Brien—he could substantiate his allegations about O'Connor's dishonesty and malevolence. Allsop's overtures came at a difficult time for O'Brien, which no doubt affected his response. He was short of money again, in danger of losing his home, and had to provide for a family unit that had grown to eight (relatives of his wife had come to live with O'Brien, his wife, and four children). O'Brien's relationship with Allsop was strained as Allsop urged him to reunite with the man he blamed for his loss of status, influence, and means of support.[13]

Allsop and O'Connor were fond of each other, judging by their surviving correspondence, but it is curious that the possibility of a reconciliation between O'Connor and O'Brien does not feature in their letters dating from 1847. Perhaps O'Connor was reluctant to discuss it. Allsop had leverage, for O'Connor was sometimes reliant on him for money, but Allsop probably chose not to press him because he thought that it was really O'Brien who ought to give way, or because he did not want to alienate O'Connor. There is a section in one of O'Connor's letters to Allsop that possibly refers to Allsop's proposal for clear-the-air negotiations between O'Connor and O'Brien, but it is undated and therefore its meaning cannot be verified absolutely. It was written at the House of Commons (O'Connor was elected MP for Nottingham at the general election of July 1847, and Parliament assembled in November; the letter seems to have been written sometime in the later weeks of 1847). O'Connor wrote: "I should much like to join you in your romantic hope but the fact is that I cannot gratify my better nature just now."[14]

Allsop was disappointed by O'Brien's attitude, but can he have been surprised? He must have known what O'Brien thought of O'Connor, and known also that O'Connor had lost—or never been given—the trust and affection of other public men. Another of Allsop's friends and correspondents, for example, was Richard Oastler, the prominent factory reformer and opponent of the New Poor Law. "I have made no treaty with O'Connor," Oastler wrote to Allsop in July 1846. Oastler's hostility appears to have abated, because he welcomed O'Connor's election to Parliament a year later, but he was unimpressed by O'Connor's Land Plan.[15]

Allsop described O'Brien and O'Connor as two planets in the same orbit and assured O'Brien that O'Connor was ready to bury the hatchet if O'Brien would do likewise, but O'Brien became indignant as Allsop persisted. He was angry that Allsop would not accept his interpretation of O'Connor's conduct.

> Gladly, most gladly, would I forget the wrongs I have endured and the principal author of them; but while the effects remain (an almost total absence of profitable and useful occupation, a virtual banishment from public life, the impossibility of serving either my family or the cause I have so long laboured and suffered for, the consciousness that I possess talents and acquirements to effect much good for my fellow creatures but am basely and tyrannically debarred from the exercise of them)—while these and their like effects remain I can neither forget any wrongs nor forgive the heartless and selfish author of them.

Allsop suggested that by allying once more with O'Connor and regaining a leadership role in the Chartist movement, O'Brien could have the same influence and respect (and earnings) that O'Connor enjoyed. O'Brien replied that he had no desire to do as O'Connor had done. O'Connor had raised himself up by destroying others. Did Allsop mean for O'Brien to do this?

> That is, organize mobs of fanatics and ruffians all over the country to put down every man that crossed my path and establish a newspaper for praising myself and running down any other man that I did not want to use at the time as a tool or accomplice. And when by this and the like means I had driven off every other man from the field and got exclusive possession of it I should then proceed to build up my own fortune on the ruins of my coadjutors—kick down the ladder on which I had climbed—and begin to dispense praise and patronage to those I had previously cashiered, enslaved, or ruined.

O'Brien kept up the familiar charges: O'Connor had damaged his newspapers, harassed his friends, interfered with his meetings, and wrecked Chartism, probably irreparably. O'Connor could not be trusted, and O'Brien was not the only one to think so. He told Allsop that other Chartists had the same opinion—indeed, the vast majority of delegates who attended the first Chartist Convention in 1839 would tell Allsop the same thing. O'Connor had tried to crush others as he crushed O'Brien. Allsop seemed to think that O'Brien had a perfect opportunity to revive his own fortunes, regain public position, and support himself and his family with ease. O'Brien disagreed. What Allsop expected of him would be false and dishonorable, for O'Connor only wanted him as a "slave" and "muzzled and tamed." How could O'Brien accept this? Why did Allsop not appreciate that the only arrangement that could work was for O'Connor to agree that he and O'Brien should leave each other alone? This was what O'Brien wanted, and he had proposed it many times through third parties. O'Connor would not consent.[16]

These exchanges between Allsop and O'Brien went on for some time, and nothing was resolved. O'Brien wrote that Allsop was laboring under a misunderstanding and could not be aware of all the facts. He pleaded with him not to believe the lies spread by O'Connor, the *Northern Star*, and O'Brien's other enemies. In letter after letter he ran through O'Connor's offenses, including the "treachery" of siding with Hetherington in 1836–37 (after, in conversation with O'Brien, he had condemned Hetherington as a "villain") and holding back witnesses who were needed to give evidence for the defense at O'Brien's trial in 1840. Furthermore:

> He has exiled many thousands of my political friends all over the kingdom. He has made it impossible for me to benefit myself and others for ten long years. During seven of those years he caused the failure of all my publications, and involved me in debts, difficulties, embarrassments, and mental suffering indescribable. He laid me three times in a sick bed from which my medical attendants did not expect me to rise a living man. He has caused me to pass nearly three years in the horrifying expectation of seeing my beloved wife carried off by excruciating illness and he afterwards had the atrocity to publish that I was the author of her sufferings. He has paraded my name in his paper as tainted with drunkenness, idleness, neglect of duty, and everything else of a similar kind calculated to deprive me of the chance of employment when it might offer. In short, I owe to O'Connor the loss of health, fame, fortune, peace of mind, domestic happiness, and every other blessing worth living for.

O'Brien denied that he was by nature—and "all who know me intimately will vouch for the truth of this"—a morbid, suspicious, unfriendly person. If he appeared so, it was the fault of O'Connor; and while it was true that he had not expressed himself to Allsop in a calm and polite manner, he wondered who on earth could when placed under such burdens ("circumstances over which I have no control"). It was not that he was unable to forgive. O'Brien had been involved in fierce disputes with Hetherington, Carpenter, and others, but after apologies all round they had patched things up. O'Brien claimed to have good relations with many in the Chartist movement, mainly because they respected each other's freedom of opinion. But not O'Connor. He was an ambitious and unscrupulous tyrant. O'Brien realized that Allsop saw O'Connor differently—but this was only because O'Connor had no reason to treat him the way he had treated O'Brien. The truth was that O'Connor did not want reconciliation. If he was sincere he could make it happen at once, with a simple statement in the *Northern Star* or before a public meeting or to O'Brien's face in front of witnesses, to the effect that he respected O'Brien's freedom of opinion and they could agree to disagree. He would not, O'Brien explained, because he was not serious about reconciliation. He just wanted Allsop and others to think he was. The whole affair was regrettable and indeed shameful. O'Brien reflected that he could have done so much more for the reform cause, and entered Parliament, and made an adequate living; and he would have accepted O'Connor as chief (he had never wanted to lead Chartism himself). He could have been useful and successful, but O'Connor had ruined everything. Even now, though, it was not too late. O'Brien told Allsop that he was willing to make a pact with O'Connor *provided* it could be done for the public advantage and without injury to himself. O'Brien was sure that O'Connor would not make this possible. What O'Connor really wanted was for him to abandon "those principles and self-respect for which I have endured years of wrong and wretchedness."[17]

It is easy to assume that O'Brien's remarks—the zealous self-justifications, emotional protests, tortuous clarifications, and increasingly extreme allegations—proceeded from an unstable mind. But the position he took was also necessitated by considerations that were both personal and public. O'Brien may have believed that he had to dissuade Allsop from accepting O'Connor's version of events or he would lose Allsop's financial help. He also saw that he could not go ahead with any form of rapprochement that would allow people to think that his statements about O'Connor were untrue and O'Connor's statements about him accurate.

Aside from personal and public reasons for O'Brien's invectives against O'Connor, his bitterness was exacerbated by financial worry and periods of ill health. After his release from prison O'Brien's circumstances were quite often parlous in the extreme, to the extent that he did not have enough money even for basic necessities. In these times his hopes and energies were sapped and he feared for his wife and children. In a letter dating from around 1843 to his friend Mathews (the forename is not given), a resident of Bungay, Suffolk, O'Brien described a pitiful situation. His income had fallen; he had not paid his rent for nine months; "I have not a shilling to spare for any purpose but actual food"; and he was seriously afflicted with pain in the head and throat. He told Mathews that he could not travel to give lectures unless he received specific invitations—presumably because this would mean he could be sure of payment. In London, he wrote, his audiences were increasing, but in the preceding weeks "they were nil." There was no money for O'Brien to write and print. "If the democrats would raise £80 or £100 for me," he would take care of his family and get back into publishing. As it was, O'Brien was sinking into depression (which would affect him more as the years passed). He bemoaned his misfortunes: "My life has been one of trouble, owing to persecution in my youth by priests and in later times by the middle classes. But I never was so completely hemmed in on all sides as I am just now."[18]

In 1844, following the failure of his *Poor Man's Guardian and Repealer's Friend*, O'Brien moved to the Isle of Man, which had free postage and no newspaper taxes. He hoped that lower costs would make it possible for him finally to succeed in the newspaper business. He began a printing and stationery concern, opened a library, and eventually launched the *National Reformer and Manx Weekly Review*. His principles were unchanged. The workers had to gain political rights in order to secure all the other improvements they needed, which meant that manhood suffrage remained the great prerequisite; but all six points of the Charter were to be sought, along with land nationalization, currency reform, and "equitable exchange through national marts." Unfortunately, O'Brien was unable to make enough money to pay off the debts he had accrued before moving to the Isle of Man. He abandoned his activities there and returned to London late in 1847.[19] John Belchem regards his activity on the Isle of Man as an abject failure. Not only did the "disaffected" O'Brien devote too much column space to remarks against O'Connor, and against the "base" and "venal" printers, publishers, vendors, and agents of London who, he alleged, had obstructed his journalistic efforts there, but he also refused to pay attention to any reform proposals other than his own, convinced that his were the best available. This, writes Belchem, showed "poor business sense for a radical publisher." O'Brien gained little support from workers' organizations such as trade unions and benefit societies because he condemned them as inadequate. He was "out of step with changes in working-class collective behaviour."[20] No doubt his personal vendettas and a single-minded preoccupation with his own radical program did affect O'Brien's prospects on the Isle of Man. Yet his shop, library, and newspaper made a profit overall—just not enough to wipe out previous debts.

Toward the end of 1847, realizing that he needed to make a change, O'Brien contacted friends for help. He sought paid work rather than handouts. Several of these requests went to Allsop:

> You will confer an everlasting obligation on me by being the instrument of obtaining for me any sort of engagement or occupation by which I can make my services worth the pay. . . . I would not press this application if there were not a great necessity for it, which every day nay every hour increases.

O'Brien spent more than a few weeks in London while he was based on the Isle of Man, trying to raise money to save his business, but to no avail. This was a sad predicament, he informed Allsop, because with more stock and a small amount of ready cash the shop would have been secure. With its closure O'Brien lost not only the shop but all the money he had put into it previously. He needed just one year to recover, he believed. If he could get enough money to live on for twelve months he would do nothing but write, earn handsomely from this writing, and "then I might be able to shape my own course." For seven or eight years he had been wanting to finish a biography of Robespierre, a history of Ireland, a treatise on democracy, a book about European politics, and essays on the land, currency, and exchange. He had been prevented by unfavorable circumstances (and here he mentioned O'Connor, as usual).

> All I want is *twelve months' command of my books and brains* that I may write historical and other works, *in my own way*, for the London market, and if God spares my health I venture to say I shall be a safe man after that. . . . But I can do nothing while I am hourly exposed to be left without a home or a bed to lie on.

O'Brien asked Allsop to contact booksellers, agents, stationers, or anyone else who could render assistance. "For want of credit and position I am incapable of doing this for myself. Otherwise be assured, my dear Mr. A., I would not obtrude such an awkward commission upon you."[21]

O'Brien distanced himself from the Chartist revival of 1848. Although he was selected as a delegate to another convention, he withdrew from this body and was further marginalized in the process (Henry Weisser quips that O'Brien "left the Chartist movement in a huff in 1848"). Almost inevitably he quarreled with O'Connor at the convention. A few days later, on 9 April 1848, he confirmed to a meeting of London Chartists that he had resigned from the convention because he regarded its majority as unsound. He was not questioning anybody's motives, he said, but he did perceive in other delegates a want of judgment (and, Gammage recorded, O'Brien "was resolved to act up to principles which he had always publicly avowed, and to which he considered himself publicly pledged").[22] Allsop shared O'Brien's misgivings about the convention. It "decided upon meeting in spite of the authorities," Allsop wrote disapprovingly to Robert Owen.[23]

O'Brien wanted a pragmatic approach, in view of the state's ability to withstand pressure, but the convention opted for confrontation, with a mass mobilization culminating in an irresistible coup de grâce. The demonstration on Kennington Common on 10 April proved to be an embarrassment for O'Connor and his associates, for the government had taken full precautions. Thereafter, different Chartist groups and leaders found it impossible to work together, and the former levels of energy, commitment, and support were never to return. O'Brien attended several meetings and joined in the negotiations between moderates and militants in London, but little came of this. He still had a personal following, mainly in London. He launched a new weekly, the *Power of the Pence*, in November 1848, intended "for those who know the look of a penny better than that of a pound," and it contained ambitious, lengthy, informative articles on current affairs, political ideas, reform proposals, and other topics of concern to plebeian radicals. But there was no light reading, which limited its appeal, and it made no money. O'Brien's health problems did not help. The *Power of the Pence* folded in April 1849. Another weekly, the *Social Reformer*, lasted for only three months later that year. O'Brien continued to appear in lecture rooms and meeting halls and found outlets in the metropolitan and provincial press, especially the popular publications of G. W. M. Reynolds (the two men had more than political ideas in common: they were both Francophiles and both careless with money). In 1849–50 O'Brien set up the National Reform League for the Peaceful Regeneration of Society, which appended social and economic aims to the six points of the Charter. O'Brien served as the NRL's president. He also involved himself in debates about Europe in the aftermath of the 1848 revolutions, and joined international "social democratic" committees. Despite penury and illness he remained active and in 1849 established the Eclectic Institution, which used several premises in the Soho district of London (including rooms in John Street, a regular meeting place for various political clubs, and Newman Street) and by 1851 was based in an abandoned chapel in Denmark Street. There he spoke several times a week on politics, religion, education, and currency and credit. The institution also offered classes in English, French, mathematics, and science.[24] The activities of the NRL and events at the Eclectic Institution were given full coverage in O'Brien's publications.[25]

O'Brien's influence held steady after 1848. Such was his fame and importance, indeed, that his name alone was "almost a programme," according to Theodore

Rothstein.[26] Gammage joined the NRL and continued to spread O'Brienite principles as an itinerant lecturer; and when he was elected to the executive of the National Charter Association in 1852, he inserted O'Brien's proposals on land and money into an address issued by the executive to the whole Chartist body. In the spring of that year Gammage spent two days with his "dear friend" O'Brien before heading out on another speaking tour that took him to Wales. His lecture in Newtown on 20 October 1852 was given over entirely to the NRL platform. It was published as a pamphlet and sold "several thousand copies" across Britain: "It was brought out in so cheap a form that all but the penniless could purchase it."[27] This indicates the continuing appeal of O'Brien's ideas.

The speeches O'Brien made at NRL meetings offer a useful indication of his post-1848 agenda and its consistency with previous statements and commitments. Addressing a "numerous audience" in the John Street rooms in March 1850, and employing his "usual lucid and humorous style," O'Brien "had no hesitation in saying that the League would one day be the strongest party in England, because all other parties, not founded on its principles, must get weaker, while the League would be daily getting stronger." Ideas and proposals that had once struggled to find acceptance were winning support—"it was satisfactory to perceive that political Chartism was now seldom advocated without being conjoined with social reform aspirations"—and O'Brien referred to a recent gathering in Greenwich, at which his proposition "that all measures of free trade shall be accompanied by a repeal in the fixed price of gold and also with a readjustment of all public burdens to a scale proportionate to the fall in prices caused by free trade" met with a friendly reception. He condemned the "commercial aristocracy" that he said ruled Britain and restricted popular liberty. The NRL, O'Brien declared, eschewed "political and social cant and hypocrisy" and represented a "neutral ground" where all groups would find a welcome, and fair treatment, whatever their political, social, economic, or religious complexion. The NRL was "the only party who consecrated the past for the benefit of existing interests" and "consecrated the future for the benefit of the whole people."[28]

In this same speech O'Brien dwelt at length on the lessons of the past and on the principles and contributions of historical figures. The usual description of Julius Caesar as a despot and his assassins as noble and patriotic saviors of Rome was erroneous, O'Brien said. The real reason why Caesar was killed related to his popularity with the common people. His reforms had benefited them, and the wealthy removed him to defend their own comforts and privileges. O'Brien thought that changing assessments of historical figures pointed to the advance of sound opinions more generally. Did anyone care much anymore about the identity of "Junius," who had written against government abuse and incompetence in 1769–72 to great acclaim? O'Brien argued that royal and parliamentary misbehavior had come to matter far less than other problems, and people were beginning to realize that they should tackle the real cause of social evils.

> Legal and conventional plunderers of the working classes were in the act of attributing public distress to anything but their own injustice, and artfully managed thereby to divert public attention from bad social institutions to mere political institutions of comparative unimportance. The power of the crown had often been egregiously exaggerated.

Queen Victoria reigned, but her ministers governed and her prerogatives were limited. The British system was oligarchical rather than monarchical, "yet popularity-hunters went about denouncing kings—those mere puppets of crafty landlords and money-lords." If there was one figure more than others who merited rehabilitation on public grounds, it was Robespierre, and O'Brien was pleased that his own efforts in this direction were bearing fruit.

> A few years ago he had been voted mad for defending Robespierre against the calumnies of historians and against popular prejudice; but now, apologists for that wise and good man were frequently appearing. . . . Robespierre was one of the truest philanthropists the world had ever seen; and the crimes which had been attributed to him were the work of his enemies—who, dreading the influence which he had acquired over the working classes, through the wise and just measures of reform he had advocated, contrived by intrigue, slander, and treachery to get him murdered before those reforms could be carried into practice. The privileged classes, who wished to keep the working classes powerless slaves to capitalists and landlords, hated and dreaded such reformers as Maximilian Robespierre, and would sacrifice them without remorse.

O'Brien added that two other admirable figures, Paine and Cobbett, were also better understood than they had formerly been. Their ideas about land and money, so useful to so many, could now be properly appreciated (and their shortcomings as well as strengths "generally admitted").[29]

Though most of his speaking engagements were in London, O'Brien traveled as much as he could to promote the NRL program in person. He went as far as Scotland, where he still retained some popularity, for a speaking and organizing tour in the summer of 1850. The main goal was to set up a Scottish section of the NRL (if it was established, it does not appear to have lasted very long).[30]

In October 1851 about 130 guests attended a supper in Wardour Street, Soho, to honor O'Brien and mark the second anniversary of the foundation of the NRL. Among the toasts were "the sovereignty of the people" and "the National Reform League and its principles," and O'Brien was applauded as the "untiring friend and teacher of the people" who "under all times and circumstances... had always been a good and true reformer." He responded by forecasting eventual success for the NRL.

> Notwithstanding the predictions of false friends and open enemies, they had outlived all the opposition that had so assiduously been brought against them, and they would, he had no doubt, live until their end was accomplished. The National Reform League was not an ephemeral body—its principles were for all time. Individual members might die, and greater numbers would supply their place, but, as an aggregate body, the League would never die until a veritable social and democratic republic should be established.

O'Brien preached perseverance and honesty and spoke "with great fervour" about "the wrongs of the people and their folly in not uniting to remedy them." He was glad to be with so many "true friends . . . who had rallied round him in the days when he had been denounced and abused by the leaders of all parties, and were still at his side, battling for the cause of human progress." He gave "a retrospective of his career," looking back over twenty years, reminiscing about Hunt, Cobbett, and others, and again defending the reputation of Robespierre. "He concluded by showing the great progress which true principles had made during late years, and sat down amid tumultuous and long-continued cheering."[31]

O'Brien followed this up just weeks later with a forthright speech on European affairs at a large meeting in Holborn chaired by George Jacob Holyoake, a friend of O'Brien and a prominent promoter by writing and speaking of radicalism, secularism, and cooperation. O'Brien was able to amend a motion on French politics to make it more hostile toward Louis Napoleon, the president of the Second Republic who had recently staged a coup to overthrow it. There were objections to O'Brien's "intemperate" language, but his amendment was carried by a clear majority. He rejected both the complaints made about his speech and the suggestion that the British government under Lord Palmerston might be persuaded to act to save French liberty.[32]

O'Brien's efforts confirm that to him, as to others, 1848 was not an ending or culmination. There was no break in his writing, speaking, and organizing. The notion that 1848 marked a "defeat" was not widespread among radicals at the time. It is likely that this concept was only generated later, and mainly by those interests in state and society that wanted to discredit Chartism and deny its importance. Although a growing number of statesmen showed themselves willing to discuss parliamentary reform after 1848, thinking this could now be done safely since mass radicalism had been checked, Chartist morale was not destroyed by the events of 1848. If there was a sense of doom and gloom in some radical quarters, in others there was defiance and expectation. Some became even bolder in their politics than they had been previously. Ian Haywood contends that Chartism entered its most radical phase *after* 1848.[33]

Chartism had from the outset been a heterogeneous movement, and diversity also typified the post-1848 strands in British radicalism. Lasting unity and ideological consistency were not to be achieved. Chartism splintered, and O'Brien participated in and commented upon several of the efforts for reorganizations and mergers after 1848. Various groups made proposals in readiness for the Chartist Convention of 1851. O'Brien argued against compromise and only entertained joint endeavors when they were designed to promote the full Charter and a program of far-reaching social reform.[34] As international perspectives came more to the fore, O'Brien approved of some of the people and ideas involved in Chartist internationalism while finding fault with others. The 1848 revolutions prompted him to cement his links with international committees and extend his conversations with political exiles in London about democracy, class, the nation, and social change. As British radicals focused on "patriots" in Europe and America as objects of praise and admiration, O'Brien wrote of the affinity between Chartism and like-minded mobilizations abroad. He stated that in France as in Britain, a democrat had to be a socialist and a socialist a democrat. Margot Finn has connected this with the rise of a "social definition" of patriotism, one that marked a departure from specific political doctrines and made patriotic language and symbol more flexible and easier to draw upon. Chartists were able to include their own values and goals in this new definition. One outcome was that when European revolutionary leaders visited Britain for political rallies and celebratory dinners, their hosts tended to pick and choose what to accept, and reject, from among the principles that these visitors expounded. They presumed to decide for themselves what the visitors stood for (in line with shifts in domestic politics). O'Brien's equivocal attitude toward Hungarian leader Lajos Kossuth, who arrived in 1851, exemplifies this tendency. He was ready to make use of Kossuth but objected strongly to some of the latter's opinions. In these years, as Finn explains, a "radical patriotism" was used to express class differences and press for reforms: "Disingenuous to an extreme, working-class radical analysis of social and economic relations accepted the overarching framework of the nation-state only to insist upon its reconfiguration to accommodate the claims of class." Kossuth did join briefly with O'Brien, who presented the Hungarian not as an antisocialist, middle-class liberal but as an "illustrious democrat" who believed in the principles of all "true Englishmen." Differing interpretations among British radicals at this time can be traced, at least in part, to the tension between traditional opposition to monarchical and state power and newer arguments about economic inequality and class power. O'Brien himself used both idioms, and though he promoted international fraternity, there were occasions on which he dismissed it as a side issue.[35]

Overt class consciousness increased from the 1820s onward, but this does not mean that old-style radicalism focusing on the corrupt state was supplanted. The two approaches can be seen in O'Brien's work. He wrote about class, property, and capital. He also continued to express familiar radical nostrums about the state. To him, there was no barrier between older and newer perspectives: class rhetoric could be employed in the very act of demanding manhood suffrage as the way to redeem the state.[36] If there was a danger of ambiguity, because of the discrepancy between an economic or class-based analysis and the radical inclination to prioritize political relationships, this was something that O'Brien was aware of and explicitly addressed. As he explained in 1838 in response to a correspondent who had asked about his opinion of shopkeepers, much depended on the *conduct* arising from class identity, not the class identity itself.

> It is because we are not opposed to Shopkeepers, merely as such, that we coined the term "Shopocrats," in order to distinguish the good from the bad, the politically honest from the politically dishonest, those to whom we are hostile and those to whom we are not. Under the present arrangements of society, Shopkeepers are almost as necessary as producers, but under no constitution of society ought there to exist the animal we call a "Shopocrat," which means a Shopkeeper or capitalist who would keep all the powers of government in his own class *through a monopoly*

> *of the elective franchise.* Now as all Shopkeepers are not necessarily, nor in point of fact, enemies of Universal Suffrage, it follows that they are not what we call "Shopocrats," or shop-exclusives, who would monopolize all political power to themselves.[37]

Radicals used a mixture of words, ideas, and symbols drawn from many sources. James Epstein points out that "tolerance for such apparently discordant ideological strains was born of neither ignorance nor ideological indifference."[38] Radical thought and action both arose from and helped to create identity and purpose.

By the late 1830s O'Brien was committed to the nationalization of the land, to result in a system of tenancies held from the state. His premise was that the land belonged to the people. It had to be taken back and leased out for productive activity, and the rents would finance social programs. Here was a way to end poverty and exploitation and landlordism—the type of landlordism that forced people into the towns where they became slaves of the commercial middle classes. The cardinal requirement for O'Brien was that the land must be recognized and used as a public resource.[39]

O'Brien's ideas about the land conflicted with an alternative vision in Chartism, developed mainly by O'Connor, who favored the expansion of private peasant proprietorship. O'Connor saw this as a route to independence, self-sufficiency, and social transformation. He wanted to offer the laboring masses an escape from urban squalor and factory oppression, but O'Brien protested that his policy would obstruct radical change and strengthen conservatism and individualism. Landholding had to be completely reorganized, O'Brien thought, because private ownership was at the root of many social and political troubles. It suited the rich and depressed the poor. It denied to producers the benefits of what they produced. O'Connor was unmoved and pressed ahead with the Chartist Land Plan. He made big promises and the response was enthusiastic, much to O'Brien's frustration. To O'Brien the Land Plan was a distraction that took energy and money away from the campaign for the six points of the Charter and an acceptance of laws and institutions that radicals should be trying to destroy. He was sure that it would not mitigate the evils of industrialization, or absorb surplus labor, or correct unfair and unreasonable patterns of production and consumption. He denied that it could really benefit the workers. The priority had to be political rights, and it was madness to expect social and economic advantages before these were enjoyed. O'Brien ridiculed O'Connor for switching from one proposal to another, responding to the failure of each by offering one more panacea, and then one more, ad infinitum. Having previously declared that social happiness would come from political equality, O'Connor now seemed to think that political equality would come from social happiness. He peddled in delusions. O'Connor responded in kind, accusing O'Brien of a number of errors and offenses.[40]

This was partly a dispute about what O'Connor's Land Plan implied: that, contrary to a long-standing tenet of popular radicalism, improvement was possible *within* the existing political system. It was also a sign that jarring ideas about the land among radicals could no longer be contained, and it was exacerbated when O'Connor changed his mind about the Corn Laws. Instead of a committing a fraud upon the workers, he decided, repeal would help them by bringing down the price of land. More of them would be able to buy land. The repeal of the Corn Laws in 1846 put these claims to the test and undermined radical assumptions about the exclusive and corrupt aristocratic state. Repeal could be presented as the act of a benign and responsive state (the banking, mines, and factory legislation of the time could also be seen in this way). For campaigners like O'Brien, however, this was nonsense and O'Connor was turning his back on fundamental change. O'Brien was certain that the Land Plan could not deliver the economic reorganization on a national scale that was necessary. "Every man who joins these land societies is practically enlisting himself on the side of the Government against his own order," he insisted. O'Connor's scheme was "a government plot to stifle in embryo our movement for the nationalization of land and property."[41]

In many cases, attitudes toward the Corn Laws reflected wider concerns relating to market forces and the politics of consumption. O'Brien was one of a number of commentators who maintained that Chartism and the Anti–Corn Law League were antithetical. While the league promised that economic freedom would bring social peace and benefit working-class consumers, O'Brien and other Chartists argued that the interests of consumers had to be promoted through regulation. O'Brien adopted eighteenth-century ideas about the "moral economy" and believed that a liberal economic order was objectionable on political and moral grounds. As Peter Gurney explains:

> Chartists vehemently opposed the Anti–Corn Law League, not because they were necessarily against free trade, but because they believed that the League's version of free trade entailed the hegemony of the abstract market, which would further erode their position as poor consumers. Chartists used what was left of the moral

> economy, in popular memory and practice, to contest what they sardonically dubbed the "extension of commerce," and they also began . . . to develop a new democratic politics of consumption which sought to maximize popular participation and control.[42]

These ideas about markets, prices, consumption, and "moral economy" featured in Chartist definitions of justice and equality.

O'Brien invariably argued that reformers must focus on the vote first. To join in the agitation to repeal the Corn Laws would be a mistake. Repeal might make food cheaper, but employers would use this as an excuse to reduce wages. The "commercial plutocracy" claimed that repeal would be good for the people, leading to general prosperity as Britain sold more abroad by allowing other nations to pay in corn. This was the deception dreamed up by "the swindling exporters of our produce, who pretend to make us rich by sending our earnings abroad and dividing the plunder with the foreigner." Middle-class businessmen posed as reformers to get the workers to trust them, but they pressed for repeal to serve only their own interests. The leaders of Anti–Corn Law League "throw obstructions in the way of real reform by their obstinate pursuit of a phantom." Repeal by itself was not enough. Yet Leaguers lashed out whenever this argument was put to them and condemned anyone who wanted more than repeal. O'Brien was adamant that the vote must come first—only then could Britain's problems be solved. Without the vote, "all other remedies will prove abortive." O'Brien did not discount rumors circulating in the summer of 1842 that league "millocrats" were encouraging disorders to put pressure on the government, or alternatively that they were colluding with the government, creating alarm to warrant emergency measures against Chartism. These men gained their wealth from the labor of the working classes, but would do nothing to help the latter: "That there are several upright and kind-hearted men amongst the League, we do not question. Indeed we know there are. But, taken as a whole, we conscientiously believe that a more selfish and pitiless bunch of tyrants does not tread British ground." One of O'Brien's central points was that free trade was not properly understood. It was only appropriate as part of a comprehensive reform program. Intelligent Chartists knew this, and they *did* want free trade: "They only desire other measures of a protective character to precede or accompany the legal establishment of free trade." O'Brien was for free trade, but not the league's version of free trade. He advocated free trade *with* the rights of labor (and stressed that Leaguers did not believe in the rights of labor).[43]

When reporting on the league's fund-raising successes, O'Brien told Chartists not to be downhearted, for the truth would win out.

> The money will be expended in bribing the press, in hiring unprincipled lecturers, in corrupting the leaders of the working classes, in purchasing electoral votes for their party—in short, it will be expended by means as unscrupulous and ungodly as are the ends they have in view. But they will fail. . . . The people will meet them everywhere at public meetings, as they have done before, and will not suffer them in a single instance to have the sanction of a public meeting, fairly convened, in favour of their desolating doctrines.

Denouncing the leaders of the league as "slave-drivers" and "tricksters," O'Brien reiterated that he was not against repeal of the Corn Laws *provided* there were accompanying reforms, especially tax cuts in proportion to the fall in prices that would result from repeal, and the adjustment of all contracts liable to be affected by the fall in prices. This was the "equitable principle" that had to be adhered to. During 1843 O'Brien urged "honest reformers" to attend the league's meetings and speak against its activities: "Not to do so would be a gross abandonment of their duty to the people—an abandonment of the field of public opinion to our most implacable and least scrupulous enemies." At the same time, he was willing to work with Corn Law repealers who would join the campaign for a democratic suffrage. Of an amalgamation with them he wrote: "We should like to know who but themselves prevent it. . . . We are always ready to receive them with open arms, but as repentant sinners and brothers, not as supercilious dictators and taskmasters." After the repeal of the Corn Laws had been approved in Parliament, O'Brien continued to condemn "pseudo-free trade" and to advise his readers that other things would benefit them more, such as a return to the old poor law system, a statutory restriction on factory hours, new currency arrangements, and of course manhood suffrage—all "worth a million Corn Law reforms." O'Brien also insisted as before that free traders' assurances about higher profits and wages were empty. When it was announced that money would be raised for a Richard Cobden testimonial, a mark of respect for the league's most effective spokesman, O'Brien was disgusted. What a travesty it was, he wrote, that this call for subscriptions resulted in the collection of twice as much money as Parliament had approved in 1846 for famine relief in Ireland.[44]

In 1848 and 1849 O'Brien claimed that many were beginning to acknowledge that his remarks about Corn Law repeal and free trade had been justified. The promised blessings had not materialized. Export industries were in trouble, and most workers' wages were still too low. Social and economic problems could not be solved without a prior political reform, such as the Charter would bring about, and the people would not get what they needed with "pretend" reforms. "What the millions want is to be able to keep themselves in independence and comfort by their own labour." Free trade had brought in a "one-sided system" that aggravated distress. "Free trade without reciprocity, without a reduction of rents and taxes, and without any guarantee to the working classes against non-employment and reductions in wages, *was* and *is* a positive evil."[45]

By the end of the 1840s O'Brien was busily writing a series of essays for *Reynolds's Political Instructor* (the first essay appeared in November 1849). These were later collected and edited by his followers and published posthumously in 1885 in one volume, *The Rise, Progress, and Phases of Human Slavery*.[46] As originally written, the essays were part of the agitation for "the Charter and something more." O'Brien stressed social demands and the labor theory of value. He argued that treating land, rivers, and mines as private property was "a perversion of natural justice." They were part of God's creation and should not be bought and sold as if they were made by human beings: "The rights of labour and the rights of property, which ought to be really one and the same, are utterly irreconcilable under such a system." Railing against idle and parasitical elites, whose "property" could not be regarded as legitimate since it was not produced by their own labor, O'Brien's essays treated workers as the "slaves" of modern capitalist society and recommended a social revolution to reverse the effects of "class" laws that gave wealth to a minority and impoverished everyone else. O'Brien elaborated upon his earlier arguments about the need for thorough reform, especially affecting land and the currency.[47]

These were among the topics upon which he lectured at the Eclectic Institution. Currency reform was by the late 1840s a staple ingredient of his radical creed. O'Brien wanted money to be regarded as a symbol of the labor content of every article and commodity, not least because the cost of living tended to change more quickly than money wages. Inflation was a cause of working-class poverty and lowered the value of savings. Deflation increased the weight of taxes and debts. State-administered marts or stores for fair exchange would help to tackle these problems, as would a nationalized banking system in which private banks of issue would have no place. Before any of this could happen, though, there would need to be a representative Parliament, in order for the people's rights and interests to be properly respected. On these matters O'Brien's approach was, as ever, strongly rational, but he also placed reform on a moral basis, as may be seen from his remarks about religion and ethics.[48]

Independently minded from his teens, O'Brien turned away from the Catholicism of his Irish parents and relatives. Though he rejected agnosticism and atheism, he had no liking either for formal Christianity. Undogmatic and nonsectarian, he condemned the organized denominations for departing from what he took to be the true purpose of Christ: to promote good conduct. He focused on a social message. The weak should never be exploited by the strong, and the haves must share with the have-nots. O'Brien saw justice and equality in the Christian Gospel, and he believed in Heaven, in an eternal life for which one's life on earth was a preparation. This being so, individuals who misused their power and wealth were endangering their own salvation. Employers who mistreated their workers fell into this category, as did church- and chapel-goers who had forgotten Christ's teachings against oppression and did nothing about the plight of the laboring poor. They tended instead to uphold the corrupt political system and turn a blind eye to social and economic wrongs. As for Church of England property, O'Brien included it in his nationalization plans and insisted that it really belonged to the public. Income from church lands should be spent on social projects, he declared. He also advocated the gradual disestablishment of the church, to stop "the march of piety and plunder" (and he considered the absence of an established church in America to be in the best interests of its citizens). As ecclesiastical officeholders died, their salaries could be put to public use, and eventually each Anglican congregation would, like the Nonconformists, pay for its own minister. O'Brien was firmly anticlerical, but he was no enemy of religious faith. His opposition to superstition and "priestcraft" did not make him a secularist. He understood that there was a spiritual dimension to human life, and, believing that misconduct was correctible, he also believed the doctrine of total depravity to be false. O'Brien maintained that religion should not become a political instrument. Above all he stressed the social and moral aspects of Christianity.[49]

Personal observation and political principle shaped O'Brien's attitude toward religion, and there were clear moral imperatives behind his mature reform program. His link with Owenism was an influence, as was his knowledge of the Enlightenment and his adoption of selected tenets of the French Revolution. To O'Brien, personal liberty required and included freedom from ignorance and superstition. He favored wide religious toleration, opposed fanaticism, and argued that equality had a form of divine sanction (much as some French revolutionaries had done); and he approved of the Chartist "churches," the most important of which was established in Birmingham in 1840 under the leadership of John Collins and Arthur O'Neill. O'Brien understood why Chartism was regarded by many in the movement as a religious crusade.[50]

He abhorred religious hypocrites, who, posing as good Christians, joined in the oppression and plundering of the people. They were

> infidels of the worst description, who acknowledge no God but money and whose whole lives are a continued rebellion against the life and gospel of Jesus Christ; villains who, while they go to mass and church, rob their fellow creatures of their birthright that they may rob them of everything else, and transform them into beasts of burden, to subserve their pride and rapacity. . . . Not the slightest compunction do they feel at seeing millions of their countrymen reduced below the brute level, abandoned to crime and misery, and robbed of all the joys of existence intended for them by the Creator. And all for what? That aristocrats may have parks and titles, and that profit-mongers may amass fortunes out of other people's earnings.

O'Brien saw this across Britain and Ireland and all over the world, but he looked forward to a change: "The supporters of such a system cannot rule always. To suppose it would be to doubt Divine justice itself." The "radical reformation" he described in 1837 covered religion and morals as well as government and law. True radicals were also "true friends of justice between man and man," while statesmen who used God's name in their own support were purveyors of "cant." "Nothing can be more offensive," O'Brien wrote, "than appeals to the Deity in reference to political subjects." He rejected the "blasphemous" and "anti-Christian" teaching that God made people rich and poor and that the poor should accept their lot. This was to make God the author of the guilt of the rich and the misery of the poor.

> God made all men to be happy and none to be miserable. He has provided enough, and more than enough, for all, if all would agree to contribute their fair proportion of service to the commonwealth, and be content with their fair share of the proceeds. . . . There is no real misery in the world but what man himself causes, and what man himself can therefore remedy.

(O'Brien later made a similar point about the Irish Famine: distress had nothing to do with so-called Divine Providence.) In 1843, joining in the controversy about

"Romanizing" influences in the Church of England, O'Brien addressed Anglican clergy directly, telling them that the people cared little about disputes over ritual and doctrinal minutiae: "They only want you to become Christians *in practice* as well as in theory, after the fashion of the early believers," and to raise "your general character and conduct as ministers of religion and teachers of the poor." Nonconformist ministers who joined the Anti–Corn Law League were also wide of the mark. Their efforts were likely to increase, not decrease, suffering and unrest. In 1847, reading of an attack on Chartism by Joshua Hocken, a Wesleyan pastor in Norwich, O'Brien declared that, essentially, Chartism was the same as genuine Christianity. Both sought to correct "the corruptions of society."[51]

The role in Chartism of "radical Christian beliefs authenticated by struggle" has been explored by Eileen Yeo, who notes the survival of older ideas (especially from the seventeenth century) and the use of Biblical language and examples in political campaigns. Although many workers found organized religion unappealing, and some turned toward infidelity, there was also a "counter-Christianity" that involved efforts by radicals to return the Christian faith to its former purity. Chartist "churches" attempted, among other things, to make Christianity more relevant and credible in working-class communities. Christian themes about caring for the poor and respecting the sacred bonds of marriage and family were especially pertinent in the agitation against the New Poor Law. Banners with religious texts were also prominent in the factory reform movement. Yeo argues that few Chartists went to the lengths of O'Brien in their negativity toward Christianity, and that collaboration between Christians and infidels in the radical cause was not unusual: "A wedge must not be driven too far between radical Christians and infidels, who shared common religious enemies, treated them with equal sarcasm and aggression, and sometimes worked amicably together, even if Christians, unlike infidels, gave special authority to the Bible and Christ." Animosity toward the established order in church and state was a basis for unity, and O'Brien was a key figure in debates about the corrupted church, how it compared with the "true church," and the people's claim to religious institutions that matched with their experiences and interests. Did the people not finance the parish church? Was the Church of England not founded on the theft of the nation's property at the Reformation? What about the role of the Anglican clergy in enclosure? Were tithes not meant to be a way of providing for the poor, rather than enriching the church? These were among the matters O'Brien addressed in his lectures and writings. He realized that his religious views offended many people, and that his newspapers lost readers as a result, but he hoped that he could partly make amends by praising "pure" Christianity and contrasting it with the abuse-ridden denominational churches.[52]

When Henry Hetherington's last will and testament was published following his death in 1849, O'Brien engaged in a heated dispute about Hetherington's atheism, taking the line that a Christian was more likely than an atheist to push for necessary reforms.

> A truly religious man, believing himself accountable to the hereafter, would no more support the present system of landlordism and profit-mongering (supposing him to understand their tendency) than he would support brigandism or murder, which are, indeed, but some of their consequences. On the other hand, we could point out shoals of Atheists, professed and unprofessed, who, though they will revile the names of Moses and Jesus, and even of God Himself, would persecute you to death's door, or shoot you like dogs, for attempting any reform that would go to rescue the toil-worn labourer from the fell profit-monger's deadly gripe.

O'Brien thought of superstition and "priestcraft" as "but gross forms of Atheism itself."[53]

In 1853 one of O'Brien's Owenite acquaintances, John Finch, published a "Chartist Bible," and, knowing that O'Brien would be interested, sent him an inscribed copy: "No man having lighted a candle puts it under a bushel. To J. Bron. O'Brien, Esquire, with great respect this volume is presented." Finch's religious views apparently coincided with O'Brien's to some extent, and O'Brien would not have faulted Finch's description of Jesus Christ as "the wisest, best, and most benevolent of moral teachers" or his definition of "true religion" as "charity, good morals, reason, and free inquiry." In his book, Finch rearranged the Bible to emphasize "truth," the basis of which was to be found in the Gospel of Christ and the Laws of Moses. Anything that did not accord with this "truth" was transferred to sections headed "corruptions," "mysteries," and "miracles." By publishing the Bible "under an entirely new arrangement in all its parts," Finch aimed to put an end to "speculative notions of no practical importance or utility to mankind."[54]

O'Brien was still writing about religion toward the end of his career. In 1859 in the *Vision of Hell*, for instance, he declared that public men who abused their position deserved the torments of "hell," and all the more so if they tried to use the Bible as a cover for sins against the people. O'Brien's object, he explained, was "to turn the tables on those preachers of false doctrine, heresy, and schism who abuse the Word of God, by using hell as a sort of artillery on the side of established power, to terrify poverty and ignorance into false submission to arbitrary and wrongful rule."

> Our logic is this. God's mercy may *mitigate*, but His justice will never let the penalty exceed the offence. If, therefore, God has ordained eternal punishment for any, it can only be for those enormous sinners whose crimes are, by their very nature, of an eternal character: such as the crimes of robbing the people of their land—of their free will—of their self-government—of all means of mental and moral culture—so as to perpetuate their degradation, corruption, and enslavement to all future generations.[55]

Such was the variety in Chartism that many Chartists rejected O'Brien and his principles. Some preferred other leaders. Some accepted much of the liberal political economy he spent his career condemning, an element within Chartism that later merged with Victorian Liberalism. This development has been described by Brian Harrison and Patricia Hollis, who offer a reminder that there was more to Chartism than opposition to capitalism and industrialization and that many Chartists prioritized noneconomic concerns.[56] O'Brien was atypical even while he was at the height of his importance in and to the movement.

In his later years his passion for reform and talent for controversy were undiminished. He could still attempt the spectacular, attention-grabbing gesture, as in the spring of 1857 when a general election was called following a defeat for Palmerston's government in the House of Commons (a motion of censure against British aggression in China was narrowly passed when Palmerston's opponents combined against him). The government won the election and increased its majority in one of the most resounding electoral verdicts of the post-1832 era; but the election is also remarkable because Bronterre O'Brien decided to stand against the prime minister in the latter's constituency of Tiverton in Devon, where Palmerston had been MP since 1835.

O'Brien cannot have expected to win. What he and his backers had in mind was a symbolic contest, with the people's champion challenging the head of the government. To radicals, Palmerston was an unprincipled reactionary. He personified the old order they so wanted to change. O'Brien was to speak for everyone who objected to Palmerston's "anti-democratic policy at home and abroad." According to the *Observer*, however, "Lord Palmerston remains true to his Tiverton constituency, and any attempt to oppose him would be futile." The *Manchester Guardian* reported the arrival in Tiverton of a "Conservative and Protestant" candidate, Sir John Heron Maxwell of Dumfries, who, realizing that a contest would be "perfectly hopeless," quickly departed. Then came O'Brien, the day before the nomination of candidates.

> On Thursday there was a report abroad that Mr. Bronterre O'Brien, a noted Chartist leader, had come down from London to beard Lord Palmerston on the hustings and arraign, in the face of the people of Tiverton, his whole foreign and domestic policy. Mr. O'Brien was actually in the town, for he harangued a meeting of the working classes on Thursday evening; but he did not present himself, we know not for what reason, at the nomination on Friday, which was consequently not so amusing as it might otherwise have been. Lord Palmerston arrived at Tiverton late on Thursday evening.

O'Brien withdrew and Palmerston and the other sitting MP, John Heathcoat, who had represented the borough since 1832, were returned unopposed.[57]

O'Brien's account of events in Tiverton survives in a letter he sent shortly afterward to his friend Mathews.

> I went there only at the last moment because the sinews of war came only at the last moment. But though I only got there on the Wednesday night and the election took place on Friday morning, leaving me but one clear day, and although I knew not even the name or address of a single individual in the town of any party, entering the town a perfect stranger with a leathern bag in my hand; yet on the following evening (7 o'clock on Thursday) I had a tremendous meeting on the hill and spoke till 9 o'clock amid tremendous cheers and excitement. At the close immense multitudes of people escorted me over the bridge that crosses the Exe—and literally stunned me—almost struck me dead—with their boisterous applause and stentorian cheers.

O'Brien addressed two indoor meetings that same night, one after the other, and was categorically assured by "six or seven of the electors" that they would place him in nomination the next morning. He looked forward to striking "a blow that would have resounded throughout Europe. I would have revealed something that the rulers of the earth would have given millions and millions to keep wrapped in night. But the promisers were meantime worked upon." O'Brien issued no printed statement, "because I wished the people themselves to take the initiative and because I was not in a condition to incur any expenses beyond my own and the bills," and the bills were only on the walls for about two hours because they had to be brought in from elsewhere. All this probably made little difference. Despite "the most fulsome and flattering language addressed to me at both ends of the town," O'Brien's nomination was prevented by threats, bribes, and indeed "every appliance" possible. Palmerston escaped a contest. "Had I got the chance of speaking upon him and his rotten parliament I would have furnished a new chapter in the history of modern Europe, worth all the chapters already published." Palmerston had faced "total extinction," and "had I been nominated I am sure the show of hands would have been at least six to one in my favour. . . . But all was lost for want of men of nerve and probity—All trembled before the threatened ruin of their families."[58]

Wishing to make the best use of his journey back from Devon to London, O'Brien arranged to hold meetings in towns along the route. Unfortunately, in Cullompton, Devon, every public room was closed against him (the magistrates had banned "Chartist meetings") and he had to stand under an archway in the street. The rain came down but the crowd got bigger and "the cheers and excitement, at last, became so great that the very uproar deafened me." After an hour the police came and O'Brien told the crowd to disperse peacefully. He tried again in Exeter, Exmouth, and Torquay, but in these towns too it was obvious that the local authorities were determined to prevent his speaking. Preferring not to endanger himself or his supporters, he decided not to linger and returned directly to London.[59]

O'Brien's ideas remained influential at this time, especially in the organizations and locations where his followers were most numerous, but physically and mentally he went into decline. Talk of another effort to stand for election to Parliament was given up. Hopes for a Chartist resurgence rose and fell. O'Brien's writing and lecturing were curtailed by illness, though he still had the energy to quarrel with other radicals, notably Ernest Jones, editor of the *People's Paper* and prospective leader of a socialist-Chartist campaign. O'Brien's friends tried several times to raise money for him, but the response was disappointing. In the mid-1850s he was lecturing several times a week and either writing or providing material for articles and pamphlets. Among the publications of his later years were *Bronterre O'Brien's Sermon on the Day of the Public Fast and Humiliation for England's Disasters in the Crimea* (1854), the *Ode to Lord Palmerston* (1856), *An Ode to Louis Napoleon Bonaparte* (1857), *A Vision of Hell* (1859), which continued O'Brien's criticism of Britain's currency arrangements, and two pamphlets discussing Robespierre and his political ideas (1857 and 1859). Sometimes, amid the whirlwind of insults and recriminations that marked Chartism's demise, O'Brien expressed regret over lost opportunities and disillusionment with the people he had wished to serve. From 1860 he suffered from a serious bronchial complaint. He died in 1864.[60]

His final years were very difficult. The correspondence with Mathews fills in some of the details. Lack of money, poor health, and family concerns were recurrent themes. In the spring of 1856 O'Brien was desperately seeking an employment for his son James, and for himself he had only "vague promises" of paid work. Six months later he wrote that he and his wife were both unwell and that James had been a great burden on the family. In this period O'Brien waited expectantly for financial assistance. Small amounts were forthcoming, but mostly O'Brien was anxious and disappointed ("I know not what my friends are doing for me in the country. I have not yet heard from any of them"). He commented, with some resentment, on other writers who found "a good berth" at this or that newspaper while O'Brien himself was struggling; and in September 1856 he reported that the hall in Denmark Street had been poorly attended over the summer and "I have had no classes for a long time." He had no doubt that he could make money by writing, if only he had sufficient funds to print and advertise. With quick sales, and a small amount to live on, the future would be brighter. O'Brien had works that were ready or almost ready for publication (including one on Robespierre and one on Christianity), but "I am stopped at every turn and kept continually in distress and difficulty for want of a sum in hand to print and advertise with. Without that I am lost to the world, my family, and myself." Another fund-raising effort was commenced on O'Brien's behalf in the autumn of 1856. He complained that the announcement should have been more widely distributed. "One hundred and some odd of our party have put forth an address for me. . . . Were the people to support me as they ought I could soon be well off and do more good in twelve months than for want of such support I have been able to do all my life." Subscriptions trickled in during 1857, but they did not alter O'Brien's prospects; and there was some discussion of his renting a smaller house or perhaps living at a "teetotal hotel" run by a friend and former Chartist named Cranston, who "seems fully bent on rescuing me from the hard life of never ending persecution and trouble I have had."[61]

The melancholic and even defeatist tone of some of these remarks to Mathews can also be discerned in O'Brien's letters to Allsop from the mid-1850s. He continued to attend political meetings, but rarely did they cheer him up. "They spoke like schoolboys," he wrote on one occasion, "with an evident want of knowledge and expression." O'Brien himself was hardly on top form. One time he could not speak as planned because he arrived too late; another time "I did not speak well for my head was very bad." To Allsop he described at length his unsuccessful efforts to find literary employment with various periodicals. Unable to support his family, he thought again of emigration ("I am rife for Australia, California, or anywhere else on the first opportunity"). When Allsop suggested that old contacts like the Owenites Pare and Finch might have money to spare for O'Brien and his family, O'Brien was dubious.[62]

O'Brien had known Pare since the early 1830s, and Pare was one of those who had encouraged him most earnestly to embark upon a political and journalistic career, but they had since grown apart. Though O'Brien had seen him at a meeting in 1854, they did not speak to each other: "He has shown me no friendship since he prospered in the world." Even so, O'Brien was willing for Allsop to approach Pare—or any other mutual acquaintance—on his behalf. Among the topics O'Brien and Allsop conferred about in these years was the condition of Owen, whom they both knew. Now in his eighties, Owen seemed to O'Brien to have lost "mental soundness," as he devoted himself to quirky spiritual and scientific pursuits.

> Poor dear good Robert Owen is, as you say, in the world of spirits—holding converse with departed great ones. Well, if it makes him happy and soothes his last days I hope he will continue under his mesmeric illusions. . . . At all events few men have better played their parts in life, and his (with all his false enthusiasm) has been a magnificent part.

O'Brien had several publications planned, he told Allsop, but he needed help. Pare was not a likely prospect, so he intended to try others, including the publisher Reynolds. O'Brien had been put off, however, by what he saw as the latter's odd behavior—sometimes friendly, other times less so—and since Reynolds already had more contributors than he needed, he probably had nothing to offer O'Brien. The best thing by far would be for Reynolds to hire O'Brien to go to America. O'Brien could send back items for Reynolds's titles, which would both enhance their appeal and allow O'Brien to earn enough to support himself and his family in the United States. This was not about to happen. O'Brien looked to other possibilities. He had conversations with writers and publishers about a new paper, only to be told that the organ would have no chance of success unless it was in favor of the war with Russia. He fell back on work he had completed that was ready to publish. He needed £100 for printing and advertising, and he was trying to find partners: "I could hardly fail, had I anything of a circulation." There was much to say about "the approaching European Crisis"—O'Brien just lacked the necessary "facilities." But he also needed a period of good health, having experienced "congestion of the brain" for five years. He often found it impossible to write because "my poor head suffers too much," and his grinding poverty caused ever more disquiet. If his remarks to Allsop are any guide, O'Brien succumbed during the 1850s to increasing loneliness and alienation: "Few are now left of those I knew when I first came to London. Nearly all are dead—dead physically or, what amounts to the same, morally and socially dead to all the finer impulses than once honoured their humanity." The world was becoming "mechanical." People were dehumanized and society was moving backward not forward, which O'Brien attributed to "the development of our manufacturing and commercial greatness."[63]

O'Brien's letters of the late 1850s continued in this vein. He referred to "very unpromising times." Reynolds was definitely not as reliable as he had formerly been, for he was growing rich and wanted to join the "fashionable world," but even worse was the defection of Samuel Kydd, the former Glasgow shoemaker who had been a popular Chartist lecturer and secretary of the Chartist executive in the 1840s, only to devote himself to tariff protection and factory regulation in the 1850s before qualifying as a lawyer. O'Brien had long regarded Kydd as "a trimmer and time-server," and now others would see him in his true colors: "Kydd knows the middle classes are the foundation or basis of every system of tyranny on the earth and has often confessed it in my hearing; but he wants money and preferment and is accordingly bidding for both." The membership of the National Reform League was growing, but times were hard and most could not pay the yearly subscription, and O'Brien was sometimes disheartened by the low turnout for his lectures:

> They are strangers that mostly come—very few of the old ones appearing oftener than about once a month or fortnight. The feeling is always good and there is no doubt I am doing much in the way of making converts, but it is at a fearful cost to myself, for while the lectures yield but a mere trifle I am effectively shut out of the press, the platforms, and institutions of every sort where money or pay might be had.

In one letter, after thanking Mathews for a gift of money and "your earnest desire to prop me up," O'Brien confessed that if he could have his time over again he would get out of politics altogether, "at least till I had made myself safe and landed a more favourable chance of influencing public opinion with our ideas." In this frame of mind he saw nothing but the "tremendous odds" stacked against him and the NRL. Further fund-raising efforts were inhibited by financial instability and slack trade, which made it impossible for NRL members to give more (O'Brien had hoped that if he could get two hundred paying members, he would be able to cover some expected printing costs). He claimed that the NRL was being persecuted through the "diabolical agency" of "sons of Mammon," and he held out little hope for Britain and the wider world. His morale was also affected, as ever, by family concerns. His eldest daughter Louisa fell ill; he needed money to facilitate the entry of another daughter, Emma, into her chosen profession; and his wife Sophia suffered from bouts of bronchitis.[64]

In the spring of 1858 O'Brien was again downcast. Despite the "sound instruction" he offered in his lectures and classes, he could not get more than half his members to pay their dues. Most of the defaulters were poor and could not be blamed, but some lacked "zeal and heart" (the suggestion was that they could afford to pay but chose not to). "They will never find another to serve them as I have and for so long," O'Brien wrote. "But God's will be done—I have done my duty." To add to O'Brien's frustration, he learned that Ernest Jones "had no difficulty in getting £40 last month from his party and he asks for £80 more this month, which he is sure to get in a few days, while I cannot get a quarter of the sum." O'Brien estimated that Jones had received at least £2,000 in recent times (Jones's *People's Paper* was in trouble and would cease to appear in 1858); yet O'Brien, after all his years of toil, could expect nothing like that sum, no matter how hard he worked or how much he suffered: "So much for popular appreciation."[65]

In 1862, in order to publish a pamphlet dealing with "all social and political systems and their founders," O'Brien asked Allsop to help him raise the necessary money. The venture was doomed from the outset, as O'Brien probably realized. The best hope for assistance seemed to be Pare, yet O'Brien told Allsop that Pare would ignore any letter that came direct from him, which is why he urged Allsop to intercede. Was there a chance? O'Brien's work *had* to be printed somehow, "on public grounds" and because O'Brien needed whatever profits might accrue to take care of his family (and again he mentioned the possibility of emigration should he find no new source of income). O'Brien was willing to vest the copyright in Pare to facilitate a bargain. It was about time for Pare to show some generosity.

> He has never, like you and others, given me any help in the long warfare I have waged against the powers of darkness, though he knows well that in consequence of my

> principles I have been for a quarter of a century systematically excluded by the aristocracy and middle classes (the latter especially) from all lucrative employment and from all means of writing and publishing the works I long ago promised the public. Indeed, but for the occasional help of private friends my family and self must have perished long ago, if we had been born with five hundred lives apiece.

Allsop did write to Pare, though O'Brien did not expect much of the latter, describing him as a man whose conduct was far removed from the doctrines he professed. Having known him for more than thirty years, O'Brien had never sensed any sympathy in Pare. He complained to Allsop that Pare might have helped many times in the past, at little cost to himself, and so contributed to a very different life for O'Brien and his family. O'Brien could have written important works "which would live as long as the English language" and "change nations." He could have been independent. He could have been elected to Parliament. "With a powerful support out of doors and a public opinion in my favour in Europe and America," O'Brien declared, "I could have done more during the last twenty years to prevent *wrong* and to enforce *right* than it would be possible nowadays to make anybody understand." The weeks went by and Pare offered no money. O'Brien cast around for other loans or gifts and briefly had hopes of Colonel Henry Clinton, of Hertfordshire, who was on friendly terms with several radicals and Owenites to whom he had given financial help in the past. But Clinton informed O'Brien that he could spare no more. He wished O'Brien had applied sooner, "before he got drained," and the best he could do now was to provide a goose for dinner.[66]

O'Brien repeatedly told Allsop of the desperation to which his poverty was driving him. If he could just be secure for a year, or even six months, the freedom from worry would allow him to earn money by writing, lecturing, and giving classes, and he could thereby repay some debts and set himself and the family up in comfort for the foreseeable future. Instead, they seemed to be trapped in an unending struggle for survival. With the approach of winter in 1862 O'Brien confessed that they lacked warm clothing. The rent could only be paid with the help of friends. Yet another event was put on in Denmark Street to raise money for O'Brien, but "though the attendance was numerous and respectable," it was "a complete failure in a pecuniary sense." He was advertising for pupils and had a few promises, but nobody had paid in advance. He was ready to write for the press at half the usual rate of pay, or do double the work, "but the public name I have got has long since closed every avenue against me"—and anyway, how could he focus his mind when he was so anxious about his family? He discussed with Allsop the employment prospects for his children (particularly abroad, which seemed better than at home); but often he simply detailed all his regrets, about things he should have done earlier in his career had it not been for family considerations or lack of money.[67]

For all the grumbling, however, O'Brien remained busy and even optimistic between the mid-1850s and early 1860s. With Mathews he discussed his speaking and writing, his plans for the future, the many activities at the Eclectic Institution, and the progress of the National Reform League. Attendance at the hall, he reflected, tended to increase as winter approached and the weather turned, and he was greatly excited by the positive and encouraging reception given to the *Odes* to Palmerston and Louis Napoleon. O'Brien wrote to Mathews upon completion of the second *Ode*, "which my friends have told me is the strongest and fiercest composition of the kind in the English language." The *Odes* "are greatly liked," and people were learning them by heart. O'Brien drew attention to a review in *Reynolds's Newspaper*:

> The notice was a most flattering and friendly one and did me much good amongst both my own party and the democrats in general who saw it. The odes sell well when they get before the public, but the want of money to advertise and the want of friends in the newspaper press makes me require ten or twenty times the length of time I otherwise should to get at the public and consequently sell what I bring out.

Such problems were not insurmountable. For example, there was the prospect of a new O'Brienite journal. "Some of our friends here are thinking seriously of a daily evening penny paper for our party," O'Brien stated in March 1856. Though the scheme was eventually abandoned, for a while O'Brien was buoyant. With £500, half a dozen good writers, and two competent editors, "the thing might answer well."[68]

During 1857 and 1858 O'Brien reported that meetings and classes were attracting more people (though one could always wish for more) and that the NRL was "rather on the march" as its principles met with increasing sympathy. The material, moral, social, and spiritual advantages of the O'Brienite program were becoming clearer. "I believe in my conscience that no other similar body (I mean having the same objects) has ever existed and that had we only members and pecuniary means equal to the magnitude of our enterprise we should swallow up all other parties and soon be the rulers of the world." Though O'Brien would wish poverty and unemployment on nobody, at least "these bad times make people reflect and that works well for our cause," and "I find the propositions of the League . . . listened to more than for a long time past."[69]

About current affairs he was opinionated as ever. He kept up with European and American events and declared that "the enlightened few . . . sigh and long for the realization of our social doctrines," since, wherever they lived, they knew that political rights must lead to the overthrow of the "land usurper and money capitalist" through "just laws upon landed tenures, credit, and equitable exchange." O'Brien was determined to reveal all about the Indian Mutiny. "The news from India gets worse and worse," he remarked to Mathews, "though they try to put the best face on it . . . It was a premeditated affair from the outset." The crisis in India was provoked intentionally, O'Brien thought, in order to provide justification for the seizure of property and wealth by British merchants, speculators, and bondholders, who "dread the truth coming out." The same thing was going on in China. In fact, all over the world there were plots to parcel out land, revenues, and produce to those who already had too much. O'Brien was confident that these plots could not be concealed—or tolerated—for much longer. "Right" would combat "might" and "feudal and mercantile power" would be resisted.[70]

In October 1862 O'Brien stressed the irony of his condition to Allsop. "Strange to say—though I was never so low in the world I am decidedly getting popular again."[71] Perhaps he had exaggerated his afflictions to friends and correspondents in order to stimulate more generosity on their part. In any event, poor health and lack of money in O'Brien's final years did not stop him from writing, speaking, or organizing. He had a loyal personal following. He continued to explain his reform program and to maximize its appeal, and there was evidently a good deal of interest in it within radical circles and beyond. In order to understand why he took the positions he did, it is necessary to look more searchingly into his core concepts. These are best explored by studying his treatment of his favorite topics, those he wrote and spoke about most often: revolutions; "National Reform" and the land and currency; America; and Ireland.

CHAPTER 3

# A Concept of Revolution

Chartism was widely regarded as a "revolutionary" movement, but recovering the meaning of this phrase is problematic. No prominent Chartist discussed, researched, or theorized more about "revolution" than Bronterre O'Brien. Despite some vagueness on the matter within the movement (understandable, in view of the counterrevolutionary resources available to the government), O'Brien worked his way toward a definition of revolution that was not without influence. Historians use the word but often fail to define it, which rather confuses the issue, but Chartists themselves were rarely concerned to explain its meaning either. There were reasons for this. They did not wish to give advantages to their opponents (such as an excuse for persecution), and they wanted to allow for adaptability in order to keep abreast of changing circumstances. O'Brien is noteworthy because he *did* try to explain what revolution was and how it could happen. This marks him out from other radical leaders of the period. The idea of revolution as fundamental change, to be achieved nonviolently, was common among Chartists; but defining revolution also required a clear grasp of what that change should look like—what the revolution should consist of and accomplish—and O'Brien made a significant contribution in this respect. The present chapter will explore the main features of his theory of revolution, and its roots, context, and application. There will also be some investigation of how O'Brien's claims related to broader trends in Chartist thinking, and what the models and inspiration provided by revolutions abroad might reveal about the international aspects of Chartism.

"Physical force" and "moral force" were not entirely separate modes of expression. Chartists needed tactical flexibility and innovation, to keep options open and maximize support, and most of them respected the diversity within their movement. Chartists who discussed revolution thought of it as a realizable set of political, social, and economic conditions that differed from those they were experiencing in their present. But there was no unanimity on the details, and revolution was about means as well as ends. Did the revolution have to be violent?

"Peaceably if we may, forcibly if we must" was the perfect slogan in the early years when excitement and optimism were mounting, for it reflected both the intentional ambiguity about tactics within the movement and a clear preference for one set of methods over another. "Peaceably," it was generally agreed, would be better than "forcibly." Malcolm Chase has pointed to the Chartist belief in the right to resist oppression and the related assumption that it was appropriate and legal to take up arms for self-defense. It is also clear that it was the bold language and defiant attitude of "physical force" that appealed, not so much the prospect of a resort to actual "physical force" behavior. Chase describes the violence that broke out in the summer of 1839 as "not calculated or strategic." Moreover, "Chartist arming and the rhetoric of resistance were extensive, but neither in itself constitutes sufficient evidence of insurrectionary intent." Yet it would be wrong to ignore or dismiss the potential for violence. As Chase remarks, "There was an implicit and near-universal endorsement of the principle of legitimate resistance to undemocratic rule."[1]

While noting the sense of danger created by Chartism, Gareth Stedman Jones contends that the level of insurrectionary intent in the movement has been exaggerated by those historians who seek to explain its failure as the result of disunity. It was easy to sow dissension among Chartists, especially on the use of violence. Nevertheless, some Chartists, albeit a minority, *were* willing to resort to violence, and violence was integral to their concept of revolution. Many more accepted the necessity for intimidation, presuming that they could win no concessions without it. In bringing to light the continuity in popular radicalism over the long term, Stedman Jones describes Chartism as the most important "though not perhaps the most revolutionary" stage.[2] Gregory Claeys argues that the "moral force" majority "hindered Chartism from setting a more revolutionary course."[3] In specific locations, Chartists moved from nonviolence to violence and back again over time. The same people in the same place could draw on a range of possibilities in their readiness to organize and protest.[4]

It is not uncommon to find in modern scholarly writing on Chartism an emphasis upon constitutional methods. The centrality of petitioning has been stressed by Paul Pickering (and O'Brien, though skeptical at times about the usefulness of petitions, energetically supported the endeavor in 1838–39). Despite the arming and intimidation associated with some elements in the movement, "the typical Chartist did not sharpen pikes, he collected signatures." Another form of self-restraint can be discerned in Chartist attitudes toward Queen Victoria and the monarchy. Chartists were conscious of the limited powers of the crown, and most of them did not consider the existence of monarchy to be incompatible with progress toward political and social democracy (O'Brien often excluded the crown from his invectives against the elitist structures that kept the people down). Here, suggests Pickering, is a reminder of "the limits of Chartist aspiration and the constitutionalist horizons of the majority of those who supported the movement."[5]

This is not to deny that O'Brien, and others, could condemn the monarchy as a waste of money, or commend republicanism as superior in practice and principle. By the time of the 1848 revolutions in Europe, the republican cause was gaining more support among Chartists. Drastic change was hoped for, but, as before, extreme methods were eschewed. The constitutionalist proclivity has been confirmed by scholars who employ such cultural forms as popular literature to re-create contemporary mind-sets. Most Chartist writers, as Ian Haywood notes, "were unwilling, unable, or reluctant to preach an openly insurrectionist message—indeed, Chartism inherited the English radical tradition that it was government intransigence and provocation, not radical demagogy or inherent working-class savagery, which was the cause of political violence."[6] Arming, rioting, striking, and similar manifestations of militancy featured in Chartist writing and were prominent in 1839, 1842, and 1848, the peak years of agitation. Yet Chartists seem not to have discarded their belief that one could be revolutionary without being violent. Whenever violence was discussed as an option, it proved divisive.[7]

In an investigation of "the Chartist imaginary" and its combination of political and aesthetic expression, especially in Chartist poetry, Mike Sanders offers further insight into the variations in Chartist identity and strategy. Chartist poems were widely published and read, and many local and national leaders (including O'Brien) wrote poetry. There was a tendency to hint at violence without openly encouraging it. This was in line with the call to attend meetings unarmed but to act on the right of self-defense should the authorities break the peace. Menace coexisted with moderation. To Sanders, Chartists were "far more comfortable with the idea than the reality of physical force."[8] When violence did occur, as in the Newport Rising of November 1839, responses were mixed; but the gap between the purported right of armed resistance and Newport as the practical exercise of that right was never quite bridged. Justifications for the rising were not numerous. Later, during and after the British, Irish, and European disorders of 1848, there was again some ambivalence.[9]

The wish may have been for revolutionary change, but the overriding desire was to achieve it without violence and illegality. Did the Chartists' opponents understand and accept this? Mostly they interpreted Chartism according to their own values and concerns and denied that it was an authentic expression of the people's will. The possibility of a violent uprising created alarm, but not much, and after 1848 the danger was thought to have passed. Social reforms and economic growth undermined the radical challenge. Britain's rulers might have been frightened by Chartism, but in general they responded to it on their own terms.[10]

The need for a top-down solution to Britain's problems was affirmed by several influential commentators at this time, notably the philosopher and historian Thomas Carlyle. No advocate of political or social equality, Carlyle nevertheless argued that the government should act sympathetically—not by extending political rights to the masses but by pursuing more humane policies. Carlyle saw Chartism as dangerous and destabilizing; therefore the right response was urgently necessary.[11] This owed a great deal to his ideas about the French Revolution, ideas shared by contemporaries who did not care for the French, or revolutions, or both. To Carlyle, the years after 1789 in France demonstrated all the evils of zealotry in a bad cause. An enemy of political radicalism, Carlyle sought to show that the French Revolution was an inevitable failure and its leaders inadequate (he depicted Robespierre as weak and defective in character and physique as well as ideology).[12] Furthermore, his eagerness to combat Chartism led him to present its methods as well as its goals—its mobilization of the masses, the Chartist "crowd"—as wholly without worth.[13]

There were many who, like Carlyle, were worried by Chartism. State repression was one response, and there were other techniques that were designed to belittle political radicals and deprive them of importance. Antiradicals attached to Chartism qualities that were impossible to admire—irrationality, immaturity, unruliness, criminality—and did all they could to ruin the reputation of Chartist leaders.[14] Some contemporaries denied that Chartism gave any cause for alarm. They included Sir

Charles Napier, commander of the army in the Northern District (1838–41), whose troops were frequently called upon to aid the civil authorities. Napier's motive was probably selfish, however, for he wanted praise for his handling of Chartism. At some times, in some places, fear was well founded.[15]

Chartist organs claimed that the movement had arisen to promote peace, stability, justice, and legality, not to endanger them. But they also took up the theme of "revolution" and frequently used defiant, threatening terminology. This was true even of the relatively moderate *Chartist Circular*, which usually sought to avoid controversy. Being moderate did not mean being timid. The *Chartist Circular* insisted that the people had the right to resist oppression. It cherished the "spirit of revolution" in Britain and Europe, though this was regarded not as a matter of blood and thunder but as "moral reformation, political amelioration, and religious changes." In a series of articles the *Chartist Circular* exposed the shortcomings of the July Monarchy in France, where the liberty promised by the 1830 Revolution had been eliminated, and paid tribute to the leaders of revolutionary struggles of the more distant past (in Europe, Ireland, and the Americas). While admitting that atrocities committed in the name of "revolution" were to be regretted, the *Chartist Circular* also held that a desire for retribution was not unnatural in anyone who had suffered under crushing tyranny.[16]

This was not what the *Chartist Circular* wanted for Britain. The hope was for "a bloodless revolution," accomplished through the repeal of all laws that existed "for the benefit of only a particular class, to the nation's detriment." The prerequisite was obvious—"Institutions must emanate from the whole people"—but the people did not have to resort to violence: "Let the oppressed become as united and intelligent as their oppressors are, and they will achieve their redemption without crime or bloodshed."[17]

In the spring of 1841 the *Chartist Circular* responded to remarks made by O'Brien ("one of the ablest political writers of the present day") on the question "Can reform be obtained without revolution?" O'Brien had stated that a violent confrontation could be averted if Britain was changed in a manner that satisfied both rich and poor: the rich should be allowed to keep their possessions and the poor should be guaranteed a better future. The first step was to place in authority the men who would introduce the necessary policies. Though the *Chartist Circular* accepted this analysis, it was not optimistic that appropriate reforms could be obtained and declared that Chartists—defined as the party that wanted change without "fierce revolution"—should "prepare for the worst," for they were sure to be resisted.[18]

This was a familiar reiteration of the moderation-with-menace motif. A sense that violence was looming, and that Chartists had to maneuver carefully if they wanted to avoid culpability, comes through clearly in the pages of the most important Chartist periodical, the *Northern Star*. During April and May 1839, when the first Chartist Convention met in London and Birmingham, the *Northern Star* praised the campaign "to establish, by all constitutional means, the rights of the whole people"—and these means, as plenty of legal and historical sources agreed, included "the right of every man to provide himself with arms. When the time shall have arrived in which the people shall feel themselves justified in using them, no man can tell, nor have the Chartists ventured to make any declaration on the subject." Chartists were not giving notice that they definitely *would* take up arms, but they did intend to proceed on the understanding that the possibility was available to them. The *Northern Star* was issuing no instructions, trusting instead to the people's judgment; and it was advocating not violence but prudence, in the hope that violence would not occur.[19] After the Newport Rising the *Northern Star* refrained from any statements of unconditional approval for the insurrectionists, but did call them "patriots," claimed that they had popular sympathy, and warned of serious consequences if the government treated them harshly.[20] Disturbances in the summer of 1842, growing out of reform agitation and workers' strikes, were deemed by the *Northern Star* to be part of a design to crush Chartism: violence had been incited by the government and middle classes.[21]

The Chartists' self-understanding and the image they sought to project through their newspapers, organizations, meetings, and other activity remained unchanged, at least on the matter of violence and illegality. They preferred to use constitutional methods, and when violence occurred they were not to blame. Their opponents were responsible. Chartists were usually the victims, not the perpetrators. Violence could be explained as the desperate recourse of overburdened people pushed beyond their limits. Violence could also be explained as the instrument of the powerful and privileged, and Chartists rushed before the tribunal of public opinion whenever their meetings were broken up, or they were assaulted, or dismissed from their employment, or arbitrarily arrested and mistreated in custody. Chartists liked to discuss "physical force," but they complained loudly when it was used against them.[22]

Chartism was variable according to time and place, pragmatic, and not ideologically pure or consistent. Many Chartists responded to events rather than set and adhere to a clear course of their own. Particular events could provoke a violent reaction, or at least a readiness to act violently. Rob Breton has highlighted an "undecided, oscillating rhetoric" in the radical platform of the 1830s. His study of the *Poor Man's Guardian* reveals an intermingling of constitutional campaigning and militancy and subversion.[23] In the 1850s, violence was not ruled out. "Peaceably if we may" was still the first choice, but European examples, and years of frustration as Chartist agitation appeared not to be working, ensured that Chartists were unwilling publicly to limit themselves only to nonviolent means. When reporting on unrest in Ireland and France, *Reynolds's Political Instructor* suggested that revolutionary violence was unavoidable and not altogether inappropriate. Recent times—with "Hungarians battling for nationality" and "Romans shedding their blood for freedom"—showed that the oppressed could do nothing else when other options were closed off.[24]

What was O'Brien's position? In the early 1830s he declared himself against conspiracy and insurrection. Direct action, he pointed out, could not achieve anything unless the army was ready to join in; and unless it did so, a violent uprising would simply prompt the government to order a clampdown, placing reforms even further out of reach. O'Brien recommended other ways of maximizing and applying pressure. The existing electoral system offered opportunities, not least exclusive dealing and the extracting of policy pledges from candidates. O'Brien also wanted to inconvenience the government. Abstinence from commodities that were taxed would decrease state revenues, and as well as refusing to consume, the people could refuse to pay direct taxes and withdraw all their savings from the banks. These financial weapons, if shrewdly employed, could not fail to bring results, especially when combined with constitutional methods—interviews with ministers, lobbying MPs, sending in petitions. O'Brien thought that the trade unions could provide an organizational basis for all this. He also thought that whatever else was demanded, a democratic suffrage was the necessary first step in any scheme of reform.[25] O'Brien's "revolution" was gradual and peaceful rather than abrupt, destabilizing, and bloody. Reformers had to be constructive, not destructive, and they had to have a plan. They could not simply tear down. They had to know what to build to replace what had existed before.[26]

It has been alleged by some commentators that O'Brien compromised, retreating from "physical force" after his conviction and imprisonment in 1840–41.[27] But even before prison he had preferred nonviolent to violent methods. O'Brien made clear statements about this before his incarceration. His main points included the following: even when violence seemed justifiable it achieved nothing; it was commonly characteristic of corrupt governments and the classes that supported them, and if the people sank to their level they would discredit reform and make it easier for rulers to amass more power through emergency laws, censorship, and proscriptions; and recommending that the people should arm if they wished, in order to protect themselves, did not amount to a desire for or endorsement of bloodshed.[28]

In 1838 O'Brien categorically declared that he was *not* telling his readers to take up arms, for this was a choice that each person had to make individually. Rather, O'Brien was describing the context in which the decision had to be made. Although it was not lawful to encourage or coerce others to arm, people had the constitutional right to arm for self-defense. If Chartists did arm, it would show their opponents that they were serious. O'Brien viewed quarrels about "moral" and "physical" force as a needless distraction, stirred up mainly by enemies of the Charter. "The only way to prevent physical force," he urged, "is to be prepared against it," and the people's oppressors would not dare to use "physical force" if they knew that the people were ready to use it against them. O'Brien also thought that arming by Chartists would be helpful in maintaining public order. To their traducers there was one reply for Chartists to make:

> Tell them that you abhor all physical force which is not strictly necessary for self-defence against those who wantonly employ it against the people; tell them that your only object in arming (if you do arm) is to protect your own personal liberties and constitutional rights, against arbitrary force on the one hand, and against anarchy on the other.[29]

It is likely that, excited by the upsurge in agitation at the end of the 1830s, O'Brien expressed himself less guardedly than he might have intended. Delbert Schafer refers to "revolutionary and inflammatory promises that he never intended to put into action." Although some contemporaries (friend and foe alike) did regard him as an advocate of violence, he often repeated that his remarks about arming and the need to subject the government to maximum pressure did not mean that he was ready to approve of conspiracy and insurrection. If he spoke and wrote sympathetically about "physical force," this was largely because of his concern for unity. He saw a need to keep all sections of Chartists moving in the same direction. Different opinions and proposals therefore had to be kept in balance—none could be rejected in case this alienated a large body of support.

O'Brien's mixture of moderation and menace in 1838 and 1839 confused some observers (and the controversy over his speaking engagement in Chichester in the spring of 1839 both arose from and perpetuated his notoriety as a dangerous firebrand).[30] But he thought he was openly adhering to a policy he had already announced: "I never recommended physical force except as a last desperate resort against tyranny, and to be used only when the popular mind has been fully enlightened beforehand."[31]

By the time O'Brien became editor of the *Poor Man's Guardian* in late 1832, he had developed a fascination with European revolutionaries and that publication had taken up the cause of liberty abroad, also commending the egalitarian teachings of groups such as the "St. Simonians."[32] The goals of this "ardent and enthusiastic party" were "1. All social institutions should have for their object the amelioration of the moral, physical, and intellectual condition of the poorest and most numerous class. 2. All privileges of birth, without exception, must be abolished. 3. To everyone according to his capacity—to every capacity according to its works."[33] The message was that Europe, and indeed Britain, would be much better off if reforms along these lines could be effected. O'Brien continued in this vein as editor. He often wrote in aid of democratic movements in Europe. He also explored the question of "justifiable assassination" in the name of freedom. O'Brien argued that extreme courses were best avoided because they brought no beneficial results, and, since they were not useful, notions of their rightness or wrongness mattered little. Oppression, he went on, was the tool of *classes*, not individuals, and therefore violence against individuals was pointless. However objectionable a Louis Philippe might be, or a Czar Nicholas I, they could not rule without a basis of approval. The immediate task was to target the classes that supported them—the propertied and moneyed elites and their hangers-on among the "shopocracy" and "bourgeoisie"—and the way to get necessary reforms was to "work rationally for rational ends." With knowledge, unity, and organization, the people could secure equal rights and equal laws. Violence was unnecessary and inadvisable.[34]

O'Brien acquired an expertise in the politics and history of France. During the Chartist era in Britain there was pressure for political reforms in France, and Benoît Agnes finds that ideas and tactics in Britain that were shaped by the French revolutions of 1789, 1830, and 1848 were less significant than French imitations of Chartist modes of agitation. There was a preference, encouraged by Frenchmen who spent time as exiles in London, for "incremental democratization" and nonviolent methods.[35] Perhaps the divergence affirmed at the time and afterward between the unstable, violent French and the peaceful, moderate British was overstated. All the same, British observers were obliged to take into consideration the insurrectionary and conspiratorial elements in French politics, the assassination attempts on Louis Philippe, the bursts of violence in the 1830s that culminated with an abortive coup in May 1839—all of which kept alive a proviolence tendency in France, the appeal of which increased as legal and peaceful avenues were blocked by the state.[36] O'Brien's writings about France helped to familiarize British readers with the issues at stake and added another strand to the debates about revolution.

O'Brien's theory of revolution had some distinctive foundations. The end he had in view, as is plain from his most advanced and mature reflections, was really a social revolution, accomplished through the fundamental alteration of British law and practice concerning the land, money, credit, and exchange, not a violent overthrow of the existing state structure. O'Brien was concerned about the same political problems that had vexed British radicals since the late eighteenth century, but there were other precepts and goals that affected his thinking. The main influences included ideas on property taken from seventeenth-century philosopher John Locke, especially the principle that personal labor gave some form of title to what that labor was expended upon. This principle was confirmed and extended in such writings as Thomas Spence's *The Real Rights of Man* (1795), Charles Hall's *The Effects of Civilization on the People in European States* (1805), and Thomas Hodgskin's *Labour Defended against the Claims of Capital* (1825). O'Brien read these works and accepted the doctrine that workers should enjoy the full fruits of their labor. On related matters there was much disputation. Should the focus be on individual rights or on fair and equal distribution, and were competition and private property to be allowed? For O'Brien, some clarification was provided by John Gray's *The Social System: A Treatise on the Principle of Exchange* (1831), which presented a form of practical socialism and identified the worker as "producer" (Gray argued that nobody else could be defined as such), and by the propositions of Owen, that labor was the source of all wealth and that the essential distinction in society was between the "productive" and "unproductive." O'Brien eagerly involved himself in discussion of these points.[37] During the 1830s he developed a "class analysis" that has been explored by Ben Maw. Borrowing from several sources and examples, O'Brien's focus became more social and economic than political as he delineated, in particular, the contrasts between the possessors and non-possessors of the means of production, distribution, and exchange.[38] All this provided a framework for O'Brien's thinking about and promotion of revolution.

O'Brien rejected the antirevolutionary aspects of Owenism, while Owen opposed political action and argued that even "moral force" was inappropriate (Owen did not take up O'Brien's idea of the early 1830s about organized agitation modeled on the Birmingham Political Union). O'Brien developed a style of what Gregory Claeys calls "social radicalism." He took Owenite elements and combined them with the more familiar radical heritage that could be traced back through William Cobbett, Henry Hunt, John Cartwright, and Thomas Paine, which focused on the system of government. By itself, O'Brien thought, Owenite cooperation could not offer a theory of revolution (and Owen was no democrat—in fact, he was widely seen as an autocrat, and even his intimates thought him too zealous in demanding his own way). But O'Brien approved of Owenite aims—abolishing competition and securing a fair reward for labor—and saw that these could be applied in revolutionary ways. To O'Brien, and to Owen, the growth of class consciousness could also have revolutionary consequences; but again, this did not mean that inequality and injustice could only be ended through violence. Owen's followers condemned the disorders of 1839 and 1842, and most of them decided not to ally themselves with Chartism, though some did so later as communitarian experiments failed and they accepted that true reform would require a transfer of political power. Chartists in turn became more sympathetic toward Owenites, and after 1848 there was probably less support in the movement for "physical force." Even so, in the splintered radicalism of this time the commitment to violence and insurrection remained strong in certain circles.[39]

The discussion in the *Chartist Circular* in 1841, about a revolution that all classes could accept, saw that paper express doubts about the prospect. O'Brien's idea that thorough reforms could be implemented in a way that satisfied both rich and poor indicates that he wanted not to facilitate the workers' victory in a class war, but to stop that war altogether. He often wrote of the need to reform without injuring particular persons or groups. He made plain the differences between legitimate wealth and influence—which had to be respected—and illegitimate wealth and influence—which had to be eradicated. Conflict and exploitation featured heavily in his writing, but he never lost his faith that they could be brought to an end.[40]

The tension between an economic or class-based analysis and the tendency in radicalism to prioritize political relationships was something that O'Brien explicitly addressed (as in his previously noted remarks about shopkeepers): one's *conduct* mattered more than one's class identity, and it was important that reformers should "distinguish the good from the bad, the politically honest from the politically dishonest, those to whom we are hostile and those to whom we are not." Before and after prison, O'Brien differentiated friendly from unfriendly members of the middle class and aristocracy. Broadly, one's class identity rested on economic function, social status, and political rights, but although the hierarchical structure of society was evil and wrong, individuals within that structure were not necessarily evil and wrong. Some of the middle class and aristocracy were *not* the workers' enemies, because they were willing to extend rights to cover the whole people.[41]

Radicals used an assortment of concepts and symbols drawn from popular constitutionalism, economic analysis, the American and French revolutions, natural rights, public and personal morality, local and national traditions, class relations, and other sources. While the "constitutional idiom" was, for many, the dominant mode of communication and spur for action, other idioms were employed as well, and the Chartist era—largely because of O'Brien—saw a merging of the older rhetoric (political corruption, aristocratic rule, monopolies, and heavy taxation) and a new paradigm (class conflict, economic exploitation, the labor theory of value, and anticapitalism).[42] It bears repeating, though, that Chartism was not monolithic and that many Chartists repudiated O'Brien's principles.[43]

From the outset, O'Brien maintained that moderate reforms were of no use. The key to everything was a democratic suffrage, which O'Brien expected to result in tangible social improvement: "meat and drink and clothing, good hours, and good beds, and good substantial furniture for every man and woman and child who will do a fair day's work."[44] O'Brien told the workers that "your poverty is the *result*, not the *cause* of your being unrepresented."[45] In other words, the people were subjugated because of a network of monopolies, in lawmaking as well as in the land, machinery, and resources. Gareth Stedman Jones regards the suffrage not as a matter of inherent individual rights but as a "practical and corporate" demand, "closely tied to the Chartist analysis of the cause of the condition of the working classes."[46] Hence O'Brien's linkage of property and representation: the workers lacked property because they lacked parliamentary representation, not the other way round.

What O'Brien envisaged was "an entire change in society," as he put it in 1833, "a change amounting to a complete subversion of the existing order of the world. The working classes aspire to be at the top instead of at the bottom of society, or rather that there should be no top or bottom at all."[47] In 1837 he exclaimed that nobody could expect hawks not to prey on doves. Why then should his readers look for morality on the part of their landed and moneyed oppressors?[48] O'Brien insisted that reforms should reduce the number and limit the power of nonproducers, safeguard for the workers the fruits of their labor, and enable the productive classes to take up a legislative role in order to promote social and moral transformation. This owed something to the ideas of Owen, but if the two men agreed on goals, they differed as to means. O'Brien continued to advocate manhood suffrage. Owen argued that the route to the better society lay through cooperative practices. To O'Brien, this offered only slow and partial change, whereas legislative power would bring immediate results. New laws could be passed and a radical program implemented (including nationalization of the land, currency reform, an overhaul of the banking system, and a role for the state in production and distribution).[49] From the mid-1830s O'Brien devoted himself increasingly to land reform. This was a matter of concern to most Chartists. In time O'Brien came up with his scheme for nationalization of the land (several commentators have credited O'Brien as a figure who connected "resumption of the land" platforms of the 1920s and 1930s with those of the late eighteenth century); he also thought of extending public ownership to utilities and related enterprises.[50] Since no law could supersede a preexisting common right to the earth and its produce, O'Brien sought to reconstruct "the institutions by which wealth is distributed" (an aspiration that Richard Ashcraft has placed within the context of rapidly evolving ideas about liberty, sovereignty, and natural rights).[51] O'Brien's position conflicted with that of O'Connor, and the latter's Land Plan became the mainspring of contention between them.[52]

The "entire change" and "complete subversion" that O'Brien described was, in his view, the necessary and achievable revolution that Chartists must seek, and its ingredients were taken both from old British radicalism's strictures upon political structures and relationships and from newer social and economic thinking about class, capitalism, the land, currency, credit, and exchange. O'Brien's perspective was also shaped by his Irish background. The district in county Longford where he was born and raised had seen considerable United Irish activity before and during the 1798 Rebellion. O'Brien grew up listening to stories about patriotism and sacrifice. Though he left Ireland at the end of the 1820s and did not go back, the Irish experience affected his opinion of violence and insurgency.[53] O'Brien was also fascinated by the United States of America. He never went there, but he was confident that America exhibited the blessings of democracy in action, and he commended its war for independence, its written constitution, and its republican system.[54] Above all else, though, O'Brien admired what he took to be the core democratic and libertarian principles of the French Revolution. Among his heroes were Babeuf, Buonarroti, and Robespierre. Hoping to facilitate a better understanding of the French Revolution in Britain, O'Brien planned to write a number of books and visited Paris several times in the 1830s to collect material. He met and conversed with Babeuf's surviving lieutenant Buonarroti (who by this time was a doyen-like figure among the initiated, the "old revolutionary" sought out by younger, up-and-coming radical leaders from across Europe—most of whom, as Bert Hoselitz has remarked, would go on to wield significant influence in their own right). O'Brien's annotated translation of *Buonarroti's History of Babeuf's Conspiracy* was published in 1836 (Babeuf was executed in 1797 after leading an abortive coup that was designed to reverse the drift toward pragmatic moderation and return the Revolution to a more egalitarian path). The first volume of O'Brien's biography of Robespierre was published in 1838. The other volumes did not appear, but there were shorter pieces on Robespierre and O'Brien presided over annual events held to celebrate Robespierre's birthday.[55]

In investigating and theorizing about revolutions, O'Brien emphasized the need for thorough social and economic reorganization. He hoped to inform and inspire by illuminating situations of revolutionary potential. America in the 1770s, France in 1789–94 and 1830, Britain in 1830–32, and most of Europe in 1848–49 provided the main lessons he wanted to pass on. All became part of his analysis, although pride of place was retained throughout by Robespierre's France.

Convinced that the priority was a democratic suffrage, O'Brien sought to popularize Buonarroti's maxim that improvements in any state would bear an exact proportion to the amount of influence exercised by the working classes. Robespierre had tried to build democracy in France, O'Brien explained, but after his demise the workers were edged out. Since then, in Britain as in France, it had become apparent that the workers would get nowhere unless they first gained political rights. These could then be used to transform society. O'Brien maintained that it was not enough simply to win the vote. Nor would the removal of this or that despot be sufficient; the principles *behind* despotism had to be destroyed. To O'Brien, equality was the aim and equality meant that everyone received a fair share of what society had to offer. Nobody would be able to take someone else's share, and success for each person would depend on merit and effort.[56]

Laws had to be framed by the people, not by a parliament or assembly. In the period since the American Revolution, O'Brien argued, the U.S. Congress had abandoned revolutionary measures and fallen into corrupt and self-serving ways, and this underlined the need for consent to be the ultimate authority in lawmaking.

Robespierre had wanted this for France, and the "democratic" French constitution of 1793 might have worked well, had external challenges, internal disorder, Robespierre's fall, and a clash of parties not interfered with its implementation. The 1795 constitution marked a betrayal because it provided for a taxpaying franchise. O'Brien declared that the French workers who rose in the "July Days" of 1830 ought to have insisted on a political system based on the 1793 constitution. O'Brien also referred to Buonarroti's belief that the 1793 constitution was a step toward the elimination of economic individualism and private property. O'Brien did not endorse these goals, because he thought that private property would be neutralized in a system that fostered social equality. If a man possessed more than his neighbor through his own efforts, this was a legitimate distinction, but he should be prevented from using the power his property gave him to steal the neighbor's property and add it to his own. The problem was not private property but the laws that governed it. This was the case in "reformed" Britain after 1832. Parliament was still not representative, and nothing could be expected from it that would benefit the people—not until the people made the laws, which could not happen without manhood suffrage. Britain after 1832, O'Brien decided, was like France in 1793. In the early stages of the French Revolution some useful reforms had been introduced, but the people had not achieved full liberty or removed the danger that aristocratic tyranny would give way to the oppression of the propertied middle classes. Robespierre tried and failed to meet this danger, and the French constitution of 1795 gave power to those with money. Britain was in a similar condition.[57]

These assertions led to O'Brien's explanation of why revolutions went wrong. The difficulty in America since the 1770s, France in the 1790s and 1830s, and Britain in the 1830s was essentially the same. When the revolutionary moment arrived and a redistribution of power was possible, the propertied middle classes acted fast to ensure that they made the biggest gains. Hence "the invariable success of the middle classes in cheating and duping the workpeople in France and America," and the defeats seen abroad were being repeated at home. The opportunity that arose during the reform crisis of 1830–32 had been lost. The 1832 Reform Act had not extended liberty. Instead, the reformed Parliament descended into "struggles between adverse bands of factionists for the right of tyrannizing." There was no democratic suffrage because too many of the workers had forgotten their own interests. Only middle-class aims had been accomplished. The results were being experienced in the legislation passed by the reformed Parliament, above all the New Poor Law, an "inhuman" and "homicidal" measure that demonstrated the wider agenda of Britain's elites. Their purpose was to ensure that all wealth, property, and influence remained in their hands.[58]

If he had to make a choice between the two, O'Brien wrote, aristocratic rule was marginally less objectionable than control by the middle classes. He pointed to the July Monarchy in France. The 1830 Revolution had given power to bankers and merchants. The right of association had been curtailed, meetings banned, the press censored. Here was a lesson for British workers. They had made reform possible in 1832 but were denied the benefits, as with the French working classes and the 1830 Revolution. Government everywhere, indeed, had to be examined and tested, and the people of Britain and France should accept the obvious: any system that would not allow them to vote was unworthy of their trust.[59]

Though historians have not made much use of O'Brien's assessment of the 1830 Revolution in France, what he wrote is echoed in recent interpretations. The preponderance of the propertied middle classes in the July Monarchy has been demonstrated many times. Yet the 1830 Revolution was made primarily by workers in the old crafts (printers, masons, cabinetmakers, and locksmiths).[60]

Observing France and Britain, O'Brien declared that it was important to understand the lessons of the past correctly, especially those that revealed something about the suitable methods and purposes of revolution. Unfortunately, history was written by the wrong people.[61] O'Brien's publications were an antidote. His book on Robespierre, for example, was meant to defend the cause of democracy and the reputation of democrats against their enemies; to advance the campaign for political and social regeneration by explaining why the first French Revolution had failed to do so; and to "shake the credit of 'history' and the authority of great names . . . hitherto used in support of liberticidal systems."[62]

Much of the Robespierre book was given over to O'Brien's evolving ideology of revolutions and its relevance to post-1832 Britain. O'Brien elaborated upon his claims that the French Revolution had been suborned by antipopular forces and turned against the principles that were supposed to be behind it. He called for a review of the known facts, "and facts, too, which you will have no difficulty in applying to the history and government of our own country." There could be but one conclusion:

> All the evils and horrors of the revolution arose from the fact that it was only a middle-class revolution; that is to say, a revolution commenced, conducted, and terminated by and for the middle classes only, the proletarians or labouring classes having had no other share in it than that of fighting, slaving, huzzaing, and starving!

Though some working-class leaders had for a time enjoyed a share in government, they were "cut off, one by one, by the middle classes till there was no leader left, and then came the *finale*—the utter subjection and impoverishment of the labouring people."[63] The "parent and supporter" of this reversal was the taxpayer franchise. It ensured that the French Revolution would mark a limitation of rights, not their enlargement. Robespierre had opposed efforts to restrict the suffrage in France with "money-qualifications," and it was not his fault that the French Revolution took the wrong path.[64]

O'Brien's interpretation of the French Revolution in some respects foreshadowed the later historiography. For much of the twentieth century it was the "orthodox" or "Marxist" approach that dominated, and the French Revolution was presented as a "bourgeois revolution" marked by class struggle.[65] A degree of continuity can be traced within this framework. Marx knew of O'Brien, adopted a number of his ideas, and later worked with surviving O'Brienites; and mention has frequently been made by historians and political scientists about the debt owed by Marx to earlier thinkers including O'Brien (who has been named as one of the "English School" from which Marx and European socialists took a lead, often without the proper acknowledgment).[66] O'Brien's interaction with European exiles in London gave him opportunities to influence them, and they in turn influenced him.[67] Even Marxists shared O'Brien's inclination toward peaceful methods. The possibility of cumulative reforms over time that could open a path to democracy was admitted, and so was the propriety of focusing first on winning the vote, although there was concern that manhood suffrage might not lead to a revolutionary program (what could be done if a working-class electorate voted against it?) and quarrels about how to define "revolution" went on. Must there be class conflict and revolutionary dictatorship? Was violence necessary, without exception, or a sign of immaturity and incompleteness? Did the revolution require a settled ideology and agreed program?[68]

O'Brien brought most of these considerations into his discussion of revolution during the Chartist years. In particular, he repeatedly asserted that the French experience had been duplicated in Britain's 1832 Reform Act. Aristocrats and moneyed men had needed a bargain on political reform, one that would not encourage "democratic spirit" or transfer power to the workers, and they got this in 1832. Landed and moneyed elites agreed to share power, and the people were to be excluded and plundered as before. The antirevolutionary schemes of dominant factions in France were also those of the elites in Britain. In both countries political rights still depended on property qualifications. O'Brien admitted that there was a mountain to climb "because the millions are everywhere kept in a double state of ignorance, ignorant in the first place of the incalculable benefits which a pure democracy would yield them, and ignorant in the next of their own innate power to establish such a democracy." The ruling elites were doing their utmost to perpetuate this. They manipulated all the media of instruction and information: pulpit, press, stage, universities, colleges, seminaries, literature.[69]

O'Brien assumed that democracy could not function without the widespread ownership of property. From the establishment of feudalism onward, he argued, the people had been dispossessed of the land that was rightfully theirs. In France, landowners had gradually taken even the wastes and commons to which the public had natural and legal entitlement. Enclosures in the eighteenth century had placed Britain on a par with France in terms of the dispossession of the people. Long wars, the massive debt, and the increasing rate of enclosure all benefited the landed and moneyed interests while burdening, impoverishing, and dejecting everyone else. For the people of France, the "July Days" in Paris in 1830 represented another lost opportunity. What emerged was not a democracy but a regime under the sway of wealthy property owners, and circumstances were not much better in Britain.[70]

O'Brien railed against the conservatism, selfishness, and discord that seemed to characterize groups that rose to ascendancy during revolutionary times.

> Such is the inevitable march of all revolutions which begin in the upper regions of society. Striking their first blows at the top, they proceed downwards through society, carrying along, and reducing to a common level, all the intermediate grades, till they reach the grade immediately above the producer, that is to say, the classes that live by buying and selling his labour or his labour's produce. There they stop, because there the various discomfited factions, having no longer anything to gain by combatting one another, find it their interest to reunite and make common cause against the producer, whose triumph would stop their plundering and ambitious projects altogether. No revolution has ever yet descended, in practice, below the profit-mongering classes. Hence they have all been failures.

O'Brien followed this line of reasoning through to a description of how revolutions could succeed.

> A revolution to be effective must begin at the bottom, instead of at the top of society. It must originate with the productive classes, and the first blow must be

> struck at the profit-monger. If you succeed against him, all the superior grades are brought down and made to disappear in due course; for they all grow out of and are sustained by him.[71]

O'Brien's ideology of revolution had one premise. For a revolution to work it had to involve the equalization of classes, and, thereby, a redistribution of political and economic power.

O'Brien developed these points in the lecture room as well as in the press. But his frustration mounted as the Chartist movement faltered. The working classes were following the wrong leaders; radical nostrums were firmly resisted in Parliament; and "elements of regeneration" were too weak. If a revolution were to be attempted, he reiterated in 1843, it would have to be nonviolent and would need first to break the influence of landed and moneyed elites. Then the people would have to be willing to carry it beyond its preliminary stages.[72] O'Brien complained that middle-class movements persevered until they made gains, while working-class movements rarely did so.[73] There was an angry tone to his writing in these years. He kept telling the workers what to do, but most of them did not respond as he recommended.[74]

He persevered, and European examples continued to impress. For some Europeans, conspiracy, terror, and dictatorship were not illegitimate techniques in the building of a better society. Instead, they were transitional stages and essential to the desired revolution. Many British radicals were unconvinced, and European exiles in London were divided on the matter. O'Brien, though he adopted some of the theories of Robespierre and Babeuf, still maintained that violence was not necessary or inevitable.[75]

Within the Chartist movement there may have been those who associated Robespierre and Babeuf with tyranny, intolerance, chaos, and bloodshed, but there were also many Chartists who accepted O'Brien's assessment of Robespierre and Babeuf. For them, Robespierre in particular was an icon and it did not seem incongruous to eulogize him in print or to drink to his memory at, for instance, a dinner celebrating the birthday of Henry Hunt. Indeed, when events in Paris in 1848 prompted a new attentiveness to French politics and history, a preference for radical solutions made Robespierre's career relevant and meritorious to many more people than before. Outside the Chartist movement, however, this preference was much weaker. In the broader spectrum of British opinion there were political, historical, and cultural obstacles that denied foreign examples a welcome, even among reformers. Linda

Colley has shown that British versions of liberty, patriotism, and constitutionalism were to some extent defined in the eighteenth and early nineteenth centuries in a way that distinguished them from, and in superiority to, French versions.[76] In this context the French Revolution was not something to be admired or imitated, and its outstanding personalities were not friends to Britain but enemies. In the mid-nineteenth century, debates about British reform, government, and nation were influenced by European (and American) developments, but, as demonstrated by Jonathan Parry and Robert Saunders, the link between these developments and Britain's situation was disputed.[77] In a similar fashion political exiles from Europe, including the Italians studied by Maurizio Isabella, were carefully selective about elements of the British political system that they were willing to sanction and later re-create when they returned home.[78] Ideological interaction between British and European reformers was hardly straightforward in these circumstances, and the dominant doctrines and figures of the French Revolution could be judged in contrasting ways.

It is possible, given his open and oft-repeated admiration for Robespierre and Babeuf and the France of the early 1790s, that anti-French sentiment in Britain inhibited the wider acceptance of O'Brien's reform proposals. Aware of this problem, perhaps, O'Brien made it clear—as in his treatment of Babouvism—that he approved of some but not all revolutionary propositions. In forming and presenting his own opinions, he was contributing to interpretive approaches that have shifted and evolved, and fallen in and out of favor, since the late eighteenth century. Many of these interpretations have rested on theory and imagination, not formal historical evidence. "Debates about the French Revolution are more often about the terms in which it is presented and represented rather than about any 'real' French Revolution which may or may not have taken place," write C. C. Barfoot and Theo D'haen.

> The French Revolution, it emerges, is not only the creator of rhetoric but the creation of rhetoric: made by tropes as well as the manufacturer of tropes. Poets as well as novelists; politicians as well as pamphleteers; journalists, essayists, historians—all are worked upon by the keywords, the slogans, the visual and verbal images, the myths and fantasies of the Revolutionary Epoch which are then worked and reworked either to affirm or to denounce the consequences and aftermath of 1789 and the Fall of the Bastille.[79]

O'Brien was one of the first serious British students of revolution to realize this and to write and speak accordingly. He helped to create, and made full use of, interpretative license.

O'Brien pursued what might be called an "anglicization of revolution." Those parts of Babouvism that he accepted he also tried to adapt, in order to apply them usefully to British conditions. He appreciated the Enlightenment background to Babeuf's thought and Buonarroti's exposition of that thought, and he was impressed by Buonarroti's comparison of Babouvism with Owenism. These two philosophies had broadly the same end in view: a thoroughly reformed society organized along egalitarian and communitarian lines, with tasks shared and the fruits of labor fairly distributed. But while Babeuf had wanted to move immediately to one great community, Owen began with small units, hoping that these would multiply and eventually unite in the one great community; and while Babeuf wanted to seize government power and use it to make the necessary changes, Owen relied on teaching and example. Buonarroti had his doubts about Owenite methods, but not the goal, which was also O'Brien's position. As O'Brien developed his ideas about how political rights, once extended, could be used to transform society, he weighed up the pros and cons of Babouvism. He did not share the Babouvist readiness to engage in violence, to kill or be killed for the revolution.[80]

O'Brien was uneasy about several aspects of the Babouvist methodology, especially the secret conspiratorial faction that would direct operations and the dictatorship and removal of opponents that would mark a transitional stage in the revolution. O'Brien preferred a revolution that carried reform forward with popular consent, expressed through democratic organs. It was important to respect the people's freedom to choose. Although leaders could educate and guide, a small minority should not try to compel everyone else into its way of thinking. O'Brien admitted that force might become necessary, to place government in the hands of the people and to make sure that the laws approved by the people were not disobeyed. But it was absolutely the last resort, and force could accomplish nothing unless and until the people were politically and socially aware. They had to understand why they were oppressed and be willing to resist this oppression. O'Brien opposed the "general strike" or "national holiday" proposed by Chartists in 1839 on the grounds that the people were not ready to join in and that, if it was attempted and failed, the movement would be badly damaged. He considered the Newport Rising a mistake and lamented that its participants had not learned the lessons of the Babeuf plot (in both cases a violent insurrection was easily put down, followed by the harsh repression of radicals indiscriminately, whether they had broken the law or not). Events of the late 1830s and early 1840s convinced O'Brien that a Babouvist coup could not succeed in Britain and that there could be no revolution unless a large proportion of the population genuinely desired it. The Charter offered the means, for it was essential to empower the people politically. Then the people could alter laws and institutions to revolutionize their social and economic experience—by attending to the land, currency, credit, and exchange. To O'Brien, the Babouvists were right to regard the obtaining of political power as the prerequisite for social change, to value democratic assemblies and the "republic of equality," and to wish for an educated working class. Radical leaders must instruct the people, O'Brien thought, to prepare them for the revolution. Here was a significant distinction between O'Brien and the Babouvists. They were willing to use violence and coercion and would educate the people afterward to explain why the revolution had been necessary. O'Brien's knowledge of British circumstances made him think that the people must be educated first. The creation of a political and social consciousness would *lead to* (rather than follow) the revolution. It all rested on consent, not violence.[81]

O'Brien was the Chartist movement's leading interpreter of French developments of the 1790s. He presented a particular rendering of the history of that time, to make it intelligible to British radicals and, above all, usable. He took what he thought was most relevant about the first French Revolution, applied it to British circumstances, and merged it with his own agenda, according to which political reform was to lead to social transformation and the "productive" would take precedence over the "unproductive" classes. O'Brien taught that Robespierre and Babeuf were guides who indicated the surest route to political liberty, social equality, and economic justice. Such claims helped to reduce, especially among British radicals, the negative connotations of terms like "Jacobinism." James Epstein and David Karr have shown that many radicals saw no difference between constitutional and "revolutionary" activity, and "adopted codes of speech and behavior associated with the Revolution alongside those of constitutionalism, inflecting British tradition with democratic possibilities previewed in France." As well as enlarging upon this strategy O'Brien influenced key figures in the rise of Chartist internationalism, particularly George Julian Harney, who first got to know O'Brien as a teenager when he was Hetherington's shop boy and O'Brien was editor of the *Poor Man's Guardian*. The two were often in each other's company in the early years of Chartism, and

Harney readily acknowledged his intellectual debts to O'Brien. Harney would later go on to organize and publicize the Fraternal Democrats, giving an international dimension to "the Charter and something more" from the mid-1840s. Thanks largely to O'Brien, the sacrifices for democracy made by Robespierre and Babeuf were debated at length in these circles.[82]

Harney it was who had protested against a move at the Chartist Convention in 1839 to exclude delegates who were said to be tainted by extremism. Objections were raised about the presence of men calling themselves "Jacobins" and known to be admirers of the revolutionary France of the 1790s. William Lovett was concerned that unity would be lost if extremists were allowed to participate: "On union their lives depended, and persons might obtain admittance who, by their speeches, might place their lives in jeopardy, and he thought they had a right to interfere with those sent here in opposition to the objects of the Convention." Another speaker, the writer and publisher John Cleave, a "moderate" (like Lovett) of the London Working Men's Association, "expressed his disapprobation of those who showed their approbation of the French Revolution . . . which was likely to prejudice the Convention in the eyes of those whose support would be of service to them." O'Brien was not present to reply, but he would have backed the remarks of Harney on this occasion. Harney insisted that one of the delegates in question, Joseph Williams, who represented East Surrey and Lambeth, had been properly elected and could not be excluded. (Along with Harney and O'Brien, Williams was a member of the London Democratic Association, a body that had engaged in disputes with the LWMA.) Moreover, Harney "knew that he had the people on his side, and he was not to be put down because it was said that he was a favourer of the French Revolution—he was for its virtues, not its vices." Harney declared that "he would rejoice in the name of Jacobin, and posterity would yet do them justice."[83]

During 1847 O'Brien pressed ahead with writing projects, and among those he mentioned to his friend Thomas Allsop were works on democratization and social change, Robespierre, and the potential for revolution in parts of Europe, especially Prussia.[84] O'Brien had good reason to focus on the latter. In the spring of 1847, Frederick William IV of Prussia called a united diet, or *Landtag*, of all eight provinces in his kingdom, seeking consent for new taxes and a state loan (to fund railway construction), but the king resisted all talk of constitutional concessions. The diet could debate measures and present petitions but had no power to initiate reforms, and its consent was not required for laws or budgets. In April 1847 there was serious rioting in Berlin, prompted by poor harvests, slack trade, and financial problems. O'Brien could see that pressure was building up in Prussia, in France, and elsewhere. Allsop agreed, referring in his correspondence to "great changes approaching."[85]

The events of 1848–49 in Europe gave ample opportunity for further comment. O'Brien was initially excited by but quickly saw the flaws in the 1848 Revolution in France, which ended the July Monarchy and led to the establishment of the Second Republic. He translated and printed the new French constitution and wrote several articles about it, and his argument was accurately summed up by the motto he adopted at this time (from Robespierre's colleague Louis Antoine de Saint-Just, who had been executed in 1794): "Those who make half-revolutions but dig a grave for themselves."[86]

O'Brien cast his gaze across Europe. Conservatives, he wrote, preferred to wait for a revolution from above. They trusted their governments to reform. Liberals trusted the middle classes to decide when a revolution was appropriate and how best to promote progress. For O'Brien, 1848 even more than 1789 taught that conservative and liberal versions of revolution must be rejected. The people of every nation had to realize that the highest form of revolution was the one that benefited the majority. Change that stopped short of this was unacceptable.[87]

O'Brien kept his readers abreast of the contest in the new French republic between democratic socialists and the moderates, liberals, and monarchists who seemed to be the likely victors. He gladly pointed to evidence of the spread of socialism while regretting the repression ordered by the legislative assembly. Counterrevolution set in across Europe, and by August 1849 O'Brien was passing on discouraging news from Hungary as well as France.[88]

The 1848 Revolutions and their aftermath, and his links with international committees and conversations with exiles in London, led O'Brien to write of the affinity between Chartism and mobilizations abroad, and he stated that in France as in Britain, democrats and socialists had common objectives. As noted earlier, when "patriot" leaders visited Britain, Chartists would accept what they liked and reject what they disliked from among the principles that these figures expounded. Though O'Brien objected to Kossuth's belief that national independence went hand in hand with liberal economics, for instance, he shared some of Kossuth's other ideas and was pleased that these had an airing on Kossuth's speaking tour of 1851. There were differing viewpoints among British radicals, however, that reflected a wide range of political, social, and economic aspirations, and O'Brien himself was a little inconsistent. Sometimes he preached fraternity and paid close attention to movements abroad, and yet in 1852 he declared that exiles from Europe could expect no help until the people of Britain had secured full rights.[89] "Kossuth and Hungarian independence" was among the toasts given at a public supper organized by the National Reform League in October 1851, but there was a degree of equivocation on the subject. It was not O'Brien who proposed the toast but NRL member George Hoppy, who, certain that an independent Hungary would assist in the promotion of liberty across Europe, added that "if Kossuth was not so advanced in democratic axioms as themselves, it was the duty of the democrats of London and of England to spur him forward in the cause of progression, until he became truly one of the Champions of the People."[90]

Another foreign visitor with whom O'Brien had dealings was Louis Blanc, the French socialist who served in the provisional government in Paris in 1848 before taking refuge in London. O'Brien reprinted a number of Blanc's works, and to some of these he attached detailed criticisms.[91] Blanc was among the Europeans with whom O'Brien frequently shared the platform in London meeting rooms in these years. They respected each other, though they were not close personally.

Blanc was the most prominent of the French advocates of a democratic and socialist republic.[92] His was only one of the jarring political philosophies that animated European exiles and their British hosts, and clashes were plentiful at meetings and in the press. The Italian Giuseppe Mazzini became a trenchant adversary of Blanc, advocating moral regeneration rather than class struggle and advancing a nonsocialist republican program that attracted some moderate Chartists.[93] Blanc dismissed these proposals. Mazzini's low opinion of "constitutional Chartism" and "French communism" put distance between him and others who were more concerned about political structures or more inclined toward socialism. Mazzini found fault with O'Brien's reform agenda and disliked O'Brien's edition of *Buonarroti's History of Babeuf's Conspiracy*, in which O'Brien had included an opinionated commentary.[94]

Blanc's friendships with British radicals were made easier by the fact that his socialism was relatively mild.[95] He did embrace aspects of the French Jacobin model and the utopian communitarianism of Charles Fourier, but in his amalgamation of these elements he ruled out violence. State intervention was to realize the necessary revolution, not strikes or riots or insurgencies. Blanc wanted no bloodshed, and in his later career, suggests Ansgar Reiss, he put republicanism *before* socialism.[96] At the time when O'Brien was acquainted with him, however, no such shift was apparent, for Blanc insisted that social justice was the first aim, taking precedence over a republican form of government.[97] O'Brien shared Blanc's suspicion of laissez-faire and his assumptions about the potential of the state as a reforming agency, and saw merit in Blanc's idea of "the right to live by labour" and in the libertarian spirit of democratic socialism. He and Blanc also had enemies in common, notably those middle-class reformers who tended to divide European exiles into two camps—liberals and nationalists (acceptable) and democrats and socialists (unacceptable). Blanc habitually defended French socialism by linking it with British radical traditions, which suited many Chartists.[98]

Blanc offered an interpretation of the 1790s in France that reinforced his case for social and political regeneration, and O'Brien used the 1790s in a similar way. They had shared concerns, not least the social aims that should be attached to the Charter and the steps required to get radical groups to join together.[99] To advance the rights of labor was a priority for Blanc and O'Brien, and one of the premises for this came directly from Buonarroti—that workers, because they lacked property and therefore particular goals distinct from universal goals, were ready to devote themselves to universal goals. As Marc Mulholland argues, this gave rise to collectivism, hostility to the market, and the wish to socialize the means of subsistence.[100] Such ideas added to the framework within which Blanc's concept of national workshops and O'Brien's manifesto for land, currency, credit, and exchange could be evaluated.

O'Brien was interested to learn of Blanc's explanation of the failure of the 1848 Revolution in France. The Second Republic would have fared better had its opponents not been able to occupy positions of power, Blanc asserted. Unfortunately, its strongest supporters had been silenced, imprisoned, or exiled, and when its very existence was at stake, there were insufficient numbers who cared about saving it. Republican institutions had helped those who hated the republic. Blanc trusted that next time things would be different. He favored common, free, compulsory education, so that people could better understand their own interests. A democratic suffrage was worthless when electors lacked knowledge. Blanc was ready to experiment—perhaps with a form of proportional representation—for a majority could be fallible and government by a majority was not the same as government by the people.[101] This was the main message of Blanc's essay "The Presidency and Universal Suffrage," published in London in the summer of 1849. Blanc believed, as O'Brien did, that political rights without social change could bring no advantage to any nation anywhere.[102] In a subsequent essay Blanc focused on the improvements that a socialist system might offer to Britain.[103] He generally chose to avoid a condemnatory tone in his writings about Britain, though he took exception to the account of the French Revolution of 1848 published in 1857 by Lord

Normanby, who had been Britain's ambassador in Paris from 1846 to 1852. In 1858 Blanc published his own book about 1848. He wanted to correct the widely held notion—based on the chaos of 1792–93, the failure of the republic of 1848–52, and the existence of Napoleon III's regime—that a republic could not function properly in France. Blanc agreed that in any nation, institutions ought to suit the character of that nation. He was adamant that republicanism did suit the French character, just as constitutional monarchy suited the British character. A difference between the French and the British was that the former wanted equality, while the latter accepted hierarchy and distinctions of rank. Britain was remarkably class conscious, but in France "the sense of equality is developed to the utmost."[104]

Many of these opinions about Britain and France accorded with O'Brien's own, and though he was willing to work within the British constitution he wished for sweeping reforms that would allow for progress toward equality and justice. After O'Brien's death Blanc remembered him for his "leading mind" and "generous heart."[105]

Blanc's association with O'Brien dismayed one of O'Brien's old Owenite acquaintances, the London publisher James Rigby. Though Rigby had given up on O'Brien (who had developed his own program, not reliant on or limited to Owenism), he expected better of Blanc. In 1856, reading of a plan agreed by O'Brien and Blanc for a union of British and French workers, Rigby was dismissive: "I never thought Louis Blanc a *first rate* mind but I am really sorry that he has joined the mad party that follows O'Brien."[106]

A different view had been taken by Thomas Allsop during the revolutionary year 1848, when the prospect of an Owen-O'Brien-Blanc combination seemed to Allsop to make perfect sense. He urged Owen (who went to Paris to make reform proposals to the new leaders there) to endorse "the French organization of labour," to use Blanc as an "example" to British workers, and to advise Blanc on how to overcome the "immense difficulties" of the French situation. Allsop suggested that Blanc "seems to have a fine mind" and was "worth cultivating." Like O'Brien, Allsop wanted the regime change in France to result in "visible fruits"—that is, the destruction of former arrangements for credit and capital and the removal from power of those classes that had benefited most from those arrangements. Allsop also advocated the "annihilation" of private property. Again like O'Brien, he was frustrated by the resurgence of "the capitalist and middle classes" and by electoral victories for "the moderate party." He noted the rise of anti-Blanc and anti-"communist" sentiment in France. The British press, "ignorant and afraid," was siding with Blanc's French critics. Allsop did not expect "socialism" to prosper until "it becomes more and better appreciated." When Blanc arrived in London, Allsop made ready to "aid and assist" him and stressed the similarities between his principles and those of Owen.[107]

While he engaged in long and detailed conversations (mostly in print) with Louis Blanc, O'Brien took less interest in the activity of another French republican exile, Alexandre Ledru-Rollin, whose socialism was more equivocal than Blanc's. It is nevertheless instructive to compare O'Brien's views with those of Ledru-Rollin.

In the immediate aftermath of the 1848 revolutions, O'Brien was prepared publicly to praise Ledru-Rollin. Later on he understood more clearly how their ideas differed, but there remained some affinities, not least because of Ledru-Rollin's respect for the French constitution of 1793 and for the cooperative movement.[108] In his *Decline of England*, published soon after his arrival in 1849 (the original was in French and the translation appeared in 1850), Ledru-Rollin argued that the hostility of British commentators toward French exiles arose mainly from bias against the 1848 Revolution and Second Republic. Ledru-Rollin insisted that the revolution and the republic merited praise, not censure, and he did not think that the British system of government, in comparison, had much to recommend it. Indeed, the example set by France in 1848 was worthy of serious reflection in Britain. Ledru-Rollin pointed to aristocratic authority, free trade, capitalism, and individualism as the main causes of Britain's problems. True freedom would not be possible until these problems were corrected, and any impartial assessment of contemporary Britain could not fail to notice that division, suffering, and injustice were everywhere to be seen. The French had realized that they needed a revolution in order to emancipate themselves from such evils. Elites had to be broken up and no path to liberty could be opened while privileges and monopolies remained intact. France was not afraid of fundamental change, declared Ledru-Rollin, but it was not clear that Britain had the same courage and self-awareness.[109] This echoed O'Brien's disappointment with the pace of reform in Britain, though of course he hoped for a change. After 1848 "the Charter and something more" seemed an attractive and viable proposition to British radicals, but, as ever, there was no unanimity on means and ends or on the relevance of foreign examples.

As did other Chartist leaders, O'Brien regularly interacted with European exiles. Many Chartists took up an international platform, and when they looked abroad they saw fellow victims of oppression, although this did not mean that they believed that underground plotting and insurrectionary combat could or should be tried in Britain. Chartist attitudes toward the exiles and European events were not uniform but reflected existing disagreements on principles and tactics. It is equally the case that most Chartists did not regard European politics as directly relevant to their own situation.[110] The impact of Chartist internationalism, though important, was limited, especially outside London. Nevertheless, internationalists such as O'Brien contributed to ongoing debates about how to secure the Charter and in doing so clarified some of the differences between the British political experience—openness and constitutionalism—and the European willingness to try secrecy, conspiracy, and violence.[111]

After 1848, international organizations multiplied in London. Often they shared venues, and many British and foreign radicals belonged simultaneously to more than one club or institution. O'Brien and his followers were part of this political culture of personal contact, intellectual cross-fertilization, and radical conviviality. O'Brien spoke at numerous events in these years. He also publicized them in his and other newspapers. These events provided an indispensable outlet and advanced the "imagined community" and "confluence of revolutionary traditions" identified by Margot Finn.[112] O'Brien's role in connecting Chartism with continental developments was recognized in 1848 and subsequently, and some exiles were drawn into his friendship group, including the Frenchman Joseph Collet.[113] O'Brien thought that reforms at home and abroad were mutually dependent, and he urged all campaigners for reform to get knowledge so that they would understand the reasons for past defeats and in future push for the things that really mattered. Manhood suffrage alone would not be enough. Louis Napoleon's victory in the December 1848 presidential election in France showed that democratic voting was not without its pitfalls.[114]

Observing the situation in France during 1849, O'Brien did not see much "democratic spirit." Republicans and socialists were weakening themselves, he thought, by competing for support only for their own pet theories. What was required was unity on an agreed program, one that prioritized land, currency, credit, and exchange. He lamented Blanc's failure to take up land reform. Without an equitable system of land tenure, O'Brien wrote, the economic relationships favored by Blanc could not exist and the working classes could not be freed from subordination to capitalists.[115]

O'Brien wondered what revolutionaries on the continent had learned and what the ramifications were for British reform. The methods that had failed in Europe were plainly insufficient. The inescapable conclusion was that there could be no revolutionary moment anywhere, and no revolutionary gains, unless two elements were present:

> First, a uniform creed for the reformers to bind them together in unity of object and of action, and second, sufficient intelligence amongst the mass of the people (by whom and for whom only revolutions can and ought to be made) to enable them to appreciate such a creed, and to make them proof against the arts and wiles and corrupting influences of the common enemy.[116]

O'Brien remained furious about the fiasco of 10 April 1848 on Kennington Common, and the apparent collapse (again) of Chartism.[117] Britain's 1848 told the usual story, of revolutionary potential dissipated by incompetent leaders and an uninformed populace. O'Brien continued to push for the nonviolent revolution as writer and orator. Though he had no newspapers of his own after 1849, he had a number of outlets in the metropolitan and provincial press and also published several pamphlets and poems. Among the latter were attacks on the counterrevolutionary "statesmanship without convictions" of Palmerston and the "abomination" that was Napoleon III.[118]

Though disappointed by the apparent failure of exertions in Britain and Europe in 1848, O'Brien spoke up for those radicals who regarded 1848 not as an ending or defeat but as a reason for further campaigning. Revolutionary possibility, it was thought, could be revived. There was increasing discussion of class conflict, "red republicanism," liberty, and nationhood. In Europe, some Chartists maintained, the priority should be personal liberty rather than the formation of the nation-state. International working-class solidarity remained a dominant trope, while nonviolent methods were still preferred by most British radicals and were often contrasted with the tactics tried abroad. Great attention was paid to France, and, as usual, opinion varied as to the relevance of French events to the situation in Britain and vice versa. Interpreting the past to plan for the future became a common enterprise for British radicals. Failures could be forgotten. Optimism could be nurtured. Mike Sanders emphasizes "the tenacity of hope" and "a reconfiguration of the movement's political temporality, as the idea of the future increasingly comes to dominate both past and present in the Chartist imaginary." This was one theme in the post-1848 reassessments and realignments in popular radicalism, and O'Brien joined others in rethinking the content of Chartism and its linkages with events abroad.[119]

In his speeches of this period, O'Brien's routine was to combine the history and tenets of British radicalism with the uprisings of 1848 and previous years in Europe. Sometimes he surveyed the careers of his radical heroes for reference points. In February 1849, at a "public festival" in John Street to commemorate Paine's birthday, chaired by Henry Hetherington and attended by at least fifteen hundred persons, O'Brien responded to the toast to "Robespierre and the other martyrs to social progress." He said that Robespierre's reputation, not only in Britain but also in France, Germany, and elsewhere, had changed in recent decades. Robespierre had been "rescued," and true Chartists now realized that he was one of their own.

> Robespierre was an advocate for the unrestricted liberty of the press; and for a national system of education, so that, from earliest youth, all might be trained equals—a portion of that system of education was the science of practical agriculture. He was opposed to state churches and would have no paid priests, whilst he gave unrestrained liberty of conscience to all. He held that a nation requiring a standing army must be a nation of slaves . . . and he held that the soldier who raised his arm against a citizen should be deemed an assassin. Such was Robespierre—his constitution was a perfectly democratic one, embracing all points of the People's Charter. (Loud cheers.)

O'Brien considered Robespierre's nickname, "the Incorruptible," to be well deserved. Even his enemies admitted that he would not have betrayed the Republic for all the money in Europe. His creed was still the one against which all others had to be measured, whether in Britain or on the continent.

> Robespierre was murdered because he said that mere political reforms were useless, except the people were taught to use them as a means to effect their social rights. Robespierre said we found the people *sans culotte*; let it be said, we left them *culotte*—that is, we found them clothesless, let us leave them well clothed; we find them ignorant, let us give them intelligence—in fine, to substitute the greatness of man for the littleness of the great. (Loud cheers.)

A few weeks later, at a meeting to mark the anniversary of the rising of 1848 in Paris, again in the John Street rooms but this time chaired by Harney, O'Brien spoke on "the sovereignty of the people and the fraternity and unity of the proletarians and democrats of all nations." He discussed Britain, Ireland, and Europe. Where a people became sovereign, he stressed, no suspension of liberties could occur. There would be no conflict or suffering; each man would enjoy the produce of his own labor; the land would be the property of all. Since the "despots, aristocrats, and money-mongers" were united in their opposition to this, the proletarians had to unite too, across national boundaries. "A proletarian was a man who gave his labour and his offspring as guarantees to the state. Could the aristocracy offer as good security? (Hear, hear.)" Proletarian unity meant that an attack on one was an attack on all. The people of Britain, therefore, were directly affected by contemporary events in Europe—as in Rome, where a republic had recently been established. Anyone who believed in sovereignty for those who worked and not for the idle, O'Brien declared, would build on such gains as these (he was not to know that the republic in Rome would last for only five months).[120]

In June 1850, hearing of a new electoral law in France that imposed residence and taxpaying qualifications, O'Brien helped to organize an emergency meeting. The "destruction of universal suffrage in France" proved that Louis Napoleon and his faction were preparing to overthrow the Second Republic. O'Brien argued that oppression in one place opened the way for oppression in another and that the British people had to join in resisting this "treason against the human race." About 50 percent of the French electorate would lose the vote, O'Brien said. Soldiers had been sent into the streets to enforce the new law, but it was not consistent with the French constitution and could not be regarded as legitimate or binding. It was the grotesque offspring of the politically ambitious propertied classes, and O'Brien was confident that the workers of France—encouraged by their comrades in Britain—would not submit.[121] O'Brien employed the same language of democracy and fraternity over the following years.[122]

At the end of 1851, having failed to obtain a constitutional amendment allowing him to extend his term of office as president of France, Louis Napoleon staged a coup. O'Brien attended a large meeting in London and was dissatisfied with the wording of a proposed resolution:

> That this meeting protests against the political changes in France, against the arbitrary and heartless means by which they have been effected; and deems it a duty to raise a public voice on behalf of a friendly people crushed under a military rule; also to call earnestly upon our government to use its political influence on behalf of the restoration of the liberties of the people, destroyed by the indefensible aggressions of organized despotism.

This was too weak, O'Brien asserted. He referred the meeting to what was known about the coup in Paris. Murder, usurpation, and treachery were not merely "political changes," and to ask the Palmerston government to help restore liberty to the people of France was "humbug." Palmerston did not favor liberty at home, let alone in other countries. O'Brien wanted different wording:

> That this meeting contemplates with abhorrence and disgust the triumphant usurpation of Louis Napoleon; an usurpation accomplished by a continuation of crimes, including perfidy, violence, and organized murder, unparalleled in the history of Europe. That we deeply sympathize with the great and generous French people in seeing their hard-won constitutional rights and liberties so foully trampled upon by brute military force, and we earnestly hope, in common with all good men, that Europe will speedily see a termination of this usurper's power, worthy of his reign, worthy of his crimes, and of his ingratitude towards the French people.

O'Brien considered recent events "the darkest in modern history." Not only had Louis Napoleon used armed force, fettered the press, and dispersed the legislative assembly, but he resorted to the most sordid lies and tricks, promising to bring back "universal suffrage" and siding with one group and then another so as to turn them against each other. The upper and middle classes would welcome the coup. It was only radicals, democrats, and socialists who were being shot, and it was only to working-class districts that soldiers were being sent. Though there were some complaints about O'Brien's remarks, his resolution was approved by a large majority.[123]

O'Brien's continuing commitment to the revolutionary bid for rights and self-determination in Europe shaped his agitation against the Crimean War of 1853–56. Some radicals took up an opposing position, swayed by press excitement and popular enthusiasm for the war, but O'Brien spoke and wrote against it. He was told point-blank by prospective partners in a plan for a new periodical that if it adopted an antiwar stance it would not be able to establish itself, and the plan was dropped. He addressed meetings of the "Stop-the-War League." When the government called for a day of fasting to assist the war effort, O'Brien responded with his *Sermon on the Day of the Public Fast and Humiliation for England's Disasters in the Crimea*, a poem that condemned the war, the fast, and those responsible for British policy:

> Well, consid'ring how these great ones rule us,
> How oft they starve, and how they always fool us,
> 'Twere surely right that such transcendent sinners,

Should go, at least one day, without their dinners;
But will they? No! despite of church and steeple,
They'll do it not—but they will *do* the people!

O'Brien's poem also condemned the many who stood by and let such enormities occur: "They who permit oppression share the crime." More generally, he argued that war was a device used by powerful elites when they wanted to draw the people's attention away from domestic evils caused by misgovernment, and he rejected claims that intervention abroad was sometimes appropriate to release other nations from those same evils. Instead of trying to topple foreign despots, O'Brien thought, British workers should first remove the despots at home. When they had secured their own rights they would be better able to assist the downtrodden of Europe.[124]

How soon might this happen? O'Brien veered between hopefulness and pessimism. His friend Allsop, who seems to have been more buoyant and sanguine, looked only to what the Crimean War made possible at home and in Europe. It could be the "devouring fire," the crisis that weakened resistance to social change. At the end of 1855 Allsop wrote that "a new and wholly different foliage ever springs up from the ashes of a widespread and devouring flame."[125]

While having to contend with personal and family difficulties in these years, O'Brien still attended as assiduously as he could to public affairs. As his correspondence makes clear, he was reading and writing a great deal, busying himself at the Eclectic Institution, and "keeping up with my London and country friends." In 1857 he focused for a time on the Indian Mutiny, which he explained as a "premeditated affair": the Sepoys were provoked into revolt as a pretext for the seizure of Indian property and wealth by vested interests in Britain. "All this and more my hearers begin to understand, and they will know much more before the winter is over." He predicted the wholesale dispossession of all "rebels" in India and suggested that similar moves were afoot in China, where British businessmen wanted to obtain commodities at low cost and foist their overpriced wares on the Chinese population. In Asia, as at home, the same system could be observed (if only by "the enlightened few")—those with power exploiting the working classes and enjoying the product of their labor. O'Brien continued to meet in London with political exiles from Europe, and reported to his friend Mathews that some of them (mainly among the French and Germans) had the right idea. They "sigh and long for the realization of our social doctrines," and they agreed that political liberty would be meaningless if it was not used to establish social equality and economic justice. O'Brien thought that the next revolution on the continent would not be against monarchs or parliaments but against "landlordism and profit-mongering," and he was excited by the prospect. In the spring of 1858 he told Mathews to expect popular challenges to "thralldom" in America and Asia as well as in Europe.[126]

The consolidation of Napoleon III's imperial regime during the 1850s made O'Brien think that another French revolution was needed like never before. In the *Ode to Louis Napoleon Bonaparte* he expressed the hope that the Second Empire would give way to an O'Brienite system.

> And oh! When France shall rise at heaven's command,
> To sweep from power and place thy murd'rous band,
> May her new chiefs be men who shall have plann'd
> Just laws on credit, currency, and land
> For fair exchange of wealth from hand to hand!
> By such laws only can republics stand;
> Without them, they are but a rope of sand.
> By such laws only, as by magic wand,
> May revolution's gulf at once be spann'd,
> And the whole earth be made one "Promis'd Land."

O'Brien's detestation of Napoleon III was increased by the "Orsini Plot" and its consequences, especially as they affected Thomas Allsop. Felice Orsini was an Italian nationalist who led an assassination attempt against the French emperor in Paris on 14 January 1858. Orsini and his group, and their sympathizers in Britain, regarded Napoleon III as a tyrant and accused him of machinations against Italian unification. Napoleon survived the assassination plot and Orsini was executed in March 1858. Orsini had been involved in revolutionary activity in 1848 and subsequently, and had spent time in prison in Rome. For a while he was close to Mazzini, but by the mid-1850s he had set his own course. He visited Britain in 1856 and again in 1857, when he went on a speaking tour. He associated with exiles in London, whose agitation and fund-raising drew in British radicals, and among Orsini's contacts in Britain were Allsop and George Jacob Holyoake, both friends of O'Brien. The "Orsini Plot" caused enormous controversy in Britain. Since the planning and arming had taken place on British soil, the French government demanded remedial measures. British authorities ordered the arrest of radicals who had been involved with Orsini's group, and Palmerston introduced a Conspiracy to Murder Bill. He had to resign as prime minister (19 February 1858) when a related motion was carried in the House of Commons against the government; parliamentary and public opinion proved averse to any hint that Britain was giving in to French pressure. Allsop was among those accused of assisting Orsini. He had put Orsini in touch with a weapons manufacturer in Birmingham and provided an old passport that Orsini used to get into France. But it was not clear that he had known of Orsini's intentions, and he had not tried to hide his actions. In a letter to Robert Owen of March 1858, Allsop's wife, Anna, wrote that she was "perfectly sure that he had no hand knowingly in the late plot." Allsop fled to the United States while family and friends lobbied on his behalf. Fortunately the government of Lord Derby (Palmerston's successor, in office from February 1858 to June 1859) withdrew the reward that had been offered for Allsop's capture and decided not to prosecute him. In June 1858 his wife told Owen that "our absent friend is now safe" and "no further steps will be taken in the matter."[127]

O'Brien was relieved for his old friend and benefactor. He kept up with European affairs and in the early 1860s still thought himself capable of writing with sufficient conviction and insight to influence opinion abroad as well as at home.[128] At the end of his career he returned to an old cause, that of the Poles, to whose liberty he had first committed himself during the 1830s. He and other radicals had befriended Polish refugees in London at that time, and O'Brien endorsed the 1837 "Manifesto" issued by the Polish Democratic Society. Some of the Poles in London went on to be active in Chartism. Rebellions in their homeland, against Russian rule, normally prompted meetings and propaganda in Britain, especially in London (and quarrels about Poland became part of wider divisions within London radicalism). In the spring of 1851 O'Brien was one of the speakers at a soirée arranged to raise money for Polish exiles. For the last two years of his life he was inspired by the Polish Rising of 1863–65. He speculated that the days of tyranny and injustice were numbered.[129]

A real revolution, according to O'Brien, would serve the interests of the many, not the few, but when he looked at the late eighteenth-century revolutions in America and France, at Paris in July 1830, at Britain in 1830–32, and at Europe in 1848–49, he did not see what he most wanted. Revolutionary moments had come and gone. No genuine revolution had taken place. This belief added to O'Brien's frustration with Chartism, for it was another lost opportunity. It did not fit the O'Brienite revolutionary schematic because leaders and followers alike had taken the wrong courses. For O'Brien, the revolution had to be nonviolent. It would begin with the securing of political rights, which could be used to effect social transformation through new legislation affecting the land, currency, credit, and exchange. The ideology that underpinned this plan developed out of O'Brien's mixing of elements from British political radicalism, from contemporary debates about class, capitalism, and labor, and from foreign revolutions, especially the first French Revolution. O'Brien's revolution would begin at the "bottom" of society and create a Britain in which "there should be no top or bottom at all."

CHAPTER 4

# "National Reform"

Bronterre O'Brien's ideology of "National Reform" confirms that he was prepared to go a long way beyond the Charter. Though manhood suffrage remained his starting point, "National Reform" was a plan for fundamental social and economic change in which "democratic landholding" predominated. "National Reform" was shaped by the merging of ideas drawn from contemporary debate about class, capitalism, and labor; from the main currents of thought in late eighteenth- and early nineteenth-century political radicalism; and from O'Brien's interpretation of the early stages of the French Revolution. As he put these elements together, he remained flexible, approving minor reforms when he thought they were likely to lead to more thorough changes and allowing for a mix of institutions and relationships in order to find a just and stable combination of public and private, collective and individual, interests. Along the way he developed distinctive conceptualizations of property, money, law, "wage slavery," and revolution, and in his rejection of the Chartist Land Plan he both underlined and contributed to the variety of radical strategies for land reform.

O'Brien published definitive statements of his mature program in the late 1840s. The remainder of his career was devoted to justifying and seeking support for his core proposals. Above all, he urged the people to get the vote and then the land. The Charter was only the beginning. It would democratize government, giving the people the power to make laws. This power would be used to implement reforms to bring about social equality and economic justice, the real goals. In January 1847 O'Brien issued the most detailed account of his scheme of reform in his career up to that point.

He began with the essential objective: all the land was to become public property. The "rational" method of doing this was to abolish private ownership of land and make all rents payable to and for the state. Tenant right and the right of occupancy would be available to everyone equally, and every leaseholder would get the full value of improvements made by him on the land during his occupancy. Restoring the land gradually to the people as existing owners died off, so that no proprietor would be disturbed during his lifetime, was "the only safe, peaceable, and humane way of effecting such settlement." When a proprietor's land passed to the nation, his heirs or representatives would receive the full money value, paid in annual instalments out of future rents. There would be no confiscation or spoliation (and therefore, O'Brien reckoned, existing proprietors had no grounds for opposition).

The national debt and all public debts were to be treated in the same manner. The capital sums would be recognized and payment of them guaranteed in annual instalments, but there was to be "no more plundering of the taxpayer and debtor interests, by everlasting usury and law expenses, kept up merely to feed a portion of the community in idleness at the expense of the rest."

Gold and silver would no longer be used as currency and standards of value. They would be treated only as "mercantile commodities." A quarter or bushel of wheat would serve as the standard of value, and its average price—measured by labor—the unit of account. The Bank of England and all other privileged corporations for issuing money were to be abolished. The government would be the sole issuer of money; and "mercantile paper" would be issued "in conformity with its denominations" and upon every type of exchangeable wealth, as well as gold and silver, but not until "ample security" was given by the issuers. This paper was to be stamped and made legal tender for all parties but the issuers, by whom it would be convertible on demand into government notes or precious metals at the market price. No privilege of any kind was to attach to the issuing of mercantile paper. The right to issue would be enjoyed equally by all who complied with the new rules and furnished the necessary security for the solvency of the issues.

Public marts would be established for the deposit and sale of all commodities, on the principle of equitable exchange. No manufacturer or depositor was to appraise or sell his own goods. These tasks would fall to salaried officials elected by the depositors. The officials would appraise all goods on delivery and give depositors the money price for them in paper that showed their value in labor or corn. This paper would have the same denominations as government notes and be convertible into the latter when required for the payment of taxes, or into gold and silver at the market price when required for exportation. All depositors, on presenting notes at the mart, would be able to purchase items to the amount of their notes. No notes would be given for the goods of a depositor "after intimation had been given to him by the officer that, after a certain time, no more goods of the same kind could be paid for—so that he might either turn to the manufacture of other articles more in demand, or devote himself to agricultural or other pursuits." This precaution, O'Brien explained, would prevent marts from being overstocked with some items and deficient in others. All accumulations not wanted in the home market could be sent abroad by agents of the depositors, appointed and paid in the same way as the appraisers at the marts.

District banks would be set up, into which rents were to be paid. In order to allow industrious families to farm land and manufacture goods, the banks would make loans to "every deserving man who could bring competent testimony as to character and fitness to be trusted with an advance." The stock and labor of each one would be "mortgaged, as it were, to the public." He would repay the loan with no more interest than was necessary to support the bank. "By this means the public property would, without loss to the public, be made instrumental in rescuing the major portion of the public from that degrading bondage to usury and employers which, nowadays, has made perfect slaves of nine-tenths of the population." The banks would belong to the public, as would the funds, and loans would go only to people who used them for the public benefit. Repayment rested on the labor and stock of the borrowers.[1]

O'Brien's commitment to these proposals deepened during the Chartist revival and European revolutions of 1848. He became more thoroughgoing and insistent. In October 1849 he announced the formation of the National Reform League. Its "fundamental propositions" were O'Brienite. To the Charter the NRL appended "social reforms" that were meant to correct a false estimate of rights and duties. Any institutions or behavior that had a contrary tendency had to be amended so that there was no interference with the production and distribution of wealth, no partitioning of society into classes or grades, no granting of privileges to some and not others, and no denial of anyone's right to whatever he produced by his own talent and effort.[2] O'Brien's "Prospectus of the National Reform League" was issued in December 1849 and debated and endorsed at meetings and in publications early in 1850. The full NRL manifesto of 1849–50 combined the Charter with seven proposals—the New Poor Law to be modified; sections of land to be purchased by the state and set aside for the unemployed; and the currency, debts, and taxation to be adjusted to lighten the burdens on the people (these were the immediate ones); and nationalization of the land; a system of national credit; conversion to a symbolic currency; and the establishment of public marts for the exchange of products (these were the permanent ones).[3]

The land was O'Brien's central concern, and had been for years. Possession of the land, and ideas about property more generally, were of primary importance to many Chartists. Although he maintains that political identity mattered most—that Chartists believed the main division in Britain to be that between the "represented" and "unrepresented"—Gareth Stedman Jones also recognizes the fundamental assumption that "politically enforced expropriation from the land" was "the ultimate source of the condition of the working classes and the growing tyranny of the money and factory lords." Opponents of the Chartists claimed that they threatened property. Though Chartists denied this, it is plain that some of them did wish for a redistribution of property and the restructuring of economic relationships. Opinions differed about how to accomplish these ends, and O'Brien was a leading participant in the debate. He developed a plan and attempted to educate his fellow radicals as to its advantages and practicability.[4]

Chartists were far from unanimous on matters concerning property. Even those who preached social equality did not expect it to mean that everyone would have exactly the same. The object was to create equality in rights and opportunities, and equality before the law, not to obliterate all distinctions between individuals. Plenty of Chartists held that social and economic competition was appropriate and that there would be no incentive for effort if property was socialized. They accepted the main tenets of classical political economy. As Gregory Claeys remarks, "Chartist views on property embraced a spectrum defined by the O'Brienites at one extreme, and committed economic liberals . . . on the other."[5] David Stack stresses O'Brien's role in expanding the "social content" of radicalism and authoring Chartism's "finest writing . . . much of which was theoretically sophisticated and recognizably modern."[6] This is also the opinion of Asa Briggs and John Saville.[7] Of all the proponents of land nationalization in this era, Claeys considers O'Brien to have been "by far the most influential."[8] One of the captains of the burgeoning working-class press, O'Brien led readers to consider big questions about power and property. According to Patricia Hollis, he showed how different issues were interrelated, "meshing them into a wider ideological analysis."[9]

Interest in O'Brien's proposals waxed and waned during his career. In some ways the mood of the times was conducive. Concern about social and economic problems heightened support for collectivist solutions, as many contemporaries agreed that public interest should come before private interest. In a limited fashion this was already happening, with parliamentary sanction, for the expansion of the railway network involved some interference with private property. O'Brien included railways and mines—as well as the land—among the assets that he thought should gradually come under public control.[10] In principle at least, people were willing to consider such reforms. But the majority, even among radicals, was resistant. There was a connection here with the aversion to "democracy," which had negative connotations. Some radicals disliked the label because of its association with equality, but others, O'Brien among them, unequivocally adopted it.[11] Such boldness antagonized their enemies. It was by design that mention was made, in a Commons debate of May 1842 on the Chartists' second national petition, of the confiscation of property. A similar outburst in June 1848, during a debate on "national representation," included a warning against "communist" schemes against property.[12] Arguments in favor of popular rights and government by consent were routinely countered by objections that manhood suffrage meant social levelling.[13]

The spirit of the age was against O'Brien's mature program, according to Noel Thompson, because objections to economic competition became more muted and less sophisticated at precisely the time when O'Brien issued the NRL manifesto, and in the following decades there was a tendency not to condemn market forces but to argue that they could be subjected to moral constraints—that the market should be *used*, not abolished. Joseph D'Oronzio has argued that O'Brien's ideas were ahead of their time and his initiatives mostly stillborn because contrary opinions and institutions prevailed when he was active, and he did not help matters by losing sight of practical politics. To John Belchem, O'Brien was too single-minded. Certain that his proposals for land, currency, credit, and exchange were best, he would not accept anything less; and instead of bidding for the support of "organized forms of working-class collective mutuality," he rejected them.[14] These remarks are a little excessive. To his followers there was nothing impractical about O'Brien's program, and had he been so utterly inflexible he would not have approved lesser reforms as steps on the way to major reforms. The NRL manifesto of 1849–50 was the result of at least twenty years of agitation and reflection and cannot be understood without reference to that shaping process.

Among the most important foundations for O'Brien's ideology of "National Reform" was contemporary thinking on class, capitalism, and labor, especially as it affected radical opinion about "true" and "artificial" property. The conviction that all property was the product of labor merged with claims that the idle classes lived off the productive effort of the laboring classes, enjoying power, status, and privileges that were unmerited and illegitimate. O'Brien made use of a range of ideas about private property and competitive commerce, the distribution of products, the source of wealth, and the workers' right to the full fruits of their labor.[15]

O'Brien agreed with Thomas Spence that without economic change the vote would be useless, and he took up Spence's point that ownership of land gave power. Spence advocated parochialization: land would become the property of the parish, whose inhabitants would decide on how it was to be used. Differences of wealth and influence would soon be reduced as the land was leased to anyone who wished to work it. Spence envisioned parishes full of small farmers, all on an equal footing. Their rents would be applied to public purposes. O'Brien approved, though in his scheme the land would be managed at the national rather than parish level. From another writer, William Ogilvie, O'Brien learned more (as Spence had) about natural rights theory and its relevance to land reform. While Ogilvie was reluctant to interfere with existing property rights, however, O'Brien and Spence had fewer qualms. O'Brien did sympathize with Ogilvie's notion of the economic and moral superiority of agriculture, a tendency reinforced by William Cobbett. Noel Thompson argues that this position, by the 1830s, was making less sense to the growing *urban* working class. But the workers were not unvarying in condition and outlook, and "back to the land" sentiments retained their appeal.[16]

Cobbett taught O'Brien more about "Old Corruption" and the ideal harmonious society based on mutual obligations between the powerful and wealthy on one side, and powerless and poor on the other. The long wars against France had changed Britain for the worse. Cobbett identified as the main problems the national debt, regressive taxation, inflation, bureaucratic growth and government patronage, and a redistribution of wealth in favor of enclosing landlords, war contractors, and the state's creditors. Most people were becoming poorer and losing their freedoms. Cobbett wanted to attack these problems at source—to him, a political source.

Government had to be sanitized. It had to become more representative. Although financial and administrative reforms made some of his claims obsolete, Cobbett remained influential. O'Brien endorsed his ideas while also moving beyond them to study economic as well as political explanations for injustice and conflict. Hence his interest in Thomas Hodgskin's concept of labor as the source of value. Hodgskin thought of profit as the most harmful of the exactions suffered by the workers. The main target had to be ownership of capital (rather than, as Spence would have it, land), for capitalism was nothing but the improper engrossing of produce. A capitalist was someone who took the produce of another's labor. Exploitation occurred mainly in the sphere of exchange, because the worker had to sell his labor too cheap for items that cost more than their natural value once their price had been pushed up by profit.[17]

As O'Brien evaluated these insights, he was also influenced by the communitarian and cooperative impulses behind Owen's strictures against competitive individualism and social antagonism. Owen, though well aware of labor exploitation, thought of interests as reconcilable, if the shift could be made from competition to cooperation. O'Brien did not deny that interests could be reconciled. In 1832, when writing to Owen of the suffering and delusion he saw all around him, he added: "This state of society will soon come to an end. If I mistake not the signs of the times—the hand of death is upon it!" Nevertheless, O'Brien was dubious about Owen's tendency to downplay the workers' sense of agency and strength (Owen maintained that human character had to be rationally altered and directed). O'Brien adopted Owen's principal ideas but applied them in his own way.[18]

Owen was confident that people would eventually understand how resources should be used and supply and demand balanced. For a less patient approach O'Brien could refer to William Thompson, a writer who agreed that labor was the source of all wealth and that workers should enjoy social equality and full possession of what they produced. In Thompson's view, the main obstacles were posed by concentrations of capital, unequal exchange, and ownership of the means of production by the few rather than the many. Thompson disagreed with Owen's claim that political reform was irrelevant, but kept faith with communitarian principles. From him, and especially from Owen, O'Brien gained a better grasp of cooperative and agrarian thinking and specific matters like the advantages of public marts and labor notes.[19]

A related line of thought was opened up by O'Brien's reading of John Gray, who was sure that labor exploitation and economic depression were connected. Gray decided that neither political reform nor Owenism offered adequate remedies. He focused more on the medium of exchange, believing that the way to balance supply and demand was to ensure that the availability of money would expand with output and decrease as produce was consumed. Gray advocated a broad move toward economic planning. He favored collective ownership, but with compensation for current owners; and the latter would be managers and advisers in the new order because they had the necessary experience and expertise. Gray's planned economy would not be organized democratically, which to O'Brien was unacceptable. Another theorist, John Francis Bray, tried to combine democratic with meritocratic and technocratic elements in a planned economy.[20]

To these analytical devices O'Brien added others, including the class framework explored by Ben Maw. O'Brien separated personal property from productive property, Maw explains, and maintained that only the former could be privately owned. This affected his understanding of class distinctions.[21] Although Maw suggests that O'Brien abandoned the simpler dichotomy of "productive" and "unproductive" to prioritize the contrasts between possessors and nonpossessors of the means of production, distribution, and exchange, it would be more accurate to state that O'Brien merged older and newer approaches. Throughout his career, from the early 1830s to the early 1860s, he retained the most useful (to him) elements from Spence, Gray, Owen, and others, adding to and adapting them to meet circumstances. O'Brien constantly refreshed his arguments for radical reform, but without discarding what was familiar and well established.

Alongside social and economic doctrine, O'Brien still employed some of the traditional political assertions of British radicalism. It was not uncommon for Chartists to celebrate the democratic organs that had allegedly existed in Anglo-Saxon times and to lament the people's post-1066 subjection to the "Norman Yoke." "The great merit of our ancient Saxon institutions consisted in this," O'Brien declared in 1843: "that they allowed every parish and every tithing and every county to legislate exclusively for its own internal affairs. . . . This is genuine democracy."[22] Claims about a better past that had been lost were also made in relation to the medieval Parliament. Another reference point was the dissolution of the monasteries in the sixteenth century. The removal of political rights, the theft of property by privileged elites, the monopolization of power by landowners: all could be clarified in accordance with this radical version of the past. As Robert Hall has argued, Chartists had to construct an amenable history in order to foster a sense of inclusivity and shared goals. If the six points had history behind them, however, it was less easy to make historically based arguments for a redistribution of property.[23]

While Patricia Hollis contends that "any socialist patina was always very thin" and that older radical ideas were not dislodged by newer theories about class, capitalism, and labor, she does admit that O'Brien was an "innovator" and that it was partly due to his writings that, by the 1850s, "some intellectual reordering had taken place" within radicalism. David Nicholls is not so sure, arguing that class consciousness and attacks on classical political economy were of limited impact. Yet their impact on O'Brien and his followers is incontestable. For more than thirty years O'Brien openly disagreed with those who considered capital and labor—unaided by a reorganization of laws and institutions—to be compatible.[24]

When demands lacked a convincing historical justification, natural rights theory could be put into service. O'Brien had read Locke and Paine and urged his followers to do the same if they wished to see why no socially established property laws could supersede the preexisting common right to the earth and its produce. O'Brien used the language of natural rights from the early 1830s along with the other idioms he employed. Popular sovereignty was similar to nationalization of the land in that it was another goal that could be explained in terms of both historic and natural rights. The meaning of "democracy" was extended beyond political rights, explains Richard Ashcraft, and a "new system of society" was to include the redistribution of property. O'Brien was a linchpin figure in this respect.[25] He joined in the continuing effort to erect "inclusive" as opposed to "exclusive" property rights, traced by Thomas Horne to the precept that the earth was originally held in common. The legitimacy of private property did not have to be challenged in the making of such claims. The point was to establish that the community retained entitlements against private owners. For promoters of "inclusive" rights, private owners were trustees, and their property was to be used to benefit everybody. By O'Brien's day "exclusive" rights had been solidified. Even if limits on the owners' use of their property were admitted, the limits were not severe. Moreover, it was widely assumed that obligations to use property for the benefit of others would encourage laziness and immorality.[26]

O'Brien argued that those with property had a legitimate claim—their natural right—only to what they produced with their own labor. The rest they held under the law. The power to make law had been stolen from the people. It had been used to take the people's property, making the claim rooted in law unsound. Most of what the propertied possessed really belonged to the people, since it had been produced by the people's labor. This meant that poor relief, for example, simply restored to the poor a portion of the produce of their labor, something that was rightfully theirs in the first place.[27]

This definition of property was integral to O'Brien's mature radical program. He embraced parts of Owenism and parts of mainstream political radicalism. Between the two there was some friction. Owen and his followers regarded political radicalism as misdirected, and radicals condemned the Owenites for paying insufficient attention to the system of government.[28] Historians often distinguish between political and social designs. Iorwerth Prothero argues that O'Brien's radicalism was political, not social. He did not condemn capitalists *as capitalists*, Prothero maintains, but as supporters of class legislation; and his principal concern was the conflict between rulers and ruled, compared to which other conflicts—over wealth, property, and labor—were secondary. Prothero's interpretation is helpful but deficient. Social and economic matters were important to O'Brien from early in his career and became more important over time, and he did not separate the conflict between rulers and ruled from conflicts over wealth, or property, or labor. Prothero also doubts that London Chartists were receptive to O'Brien's ideology, for their outlook had more to do with traditional "artisan radicalism." A similar view is taken by other scholars who emphasize the political nature of Chartism ahead of O'Brien's social teachings and agree that London Chartists had little time for the latter. Yet O'Brien had more followers in London than anywhere else, and Prothero's point about "artisan radicalism" seems not to be in keeping with his notion that O'Brien cared more about political than social issues. The argument that Chartism was really a *political* movement has been forcefully made not only by Prothero but also by Gareth Stedman Jones and James Epstein.[29] Though the importance of social and economic theory (including ideas about the land) is recognized by H. T. Dickinson, he also treats Chartism as a political movement and erroneously assumes that O'Brien and others only took up "socialism" *after* the failure of the third national Chartist petition in 1848. A different thesis is presented by Theodore Koditschek—that Chartism was shaped mainly by concerns about what capitalist power was doing to economic relations. Koditschek explains the failure of Chartism as an ideological failure: its alternative social vision could not dislodge conservative hierarchical or liberal individualistic values.[30] Another interpretation of radicalism, seen in the work of David Worrall and Craig Calhoun, is that it was a form of politicization rooted in kinship and locality and had nothing to do with class consciousness.[31]

There were many reasons why people became radical, and it is clear that the determination to alter political structures could also be a determination to reshape society. Nevertheless, there was disagreement on this between political radicals and Owenites—and *within* each camp—and O'Brien's answer was to stress cooperation more than communitarianism and, in time, to propose mechanisms that would satisfy both private and public needs and respect both individual and collective interests. Although O'Brien believed that cooperation was economically and morally appropriate and that individual competition, arising from private property, caused low wages and unequal exchange between capital and labor, he doubted that many people would wish to withdraw into communities and give up their rights to the group. He decided that it would be better to establish labor's just title to property. The need was not to abolish individual property-holding but to make sure that property could only be acquired legitimately.[32]

One of the difficulties Owen had in establishing model communities was that he could not raise the necessary capital. Eventually he accepted the idea that land should be taken over by the state. O'Brien was gratified, and described the form of Owenism that provided for state action as eminently practical (not utopian). He had tried long and hard to persuade Owenites that the nation should own the land and to get Chartists to accept that the best system of production would include cooperative elements. Even so, the NRL program of 1849–50 indicates that O'Brien's collectivist tendencies did not exceed his respect for individualism. He wanted to nationalize the land, but parcel it out in smallholdings for individual cultivation.[33]

While O'Brien had no doubt that many of Owen's ideas were sound, he maintained that they could not be implemented prior to political reform, the great prerequisite. O'Brien also concluded that justice counted for more than equality, in which case community of goods was not essential (his thinking was probably affected by the collapse of communitarian projects). Those who contributed most to society would also have the most, a result O'Brien pronounced to be both salutary and democratic. For this to happen, though, the people had first to gain political rights. When the workers had their proper role in government, they could bring closer the reallocation of the land (which would take much longer under Owen's system), and they could also make other changes, not least by ending the "robbery" of "producers" through tithes, rent, and profit, and by placing the supply and value of money under collective control.[34]

Before the Chartist period O'Brien had clarified these points in the *Poor Man's Guardian*.[35] In these years, and subsequently, he explicitly endorsed the core principles of Spence, Gray, and Owen.[36] He also built upon the intellectual foundations provided by traditional radical nostrums about the land, on which the key writings were by Paine and Cobbett. Paine had argued that the people had a natural right to the land. He also defended the inviolability of property rights, as did Cobbett, and O'Brien accepted this too, meaning that—in developing his scheme of land reform—he had to permit some principles and practices to remain intact. It was less difficult to establish the *need* for land reform than it was to specify what that reform should consist of; Patricia Hollis has shown how easily, for example, the "Norman Yoke" motif used by Cobbett could be married with Spencean claims that property was theft.[37] Ben Maw (whose focus is on the 1832–36 period and not later) asserts that in considering class conflict, O'Brien dispensed with Cobbett's antiaristocratic allegations and gave attention instead to profit and to the ownership of productive resources. O'Brien also decided that Owen's emphasis on competition was inexpedient because it was only one factor in production, distribution, and exchange.[38] But in the Chartist period O'Brien still employed old radicalism's diatribes against aristocratic government (especially political corruption, monopolies, and taxation that redistributed wealth upward), while also writing and speaking about the evils of capitalism, the discord between producers and nonproducers, the exploitation of labor by landed and moneyed elites, and the divergent lifestyles and conditions of the "useful" and "useless" classes. He personally identified with the abused and dispossessed—which is why, early in his career, he adopted the name "Bronterre," or "sorrow of the land."[39]

Some of O'Brien's angriest speeches were made in 1839 as Chartist agitation peaked and there was an expectation within the movement that its demands would soon be met. As reported by Gammage, O'Brien told audiences that oppression was a class action discernible not only in the political system but in social relationships and financial dealings (the national debt, rents, stock values). His list of villains was growing all the time. He attacked "the fellows who live by profits, who live by usury," "a rascally crew of attorneys, bishops and parsons, pawnbrokers, and stockjobbers," "military officers," and even "brothel-keepers in London," all of whom were "men with no interest in the welfare of the country."[40] Much of this was reminiscent of Cobbett.

On moving from Ireland to London in 1830 O'Brien had met Cobbett and become more familiar with his land and money ideas, and O'Brien's interest in currency questions grew during his time in Birmingham in 1831–32, when he edited the *Midland Representative and Birmingham Herald*. The reform movement in Birmingham was largely under the direction of banker and ironmaster Thomas

Attwood. O'Brien was unimpressed by Attwood's support for an inflationary paper money system.[41] (This was one of the reasons why O'Brien advised Chartists in 1838 to obtain political pledges from Attwood and the Birmingham Political Union, rather than simply follow their lead.)[42] While Cobbett uncovered the parasitism he regarded as inherent in a paper money system, O'Brien carried the analysis forward, linking control over the currency with political power and pointing out that workers were exploited because they lacked both. He was also drawing attention to control over exchange, which could be related to the mechanization of production.[43]

O'Brien thought that the moneyed interests had taken opportunities presented by the French wars to ensure their future expropriation of the product of labor by such means as manipulation of the national debt. In order to prevent their capital from losing value, they found new fields for investment. They loaned more than £500 million to the British government to pay for the wars. This brought a double advantage, "helping to destroy French Democrats and the Rights of Man on the one hand, and securing for themselves and their posterity the privilege of being everlasting pensioners on the nation on the other hand."[44] On this matter O'Brien made use of Cobbett's ideology. At the same time, he did something else. Cobbett had stressed wartime bureaucratic expansion, high taxes, and the untrustworthy paper currency in making a case for smaller government. His focus was fiscal, and he wanted to restrict the influence of the state.[45] O'Brien agreed that the state was corrupt, but he looked into ways of reforming it and using it for good.

Cobbett's attack on "Old Corruption" retained its force into the 1840s, and Matthew Roberts has shown that his financial prescriptions—abolition of paper money, equitable adjustment, lower taxes, and reduction of the national debt and civil list—found favor with many Chartists. Roberts goes on to explain that financial questions, and Cobbett himself, came to matter less to Chartists owing to recriminations over the failed tactics of 1839 (the "ulterior measures" included the use of financial weapons) and as a result of the policies of Robert Peel's administration of 1841–46, which provided for a stable currency and economic expansion and appeared to solve some of the problems about which Chartists were most concerned.[46] But O'Brien does not fit into this pattern. Financial matters were still central to his radical platform in the 1860s; he was a firm opponent of Peel's measures; and insofar as his creed included selected principles of Cobbett, he kept these alive in his writings and speeches long after other Chartists—according to Roberts—had discarded them. O'Brien assimilated Cobbett's ideology, but he was not limited by it.[47]

O'Brien repeatedly railed against bankers and speculators, as in a lecture on the national debt delivered in Manchester in 1839.[48] He was disturbed by the Bank Charter Act of 1844. Under this measure, only the Bank of England could issue new banknotes, other banks would have to withdraw their existing notes in the event of a takeover, and all of the Bank of England's note issues had to be backed by gold or up to £14 million in government debt. O'Brien opposed these provisions and continued in later years to condemn the prime minister of the time, Peel, and the measure's main author, the banker Samuel Jones Loyd, who was raised to the peerage as Lord Overstone in 1850. Peel was regarded by O'Brien as doubly culpable, for he had also chaired the parliamentary committee that recommended the resumption of cash payments and return to the gold standard in 1819 (cash payments had been suspended during the French wars to save the economy from ruin and allow for a flexible money supply). O'Brien often brought these matters up in his journalism, and in 1859 he published a satirical poem, *A Vision of Hell*, in which he again attacked Peel and Overstone.[49] In an address put together by O'Brien's supporters after his death, *A Vision of Hell* was commended as "a serio-comic production" that dispensed "a full and fair measure of justice to great offenders against the Laws of Providence."[50] The poem describes Overstone's descent into hell, where he meets his friend Peel. Both men are punished by representatives of all the interests they had helped—to the nation's disadvantage—when they were in power.[51]

Paper money was one of the subjects on which O'Brien clashed with Feargus O'Connor after their split of the early 1840s. Challenging O'Brien's claims to consistency and seeking to undermine his reputation as a friend of the working classes, O'Connor maintained that O'Brien had become a defender of financial and commercial arrangements he had formerly condemned (mainly because he needed the patronage of the wealthy for his newspapers). In 1845 the *Northern Star* carried extracts from items published by O'Brien in 1832 and 1837, in which O'Brien championed a metallic currency and rejected the paper money favored by "Bank-note schemers." O'Connor argued that O'Brien had completely changed his tune, for he was now insisting that he had never preferred a metallic to a paper currency. Having once sided with the Cobbett school and its extolling of gold against the Attwood school of paper enthusiasts, O'Brien was going back on his former professions.[52]

This was an oversimplification that blurred the details of O'Brien's currency ideas and the way his thinking about money had evolved in line with his thinking about land, credit, and exchange. What O'Brien wanted was "purely symbolic" money, not money that had intrinsic value. Gold and silver, therefore, should not be treated as the measure of value. They were commodities. O'Brien agreed with Owen that conventional money ought to be replaced with labor notes; but until this happened O'Brien was willing to support the most useful currency reforms that were possible in prevalent circumstances. One step in the right direction was better than no step at all.[53]

The different elements in O'Brien's *mature* thought held together, and over time he was able to explain the links between them. If he failed on occasion to do this in the 1830s, by the mid-1840s there was no such deficiency. Charges of inconsistency or opaqueness carry little weight. Even in the 1830s, contends Ben Maw, O'Brien's ideas about class and capitalism were coherent and comprehensible—part of a "macro analysis" that became "the first example of a genuinely democratic anti-capitalist political economy."[54] Gregory Claeys argues that O'Brien was treating land and money as separate matters by the end of the 1830s: land, the gift of nature, should not be private property; money was not a gift of nature but a false system of exchange, and its issue and regulation should not be controlled by special interests.[55] While O'Brien understood that difficulties with land and money had arisen in different ways, he did not regard them as unrelated. Increasingly, he discussed them not as separate matters but as interconnected, and in his mature thought land and money were treated as problems that had to be addressed together as part of a comprehensive plan of reform.

In the years before the advent of the Charter, O'Brien had repeatedly urged that the workers must gain political rights not as ends in themselves, but in order to transform society.[56] Owenites cared nothing for the democratization promised by the Charter, maintaining that the system of government was irrelevant.[57] O'Brien was frustrated by this.[58] He wanted Chartists and Owenites to combine their efforts, and he went on arguing that it was possible to steer a middle course between public and private interests, state intervention and individual rights, economic freedom and communitarian values.[59]

These thoughts about the main attributes of a just and stable society featured in the discussion in the *Chartist Circular* in 1841 about O'Brien's notion of a "revolution" that all classes could accept.[60] O'Brien preferred reforms that would not injure particular persons or groups.[61] In 1835 he stipulated that redistribution of the land should not go ahead without some form of compensation to the present owners, and he advocated not the wanton seizure of church property and fundholders' stock but their *purchase* by the nation. Capitalists, moreover, would still receive a return on their money and machinery. The main changes would include the sharing of profits, the availability of loans without interest, the prevention of large accumulations of property, and other such measures that would close the gap between rich and poor and facilitate the usefulness of all.[62] O'Brien described compensation as a way to avoid inconveniences and neutralize opposition, not as an act of fairness, for what the landed and moneyed elites really deserved was the harshness they had meted out to the workers in the past. O'Brien was ready to let this pass in order to move more quickly to a new system.[63]

He wanted the land to be a public resource and under democratic control, but also assumed that some aspects of private property ownership would continue, at least for a time. Most radicals, indeed, had no objection to property ownership and did not think it incompatible with reform politics (although the growth of the freehold land movement in the 1840s and 1850s was less about political rights than about the moral, social, and economic concerns of its promoters).[64]

As indicated earlier, O'Brien's awareness of the lingering tension between a class analysis drawing on economic theory and capital's treatment of labor, and the tendency in old radicalism to focus on political relationships, led him to try to remove ambiguity, as in 1838 when he wrote that class identity mattered less than the behavior arising out of that identity. Anyone who was ready to share power with the workers was not to be treated as an enemy, whatever that person's class background.[65] According to Mark Bevir, "O'Brien concentrated on the undemocratic nature of the British political system. He argued that social evils had political causes." If O'Brien continued to hold this basic assumption, he added ideas drawn from a range of social and economic philosophies. Though political reform was the necessary first step, other goals commanded his attention, especially the need to break the land monopoly, end the manipulation of currency and exchange, and ease social divisions. To Bevir, "The fundamental oppositions in O'Brien's writing were those of popular radicalism. He pitted rulers against people, and idlers against workers." Again, this interpretation is too limited. By the time of the NRL program of 1849–50, O'Brien had assembled a more advanced analysis than the one he had disseminated in the early 1830s. His proposals developed over the years. Bevir exaggerates the extent to which O'Brien confined himself to the mind-set of old radicalism. Bevir also thinks that "at no time did he demand collective ownership of the means of production," which is questionable, particularly if land is regarded as a means of production.[66]

In 1838 O'Brien clarified his position with two notably forthright and detailed statements. In a letter to the *Northern Star* he insisted that he had no wish to abolish private property. He would not take from the rich anything that justly belonged to them, nor give to the poor anything to which they had no right. O'Brien was ready to leave the rich in possession of the entire value of their property, however acquired, if that acquiring had been sanctioned by the laws. He wanted the rich to understand that he did not advocate the seizure of their property. Rather, he sought to end the version of "property" that gave its owners "an unlimited power of murder and robbery over the rest of the population." The rich had this power. "The natural right of property having long since given place to the conventional right, property is now wholly and solely the *creature of law*. Every new act that is passed, every old act that is repealed, affects the disposition of property," O'Brien explained. Therefore "you cannot possibly perform the function of a legislator without interfering with the rights of property." The "Peel Act" of 1819 had transferred property from debtors to creditors while also injuring many creditors by destroying the means by which their debtors could pay them back. Just one measure thereby had enormous consequences. The main losers, O'Brien went on, were small capitalists and masters, and some of them responded by pressing for parliamentary reform, obtained in 1832. In 1832, however, they did not recover all they had lost since 1819. So they had to continue pressing for a change in policy, and fell in behind the Birmingham group and its "cheap currency projects," another proof that "property is altogether a creature of law" because the Birmingham men had only wanted to reform Parliament in order to repeal the measure of 1819: that is, to occasion another transfer of property, this time to their benefit.[67]

Five months after the publication of this piece, O'Brien discussed political rights, wages, and "the conflicting claims of labour and capital" in a front-page editorial in his *Operative*. To those commentators who denied that wage levels concerned anyone other than employers and employees, and who told the workers not to bother demanding the vote because manhood suffrage could have no impact on wages, O'Brien delivered a contemptuous rebuttal. Multiple obligations (rent, taxes, tithes, loans, risks) meant that most employers could not pay higher wages even if they wanted to, and this situation involved not only the employer and employee but also "the landowner, house-landlord, tax-gatherer, fund-holder, parson, insolvent debtor, and God knows how many others besides," all of whom looked to benefit by depriving the worker of the real value of his labor. New laws were needed, to allow "a fair day's pay for a fair day's work." To trust in promises about "minimum wages" or "maximum prices," instead of obtaining the vote, was idiotic, O'Brien declared. Nothing would change until the right laws were in operation.

It was clear that society's burdens should fall on property and that the productive classes should enjoy "a concurrent power with the other classes over the *land* and *currency* of the kingdom." The possessing classes, O'Brien complained, could cultivate or not cultivate the land as they chose, and contract or expand the currency as they chose, and this "two-fold monopoly" made them "irresistible." Once the people had legislative authority, the first task was to make the nation the sole landlord. The next task of a self-governing people was to "restore commerce to its original purpose"—exchanging the different and surplus products of one place for those of another.[68]

From the foregoing discussion it is evident that O'Brien had most of his essential ideas in place by the end of the 1830s. Many of these he derived from others, joining them together and applying them in combination with his own thoughts and observations. Alongside some of the familiar concerns of political radicalism, and the perspectives shaped by newer ideas about class, capitalism, and labor, O'Brien's ideology had a third major source, the lessons of the French Revolution. O'Brien applied these, selectively, to British circumstances, retaining what was most serviceable in keeping with his present purposes. Miles Taylor's statement that O'Brien advocated "a Jacobin-style overthrow of government" is inaccurate.[69] Certainly O'Brien adopted what he took to be the core democratic and libertarian principles of the French Revolution in its early stages, and he respected Robespierre, Babeuf, and Buonarroti. But he did not want or expect to re-create the French Revolution at home.

O'Brien promoted his own adaptation of Babeuf's revolutionary creed. While he dispensed with parts of this creed that he saw as unworkable in or otherwise inappropriate for Britain (violent insurrection, dictatorship, and repression of political opponents), he approved of some of the ends the Babouvists had in view, the social changes to be accomplished with the aid of a democratic constitution. O'Brien applauded Buonarroti's transmission of Babeuf's ideology to a new generation, and he took up Babeuf's ideas about property held in common, wealth and labor regulated for the good of all, popular sovereignty, and social equality. Suspicious of private ownership, Babeuf had wanted to limit it strictly to what people actually used or needed for their work and leisure. He favored big government, education and training for all, collective control of production and exchange, and equal distribution. Everyone was to contribute to the common wealth with different talents and efforts. Political reform would not be enough. Social relations and economic behavior had also to be corrected. With this conclusion O'Brien was in complete agreement.[70]

Buonarroti fused common ownership with Jacobin democracy but had no concept of a mass movement, retaining the Babouvist faith in minority conspiracy. O'Brien did not profess this faith. Yet he helped to sustain Babouvism with his writings about it, especially his translation of Buonarroti. While Samuel Bernstein recognizes O'Brien's translation of 1836 as not only the first but also the most important, scholars disagree about O'Brien's book and indeed the long-term influence of Babeuf.[71] It is notable that Ian Birchall, for instance, glosses over the authoritarian aspects of Babouvism and argues that Babeuf was more pragmatic and democratic than other commentators have appreciated. To be sure, Babeuf had a strong commitment to social justice and was critical of the Jacobin regime (1793–94) for its persecution of political opponents and neglect of the poor. At the same time, Babeuf agreed with Robespierre on the "rights of man," on subjecting property to subsistence requirements, and on the merits of a smallholding democracy. Buonarroti stressed the connections, not the differences, between Babouvism and Jacobinism.[72] Robert Rose and Pamela Pilbeam consider his account of the Babeuf conspiracy to be misleading.[73] Buonarroti wrote long after the event and exaggerated the commitment to revolutionary dictatorship (as did prosecutors at Babeuf's trial). It seems that Babeuf preferred democracy to dictatorship. He wanted no permanent, institutionalized dictatorial powers for the government, and any withholding of popular liberties would be for months, not years. In expressing his own misgivings about revolutionary dictatorship, therefore, O'Brien was adhering quite closely to Babeuf's ideas.

Having admired Buonarroti from afar, and then making his acquaintance, O'Brien may have been hesitant about challenging his claims, and he was impressed by Buonarroti's comparison of Babouvism with Owenism. O'Brien also echoed Buonarroti's response to critics who dismissed egalitarianism as unrealistic if not pernicious. There was no presumption of *absolute* equality in the division of tasks and products, for the personal differences between individuals were to be accepted. The main consideration was not how much work a person did, or how difficult that work was, or what was produced and consumed by that person. Rather, the priority was to ensure that all members of society contributed according to their ability and received according to their need. The danger that people would not work if they knew their needs were sure to be met did not in fact exist, because work was mostly avoided when it was excessive, and in an egalitarian order the load would be easy as tasks were shared and nobody was idle.[74]

Many British radicals agreed with these ideas, though none articulated them as effectively as O'Brien. His research into Babouvism made him an authority, and this component in his thought led him in the same direction as the others, not least by reinforcing his convictions about labor as the source of wealth, about the identity and role of producers and nonproducers, about democratic institutions, and about political reform giving rise to social transformation. On this latter point, he reiterated throughout his career that nothing could happen without manhood suffrage. Rejecting the Owenite claim that society could be changed irrespective of the system of government, O'Brien also rejected the Babouvist mode of revolution in favor of a "revolution" that was nonviolent and based on consent, and unlike Babeuf and Buonarroti he did not think that private property should be abolished. Toward the broader principles of Owen and Babeuf O'Brien remained sympathetic, but no "revolution" could succeed, he maintained, unless the people saw its necessity and were willing to join in. Bernard Moss appears to underestimate O'Brien's preference for nonviolent tactics and to exaggerate the extent to which his admiration for Babeuf and Robespierre alienated his fellow radicals.[75]

O'Brien never tired of repeating that, by itself, political reform could not be satisfactory. In making this point he often used the example of America. Like other radicals, O'Brien praised America's democratic institutions and hailed it as an exemplar. The United States seemed to provide a model for reform at home, and of special significance was the availability of land there. Despite its strengths, though, America also had weaknesses, and in the Chartist period there was a growing skepticism about the United States. Some Chartists decided that America was failing to live up to its promise. They saw defects there *despite* manhood suffrage, especially social inequality, the exploitation of labor, and large accumulations of wealth and property. To these observers, America was probably no better than Britain (though they usually made a distinction when referring to its system of government).[76] While generally complimentary about America, O'Brien regretted that its form of representative government had not brought greater social and economic improvement. America offered a reminder that political reform alone would not be enough for Britain. O'Brien's writings about Ireland also had this tendency. After joining in the campaign to repeal the Union in the early 1830s, he decided that the most effective way of helping the Irish people was not legislative autonomy but land reform, because the main problem in Ireland was the same as that in Britain—social and economic inequality.[77]

Another prominent Irish-born land reformer, Thomas Ainge Devyr, followed an intellectual trajectory similar to O'Brien's (Devyr was born in county Donegal in 1805, O'Brien in county Longford in 1804). Devyr's early influences included Paine and perhaps also Spence. He embraced the Enlightenment theory of natural rights, and though his first involvement in popular agitation was in the movement for constitutional solutions for Ireland, by the mid-1830s Devyr was recommending a system of "limited ownership" of the land (a form of proprietorship that would oblige landlords to respect the general interest by granting perpetual leases and living on lower rents). The paternalistic aspects of this were soon abandoned. Devyr became a Chartist and journalist in London and then Newcastle-upon-Tyne, where he addressed meetings with O'Brien when the latter was in town. Both were accused of political offenses. O'Brien had to stand trial. Devyr fled to America. In the United States from 1840, Devyr joined in the antirent movement and took up increasingly radical positions on the land question, favoring direct interference with existing landholding arrangements. He decided that access to the land was no solution, that an equal right to the land itself had to be recognized, and that there could be no social harmony if private property in land continued, though he was content to move toward its demise gradually. Too extreme for some reformers, Devyr proved to be a divisive figure in America. His use of Biblical imagery, the labor theory of value, and the democratic ideal of redistribution and independent smallholdings struck a chord, but there were inconsistencies in his thought. They added to and reflected the disunity among reform campaigners. Some went on using natural rights arguments, while others preferred to stress legal title.[78]

O'Brien was disappointed by land policy in America. A worthy experiment in democratic government had not created a better society, and the need for "social revolution" was as acute in America as it was in Britain:

> What means a social revolution? I mean by it a gradual reform in the relative duties and positions of the different classes of society. Political revolutions seldom go beyond the surface of society. They seldom amount to more than a mere transfer of power from one set of political chiefs to another. At best they only substitute one aristocratic form of government for another, and hence all political revolutions of which history makes mention have left the world pretty much as they found it—not happier, not improved in any one essential particular.

> The American Revolution of 1775 is the most perfect revolution of its kind that has hitherto been effected in the world. Taking the states collectively the franchise is sufficiently extended to entitle the government to be called a Democratic Republic. At all events it is the most perfect government of its kind that has hitherto been known to exist. However, the American people are fast sinking into poverty and slavery. Various are the assigned causes of this downward progress. The genuine cause is BAD PROPERTY INSTITUTIONS which allow property to be dishonestly acquired and dishonestly transmitted.[79]

These institutions had not been corrected, for the American Revolution was only a political revolution and had not led to a direct attack on social evils. O'Brien routinely publicized and praised agrarian reformers in the United States, certain that some of them were moving in the right direction.[80] He advised against a more conservative option, of something like O'Connor's Land Plan, and urged them to seek thorough land reform; and he recommended smallholdings, with the rents devoted to public purposes. As Jamie Bronstein has demonstrated, however, most American land reformers did not think this way. They preferred large homesteads and passed over the question of how rents could be used for the public advantage. The failure of the O'Brienite colony in Kansas in the mid-1870s might indicate, moreover, that O'Brien and his followers misunderstood American conditions. They had bold ideas but neither the funding nor the practical know-how to implement their principles successfully in the Kansas context (Gary Entz shows that inexperience in prairie farming and an underestimation of the amount of land needed by each settler family were serious flaws—though to be fair to O'Brien, he was never a strong supporter of emigration, maintaining that what the workers really needed was the reform strategy he was advocating).[81]

There was no O'Brien-like figure in the U.S. land reform movement. Leaders there did not talk about social revolution. Bronstein describes their position as an "ideological middle ground." They wanted to press for the democratization of property ownership, but in a moderate way and with an inclusive broad-based campaign. They did not wish to be associated with nationalization or the elimination of private property and refused to accept some of the suggestions O'Brien made to them. Bronstein agrees that he failed fully to appreciate the American situation, especially the perception of the "frontier" and the expectation that as the United States expanded geographically, plenty of land would become available.[82] America was not Britain. In the 1840s, the U.S. economy was less complex than the British.

America was mainly rural, much of its land was cultivated by slaves, and most of its manufacturing was carried out in small units. Nevertheless, there *was* growing pressure for land reform. Workers believed that wider ownership would bring benefits, and there was a shared intellectual heritage in Britain and America.[83] One American leader, Lewis Masquerier, was heavily influenced by O'Brien during the 1840s. Abandoning Owenite communitarianism, Masquerier looked to combine public and private interests. He approved of O'Brien's proposals for nationalization of the land and its cultivation in individual holdings, though he did not wish to give the state full control.[84]

Subjection to landed and moneyed elites, and of course the people's own lack of land and money, became O'Brien's constant refrain. In *Reynolds's Political Instructor* in 1849–50, he traced the rise of this "human slavery" back through history (these were the articles republished posthumously as *The Rise, Progress, and Phases of Human Slavery*). O'Brien argued that personal slavery, accepted in the ancient world but phased out with the spread of Christianity, had been replaced by "wage slavery," which was even more grotesque. In "modern proletarianism," the "wage slaves" had few rights and were dependent on the purchasers of their labor, who controlled the instruments of production, ran the government, and used their ascendancy to appropriate most of the workers' product. The dominance of these "landowners and money-lords" could only be broken by new laws facilitating popular access to land, money, and credit, and to get these new laws the people needed first to gain political power. O'Brien urged his readers to reflect upon the ill effects of recent legislation. The Bank Charter Act of 1844, like the "Peel Act" of 1819, had made money scarce. Free trade budgets and the repeal of the Corn Laws in 1846 had intensified competition and lowered wages. O'Brien attacked "false principles at the root of our system," especially "that laws may make property for one set of people at the expense of another set, without the consent of the latter, and without giving them an equivalent." What the legislature had done could be undone. The notion that it would be wrong and harmful for the state to intervene was absurd.[85]

The "human slavery" articles represent a justification for the NRL program, which was to be introduced after the establishment of a democratic form of government. The Charter was available in Britain; and in a more global sense, O'Brien thought, Robespierre's projected French constitution of 1793 was also exemplary. To O'Brien, Robespierre was the model democrat and had the right idea about property.[86] He had not intended to abolish private ownership. Instead, he wanted it to be clearly defined as referring to articles guaranteed to an individual *by law.* O'Brien developed this theme in the *Poor Man's Guardian*, in *Buonarroti's History of Babeuf's Conspiracy*, and thereafter. Since property rights had to be legally expressed, anything that was not defined by law was not to be regarded as property. When the people gained political power and could make the laws, all difficulties surrounding property could be removed, and if in time the people decided that private property should be abolished, this could be accomplished. But (following Robespierre) O'Brien did not think that social happiness was incompatible with the existence of private property. The essential need was to change the laws affecting property, not least to ensure that all useful labor was fairly rewarded. Equality before the law would make private property unobjectionable, and individuals could enjoy more or less depending on their own efforts. Property would no longer mean plunder. O'Brien did not share the Babouvist and Owenite view that the institution of property was itself an evil. As Robespierre had seen, the problems arising from private ownership were best addressed through legislation, not outright abolition. The working classes did not need abolition to obtain the full fruits of their labor. Abolition might deprive the landed and moneyed elites of the property they had improperly acquired, but it would also negate the workers' right to what they produced. O'Brien sought to prevent this. It was far better, he wrote, to introduce laws that would vouchsafe property to those who created it and deny it to those who had not created it. "If all men are placed equal before the law, if the means of acquiring and retaining wealth are equally secured to all in proportion to the respective industry and services of each, I see no objection to private property."[87]

It is likely that these ideas were shaped in part by O'Brien's knowledge of French political and economic debate. In the early decades of the nineteenth century, some French commentators treated laissez-faire and free trade as timeless and universally valid, while others argued that they were but stages in the evolution of representative government. Some taught that the state could be trusted to look after the interests of all its citizens. Others wanted the people to have more say in lawmaking, especially in the economic sphere.[88] O'Brien's ideas were also shaped by a concept of "labour-power" as a form of property. Marc Mulholland points out that some Chartists espoused a variant: "democratization as a necessary stage toward having legislation passed that would bolster labour as a form of property by which a person might securely and independently live." This was a result that O'Brien had in mind: labor, as a type of property like land or capital, was no less deserving of respect and influence. Mulholland emphasizes an inclination that O'Brien, and before him Babeuf and Buonarroti, to some extent relied upon, "the tendency for wage earners to support socialized mechanisms for the protection of individual labour."[89]

Many of them were more traditionalist than progressive in attitude, however, and even in the most industrialized districts there were workers who respected their "betters," harked back to hierarchical and paternalistic relationships, and had no disposition toward independent working-class action. Some embraced "agrarian utopianism," inspired by a sense of attachment to the land, which helps to explain such phenomena as the push for allotments (to some radicals, a form of social control) and the appeal of the Chartist Land Plan.[90] Historians sympathetic to the political Left have often been accused of exaggerating the strength of "social revolutionary sentiment" among the working classes.[91] It is possible that even in regions where radicalism appeared to be weak, it was really more covert than weak.[92] But the fact remains that Chartism did lose its mass following. Many workers decided that their lives could be improved without the suffrage, or the assault on capitalism, or the other panaceas that were discussed in the Chartist era.[93]

The Land Plan, developed by O'Connor, grew out of local efforts by Chartists who wanted to try retail cooperation or who had set up benefit clubs for the purchase of smallholdings. Most of all it grew out of O'Connor's determination to revitalize the Chartist movement in the mid-1840s and to confirm his own primacy as national leader. The Land Plan—which provided for the purchase of estates and their division into smallholdings, to be distributed by ballot among members who had paid into the venture—was presented as a major boon to the working classes, but by 1851 it had all but broken down. (In the words of Richard Oastler, the paternalistic critic of the factory system and New Poor Law, the Land Plan became the "Land-Bother.") Malcolm Chase concludes that it was too big, too ambitious, and that it might have fared better if managed in a more devolved way, at the local level by smaller land societies with fewer members. Chartists remained interested in land reform, whatever the shortcomings of the Land Plan, and in a move that might be regarded as a form of vindication for O'Brien, a majority of delegates at the Chartist Convention of 1851 were willing to endorse public ownership.[94]

Some observers had long seen this coming—a splintering of radicalism, that is, brought on by differing social and economic preferences. In November 1842, for instance, O'Brien's position was discussed in a letter written by Richard Cobden to another of the leaders of the anti–Corn Law campaign, Charles Pelham Villiers, MP for Wolverhampton. Cobden knew that O'Brien had broken with O'Connor and that the two were enemies, but he considered O'Brien the more vehement opponent of the liberal economic order desired by the Anti–Corn Law League: "I was amused yesterday at reading the *British Statesman*—O'Brien's abuse of O'Connor is only surpassed by his tirades against *us*." Cobden thought that this, along with O'Brien's links with Joseph Sturge and the Complete Suffrage Union, gave a useful indication of Chartist opinion about free trade, the Chartists' refusal to put anything before winning the vote, and the flirtation with "socialism" in sections of the movement.[95] O'Connor was an avowed opponent of socialism and believed that the Land Plan offered workers the personal independence and self-sufficiency that obviated the need for socialist prescriptions. His Irish landowning background predisposed him to such sentiments, but there were also serious ideas behind the Land Plan. In 1843 O'Connor published *A Practical Work on the Management of Small Farms*, and he was recommending "my farming book" at the very time he was also seeking funds for the Land Plan. He assured Thomas Allsop that "a thousand pounds vested in spade cultivation" would bring "ten times as much profit . . . as you will receive from any the best mercantile speculation," and he hoped "that your agricultural ardour will not cool. Many of our best friends in the counties of York, Lancaster, and Nottingham are vesting some hundreds in the spec."[96]

O'Brien vilified the Land Plan, and though Ray Faherty has highlighted the personal clash between O'Brien and O'Connor, there was more to their quarrel than this. O'Brien genuinely believed the Land Plan to be disastrous: it would strengthen conservatism and individualism; it was socially regressive and would turn workers against their own class; and it was badly organized and based on flawed assumptions about the price and availability of land, the cost of building cottages on each plot, the readiness of the moneyed interests to provide mortgages, the other expenses that would have to be covered, and the extent to which land values were likely to go up. Yet Jamie Bronstein deems the Land Plan "probably more feasible" than O'Brien's "impractical" scheme, which could not guarantee that every worker would get land, involved the growth of government when most workers were suspicious of government power, and cut across the workers' respect for private ownership.[97]

There might be something in Bronstein's remarks, but it ought to be remembered that only a small proportion of supporters of the Land Plan ever gained the plots that were promised (and they had to pay rent), and that O'Brien did not expect everyone to settle on the land under his scheme. The goal was to democratize landholding so that anyone who *wished* to cultivate the land could do so. It is also likely that government growth would not have been unacceptable once that government was reformed by the Charter, creating a system in which the people made the laws; and the workers' respect for private property, even if it was as strong as Bronstein supposes, might have come to matter less to them as they saw the benefits of other social and economic arrangements. O'Brien was attempting to guide them along these lines, and in his design some of the features of small proprietorship would remain (albeit with the nation as landlord): individual plots, self-reliance, and personal independence.

The rise of the Land Plan suggests that most Chartists desired a version of "home colonization" rather than collective ownership or some similarly dramatic upheaval in property rights and relationships. The idea of "labour's own land, purchased with labour's own money" had more to do with Victorian self-help tendencies than with O'Brienite land nationalization, and it excited many workers, especially among the northern unskilled. The names of the streets in the community of "O'Connorville," at Heronsgate in southwest Hertfordshire, where settlers began to arrive in May 1847, reflected the places they came from: Halifax, Bradford, Stockport, and Nottingham. Ten years later, the Land Plan having collapsed and many workers having turned to other options, the plots at Heronsgate were auctioned off. Original residents had already started to leave well before this. The first to do so—and he came in for much criticism within the Chartist movement—was James Greenwood, from Hebden Bridge, Yorkshire, who sold his house to a London tradesman. The latter was looking for a retirement home. While some of O'Brien's claims about the Land Plan were borne out, it is also clear that plenty of workers did want what O'Connor said they wanted. "As a businessman he failed," writes Paul Barker, "but he planned better than he is given credit for. A semi in the country, with garden, has become the enduring English ideal."[98]

Opponents of the Land Plan got it wrong, according to Dorothy Thompson, for it was an advantageous and realistic undertaking that gave Chartism a focus and probably saved the movement from rapid disintegration. In addition, it did not mark a diversion from political goals, and it met the workers' need for their own institutions and strengthened their attachment to self-help and the dignity of labor. That the Land Plan was not eccentric or misguided is also the view of James Epstein, who is concerned to defend O'Connor's reputation and explains the Land Plan in terms of British radicalism's "essentially artisan vision" of "an egalitarian society of small producers based upon small commodity exchange and some form of labor credit." Undeniably, the Land Plan (at least for a time) captured the imagination of many Chartists. O'Connor made it very appealing.[99] Apparently it was easier for workers to understand and accept the Land Plan than to commit to O'Brien's proposals. Malcolm Chase regards nationalization as "tangential to Chartist thinking" and adds that although O'Brien and others who favored state intervention and collectivist principles were glad when the Land Plan broke down, they were in the minority. Numerous workers had taken up the goal of private smallholdings—to the extent that if they could not obtain land through the Land Plan they tried other means, especially the freehold land societies. The two methods were related (although promoters of the Land Plan and freehold land societies often reproached each other). It seems that one was strong in areas where the other was weak.[100]

If contemporary and subsequent denunciation of O'Connor and the Land Plan was excessive, it is also the case that the vision described by Epstein was somewhat limited. The Land Plan could not lead to the kind of transformation promised by O'Brien's policy of land nationalization; and while Epstein suggests that O'Connor's focus on the land was a gradual and logical development, it can be regarded differently. Gregory Claeys thinks it a drastic reversal, "a capitulation before the charge that social reform had necessarily to precede political change" and "a vital failure of an entire tradition of political language and logic, whereby attaining the Charter was to produce economic wellbeing for the poor, unemployed, and labouring classes." In the early twentieth century there were commentators who sided with O'Brien against O'Connor. Walter Hall, for instance, thought of O'Brien's land nationalization as "more practical" than the Land Plan.[101]

Notwithstanding these later verdicts, as the Land Plan took off in the mid-1840s O'Brien's opponents were pleased to use any evidence that he was struggling to make headway. In September 1845, when he delivered two lectures in Rochdale, Lancashire, the liberal *Manchester Guardian* ridiculed his efforts under the heading "Another New Chartist Movement." According to this report, "The lecturer maintained that all land should belong to the government, and be applied to national purposes, and expressed his disapproval of O'Connor's plan of small farms. The lectures were thinly attended."[102]

O'Brien continued, regardless of setbacks, to broadcast his objections to the Land Plan and press forward with his own agenda. He expanded upon his view that social variety was better than uniformity and insisted that in the new order there would be a place for small farms (not unlike the peasant proprietorship to be facilitated by the Land Plan) and cooperative communities (not unlike the method favored by Owenites).[103] O'Brien was reluctant to omit policies or institutions that could help to increase the availability of land for the people. Despite his negative view of the Land Plan he favored smallholdings, which O'Connor intended the Land Plan to create. Malcolm Chase argues that although the Land Plan was a negation of the nationalization that O'Brien ultimately wished for, it was also likely to devolve the economic and political power arising from private ownership, which, after all, is what O'Brien (and before him Spence) wanted. Chase presents a picture of O'Brien, "almost alone among non-communitarian radicals in developing a coherent case for the nationalization of land," also "advancing the case for smallholdings, and by implication small owners." This fits in with the thesis that popular agrarianism ought not to be regarded as a socialist alternative to capitalism. Ben Maw has stressed that O'Brien was not a socialist, because he accepted possessive individualism and envisaged rewards in line with effort and contribution. Alfred Plummer states that O'Brien did not offer a socialist theory but a plan of reform that would make government respond to the problems created by Britain's economic development (yet Plummer also thinks that O'Brien's most significant contribution was in shaping the socialist critique of nineteenth-century capitalism). To G. D. H. Cole, O'Brien was not a socialist but an antimonopolistic radical reformer, a "social democrat" whose ideas helped to shape later evolutionary socialism. Delbert Schafer notes that O'Brien used the term "socialist," but not about himself.[104] Though he did incorporate socialist principles into his mature program, he clearly thought of his own position—"National Reform"—as distinctive. This needs to be placed into its proper context: O'Brien's mix of social and economic arrangements, his enthusiasm for political democracy, and his "revolution" that was acceptable to both rich and poor.

Chartists came up with a range of strategies for land reform, of which the Land Plan was the most favored and best known. Malcolm Chase has shown that these strategies shared three characteristics: disapproval of large accumulations of land, suspicion of the state as the owner or manager of the land, and preference for shared access, usage, and control instead of possessive individualism. Chase believes that "access to—and control of—the land, rather than the democratization of ownership itself, was the essential basis from which all Chartist land reform emerged."[105] This does not apply to O'Brien and his followers. It is true that O'Brien opposed large accumulations of land and thought of redistribution as just and necessary, but he also accepted that some farms would be larger than others, since there had to be proper rewards for achievement. Differing amounts of property and wealth were to be expected. Those who did more should receive more. As for suspicion of the state as owner or manager of the land, O'Brien looked forward to a state democratized by the Charter. On this basis, it would be safe to allow the gradual and compensated transfer of land from private into public hands, and eventually the state would be the sole landowner in Britain. What of the preference for shared access, usage, and control instead of possessive individualism? Up to a point this was O'Brien's position. He favored diversity, however, and although he had no desire to inhibit communitarian and egalitarian urges, he also wished to provide scope for individual labor, enterprise, and possession.

In Chase's opinion, O'Brien joined in the "idealization of spade husbandry" and "idealization of small property ownership" of many radicals at this time.[106] To some extent he did, while also recommending nationalization of the land. He was not being inconsistent, for the end in view was the nation as landlord and the nation renting out the land for cultivation in small amounts. Farmer-occupiers would also be owners, because all the land would belong to the people. O'Brien had decided, moreover, that it was appropriate to push for lesser reforms until circumstances made possible the greater reforms. If an idea or organization or policy was useful, and represented a step toward the ultimate destination as described in the NRL propositions of 1849–50, O'Brien was ready to support it.

It is therefore unsurprising to find O'Brien regularly publicizing a range of endeavors, including "freehold provident societies," "land and building societies," "communist farms," "cooperative leagues," "anti-enclosure associations," and "provident and benefit societies," and in connection with this he corresponded with and wrote about the activities of Thomas Edward Bowkett, a London surgeon who promoted popular landholding along with self-help practices and cooperative nonprofit institutions that could provide loans without interest. O'Brien did not agree with all of Bowkett's proposals, but he was willing to treat them as a move in the right direction.[107]

By 1850, though he no longer had his own newspaper to guide and instruct, O'Brien thought he observed tokens of support for his program. There was now an organizational structure, with the NRL, and there was an outlet in the popular periodicals of G. W. M. Reynolds, who claimed that O'Brien deserved to be regarded as one of the prophets of the age.[108] The accord between O'Brien and Reynolds was exactly the kind of development that antireformers seized upon in their efforts to lampoon radicalism and brand its leaders as foolish and disreputable. Ian Haywood has noted in this respect the "honour among thieves" trope and warnings about the expropriation of property,[109] but O'Brien's intentions were not those attributed to him by detractors.

"National Reform" attracted considerable attention. Circumstances in the aftermath of the 1848 revolutions were promising for O'Brien. David Stack refers to "a new beginning." Though the mass campaign was finished, Chartism survived as a smaller and more intellectual movement. Eldon Barry regards as pivotal the Chartist Convention of 1851, which demonstrated that the movement would be smaller but more cohesive, with clear social goals attached to the Charter. There was growing approval for nationalizing the land, and "O'Brien was at the height of his influence" (even if "it was the tragedy of Chartism that political maturity came too late").[110] O'Brien's friend Thomas Allsop thought that 1848 represented opportunity. At last, he wrote, radical solutions could be tried and questions relating to property, the rights of labor, capitalism, and credit better explained and addressed. People were beginning to see that the government was incapable of doing what the times required. It was "at sea without chart, rudder, or compass, ignorant of the tides and currents." Allsop also suggested that there might be bloodshed (though he appears to have considered this much more likely in France than in Britain).[111]

O'Brien himself was optimistic. At a meeting of the NRL in December 1849 he claimed that the 1848 revolutions "had added 500 per cent to the moral power he formerly possessed while advocating those principles of National Reform for which he had so long contended, under so many and such various disadvantages." Despite its limited means, the NRL was advancing. Land nationalization had been sanctioned by other groups and was being discussed in many newspapers. People were talking about the NRL's program. This "evidence of progress" was in stark contrast to earlier times, when, O'Brien remembered, to put forward Spence's idea of "the people's farm" was to run the risk of persecution if not prosecution.

> Twenty years ago the doctrine of making land public property would subject the man who held it to the imputation of being either a fool or a rogue; and even Cobbett could find no better excuse for poor Spence than that he was half-cracked. But now, thank God, the doctrine had ceased to be considered either knavish or ridiculous.

Increasing debate about the land was pleasing, as was the fact that O'Brien's proposals were gaining wider support. A number of prominent reformers seemed to be coming round, Owen among them. "Owen had formerly expressed his belief that the changes he proposed for society would be accomplished by the voluntary acts of all parties—that capital, skill, and labour would cordially amalgamate, and go at once into community." O'Brien paid tribute to Owen, "who, in trying to work out the problem of communism, had enunciated many truths of great benefit to the world." Now Owen was arguing that the government should buy up land for public purposes. O'Connor had been saying a similar thing in response to criticism of the Land Plan.

O'Brien then turned to free trade, which he said had caused bankruptcies and pauperization. Across Britain, agricultural prices were down, profits had been slashed, and farmers could not employ workers or pay rent. The purchasing power of money was falling while the cost of living was rising. This led O'Brien to the gold standard—it was "easy to perceive what an unjust and unfair power this gold standard bestowed upon capitalists and usurers"—and the Bank of England, which stood at the center of an "anomalous system" of finance.[112]

O'Brien regarded the NRL propositions as the best way forward, and he was quick to respond in print and on the platform when they were denigrated. In response to the allegation that "democratic landholding" would bring excessive subdivision of the land and lower agricultural output, O'Brien presented evidence from France, America, and Ireland, as well as Britain, to indicate otherwise.[113] He also went on offering detailed analysis of alternative proposals, in order to show why they did not compare well with his own. Early in 1849 he focused on the financial plan of Cobden, now MP for the West Riding, who had called for a return to the government spending levels of 1835 and a substantial cut in taxation.[114]

The 1848 revolutions prompted O'Brien to clarify his opinion of socialism. He did not object to "any form" of socialism, he explained, and he would not deny that this or that form might one day be capable of implementation, but he was adamant that such implementation had to be voluntary, not coerced, and that to abolish private property altogether would not be appropriate. The crusade for common property, O'Brien complained, strengthened "the present anti-social system" by conflating the just with the unjust and the possible with the impossible. More discernment was needed.

> We have no right to take any man's money or goods from him; but we have a right to produce goods for ourselves out of the land and the raw material in it; and we have also the right to establish what system of money and exchange we think proper, for the free and equitable interchange of the commodities so produced. Again, we have no right to tax the rich for our benefit, or to force them to make loans to us out of their private property. But we have a right to nationalize landed property,

> on the principle of indemnity or compensation . . . and with the rents of the lands so acquired to the public, we have a right to give the poor the advantages of public credit, for in so doing we despoil nobody, and the public is no loser by the loan. Why will not the Socialists and Communists make these just and obvious distinctions between what we have the right to do, and what we have not, and postpone the demanded application of their theories till the people have obtained their social and political rights?

Socialism had been tried in different times and places on a small scale and had failed. For O'Brien, the new order was to emerge gradually through nationalization of the land and the currency, exchange, and credit reforms he had enumerated.[115]

He was still writing extensively on these topics. In a letter to Allsop dated December 1847 he referred to "tracts" and "essays" on "landed tenures and currency and equitable exchange" among the works he had in progress (most of which, he feared, might not go to press unless he could secure the necessary funds).[116] In the 1850s he kept his program before the public through his publications and lectures and through the work of the National Reform League and the instructional and convivial activities at the Eclectic Institution. Attendances at the latter sometimes waned, but O'Brien's correspondence also refers to times when he was much in demand as a speaker, "making converts," and fully occupied at the institution, with little opportunity to attend to anything else. Sickness, financial need, and persecution (real or imagined) did not halt the articulation and advancement of "National Reform." As O'Brien wrote to his friend Mathews, "sound instruction" had to go on so that people became fully aware of the landed and moneyed elites' abuse of their power and the need for land nationalization, symbolic currency, national credit, and public marts for the exchange of goods.[117]

The *Vision of Hell* of 1859 included an assault against "liberal" economic and financial measures. Britain had been taken along a path that was quite unlike the one O'Brien recommended, and in his poem he depicted groups and individuals coming too late to the realization that "liberal" policy was destructive and evil.

> Your Economic schools barbarian
> Taught us to scoff all nature's rules;
> Your laws commercial and agrarian,
> To make our brethren slaves and tools
> And fill the land with cheats and fools.

You made us millionaire-aspirants,
Remorseless knaves, and rav'nous tyrants,
Gorging with appetite satanic,
On general bankruptcy and panic.

O'Brien insisted that only the NRL program could redeem the situation. Only the NRL program could transfer political, social, and economic power to those who should have it from those who had been wrongly gathering it to themselves for too long:

Loan-mongers, landlords, millionaires,
Contractors, usurers, speculators,
Stock-jobbers, brokers, bulls, and bears,
Blacklegs, monopolists, regraters,
Dealers in spiritual wares;
And House of Commons sham-debaters,
Yes, the whole tribe of legislators,
Who cater for these depradators,
Most of them rotten fornicators,
All of them licensed spoliators,
Tramplers on right, and people-haters,
Rogues, every man, and all first-raters,
With swarms of hunters after place,
A hungry, servile, graceless race.[118]

In 1862 O'Brien was working on a study of "all" social and political systems. He recommended it to others on the grounds that "it contains the only kind of matter of its class that the public would read nowadays in its present morbid condition. It is probably (with the notes) the only complete anatomy of society (as it now exists) that our language contains either in prose or verse." O'Brien was certain that his influence was growing.[119] Unfortunately, the study referred to was not published at the time O'Brien wrote it; but it probably informed the editors of writings that appeared posthumously.

The long address composed by some of his followers shortly after O'Brien died was designed to raise money but also to pay tribute to him and to shape the wider perception of O'Brien and his principles. This address formed the basis of statements and appeals that subsequently appeared in the radical press. The section dealing with the formation of the NRL stressed its "celebrated Seven Propositions," which were of "worldwide repute." Supporters of the NRL remained absolutely loyal to O'Brien's program: "For the last fifteen years we have endeavoured to keep the flag of liberty unfurled." Now that their leader was dead, they wanted to accentuate his vital contribution.

> In all his numerous writings and speeches, Mr. O'Brien never ceased advocating and enforcing those great social reform principles which he saw were essential for the people's freedom. He ever contended for *social* rights along with *political* rights on behalf of the entire people. He thoroughly understood and explained the great question of a national currency and a national system of exchange for the masses in contradistinction to the false and ruinous system which now obtains and which is intended solely for the aggrandizement of a set of merchants and usurers. He enunciated the laws which should prevail on the tenure of land, the foundation of all real reform. He never ceased denouncing the twin enemies of the working class—the landlord and the profit-monger—namely, those who usurp the ownership and occupation of the soil, which should be the inalienable inheritance of the nation, and those who seize on the profits of labour, regarding the labourers as private property and using them as mere machines for producing wealth for a race of idlers and swindlers who do nothing but plot the subjugation and debasement of honest working men.[120]

Such remarks testify that O'Brien had taught his followers well and that, to them, it was clear why he was important and what his priorities had been.

O'Brien's arguments about the land continued to influence social and economic theory long after his death. In late Victorian Liberalism there was a fundamental disagreement on the land question—essentially on whether or not there were circumstances in which interference with private property was appropriate. Those who were willing to accept such interference echoed the claims that had been made by O'Brien. Several of the purposes in view were the same, though the methods might have differed. At the end of the nineteenth century a favorite idea was to use changes in taxation to deal with the land question. It would be going too far to make the people the owners of the land, it was thought, but it *was* possible to give them some of the advantages of landownership. Ursula Vogel has demonstrated that there was considerable distance between a proposal to end "aristocratic monopoly," or bring in "free trade in land," and one to abolish private ownership. Nevertheless, the radical principle that land should not be protected or exceptional had growing support. O'Brien would have approved. With the willingness to rely on market forces and the rejection of state policy or coercion, however, he would have had no patience. Late Victorian Liberals were averse to socialism, but more than a few of them were ready to talk about an equal right to the land, or its equivalent, for anyone for whom a return to the land was practically impossible. They also discussed wage and rent "slavery," natural rights, tenancies held from the state, and the moral case against laissez-faire. They mostly separated all this from a community of goods, pointing out that an equal right to the land was not the same as an equal share in what was produced.[121]

Interest in these matters was boosted by the campaigns of American reformer Henry George, who argued that land, the most important of all economic resources, ought to be shared rather than privately owned. In his best-selling *Progress and Poverty* (1879) he stated that the land should be treated as public property. He advocated the "single tax," to rest on land, so that society could recapture the value of its common inheritance. This would eliminate the need for taxes on productive activity; and it would discourage land speculation but not the continuing development of the land, because landlords would not suffer tax penalties for any edifice constructed on their land or any industry carried on there. George's influence over British reformers grew as he completed two speaking tours of Britain during the early 1880s. O'Brienites who had emigrated met George in America, read and discussed his works, and went on to lead and participate in radical organizations in the United States. When George was in Britain he made further acquaintances among the O'Brienites. It was falsely claimed in the 1880s that George, far from being an original thinker, was merely regurgitating what he had learned from a follower of O'Brien who had settled in the United States years before. O'Brien's program and George's "single tax" featured in wider debates at this time about land tenure, housing for the working classes, and the link between property and political rights. During the 1880s, discussion about public ownership of the land involved the direct transmission of ideas from O'Brien in the 1830s and 1840s.[122]

Some of the foremost intellectuals of the age joined in. Before Herbert Spencer's conversion to "unfettered competition and absolute private property," he advocated nationalization of the land by a democratized state, this land to be rented out by auction and the rent paid into the public funds as a recompense to all those who had not been able to acquire land. John Stuart Mill's plan included the provision of small plots for laborers, rural cooperatives, the setting aside of common land for public purposes only, the compensation of all existing owners who lost rights or property as a result of the reforms, and a guarantee that the reforms would not be retroactive, so that past acquisitions would stand. Mill agreed that land could not be treated in the same way as other property and that in some circumstances private ownership of land was neither just nor expedient. He did not approve of O'Brienite nationalization (preferring other solutions—peasant proprietorship, tax reforms that would allow the state to benefit from increasing land values, and public control of wastes and commons to facilitate the setting up of agricultural cooperatives); but Mill had sympathy with parts of the NRL manifesto of 1849–50. It is likely that Henry George was also impressed by the NRL manifesto. George asserted that people could not be free unless they had access to "the natural means of production" and that they were reduced to "wage slavery" through dependence on the owners of the principal productive resource, land. In order for the people's right to the land to be respected, George concluded that the best method would be not confiscation but measures to socialize the land's blessings. He insisted that political liberty and social justice were inseparable.[123] Most of these goals, ideas, and provisions had also featured in O'Brien's mature program, though he may have emphasized some more than others.

The remedies of Spencer, Mill, and George were advanced on the basis that the mainstream liberal position, "free trade in land," was inadequate. The latter focused on eradicating aristocratic land monopoly and its props, such as primogeniture and strict settlement; stopped far short of any direct interference with private property; upheld the ideal of peasant proprietorship; and appealed to "economic laws" and market forces.[124] Anthony Howe considers the failure of "free trade in land" as almost inevitable. Its opponents were strong, its supporters not united, and it was troubled by ideological and tactical limitations that robbed it of momentum in adverse circumstances (during an economic boom, for example, or when public attention was gripped by a foreign crisis).[125] Perhaps the weakness of this liberal alternative made O'Brien and his followers all the more convinced of the merits of their program.

Approaches to the land question in the nineteenth century had various determinants, including nostalgia and differing interpretations of British history, political affiliations, and the experience of both prosperity and slump. One of the long-term continuities, as noted by Matthew Cragoe and Paul Readman, was the survival of older ideas.[126] By the 1880s there were several influential and irreconcilable positions on land reform, and O'Brien's was among them. The debate was influenced by concerns about class antagonism, the government's areas of responsibility, and the changing nature of the British economy, and by moral as well as economic arguments about landlordism and capitalism. Contention about the tax system and welfare provisions played its part too. Radical criticism of the "wealthy" (a broader category than just landowners) did not diminish, and there was regular repetition of by now familiar opinions about the public interest and private property. Opposition to democracy and nationalization was as strong as ever.[127] The most important features of this late nineteenth-century controversy had been anticipated in O'Brien's journalism and reform endeavors.

The "Charter socialism" to which O'Brien made such a telling contribution has been characterized by Noel Thompson as a "social democratic political economy" that focused on the social and economic change that political reform would make possible. "Charter socialism" was distinctive because, unlike some earlier radical programs, and more than others, it aimed at political reform in order to serve the interests of labor and put a stop to class exploitation. The message was clear by 1849–50 when O'Brien issued the NRL manifesto. Political power was the means to other ends. The evils of "Old Corruption," especially those relating to taxation and expenditure, had still to be tackled, but more important was the need to prevent the robbery of the workers by the landed and moneyed elites. Class conflict could be mitigated, and economic and social improvement assured, by the nationalization of resources—the land most of all—and by adjustments in the relationship between producers and nonproducers and between owners and nonowners of the means of production, distribution, and exchange. Here was the merging of Chartist and anticapitalist doctrines. To reach this consummation, O'Brien looked back to ideas and plans advanced by the other radicals and theorists mentioned earlier, and he also looked forward to the kind of Britain that he thought *could* be created if the NRL propositions were acted upon.[128]

O'Brien has been condemned by some modern commentators for his biases and errors. Delbert Schafer dismisses his defense of Robespierre and his notion that the middle classes obtained wealth and property through their control over government. Schafer contends that O'Brien opposed the things that made Britain prosperous, free trade and manufacturing, and did not appreciate the benefits of industrialization, especially for workers, most of whom became better off. O'Brien wanted British society to remain predominantly agricultural, Schafer adds, and it is not clear that this would have solved the problems he identified. The poor would not have fared very well under an O'Brienite regime.[129]

These assertions, though not groundless, are too severe. Schafer rather abuses his benefit of hindsight. O'Brien was grappling with issues that vexed many of his contemporaries, and he offered comprehensive proposals that, in unison with the political democratization promised by the Charter, were at least as sensible and viable as other schemes available at the time. Ben Maw argues that O'Brien's program could not have worked as he intended: "O'Brien overestimated the power a newly enfranchised working class would be able to exert in transforming state institutions into democratic and effective organs of social justice, and underestimated what we know today to be the protean nature of capitalist power."[130] But from his observations of state and society in the 1830s and 1840s, was it really so unreasonable to propose the reforms he did? If the tensions and struggles of the era reveal anything, they show that contemporaries did not uniformly approve of the way things were; nor did they accept the inevitability of "what we know today" about how industry and agriculture, capitalism, finance, government, representation, and property ownership were going to develop in the second half of the nineteenth century and into the twentieth.

O'Brien's ideology of "National Reform," which influenced many later radical campaigns[131] in Britain and beyond, was a bold attempt to deal with inequality, exploitation, corruption, and injustice. Building on ideas about class, capitalism, and labor, on the familiar concerns of political radicals, and on a personal reading of the French Revolution, O'Brien presented a manifesto for the gradual but fundamental reorganization of state and society. Political reform had to come first but was only the means. A democratic form of government was to be used to effect social transformation along the lines indicated in the NRL manifesto of 1849–50: nationalization of the land; a system of national credit; conversion to a symbolic currency; and the establishment of public marts for the exchange of products. While private property would not be abolished, land was a specific exception. Land should not be privately and individually owned, although, at the same time, O'Brien did not champion collective cultivation. His mature program, to be accomplished through the nonviolent "revolution," rested on a mix of social and economic arrangements that balanced individual and public interests. “National Reform” was one of a number of projects taken up by radicals in the mid-nineteenth century, and underlined the variety and complexity of contemporary philosophies and methods of reform. O’Brien was willing and able to describe an alternative future, with “democratic landholding” to sustain the better life that everybody deserved.

CHAPTER 5

# America's Democratic Promise

Before, during, and after O'Brien's time, most reform groups in Britain were generally well disposed toward America. They admired its written constitution and guarantee of personal rights; its republican system and democratic suffrage; its religious toleration and the absence of an established church; its freedom from the weight of tradition, rank, class, and aristocracy; its well-developed local government and sense of active civic participation; its promise of liberty, opportunity, and progress. America seemed to represent what Britain could and should be. From John Wilkes in the 1760s, through John Cartwright and Thomas Paine, through William Cobbett in the early nineteenth century, and on into the mid-Victorian years, there was an unbroken thread in British radicalism, one typified by tributes to and friendship toward America. Chartists were influenced by this tendency and helped to prolong it. The United States offered them a model. O'Brien encouraged them in this optimistic conceptualization of America, and one of the striking consistencies in his career is the way he thought about and used America in his political activities.

The American Revolution added to the radical tradition and its vocabulary in the late eighteenth century and was a motive force for campaigners of subsequent generations.[1] America's contribution to Chartism went beyond inspiration and ideas. There were also personnel. One American-born leader of early Chartism was Augustus Beaumont, who became active in London politics before founding the *Northern Liberator* in Newcastle-upon-Tyne in 1837.[2] O'Brien knew him well. He considered Beaumont "as noble and kindly a spirit as ever breathed in human form. . . . Honoured be his name, and cherished be his memory for the good he has done!"[3]

Respect for the U.S. Constitution was reflected in some of the proposals for reform in Britain. Chartist propaganda was filled with American references. The vote as a prerequisite for freedom was a constant theme, and the wide suffrage in America was regarded as a security against tyranny and corruption. Chartists also discussed the British worker and the slave in America in the same breath. The latter had no rights, but British laborers were also the "enslaved many," as an address from the Chartists of Finsbury put it in 1839.[4] Chartists could therefore use negative as well as commendable features of American society in their reform mobilization at home.

At the time of the Bull Ring Riots in Birmingham in 1839, it was claimed that the authorities had moved against the Chartists without just cause. Many made a comparison with the Boston Tea Party of 1773 and repeated the slogan "No taxation without representation." As Malcolm Chase explains, "Both were defining moments that misled government into supposing it had justification for suppression." Chartists openly venerated historical figures who had committed themselves to the cause of liberty, especially during the American Revolution. George Washington and other American heroes were a staple part of Chartist iconography. Portraits, statuettes, and other symbols could be found in the home as well as on display during meetings and processions.[5]

The Liverpool Chartist William Jones told a meeting in September 1841 that a spirit of freedom was rising up in Britain, as it had done across the Atlantic at the time of the American Revolution. In both cases it was the life spring of true patriots who wished to deliver their country from oppression. This was the spirit that had "induced the brave inhabitants . . . to stain with their heart's blood the wild fields of America, rather than submit to the tyrannical impositions of insulting Britain."[6]

Chartists were deeply interested in events abroad. They sympathized with reformers in Europe, but America held a special fascination (though it was not above criticism). In the United States, political freedom was enshrined in the Constitution and an array of individual rights bulwarked by the wide suffrage, a free press, and cheap land, and Chartist periodicals gave support and publicity to working-class organizations in America.[7] Sometimes there were protests, as in 1846 when the Oregon Dispute raised the prospect of war and a Militia Bill was prepared for introduction into Parliament. Chartists declared that they would refuse to serve. "No vote, no musket" was the cry, and in the Chartist press there was increased discussion about solidarity between British and American workers.[8]

In search of a better life and often in order to escape repression or dodge prison, many Chartists went to America (mostly in three waves: after the Newport Rising of 1839, the riots of 1842, and the apparent defeat of Chartism in 1848). Emigration affected the movement in Britain, especially at the local level. When it was a leader or organizer who departed, Chartism was weakened because it was not easy to replace those who left. Some prospered in America. Others did not, and in numerous cases America did not live up to expectations. Indeed, there were Chartists whose experiences in the United States undermined their radicalism, or prompted them to return to Britain, or both. But there were also plenty of satisfied emigrants who farmed the land, found factory work, started shops, joined the army, wrote for newspapers, practiced law, and joined reform societies and trade unions. Some congregated together and, proud of their past, continued to call themselves "Chartists." They enjoyed living in a society where they were not treated as inferior or exploited by aristocratic and commercial elites.[9]

America's political system and social mores influenced Chartists whether or not they went there. For those who did not go, the Chartist press featured so much material about America that they probably felt they knew the place well, a sense that was heightened by the Chartists' tendency to see in America what they wanted to see. There was, writes Hamish Fraser, "much admiration of things American."[10] During 1840–41 the Glasgow-based *Chartist Circular* claimed that Americans knew only peace and happiness: "A hundred millions of co-sovereigns, recognizing no laws but the recorded will of a majority; no end of law but mutual and equal good; no superior, but God alone." The American nation had been founded by workingmen (Washington was a farmer; Franklin a printer; Paine a stay-maker) and the different classes were on good terms with each other because they lived under a system of equality, with representative bodies, limits on government power, and popular sovereignty.[11] Other Chartist papers also covered American topics in depth.[12] A great deal of Chartist material was sent to America, and American publications found their way to Britain, including the *National Laborer* of Philadelphia and the *Working Man's Advocate* of New York City. There was a demand for radical literature on each side of the Atlantic, and a conviction that some political, social, and economic problems were international in nature. Awareness of developments abroad helped to sustain radical activism in Britain.[13]

Respect for America was high during this period. The Charter, offering a plan for representative democracy, has been described as "essentially a proposal to reorganize British politics along American lines."[14] Many Chartists saw America as exemplary. "The inhabitants of the United States are governed on the principles of Chartism," it was declared in 1839, "the consequence of which is that all legislation is bent towards the welfare of the many and not of the few."[15] In 1845, the *Northern Star* contrasted virtuous republican government in the United States with corrupt aristocratic rule in Britain, extolling the independence, love of country, sound principle, social equality, economic opportunity, and popular sovereignty it ascribed to the American system.[16]

This theme was pursued by Chartist lecturers such as the Yorkshire-born Joseph Barker, a former Methodist preacher, who gave talks on "The American Republic" after visiting the United States (he eventually settled there). Like others, Barker stressed those aspects of U.S. politics and society that could be presented as superior, so as to reinforce the Chartist denunciation of Britain's institutions, and paid less attention to black slavery and other blots on the American copybook. Barker's career also illustrates the point made by Denis Paz: "The lecture was a transatlantic phenomenon, and lecturers themselves were transatlantic birds of passage."[17]

Chartism developed, thinks George Lillibridge, "within the framework of the American experience." America was "a blueprint."[18] Yet Chartist opinion about the United States was not uniform. Some turned against America because they came to see it as a place of inequality. These disillusioned Chartists decided that political rights alone could not create democracy. They lamented the fact that workers in America, as in Britain, had no property and that the benefits of economic development were not fairly distributed.[19] Still, the fact that many Chartists went to America and were disappointed by what they found there probably reveals as much about the emigrants as it does about the United States. Ray Boston has stressed the "unqualified paeans of praise about America," which created a "Chartist myth" concerning the link between material welfare and political institutions. Inevitably, when British workers realized their mistake, the popular notion that America was fundamentally different began to die away.[20]

Even the most sincere of reformers—Chartist or otherwise—could take a dim view of the American version of "democracy." Much was made of electoral corruption, party machines, the spoils system, "tyranny of the majority," and untalented nonentities and rabble-rousers rising to high office. To the skeptics America was *not* an exemplar. That the U.S. system of government—to its discredit—was not in tune with British values, history, and political and social conditions was a conclusion reached by admirers of America as well as by America's detractors. "Save us from America" was a slogan of reformers who wanted the British system to be more representative and participatory, but only *in line with* existing behavior and institutions. "The object," writes Robert Saunders, "was to broaden the basis of the electorate without tipping over to democracy, serving not as an approximation to American politics but as an alternative to it."[21]

Nevertheless, affection for America was strong within the Chartist movement. Conditions in Britain were viewed in a way that made America seem better: wages were higher there, government cost less, taxes were lower, elected representatives were conscientious servants of the people, economic opportunity was available to all, and liberty and progress were guaranteed by such phenomena as the separation of church and state, freedom of the press, and public schooling. Chartist leaders generally did not advocate emigration, but to many British workers it looked like a good idea.[22] What is remarkable is not that some British radicals changed their minds about America, but that resistance to the negative portrayal of America was so strong. The United States remained "a place of dreams, of populist yearning," writes James Epstein, and "the populist vision of America never really vanishes."[23]

The image of America created by O'Brien was sympathetic and flattering. If he saw shortcomings, he tended not to dwell on them. Instead, his priority was to preserve the unique status of America as an example and inspiration for British radicalism. Perhaps he feared that if he did not do this, the radicals would lose an essential weapon in their political arsenal. It is likely that, with this in mind, he felt obliged to ignore, minimize, or explain away those aspects of American politics and society that did not fit his purpose.

O'Brien's commitment to political democracy, social equality, and economic justice had a direct bearing on his interpretation of America. As was true of many reformers, America had a special place in O'Brien's thinking. He believed that one of the main causes of the French Revolution was the return from America of French troops who had been exposed to new political ideas. He also thought that Chartism was based on principles that had been established by the American Revolution and clearly enunciated at that time by British radicals, especially Cartwright, whose influential *Take Your Choice* dated from 1776, and members of the Westminster Committee of 1780. O'Brien knew of Cobbett's experiences in America (1792–1800 and 1817–19), for he read Cobbett's works and became acquainted with him soon after moving to London. The point was frequently made in O'Brien's publications that most U.S. states had elements of the Charter already in place. Several of his Chartist allies and acquaintances left Britain for the United States, and sent him information from their new homes, and O'Brien himself considered emigration to America in 1841 and 1843 and again in the mid-1850s and early 1860s. More so in the 1850s and 1860s than earlier, O'Brien was moved by his financial circumstances rather than political principles. He was trapped in poverty and thought it would be easier to support himself and his family in the United States. To his friend Thomas Allsop he mentioned California as a likely destination, or perhaps Virginia, "where good hopes are held out to us by some American gentlemen of influence." It is not clear that this was anything but a vague possibility. O'Brien made no definite plan to leave. He lacked the funds, and by 1862 he thought he should delay in view of the American Civil War. He also wanted to find out if his prospects would be better in Australia than in America.[24]

O'Brien took a keen interest in schemes to set up model communities in America—as may be seen from his coverage of the "Rappist" settlement in Economy, Pennsylvania, and the activities of John Adolphus Etzler.[25] At the end of the 1840s O'Brien became closely involved in arrangements to establish a community in Texas.[26] Although these efforts were later ridiculed by some commentators as naive and "utopian," at the time they were widely commended.[27]

In early 1840 O'Brien and his *Southern Star* became involved in a dispute that highlights the range of opinions about America that could be entertained within the Chartist movement. A proposal had been made for a formal appeal to the president of the United States (this was the fourth year of the presidency of Martin Van Buren). A memorial was to be composed, asking the president to use his friendly influence to intercede with the British government on behalf of the British people, who were suffering under the combined weight of aristocratic misrule and material hardships and who longed to enjoy the same rights and opportunities as the people of America. O'Brien considered this plan worthy of support, but it was strongly opposed. Many Chartists claimed that a memorial would achieve nothing and that the proposal was unwise and possibly illegal. Some thought it would be a sign of weakness to seek outside help. Others insisted that Americans were not outsiders but close kin—by political values as well as blood. There was no consensus. Those who looked to America were outnumbered, on this matter at least, by those who did not. The memorial was not sent, mainly because Chartist leaders, facing persecution, were worried that an appeal to a foreign power would entail serious political and legal ramifications at home.[28]

America offered reference points for reformers in Britain, and O'Brien was quick to elucidate examples and lessons. Was America the land of the free? O'Brien thought so, albeit with a few provisos. He admitted that obstacles to liberty and equality were not easy to break down, even in republican America, but he was confident that the United States pointed the way to a better future for the whole world. Americans had within their reach the peace and happiness that could not be enjoyed anywhere else, especially not in Britain. America had amazing potential, O'Brien insisted. The sharing of property, common access to education, and "equal distribution of enjoyments and of labours" were achievable goals, although there were different ideas about the method to be employed. The Babouvist, for example, would seek to do everything at once, while the Owenite would seek gradual change, one community at a time, setting a good example and relying on persuasion.[29] O'Brien feared that if the gradual method failed, people would give up. They would conclude that equality was impossible to establish. Therefore, he declared, fundamental change could not come only through education and persuasion. Political authority was needed too. O'Brien admired both Babeuf and Owen but decided that in some respects their theories were inadequate. For him, the laws had to be directly made or approved by the people, and popular control over lawmaking was not guaranteed even in systems—like the American—that had elected assemblies.

> The temptations to abuse are too great for any Parliament to withstand. Hence there has hardly ever existed a representative body that has not, at some time or another, prostituted its mission to sinister ends. Even in Republican America the representative chambers are little better than gangs of smooth-tongued lawyers and profit-mongers, who make all the institutions to favour their own class.[30]

One of O'Brien's abiding concerns was to show that political rights, though the priority, would only be a starting point: workers would have to *use* them to change society. In 1837 he argued that if America was ahead of Britain, it still had some way to go. Many could vote, but the society as a whole had not yet resolved the problems posed by a flawed system of property holding:

> BAD PROPERTY INSTITUTIONS . . . allow property to be dishonestly acquired and dishonestly transmitted. 1775 did not change the system of acquiring and transmitting property. It was a mere political revolution. In leaving the institution of property where it found it, it left all the germs of social evil to ripen in the womb of time, and these germs remaining, it was of little consequence what the particular form of government was, or might be.

If there was class struggle in Britain, O'Brien saw it also in America because there, too, the propertied middle classes blocked reform.[31]

In both countries, problems related to control over and access to the land had to be resolved. Discussion of the land question led O'Brien to study the communitarian efforts of Etzler in Pennsylvania and Ohio. O'Brien admired Etzler's *The Paradise within the Reach of All Men*, published in 1833. He considered some of the book's claims extravagant, but shared Etzler's vision of a community based on equal rights. In 1836 O'Brien reflected that people could not be forced to live this way, even if it was the best way (so he veered more toward Owenite than Babouvist tactics). In 1842 O'Brien warmly praised Etzler's book in his *British Statesman* and called the author "one of the greatest benefactors of the present age." He repeated this sentiment the following year in the *Poor Man's Guardian and Repealer's Friend*, which became one of the main organs of Etzler's followers in Britain. O'Brien also published a sixpenny pamphlet, the *Dialogue on Etzler's Paradise*. O'Brien was struck by land reformers' use of the Biblical concept of "jubilee" (which involved the return of land to its original holders, the cancellation of debts, cessation of labor, and freeing of slaves). In 1846 he wrote in support of a group of East Coast reformers in the United States and their creed of communal ownership—in short, "this most glorious of revolutions, the general jubilee for the restitution of the soil to the people."[32] Though conservative versions of "jubilee" vied for acceptance with radical versions, the "jubilee" trope was important in Chartism; and late nineteenth-century debates about land reform in the United States were still being influenced by O'Brien's ideas, most notably through figures such as the writer, economist, and politician Henry George, who had read O'Brien's writings and mixed with O'Brienite emigrants to America.[33]

During the mid-nineteenth century there was, as Reeve Huston describes it, a "scattered and uneven transmission of English agrarianism to the United States" and a "transatlantic culture of land reform." O'Brien was partly responsible for this. He advised land reformers in America and reported on their campaigns in his publications. He was well acquainted with the ideologies upon which they drew (Paine, Spence, Owen, Fourier, St. Simon) and he knew activists who had arrived in America from Britain. They included the aforementioned Thomas Ainge Devyr. Reaching the United States in 1840, Devyr soon took up with George Henry Evans, a journalist and trade unionist who had lived in America since 1820. O'Brien and Evans carried on a correspondence (some of which was published) during the 1840s. Devyr became a champion of the antirent movement, which aimed to break up large estates and redistribute them in sections to the families that farmed them. Evans persuaded him in due course to alter some of his ideas so that they better suited the American context. Believing in an individual's right to as much land as he could properly cultivate, Evans used the vocabulary of republican liberty to make this case. Though he agreed that private property in land was a violation of natural rights theory, he focused more on the claim that Americans should each have enough land to enable them to enjoy liberty. Evans advocated no drastic interference with existing landholding arrangements. Instead, he called for a legal limit on the amount of land that anyone could own, the exemption of a minimum amount from seizure for debt, the allocation of federal lands to settlers free of charge, and a ban on accumulations of more than 160 acres. Devyr approved, and while he continued to use natural law and the labor theory of value in framing his arguments, he accepted Evans's advice that to argue for a redistribution of *all* the land would be to alienate rather than win over public opinion. Devyr was still too extreme for some American land reformers, however, and the latter were already divided among themselves on market forces, legal title, and natural rights.[34]

Transatlantic communication went on, and Devyr has been identified by Mark Lause as the "chief propagandist" for an O'Brienite section of the International Workingmen's Association, established in London in 1864, the year of O'Brien's death. Among the members of this body who reached out most effectively to U.S. colleagues (as was noted at the time by Marx) were two of O'Brien's closest friends, Martin Boon, a mechanic, and George Harris, a bookseller.[35] Clearly, Devyr was closer intellectually to O'Brien than to Evans. Jamie Bronstein has pointed out that O'Brien's ideas about the land (based on public ownership combined with individual cultivation) were unlikely to gain much support in the United States, where private ownership was so entrenched. O'Brien became frustrated when land reformers in America failed to take his counsel. At the same time, some of them did regard him as a guide, and although Bronstein gives useful insights into the interaction between Britain and America on the land question, her sweeping assertion that "leaders in neither country took land reform to its farthest possible conclusion—elimination of private property" is questionable. O'Brien did, and he built up a committed following on both sides of the Atlantic.[36]

O'Brien wrote about the United States in most of his publications. By the 1840s he was engaged in a running commentary on American affairs. In the summer of 1842 it was the Dorr Rebellion in Rhode Island that commanded his attention. The issue at stake was voting rights. Rhode Island had a narrow property-owning franchise dating back to a seventeenth-century charter. The rebellion, led by lawyer and politician Thomas Wilson Dorr, resulted in a reform of the electoral system in 1843. O'Brien approved. Nothing wholesome could come of inadequate representation, he declared, and the linkage of political rights to property qualifications was unacceptable. He found it odd, moreover, that rules in place before the American Revolution—and invalidated by it—could have apologists so many years later. In America of all places, the principle of "one man, one vote" ought not to be disregarded.[37]

Following the U.S. midterm elections of 1846, O'Brien noted that the Whig Party was set to take control of the House of Representatives from the Democrats. He attributed this result to local alliances between Whigs and reform groups that were pressing for democratic rights and new land laws. The antirent movement was of particular importance (tenant resistance to the demands of large landowners had greatest effect in New York state politics at this time). O'Brien reported that reform groups held the balance of power in states that had a wide suffrage. British Chartists could learn from the American reformers:

> They cashier Democrats, when Democrats prove tyrants, and they elect Whigs to fill their places the moment Whigs acknowledge and pledge themselves to what is right and just. Oh, if the Chartists would act this wise and spirited part—if they would discard mere *names* or *sounds* and judge men and parties by their *acts* and *conduct*—how very different would their position soon be!

There was talk that the Whigs disliked taking office with the help of reformers and planned to disfranchise counties where the latter were strong. This, exclaimed O'Brien, would be a mortal offense against the American Republic. It would cause civil war. He urged the reformers to use their leverage. They might wring important concessions from the Whigs, and here was another lesson for radicals at home:

> The same would happen in England, if the English people had votes. Instead of being kicked and bludgeoned, as they now are, at contested elections and at public meetings, when they attempt anything for themselves, they would be courted and caressed by both factions, for the sake of their votes. And if (like the Anti-Renters) they had muskets also, to protect the independence of their votes, there is not a Peer or Commoner in the realm that would not treat them with profound respect.[38]

The rise to popularity of the Chartist Land Plan made O'Brien more determined to influence American opinion. The Land Plan was no good for Britain, he argued, and land reformers in the United States should not approve of it or pursue a similar scheme in their country. It was too conservative. A much more thorough change was needed. Why not nationalization, the centerpiece of the NRL program? Individual smallholdings were recommended by O'Brien even though they were part of the Land Plan, but he added the rider that rents must be devoted to public purposes. He also maintained that the allocation of large tracts was best avoided. Unless it was discontinued, the Americans would run out of land. Despite his best efforts, O'Brien would find that most American land reformers preferred large homesteads and were not greatly concerned about using rents for the public benefit.[39]

O'Brien kept up a regular summary of developments in U.S. politics. During the presidency of John Tyler (1841–45) O'Brien discussed such matters as intervention by the federal government in the individual states and the executive's discretionary power in times of crisis (as with the Dorr Rebellion), the role of ex-presidents (Martin Van Buren and John Quincy Adams), attitudes toward the standing army, Tyler's use of the veto ("It certainly is as strong an act of monarchical authority as could be practiced by any Sovereign of Europe, and may give rise to some alteration in the American Constitution"), economic policy, diplomacy, foreign loans, government waste, municipal politics, and the likely candidates for the presidential election of 1844.[40] During the presidency of James Polk (1845–49), O'Brien continued in this vein, keeping readers informed, in particular, about the relative strengths of the Whig and Democratic parties in specific states.[41] He also inserted items from the American press into his own newspapers.

There was sustained analysis of American affairs in O'Brien's *Power of the Pence* in 1848–49. As was his usual practice, O'Brien wrote less about the apparent shortcomings of America than about the reasons why it was to be admired and emulated. He rejected the negative comments made by high-profile visitors to the

United States, minimized the importance of slavery there, and highlighted only the most favorable evidence provided in travel books, correspondence, and other sources. The *Power of the Pence* did not claim that America was perfect, but it did insist that America proved "the successful results of democratic government in all really essential particulars."[42]

O'Brien thought of America as synonymous with progress. The benefits of democracy were spreading; the comforts of life were increasing; sound opinions and habits were rapidly gaining ground. In America people of different classes mixed together and education, religion, and social relations all had their basis in equality. A free press and public schooling meant that the diffusion of knowledge was unhindered, which also facilitated constant scrutiny of the government by the people. "The American feels all the pride and dignity of a freeman," O'Brien argued, "whilst the Englishman feels and knows, when he thinks at all, that he is kept in leading-strings, lest he should become mischievous." People who did not choose their own government lacked spirit, energy, talent, and aspiration. This was Britain's curse and America's advantage. Out of self-government arose greater patriotism and unity and higher moral standards, seen in the respect for women, religious toleration, charity, dress and dwellings, physical health, low rate of criminality, protection from "cruel and unusual" punishments, and intellectual elevation that characterized American society.[43]

Unfortunately, there were dangers posed by landed and moneyed elites and the United States still had some distance to go, but O'Brien claimed that the Americans were much further down the road to true liberty than were the British. Every day, more Americans were joining in reform campaigns and thinking the right way about political change, "free institutions" and "national education," the land, taxation, public services, currency and credit, monopolies, employment laws, the liberty of the press, the judicial system and penal code, and war.[44]

In one of his long and detailed essays, "The Testimony of European Writers on America," O'Brien offered a précis that reflected his own predilections. In this selective reading of well-known texts, he posited a "uniformity of opinion" on the impact of democracy and made connections between the United States and a Europe in which the 1848 revolutions were (O'Brien hoped) opening the way for political and social improvement. Among the comments of non-British writers, O'Brien was particularly drawn to those of Alexis de Tocqueville, Friedrich von Raumer, and Michel Chevalier. The French historian, philosopher, and politician Tocqueville visited America in 1831–32 and published *Democracy in America* in two volumes, in 1835 and 1840 (and his work is still appreciated as one of the shrewdest insights into U.S. political culture and social life that has ever been written). Von Raumer, the German historian and statesman, visited America in 1841–43 and 1853–55. His *The United States of North America*, published in two volumes in 1845, compared the U.S. Constitution with Europe's differing polities and analyzed American religious movements, political parties, and foreign policy. Chevalier, the French engineer, statesman, and economist, visited America in the early 1830s and published *Society, Manners, and Politics in the United States: Being a Series of Letters on North America* in 1834.

O'Brien was adamant:

> All the writers upon America agree in testifying to the vast superiority of the Americans over the people of the old world in material comfort, intelligence, and independence. De Tocqueville, Von Raumer, Chevalier, and a host of continental writers attribute this to the effects of democratic institutions and laws; and there can be no doubt that their writings have powerfully contributed to bring about the recent glorious events in France, Germany, and Italy. . . . Our principal English writers concur in this opinion; and all of them speak in glowing terms of the comfort and prosperity of the American people.

Even antidemocratic writers could not overturn the respect that was America's due. Indeed, if anything, their remarks reinforced rather than eroded that respect. O'Brien included Frances Trollope, Thomas Hamilton, Frederick Marryat, Charles Dickens, and Charles Lyell in this group.[45] In each case, he contended, the censure was less consequential than the praise, and for every negative remark O'Brien had an offsetting explanation. For example, Mrs. Trollope was describing a society that no longer existed, for America had changed since her time there; she failed to substantiate her claim that the U.S. political system would not suit other nations; and the prosperity she saw in America certainly *would* suit other nations. Hamilton's idea that this prosperity rested upon an abundance of land and would diminish with population growth was incorrect, because thinly populated countries were not necessarily prosperous (as exemplified by Russia). His strictures against the American system of government, moreover, proceeded from a misunderstanding of the U.S. Constitution, and his complaints about the quality of public men in America could just as easily be made about Britain. Marryat, though an opponent of democracy, could not deny that some institutions tended more toward the comfort of the people than others, and that local self-government in the United States was a definite boon. The logical corollary of this, O'Brien asserted, was that other elements of democracy had the same outcome. As for Dickens, O'Brien sided with those who read him as more of a friend than an enemy to America, and Lyell's aversion to popular suffrage had to be balanced against his recognition that, in America, it was a buttress for religious toleration and mass education, and that the United States might not have advanced so far under a nondemocratic form of government.

Turning to writers who were not unfavorable to democracy, O'Brien gave their opinions an enthusiastic endorsement. In this group he included James Stuart, Harriet Martineau, James Silk Buckingham, and George Warburton.[46] Stuart approved of manhood suffrage and offices open to talent, argued that the U.S. Congress was more effective and dignified than the British Parliament, and saw America as superior to Britain in terms of living standards, morality, education, and respect for the law.

> Mr. Stuart vigorously defends the Americans from most of the charges brought against them by hostile English writers, and exposes the despotic character of the British government, the ignorance and bigotry of British statesmen, and the awful consequences of British misrule; but he acknowledges the pernicious effects of slavery upon the character and condition of the free people in the slave states.

Martineau noted the independence and prosperity of the American people, and the absence of servility, insolence, ignorance, and poverty. Buckingham thought that in their physical, moral, and mental condition, Americans had surpassed the people of Britain and that this was largely attributable to their system of government, and although Warburton was no admirer of republics, O'Brien highlighted his confession that America's rate of progress was faster than Britain's.[47]

O'Brien responded to anti-American material, therefore, by attempting to mitigate it or by casting it aside. This activity was becoming all the more needful. Allan Nevins has shown that defenders of America came under increasing pressure after the 1820s. Compared to earlier decades, when most British visitors to America had been complimentary, this was a time when the approach was less so. The context was changing. Transatlantic travel was easier, new types of visitor arrived in the United States, and there was greater knowledge and more discussion of American politics and society. A growing amount of negative comment about America created the impression there that this was the norm for British visitors, but

Nevins suggests that Americans who took this view made a misjudgment. Rejection of negative accounts of America by such commentators as O'Brien appears to fit the pattern described by Nevins, whereby a reaction against this negativity (a negativity cultivated mainly by antireformers) was prompted by political events in Britain, evidence of America's wealth and power, and an awareness that previous insults and complaints had stirred up tension between the two nations.[48]

There are not many disparaging statements about the United States in the *Power of the Pence*. Those that do appear relate mainly to inequalities of wealth and property; politicians who did not care about the general good; greed and patronage in legislative bodies and in the private companies that provided public services; delay and confusion in the funding of improvement schemes and the disposal of public lands; an unclear division of responsibility on some matters between the individual states and the federal government; inadequate newspaper support for radical reform, despite a free press; underspending on poor relief, the penal system, and the courts; and tax laws that did not distinguish between productive and unproductive property.[49] But all this pales into insignificance in comparison with the admiring, celebratory, and commendatory remarks that O'Brien published.

He had no doubt that American democracy provided a model for Britain. "It is the mission of democracy to introduce an entirely new system of society, in which mankind will advance to a state of real, instead of nominal, liberty, equality, and fraternity." America had taken this path. O'Brien denied that conducive social conditions there were simply attributable to its small population and abundant land. He also rejected the claim that as America became more densely populated its citizens would discard democracy and imitate Europe by opting for aristocratic and monarchical institutions. The truth was that America's happiness and prosperity were the results of "the excellent constitution and laws which emanate from popular representation and government." America used to be like Britain, O'Brien wrote. It had exhibited "the ancient form of society," one based on coercion and custom, with the many kept poor and subordinated by the few who enjoyed land, wealth, and luxury. This type of society could not stand up to "impartial examination." Its flaws had become well known, and if anybody wished to learn more about rights, interests, and duty, America was the place to look.

> It is but three score years ago that a new community on the other side of the Atlantic recognized the fundamental right of the people to appoint their own rulers to office and to remove them from office, as well as that other invaluable right of every

> citizen to be chosen to any, even the very highest, office in the gift of all. It was but yesterday our eyes saw the luminous political example of America followed by a procession of all the enlightened countries on the continent of Europe, under the lead of Republican France. And now is the time at last, when, having secured the first great step in the movement onward and upward, we are to engage ourselves in consolidating that invaluable possession, and also begin to extend our vision to the ultimate object of a social revolution.

Democratic republican institutions offered the framework, and without the appropriate political system no nation could enjoy lasting prosperity, peace, liberty, and justice. Democracy was pointless if it did not remove physical want and promote moral and intellectual progress.[50]

O'Brien's notion of "democracy" rested heavily on egalitarian and communitarian principles, the rights of labor, and a belief in social welfare provisions. Many people in America, he wrote, shared these values and commitments, and some were living them out; but O'Brien also recognized the majority's attachment to economic competition and private property—to what was unregulated, selfish, excessive, and destructive. In O'Brien's opinion, democracy should mean that the choices open to people were always on the increase. Through choice, under a government that emanated from the people, rights would have their correct basis and liberty and property would become available to everyone. O'Brien wanted it to be clearly understood that "by each person being allowed to work out his own individual interest, the interests of all are woefully sacrificed, as no man can gain his interest beyond a certain point without abstracting from others a share of their just dues." There were Americans who knew this, which augured well for "a fairer distribution of fortune's favours."[51]

Evidence that America's system of government was more efficient and less expensive than Britain's was often used by British radicals to highlight the need for reform at home. O'Brien offered many illustrations. In December 1848 he focused on the Royal Mint, which made and issued coin (as a government monopoly) and was central to the financial operations of the British state. In the United States, coin was made and issued much more cheaply, and the whole of government was more cost-effective because salaries were properly in line with service. In Britain, huge sums were paid to functionaries who served no useful purpose. Other examples of America's superiority over Britain included a legal system in which the courts were more accessible and justice was administered cheaply and efficiently; a tax burden that fell primarily on the land; religious freedom; a free press and easy access to education, which facilitated the spread of knowledge; freedom of expression and association; public works such as canals and railways (O'Brien stressed that although individual states took on debt to pay for these, they soon became valuable assets and yielded revenue that could be used for other public purposes and to keep taxes low); social mobility and rewards for talent and aspiration; a wider diffusion of wealth, aided by sensible property laws (no entails, the transference of land between individuals at little expense, the division of the property of intestates); an abundance of land, which added to the ease and independence of life and created opportunities for employment; a multitude of small, owner-occupied farms that were more productive overall than Britain's agricultural system; higher moral standards, linked with political and social equality and the rejection of monarchical and aristocratic values; and authentic self-government, with representative organs and a rational federal system that O'Brien thought would suit Britain and its empire. In his articles about the blessings of democracy and the constitutional, social, and political differences between America and Britain, the latter came off worse every time. "It would be wonderful indeed," O'Brien commented, "if a people who governed themselves did not secure the general welfare; and it would be equally astonishing if we found, under the English or any similar government, an intelligent, moral, and prosperous people."[52]

In 1833 O'Brien had expressed concern that antagonism in the United States over economic policy and states' rights would give encouragement to the defamers of America and democracy (it was a gift to "despots" and "usurers").[53] This remained a problem for many decades. As Simon Morgan observes, "American protectionism posed a dilemma for those whose promotion of free trade was accompanied by a belief in the benefits of democracy." High U.S. tariffs were condemned by many in Britain, but some claimed that America was not to blame. They argued that America was only responding to the policy of its main trading partner Britain, where a selfish, landowning, aristocratic Parliament was clinging to such outmoded measures as the Corn Laws (which, by keeping out American grain, caused the United States to maintain barriers against British manufactures). Others did blame America for its protectionist stance, citing the flaws of democracy and presenting a picture of "a fragile Union, riddled with sectionalism," with contention over slavery as well as tariffs inhibiting progress.[54]

O'Brien often reminded his readers that events in America had an impact in Britain. He was eager to clarify the effect of gold discoveries in California on trade and the currency, for instance. In 1849, when promoting his "National Reform" propositions, he reiterated that using gold as a standard of value damaged living standards and corrupted commerce. He hoped that currency reformers in America as well as Britain would get the message.[55] This followed O'Brien's earlier coverage of reform associations in New York and other states, which had campaigned for changes in banking, credit, currency, and business (on some specifics, O'Brien thought, they did not go far enough); and his articles on tariff disputes and periods of "financial gloom" in the United States, as in 1842, when he analyzed the indebtedness of the federal and some state governments. The struggle between free traders and protectionists, and discord about the best way to maximize corn and cotton production and the output of other commodities, seemed to O'Brien to be getting away from the main point: for the American democratic experiment to succeed over the long term, the appropriate social and economic practices and structures had to be put in place. Special interests had to be restrained. America had the opportunity. The prospects for reform were better there than elsewhere.[56]

On urbanization, communications, and infrastructure, O'Brien took an equally clear position. Noting the calls for railway regulation in Britain, he suggested that American practice regarding public works was superior and that Americans were increasingly motivated by the principle that essential services should be performed by public bodies at public expense. Allowing private companies to intervene had created a "mass of plunder," and journalists, reformers, and legislators in several U.S. states were beginning to change things. O'Brien gave plentiful column space in his *Power of the Pence* to debates in America about the funding and management of internal improvements and the disposal of the public lands, and when comparing American and British cities he stressed that local taxes in the former were invariably lower, even though their expenses were high (for "paving, draining, cleansing, lighting, and watching"), and that most of these expenses were covered by the owners rather than the occupiers of urban property.[57]

Another discussion thread in the *Power of the Pence* brought together colonialism, land policy, and political institutions, principally with respect to Canada. O'Brien sympathized with Canadian complaints about British rule and contrasted Canada with the adjacent United States. In America, when a new territory was organized and settled, public lands were reserved to provide a source of revenue or used in some other way that benefited the people, irrespective of sect or party; but in Canada, one-seventh of all land was "given to an ecclesiastical fraction of the community, possessing no apparent claims above their neighbours." In America, the people could control their own affairs. Most issues were dealt with at the local level. Other matters had to go to Congress, but each state had its representatives in Congress and they could attend to local needs there. Canada had no representatives in the Parliament at Westminster, however, and its internal affairs were subject to the whims of the British government. Leaders of parties and sects in Canada could gain "all the pickings of the state" by colluding with and recommending particular policies to that government. In America people and legislature were one, but in Canada this was not the case. Indeed, the imperial Parliament did not know or understand the people of Canada. A related problem was the cost of administration in Canada, where the salary of the governor-general, for example, was about 50 percent higher than the salary of the U.S. president. Canada was plagued by "foolish laws," unlike America, where the people who had to obey the laws played a part in making them. To O'Brien, a sure sign of the unfortunate situation of Canada was the fact that British investors preferred the United States. He agreed with one Canadian journal that the best course for Canada was neither separation from Britain nor incorporation into the United States, but greater autonomy. O'Brien believed that the people of Canada should be in charge of their own trade, revenue, land, education, and public works.[58]

He was uneasy about the fondness for military aggression evinced by some American politicians and supported the agitation against the Mexican War of 1846–48. In the United States (as elsewhere) it seemed, most people had more sense than those who presumed to lead them. O'Brien wrote that America was not being well served by its statesmen, for "there is not a great national question upon which the two principal parties in the United States are completely antagonized. It follows that the contest between them is for the offices only in most instances." The annexation of Texas and war with Mexico were not opposed by the Whigs "as a party . . . although many Whigs, and but few Democrats, raised objections."[59] In the early 1840s O'Brien had reported on the struggle for Texas with some disquiet (there was a Mexican invasion in 1842 as tension mounted following the Texan declaration of independence from Mexico in 1836). During 1846 and 1847, as he reported on the progress of U.S. arms against the Mexicans, he lamented the detrimental impact of the war on American politics and society. Reform, he feared, would be impeded. Americans enjoyed a wide suffrage, but what good was that if it was not used to determine the course of government policy? O'Brien asserted that the U.S. soldiers risking their lives for Mexican land would not get to own any of this land. They would do better to return home and demand new laws in America, so that land went only to settlers and not to speculators and entrepreneurs.

> A strange animal is man! For the priest-ridden slave of monarchical Europe there may be many excuses made. There is no excuse at all for the Republican of America. Born and bred a free man, he renounces his own birthright in the land of his home and becomes the hired slave of tyrants, to help them to rob others of their birthright abroad. There is no excuse for such a man. He deserves to die as he has chosen to live—a landless, graceless slave.

The Mexican War was like other wars. The productive classes were tricked into fighting for the benefit of the landed and moneyed elites.[60]

In this period the United States and Britain clashed over the Maine and Oregon boundaries. O'Brien was angered by the quibbling and posturing that delayed the settlement of these disputes and relieved when treaties were agreed. He much preferred mutually beneficial interaction between Britain and America to accusation and conflict (and one of the reasons why he admired Owen was because of the latter's efforts to prevent war and promote friendship between the two nations).[61]

Remarkably, there was little in O'Brien's writings on America about black slavery. He mentioned it infrequently, and only in passing. It came into his coverage of the Dorr Rebellion because he saw parallels between restrictions on voting in Rhode Island and the denial of rights to slaves in the American South. For some in America, evidently, "the people" meant only "a majority of the white population." O'Brien stood for a democratic suffrage, though he did not explicitly approve of black voting. He went no further than to opine that "if property be no qualification, or the want of it a disqualification, surely the colour of one's skin should be even less so! Slavery is a sad blot on the American character. What inconsistencies the defence of it gets them into." Later he participated in a debate about whether or not, in view of slavery, the United States could properly be called "a democracy." Hoping for land reform in America, O'Brien asserted in 1846 that "land freedom" was the only way to ensure other types of freedom—and independence from "money-mongers"—and he rejoiced that American reformers were protesting against "wage slavery." "Yes, men of England, and men of America! *Wages*-slavery is, in its results, ten thousand times more horrible than *chattel*-slavery. It has killed millions, where the other has but killed its thousands." All the same, O'Brien was not unmoved by the plight of blacks in America. He included a piece on "Slave Auction Scenes" in his *National Reformer and Manx Weekly Review* early in 1847, reprinted extracts from a biography of runaway slave and abolitionist leader Frederick Douglass, and condemned the design to extend slave cultivation in territory wrested from Mexico. Joining in a controversy over the sale in Mississippi of a boy with blue eyes, auburn hair, and a pale complexion, O'Brien wrote:

> The public press have levelled their stoutest exclamation points at this transaction, while the sale of millions of darker hue has escaped their inky bayonets. Why is this? If any kind of slavery is sanctioned by the Scriptures, it is white slavery. There were probably far more slaves of very light complexion, with auburn hair and blue eyes, in the day of Christ and His apostles, than of those of African descent. We should as lief see a white man sold as a black man.[62]

To many Chartists who professed feelings of solidarity with workers in the United States, and admiration for the American political system, slavery was a source of regret. In fact, slavery was a divisive issue in Chartism. While some expressed sympathy for the abolitionist cause and claimed that America's acceptance of slavery brought shame upon its people and institutions, others thought that time and energy would be better spent on combating "slavery" at home. O'Brien was in the latter camp. He condemned the leaders of the antislavery movement in Britain for ignoring the misery of the laboring poor, the wage slaves who knew only toil and pain. State and society could not function without them, and Britain's purportedly "civilized" and "respectable" antislavery spokesmen were really part of the apparatus that kept the workers down. In Britain, O'Brien argued, the employer noticed his "slaves" only when he needed them. In America, a slave master had to support his slaves whether he had work for them or not, and emancipation would enable the master to get more labor at a lower cost. O'Brien hardly referred to American slavery in the *Power of the Pence*. He counseled emigrants from Britain to avoid the slave states, presumably because they would have difficulty finding work where they had to compete with slaves. Noting the lack of genuine disagreement on slavery between the Democratic and Whig parties, he added that politicians tended not to get elected if they openly opposed slavery (he suggested that this might change as the populations of the northern states expanded). He gave column space to both pro- and antislavery opinions expressed by British visitors to the United States, but he did express the hope that slavery would be excluded from the new states in the West and eventually abolished throughout America, and he reported that liberty was more restricted in the slave states ("Slave-holding needs sedition laws for its support like those of England"). Nevertheless, O'Brien considered slavery in America a relatively unimportant matter and was rarely firm or categorical when objecting to it.[63]

Antislavery groups in Britain and America did not always agree with each other, and the abolitionist cause divided British radicalism during the nineteenth century. O'Brien's position was not that of all radicals. Iain McCalman has shown that for some activists, hostility to chattel slavery was a *core part* of their political radicalism, that this tendency was present in Chartism, and that different combinations of Spencean, Cobbettite, O'Brienite, and other arguments could result in different levels of opposition to slavery. To many radicals "liberty" was for all, whatever their race and location, and black slaves and British workers had common problems. The passing of time, McCalman thinks, brought "less the emergence of a new, pervasive class-conscious hostility to abolitionism than a persistence of the old ideological diversity."[64]

After 1849 one of O'Brien's main outlets was *Reynolds's Newspaper*, which admired and flattered America, though it also attacked slavery and complained that slavery damaged America's reputation. This was an O'Brienite claim. Another tie-in with O'Brien was *Reynolds's Newspaper*'s condemnation of British abolitionists who showed sympathy for blacks in America but none for the laboring poor at home.[65]

In challenging the abolitionists of their own time, O'Brien and other radical spokesmen were dismissing abolitionism as a selective response to labor exploitation. Yet the basis of their position is not absolutely clear, raising the questions posed by Thomas Haskell:

> Did labor leaders work from a more advanced humanitarian perspective that really assigned equal importance to all varieties of exploitation, whether of slave or free labor . . . or did they simply assign a higher priority to the problems of wage laborers (nearby and racially similar) than to those of enslaved laborers (far away and racially different)? To what extent was the workingman's criticism of abolitionism a pragmatic tactic for drawing attention to his own cause rather than a considered judgment of the equivalence of the exploitation in the two cases?

Greater clarity emerged from the 1840s, in a theoretical framework that included a view of suffering that was wider than that of the abolitionists, but Haskell warns against taking the arguments of "a few extreme figures" as the norm. Some contemporaries might have accepted these arguments, but some did not, and the reasons why these choices were made are open to debate. Malcolm Chase has pointed to an element of racism in Chartism, seen in attitudes toward Jews and Negroes and especially in the equivocation over slavery. Equating the labor system in the American South with the "wage slavery" in Britain's factories was, Chase thinks, a "clumsy association," and reflects ignorance of the real condition of slaves in America.[66]

Allegations of exploitation and solicitude for the rights of labor often featured in polemical discourse, travel writings, and other forms of cultural and political interaction between Britain and America. "Wage slavery" was just one of a broader set of ideas about the nature of work, ideas in which class and race played an influential but flexible role.[67] American attitudes might have overlapped with, but they also differed from, those expressed by British observers like O'Brien, and British observers sometimes misunderstood American circumstances. British radical perspectives on this, as Chase suggests, were affected by racial prejudice and ignorance of American slaves' real-life experiences. Even so, as British knowledge of America increased during the nineteenth century and transatlantic communication had greater effect, opinions about work, liberty, class, and race could more easily pass back and forth.

Most white Americans did not think in terms of economically defined classes, and U.S. political parties did not pursue specific class aims. There were labor disputes, and class language was used by some participants, but class allegiance mattered more in Britain. Popular participation in organized politics came earlier in the United States than in Britain. The wide suffrage, decentralized government, and locally based mass parties in the United States brought American workers into politics as neighborhood and ethnic groups rather than as an economic class.[68] Meanwhile, within British radicalism, disadvantages attaching to race were usually regarded as less immediate and urgent than those relating to class. By the mid-nineteenth century racism was probably increasing in British society, strengthened by contemporary debates about status and hierarchy. There was an acceptance and even, by some, an active defense of distinctions of rank.[69] Class consciousness accentuated British workers' compassion for slaves in America, as an oppressed labor force, but it might also have encouraged them to concentrate more on winning victories for themselves at home. Some were simply not interested in the lot of America's slaves. Some were racist. Yet there was no dramatic rise in discrimination against acculturated blacks in Britain in the mid-nineteenth century; and if class was more important than race, blacks could have been regarded and treated as individuals according to their perceived class status. Historians have pointed out that there was no single "black experience" in Britain, and considerable resistance to racism. They have also highlighted the distinctions made between slaves in the United States and the natives who fought wars against the British in Africa (African chieftains were well received when they visited Britain).[70] Racist ideology and behavior were more typical in the empire than in Britain. Controversies about race were heightened in the multiracial colonies and in relation to Britain's imperial policy. Still, it is likely that in Britain, in some circles (radical or otherwise), racial and class attitudes could merge and support each other.

British admirers of the United States found it difficult to discuss slavery without contradicting their praise for America. This was true of many Chartists. The way individuals regarded slavery in America depended on time, place, and circumstance, and the motives of those who visited and wrote about what they saw in America were varied, as were the levels of antislavery conviction. "It appears that many travelers felt a sense of obligation to jot down a few perfunctory words about the intrinsic injustice of the institution," writes Thomas Murphy, "only to move on swiftly to another topic." Abolitionism gained adherents, primarily for moral but also for economic reasons (the assumed inefficiency of slave as opposed to free labor), and there was a consensus that slavery was an evil. But the responsibility for it was sometimes transferred. Since Europeans had started the transatlantic slave trade, it was reasoned, guilt could be redirected toward Europe. Murphy also notes that slavery was romanticized. The inference was that conditions for the slaves were not so bad and that most slaves were happy and well looked after. Here was "a means of either coping with or rationalizing patent contradictions in American republicanism or of smoothing over some of the associative responsibility for slavery in America carried from Europe."[71] One effect was the reinforcing of British radicals' wish and ability to prevent slavery from getting in the way of their pro-American eulogies.

Before repeal of the Corn Laws in 1846 there was an argument that American slavery was being sustained by the self-interested aristocratic government of Britain. By allowing cotton in and keeping corn out, this government was diverting capital from the expanding farmlands of the American Northwest to the plantations of the southern slave states. For many radicals, though, it was the role of America in discussion of the pros and cons of manhood suffrage that mattered most. The clash of ideas about race in the mid-nineteenth century prompted quarreling over the status of blacks in a white-dominated democracy. Did a democratic suffrage mean a nonracial suffrage, or was meritocratic selection for the vote necessary? To some observers, as Richard Huzzey has demonstrated, "the frailties of whiteness made it a poor test of political responsibility." Once the claim was accepted that rights must be restricted for the general good, the question resolved itself into the matter of how best to define and impose qualifications.[72] In 1847 the *Northern Star* was moved to comment that the U.S. polity was excellent *except* for the denial of the vote to free blacks.[73] This highlights again one of the main difficulties faced by British radicals as they tried to use America in their campaign for reform at home.

O'Brien's concept of wage slavery was part of a worldview in which all forms of wealth, privilege, and power belonged to the wrong people. One of his clearest statements about this seminal predicament came in an article of March 1849. O'Brien stated that the consolidation of farms and enclosure of common lands "stand, undoubtedly, at the head of the list" of the "principal causes of the rapid decline of the British working classes, relatively to the higher and middle, during the last century." He then embarked on an analysis taking in British and international history, Britain's national debt and other financial arrangements, the land question, wars and taxes, labor, trade and imperialism, class oppression, and the inadequacy of prevailing institutions (including political parties). One of the key passages in the article was as follows:

> The ejection of the small farmers and labourers from the soil, gave to the manufacturing and mercantile classes an inexhaustible supply of slaves. The produce of these slaves' labour, aided by machinery and steam power, glutted the markets of the world. New markets had to be found; our empire was extended by the annexation of new colonies; to secure these, and to force a trade on new tribes and remote regions, our naval armaments were carried to an unprecedented extent. The result of all is, the richest aristocracy, moneyed and landed, in the world—the most numerous and opulent middle class, in proportion to the population—and the most overworked, oppressed, and despised labouring population on the face of the earth.[74]

Slavery in America did not strike O'Brien as being any more evil or inappropriate than wage slavery in Britain. One of the premises of his series on "The Rise,

Progress, and Phases of Human Slavery" of 1849–50 was that "chattel-slavery, with all its abominations, is less destructive of life, liberty, and happiness than the wages-slavery of modern proletarianism."[75]

Few visitors' accounts of America failed to mention slavery and racism, and in the 1840s and 1850s there were British observers who predicted that the slave states would eventually secede from the Union.[76] Discussion of American slavery was complicated by quarrels between British and U.S. abolitionists and by splits within the British antislavery movement, and another talking point was the economic strength of Britain's colonies in the West Indies, which faced an awkward transition from slave to free labor after 1833. America's victory in the War of Independence had removed from British politics the American lobby that previously defended slavery in alliance with the West Indian planters. J. P. Greene points out that in America the U.S. Constitution, by preserving local autonomy (a bedrock of "English liberty overseas"), made easier the defense of slavery. Peter Onuf stresses the American zeal for property rights, including the right to own slaves. By O'Brien's day, the rise of the United States had vindicated the claim that there could be no liberty without property (and as Onuf explains, "The democratic devolution of authority to local governments and ultimately to slave-owners themselves reinforced the link between liberty and slavery").[77]

This ideological ferment affected British attitudes. The economic and imperial aspects made for confusion and discord because the quickening shift from one kind of empire to another—from mercantilist policies, colonies under close economic control, and the empire as a regulated trading bloc, to freer trade and an outward focus—was problematic. It was not clear what the empire would look like in the future, which had repercussions for Britain's own political and economic prospects. American as well as British observers were aware of this. They were acutely aware also that the West Indies went into economic decline after the abolition of slavery there. If in some circumstances free labor was *not* more efficient than slave labor, abolitionism would lose one of its main props; and reliance only on moral and humanitarian arguments against slavery was insufficient when claims could be made about the welfare provisions made by slave owners across the American South, as opposed to the retreat from paternalism of employers in industrial Britain, and about slaves being fed, employed, and civilized in the United States, which had not been their lot back in Africa. Seymour Drescher has demonstrated not only that the condition of Britain's "ex-slave colonies" was a deterrent to change for slave owners in the United States (and Cuba and Brazil), but also that racist assumptions were stimulated as commentators tried to explain why Britain's experiment in emancipation could not be judged an economic success.[78]

Disagreement about slavery among British Chartists did not diminish. There were Chartists who believed in a common cause. Since nobody could be free without the appropriate entitlements, especially the vote and education, it did not seem incongruous to demand these things for the black labor force of the American South as well as for the British working class. Despite this, many Chartists continued to treat American slavery as a side issue. To them, the focus had to be on the fight for popular rights at home. To bring in extraneous goals would be a hindrance. Yet the abolition of slavery in the empire in 1833 did have an impact on Chartist thinking because it was related to domestic problems that concerned them directly. Abolition featured in discussions about Britain's economic strengths and weaknesses; and the price of sugar, for example, was both a major political and economic issue and a central point in discussion about working-class living standards. Reports that wages in the West Indies were rapidly increasing led British labor to complain all the more about its straitened circumstances and reinforced Chartist animosity toward the affluent middle-class and aristocratic leadership of the British antislavery movement. By the early 1840s it was not uncommon for Chartists to disrupt antislavery meetings in Britain. Instead of looking across the Atlantic, they argued, something ought to be done first for the "slaves" at home. Such claims were likely to gather more support when combined with the racist ideas that gained a purchase in this era.[79]

During the late 1840s the *Northern Star* highlighted the "deplorable state" of "our West Indian colonies," which it linked with the amendment of the sugar duties (after 1846 the West Indies lost their protected status). Parliament had not thought the matter through with sufficient care, another proof that it was not fit for purpose; and the influence of both the "Anti-Slavery party" and the "Free Trade party" had been shown up for what it was, selfish and destructive. The *Northern Star* did not deny "the horrible cruelties and gross immoralities of slavery," but its main target was the British state.

> If England still retain its horror of slavery and slave-grown sugar, let us discourage these things in every possible shape.... If the Legislature is not prepared to do this, if cheap sugar is more important than the Suppression of the Slave Trade, then we say it is bound to act distinctly, unequivocally, and consistently upon that principle.

To the *Northern Star* the solution was obvious: abandon the naval patrols off the coast of Africa, which had signally failed to inhibit the slave trade, and allow the West Indies to get their labor "where they can, how they can, and at any price they can."

> Perhaps there is not a single instance in the whole history of our extravagance and folly, which more aptly demonstrates the reckless and insane manner in which we squander public money, and the pretences upon which we are induced to do so, than that of the Blockading Squadron on the African coast.

Antislavery activists liked to appear moral and philanthropic, but their intent was to pour out the people's treasure "in support of their Utopian and impracticable crotchets." The squadron cost about £1.25 million a year, and this on top of the £20 million set aside to compensate West Indian planters for the abolition of slavery, "every shilling of the interest of which has to be paid by the English labourer before he can receive a farthing of wages for himself." The time had come for a fresh approach. The *Northern Star* did not wish for a reestablishment of slavery in Britain's colonies (the dignity of labor had to be universally upheld). Rather, "the experiment of free labour" had to be given "a fair trial . . . in such a way as effectually to extinguish the slave trade."

> The money now most wastefully expended upon the African squadron, if applied for a few years to promote the immigration of free negroes to our own colonies, under arrangements which would secure just and humane treatment, would not only—if all parties went to work in good faith—save these colonies, but relieve this country from a useless and heavy burden.

The burden, taking into account indirect as well as direct costs, was at least £50 million.

> What might have been done with such a sum? What schools might have been built and endowed; what wastes and bogs reclaimed; what a healthy, prosperous, and happy yeomanry created! What harassing, oppressive, and unjust taxation reduced! But while pauperism and poverty have been stalking rampant among our own labouring population—while ignorance and want have degenerated into brute apathy, or active criminality—while workhouses, hospitals, and prisons have

> overflowed with the ever-increasing tide of destitution, disease, and vice—the Government and Legislature have gone on and mean now to go on . . . in this most wanton, mischievous, and profligate manner.[80]

Remarks like these helped to shape the framework within which O'Brien's ideas about slavery in America and "wage slavery" in Britain could evolve and be understood. Some connections between political struggles in Britain and events in the empire also had their effect. Abolitionists became more of an electoral force in Britain after a slave rebellion in Jamaica in 1831 and the passing of the Reform Act of 1832, and quarreling about the abolition of slavery in 1833 coincided with debates about factory legislation. While factory reformers used antislavery rhetoric to win backing for their cause, evidence about the distress of British factory operatives was used by the opponents of slave emancipation (life expectancy among slaves in the West Indies was revealed to be much higher than for workers in the manufacturing towns of Lancashire and Yorkshire). The New Poor Law of 1834 intensified the acrimony. Stigmatizing pauperism and restricting relief, it was regarded by British workers as a disgraceful piece of class legislation. Meanwhile, the £20 million awarded by Parliament as compensation to the West Indian interests was three times the sum spent in 1833 on relieving the poor. The total revenue of the British state was only about £50 million, meaning that the compensation would entail more public debt. The government was accused of taxing the British poor to pay for emancipation. In addition to all this, the theory that free labor was more efficient than slave labor was challenged, and, as economic problems mounted in the West Indies and the sugar duties were included in analyses of prices and consumption in Britain and the revenue needs of the British government, bolder statements could be made about the suitability of slave labor for particular regions and climates. Abolitionists had denied that working conditions and living standards in Britain had any relevance to the debate about colonial slavery, but in the 1840s it became more difficult for them to answer their critics, especially the many who insisted that the plight of British labor should be addressed first, before anything more was done about the West Indies.[81] Slavery was obviously a sensitive issue for O'Brien. In his determination to strengthen America as an ideal, a motivating force, and a rhetorical device for use in reform struggles at home, he was not unwilling to excuse certain things in order to do this.

The career in America of a former colleague of O'Brien, John Campbell, illustrates the often complicated intermingling of ideas about class and race, and while O'Brien never adopted an overtly racist position, Campbell emphatically did. Born in Ireland, Campbell was a weaver in Manchester by the mid-1830s and active in radical politics by 1840. He rose through the ranks in the Chartist movement, having attached himself to O'Brien, but then he turned against O'Brien after the latter's breach with O'Connor and the National Charter Association. In 1843 Campbell relocated to America. He became a labor leader and bookseller in Philadelphia. Formerly an opponent of black slavery in America, Campbell changed his mind as debates about race and immigration intensified and as the 1848 revolutions in Europe seemed to open up new political possibilities. The "producer versus nonproducer" analysis he had learned from O'Brien was retained, but in America Campbell altered the categories. The natural laziness and inferiority of Africans, he decided, placed blacks in America among the idle nonproducers who lived off the labor of the producing classes. He was still the enemy of political, social, and economic inequality, but now he understood it differently. Andrew Heath has suggested that Campbell's ideological shift was motivated in part by personal ambition—he wanted to gain attention and influence—and by his bond with Irish immigrants who were prejudiced against blacks. "Taking as an axiom that the true source of wealth lay in labor," Heath comments, "workingmen and their allies endeavored to divide the world into the productive and the idle, a task that against the backdrop of tumultuous national and international events forced them to grapple with questions of ethnicity, race, and slavery in often unpredictable ways."[82]

After the regular discussion of America in the *Power of the Pence* in 1848–49, there were further points of contact between O'Brien and the United States. In his next journalistic venture, the *Social Reformer,* he offered advice to prospective emigrants to the United States; publicized the North Texas Colonization Society; inserted letters from American correspondents and added comments of his own; stressed the futility of mere "organic, financial or fiscal" reforms in America as well as in Britain; and held up the United States as a model for the new Europe that he hoped would emerge after the 1848 revolutions.[83]

America was frequently discussed in those pieces O'Brien wrote in 1849–50 that were republished later in a single volume. He repeated his positive assessment of the U.S. system of government—its structure and the theories behind it—while pointing out that America was "incomplete and unfinished" and that the program of the National Reform League would bring improvements there just as in Britain and Europe.

> It is the land and money laws of a country that must ever mainly determine the social condition of its people. In other words, without just agrarian and commercial laws—laws that shall establish for all classes equal rights to the soil and equal advantages from the use of money and credit (so as to secure equitable exchange in trade)—no country can be prosperous, be its form of government what it may.

Despite America's existing political and social advantages over other nations, there was still a gap between what America was and what it *ought* to be. O'Brien began to wonder if America's advantages had less to do with its political institutions than with other factors: its natural resources; lower levels of public and private debt (because it was a relatively new country); the availability of land; and the fact that the landed and moneyed elites were smaller there than in Britain and Europe. At the same time, O'Brien thought that the heavily populated northeastern region of the United States was not unlike Britain and Europe in that most of the land had already been appropriated, creating unemployment, squalor and hardship, extremes of rich and poor, and desperate need alongside conspicuous plenty. This situation pushed many Americans into wage slavery. A democratic suffrage gave little protection by itself, and the history of Europe showed how easily the privileged few could sweep such protection away. As O'Brien had often insisted, "Universal suffrage is no guarantee at all for liberty, unless it be accompanied, on the part of the working classes, with a knowledge of their social rights and a consequent determination to use political power for their establishment." O'Brien compared the United States with ancient Rome, Sparta, and Athens and Robespierre's France. Though he praised the love of democracy in America, the efforts to prevent the extension of black slavery into the West, and the call for free homesteads for settlers, he warned that America would go the same sorry way of the "Old World" if the NRL propositions were not implemented.

> Her agrarian laws are not a jot better than those of France or England; and her commercial spirit is even more ravenous and unscrupulous. In one respect she is worse than either. We allude to her preference of metallic money to symbolic money; which is a result of the fraudulent paper-systems she has so often smarted under. There is no subject upon which the American working classes are so lamentably at fault as the subject of money. They fancy that an honest paper system is impossible, because they have been so often cheated by the worthless rags of

> fraudulent usurers; and in this suicidal delusion the bullionists and usurers take good care to confirm them.[84]

O'Brien continued to think that America was a place of promise but that its promise might dissolve into futility and fruitlessness, for social and economic problems would not be removed unless political rights were fully and wisely exercised. He wrote about unemployment, hunger, high prices, banking scandals, and a host of other concerns, both in his private correspondence and in his published remarks. In 1857 he discussed with his friend Mathews the flaws in American society that were likely to stop all progress even in "the land of liberty." He went on to reminisce about a group of Mormons who had attended meetings at the Eclectic Institution. With them O'Brien had broached the possibility of persecution at the hands of the U.S. authorities, and this now appeared to be happening with the so-called Utah War of 1857–58.[85]

Mormons had been settling in Utah Territory (an organized incorporated territory of the United States) for about ten years. They had obtained recognition of their right to self-government and religious freedom, but matters were complicated by disputes about the westward expansion of the United States, and slavery, and by the theocratic dictatorship that many Americans thought had been erected in Utah—added to which there was still much condemnation of Mormon practices (which had prompted the Mormons to move west in the first place), identified by O'Brien as fanaticism, polygamy, and the "depreciation of morals." Federal officials in Utah complained about the Mormons and so did many Americans who had to pass through on their way to California. In the summer of 1857 federal troops were sent in and there was bloodshed as the Mormons resisted, fearing that their way of life was under threat. A settlement was agreed in 1858. Utah would be converted from a territory into a state in 1896.

During the conflict of 1857–58, O'Brien wrote that it had one main cause: opposition to the creation of a "commonwealth" where workers could produce wealth for themselves "without the leave of landlords and profit-mongers . . . lest one such example might prove contagious." Applying his own paradigm, and regarding Utah as yet another location where a reform plan like the NRL's could and should be implemented, O'Brien hoped that the Mormons would defeat the attempt to plunder and "civilize" them. He thought that they would have sympathizers in Britain and in America, "less from love of their peculiar tenets than from hatred of the common oppressor." Some of the region's Indian tribes might help, he thought, for they were also facing the disruption of their political and social institutions at the behest of the privileged elites that ran the government and controlled the army. Some Mormons in Utah knew O'Brien to be a friend, and one of them contacted him in the spring of 1858 to inform him of recent developments. He grew pessimistic. Realizing that the Mormons might not be able to win their struggle for liberty, O'Brien declared that this was a fight that would have to be taken up again and again across the world because the elites would suffer nobody to live honestly and independently. He lectured on the "Utah War" several times, fleshing out his interpretation of what was happening with news sent to him directly from the territory.[86]

Despite his disappointment that America seemed not to be adopting the values and policies he advocated, O'Brien had no doubt that the "New World" was ahead of the "Old World" in many respects. During the 1850s, as London continued to be a haven for political refugees from Europe, O'Brien went on meeting with them, and among the topics on which he lectured was the way in which America as well as Britain might assist in freeing Europe from tyranny. *Reynolds's Political Instructor*, on 30 March 1850, included a biographical piece on O'Brien and stated that his ideas were as well known in the United States as in Britain, and in 1861, when the council of the National Reform League issued an appeal for funds on O'Brien's behalf, it was stated that "his disciples are scattered all over the earth," including America. At a "tea and soirée" in O'Brien's memory, held at the Eclectic Institution in February 1867, the icons on display included the U.S. flag and a portrait of Abraham Lincoln, as well as a bust of O'Brien. After O'Brien's death a plan to establish an O'Brienite community in the United States was floated at various times. Among those followers of O'Brien who spent time in America was the Manchester-born cloth maker Harrison Riley, who returned to Britain in 1871, associated with Marx in London, and became a radical journalist, first in London and later in Sheffield. Riley was one of the activists who linked the Chartism of the 1840s with the socialism of the 1880s.[87]

There were many others. O'Brienites went to America during the 1840s, 1850s, and 1860s. O'Brien was sure that the United States offered the best prospects for emigrants from Britain, and he advised them to journey there rather than to any of Britain's overseas possessions (where, as at home, the resources that should belong to everyone were cornered and abused). O'Brien described the economic opportunities available in America and, as outlined earlier, he was explicit about the interconnectedness of political institutions and material prosperity. No "aristocratic spirit" prevailed in America, which meant that workers could find the rights, wealth, and comforts they deserved. The ideal was to clear some land and farm it as a family concern. There was no need to hire labor, no need to take more than could be consumed, no need to compete unfairly. For those who wished to work in a city rather than the countryside, there were options in the thriving ports, manufacturing centers, and service industries. Moreover, the fact that most U.S. states had the Charter, or elements of it, gave workers in America a higher political status than they had in Britain. Each state was its own little republic, with safeguards for individual liberty and genuine progress toward economic justice and social equality. "Each man feels his own importance in society," O'Brien observed, "and it becomes the fashion to treat every voter with respect."[88]

O'Brien published correspondence from the United States from his personal and political acquaintances, especially those who were trying to live by and win approval for his principles. The first number of the *Power of the Pence* featured "A Letter from the Far West." The author was Thomas Hunt, "a true democrat, who has located himself in the distant province of Wisconsin." Hunt had associated with O'Brien in the Chartist movement before emigrating. The main purpose of his letter was to fortify British radicals against compromise. They should increase their demands, Hunt argued, not rest at only moderate reforms. Hunt used American examples. Without vision and intelligence, the "industrious classes" were liable to be defeated by the classes above them, and it was not enough to win the vote. The vote had to be used effectively. This was the case even in the "model republic" of America. Although "the people of the United States have been in possession of the Charter for more than seventy years," their salutary quest for liberty was not over. They had the liberty to vote, but now they had to vote for liberty. In true O'Brienite fashion, Hunt insisted that political rights were meaningless if they did not lead to social improvement and access to the land. These matters were related by Hunt to the ratification of a constitution for the new state of Wisconsin, taken into the Union in 1848. He urged radicals in Britain to take notice.[89]

It was at this time that O'Brien backed a scheme to establish an egalitarian community in Texas. In October 1848 a group set out from London led by a Scot, John Alexander. Things did not go well in Texas, and at home the decline of Chartism did not help. The settlement was soon abandoned. Alexander began to turn against American democracy, not finding it to be what he had expected, but O'Brien persevered in supporting and publicizing the North Texas Colonization Society, "composed of intelligent working men" who wished to go to the United States, "where the soil is fertile, the climate healthy, the government popular, and the people free." When printing letters from Alexander, he added a commentary in order for readers not to become discouraged. O'Brien confessed that Alexander had initially faced difficulties in America, but once he saw more of the country and found employment (as a joiner) his opinion of the United States changed. Though Alexander still had misgivings about some U.S. institutions, and about the influence of landed and moneyed cliques, it was also obvious from his letters that the wide suffrage gave American workers an opportunity to secure rights that workers in Britain did not yet possess. This, at least, was the message from Alexander that O'Brien wished to inculcate.[90]

About twenty years later a group of O'Brienites led by John Radford, an engraver and metal worker, and James Murray, a bootmaker, formed the Mutual Land, Emigration, and Cooperative Colonization Company. Inspired by O'Brien's program, and backed by the National Reform League, the company sent out six families in 1869 to set up a community in Kansas. More families followed and before long there were fifty. Though O'Brien was dead his most devoted followers were determined not to give up on his vision, and the Kansas experiment sustained hope and commitment. In Kansas, it was thought, individual and collective interests could be practically and successfully merged (or, as one of the company's addresses put it, the colony offered "individual sovereignty as well as all the advantages of socialism"). Debate about the NRL manifesto of 1849–50 was as lively as ever, and some of the Kansas settlers would go on to participate in later radical movements (including Populism), as would the colony's promoters back in London. Gary Entz has argued that O'Brien, who had not regarded emigration as the best remedy for labor exploitation at home, would not have approved of the Kansas venture; but Entz exaggerates the "utopian socialist" elements in O'Brien's philosophy and underestimates O'Brien's approval for model communities and related efforts as practical steps on the way to the ultimate reforms he advocated. It is true enough that in O'Brien's mature program, evidenced by the NRL manifesto, emigration and colonization were not priorities. Nevertheless, his followers thought it appropriate to set up a community in Kansas to demonstrate and vindicate his ideas. They wanted to stay close to his teaching and were probably also frustrated by the slow pace of reform in Britain. They collected money, set up a colonization company, sent out settlers, put on meetings and lectures, and published a monthly paper called *New World*. They established relationships with American radicals, notably the veteran Josiah Warren, who had developed a social theory on cooperative, mutualist, individualist, and anarchist foundations. In an article in the *New World*,

Warren argued that labor's reward should always reflect the nature of the tasks performed. Unfortunately the O'Brienite colony suffered a lack of funds throughout its existence. The company directors in London had limited understanding of conditions in Kansas, and settlers began to object to rules about social equality and common landholding. Some abandoned the colony. In London, bad news was suppressed. Confident assurances were given as to the colony's principles and prospects. Eventually, desperately short of money, the colony's promoters had to accept assistance from persons who were not O'Brienite and had little regard for the colony's original goals. Talk of recovery petered out. By early 1875 the O'Brienite colony was on the verge of collapse. Climatic and other problems made farming difficult, and the availability of cheap land all around the colony undermined collective spirit and communal living.[91]

This was, as Entz contends, "a remarkable social experiment . . . A group of marginalized people challenged the status quo and attempted to demonstrate the feasibility of radical, intellectual ideas in a practical setting." Like many similar experiments in Britain and America, the O'Brienite effort in Kansas is important because of its connections with communitarianism, the labor movement, socialist programs, and radical politics. It helped to keep alive the aims and methods of earlier reformers, ensuring that a legacy of thought and activity would be available to campaigners of the late nineteenth century.[92] This was the kind of abiding influence that O'Brien himself wished to have, and in view of his many writings about America and his belief that there was more liberty, equality, harmony, and abundance there than anywhere else, it was quite fitting that his followers should focus on an American undertaking in the years after his death.

Logically, O'Brien should have been disappointed with the United States. He had expected political democracy to put an end to social injustice and economic inequality, but in America, the great testing ground, this had not happened. He preferred to think that it had not happened *yet*, that it would happen soon, and that America *would* complete its journey and its mission. As did others, O'Brien saw what he wanted to see in America. It did not matter if his statements about America were true or false. What mattered was that America was a prototype and model, a source of hope, a reason to persevere in agitating for fundamental reform. There were things he disliked about the United States, but he could not draw attention to them because of the risk of weakening the ideological, political, and rhetorical power of America as a tool for British radicals. The example of America was to be utilized and enhanced, not jeopardized.

CHAPTER 6

# The Irish Dimension

O'Brien's Irish experiences and identity were among the most important of the influences that shaped his radical ideas and activity. He often wrote and spoke about the politics, religion, economy, and society of Ireland, and he was convinced that Ireland desperately needed the reforms he was advocating. Ireland was a cradle for and a prospective beneficiary of the O'Brienite program. Chartism, though weak in Ireland, was not insignificant there, and O'Brien involved himself in efforts to make the Charter relevant and appealing. He also went beyond this. His thoughts about Irish issues circulated widely for a time, and they offer suggestive revelations about Ireland's importance to radicals of the Chartist era and about contemporary concepts of Irishness.

Irish aspects of O'Brien's career have generally been neglected. There has been little analysis of O'Brien's perception of Ireland and Irishness, his proposals to improve his homeland, and the connections he made between Ireland and broader questions about reform in the nineteenth century. O'Brien did not rate an entry in the *Oxford Companion to Irish History* published in 1998, though he is briefly mentioned in the entry on Chartism. O'Brien features in a pioneering essay by Dorothy Thompson, "Ireland and the Irish in English Radicalism before 1850," though this piece is more introductory than substantive. Irish affairs are not overlooked in a more recent book by Paul Pickering, but O'Brien is mentioned only twice in the whole of the work. More forthcoming is Timothy Keane, in his exploration of "Ireland" and the "Irish" as "conventions" in Chartist discourse. These "conventions" informed political arguments and action, providing ideas, symbols, and other means (especially in literary form) by which Chartists could articulate grievances, incite protest, and frame demands. Keane does not discuss O'Brien in detail, but does point to him as a figure who both embodied and promoted linkages between Irish issues and British reform (as when he evaluated the leaders and heroes of Irish nationalism in his newspapers). Takashi Koseki made a valuable postgraduate study of O'Brien's relationship with Irish nationalists before moving on to focus on other areas of specialty.[1]

Born, raised, and educated in Ireland, O'Brien never denied or tried to hide his personal roots. His home district in county Longford had seen United Irish activity in 1798 and O'Brien grew up in an environment of struggle, sacrifice, storytelling, and patriotism. These early memories stayed with him. Perhaps his independent and often truculent spirit arose from his background (his enemies claimed as much later on, using negative fixed characterizations of the Irish to insult and undermine him). Certainly Irish conditions played their part in influencing O'Brien's position on political, social, and economic reform and helped to make him a strident democrat. The Irish background was important to his self-understanding and indeed to the identity and image he sought to project as a radical celebrity in England from the early 1830s. The name "Bronterre" had unmistakably Gaelic roots (*brón* and *tír*).[2]

O'Brien's ideology and program developed mainly on the bases provided by old political radicalism, newer theories about class, labor, and capitalism, and what O'Brien took to be the ethos of the French Revolution in its early stages; but another component in his political philosophy was Ireland. O'Brien's interests and commitments were not without relevance to Ireland. He stood for social revolution, the rights of labor, class-conscious politics, manhood suffrage, a restructuring of lawmaking and government, and the democratic disposal of land and resources. Each of these could be applied, he thought, to the Irish situation. Yet there was an awkwardness and ambivalence in O'Brien's makeup with regard to Ireland. Though he was proud of his background, he did not go back to Ireland after leaving in 1830.[3] The hardships of his youth left an impression. In later life, as shown in the correspondence studied by Ray Faherty, O'Brien could be irritable and was prone to dwell on personal disappointments.[4] His experiences in Ireland and continuing solicitude for his homeland were related to this, and his adoption of the name "sorrow of the land" indicates an attitude of despair and affliction even if it could also be bold and affirming.

There was no single or agreed concept of Irishness in O'Brien's day (or today for that matter). Ireland was divided religiously, economically, and culturally, and Irishness could be expressed in contrasting ways. Identities were largely determined by religious affiliation and by the distinctions between those who occupied the land and those who owned it, and divisions had been exacerbated by the rapid economic and social changes in Ireland since the mid-eighteenth century. Even within identifiable groups there was tension—among Catholics, for example, between farmers and agricultural laborers; and among nationalists, between constitutionalists and insurrectionists. Protestantism, the minority creed, was itself far from homogeneous. Another difficulty concerned "Anglicization" and whether or not Ireland should or could become more like England. Would Irish people change? Could they be *made* to change? Was Irish society inherently unstable, violent, and backward? Was it incorrigibly Anglophobic? At a time when nationalism was sprouting in different directions across the whole of Europe it was also legitimate to ask if "Ireland" was, more than anything else, a romantic, literary, intellectual construction. Much depended on perceptions of Ireland that developed among the *non*-Irish. An idea persisted that Ireland's problems were frequently exaggerated for ulterior reasons. Meanwhile, both in Ireland and beyond, claims about the need for fundamental social restructuring conflicted with a preference for traditional values, relationships, and institutions. For Irish people of O'Brien's generation, there were key events in their recent history that had directly shaped current discourse: the recognition in 1782 of the exclusive right of the Irish parliament to legislate for Ireland and the authority in Ireland of Irish courts; the 1798 Rebellion; the Union between Britain and Ireland implemented in 1801; and the Catholic emancipation won in 1829. The meanings attached to these events were shifting and contested.

Irishness was really an amalgamation taking in class, race, faith, kin, locality, interest, status, power, and other variables, and it could take on discrete forms. O'Brien appreciated its complexity, but in his work he tended to keep things simple in order for his arguments to be persuasive and intelligible. He had no definitive version of Irishness in his own heart and mind. Irish elements were present, but they coexisted with other sources of identity and rarely achieved ascendancy. Graham Davis suggests that O'Brien's radicalism emerged from an Irish grievance mentality and the belief that Ireland had been ruined by military occupation, economic discrimination, poverty, and landlord absenteeism. It is clear that O'Brien saw these as imposed and avoidable problems. Less convincing is Davis's idea that the facility with words, rapport with popular audiences, and sympathy for the poor demonstrated by O'Brien are specifically *Irish* qualities. But it is also clear that some commentators built upon their own dislike of the Irish to argue that Chartism was wrecked by its Irish-born leaders, its association with Irish issues, and its adoption of methods and rhetoric that came out of the Irish experience.[5] O'Brien took up "justice for Ireland" in the 1830s along with many British radicals. He thought that Chartism arose partly because of opposition to the policies pursued in Ireland by the British government, especially the Coercion Act of 1833. One of his most forthright statements about the New Poor Law, meanwhile, was that it would reduce English workers to Irish levels of suffering.[6] In this instance Ireland served as a warning to England, not as something to be celebrated and asserted personally or politically. O'Brien was a radical who happened to be Irish rather than a radical *because* he was Irish. Personal experience was no less a factor in his radicalism than ideological conviction, however, and it would be inappropriate to dismiss his Irish background completely.

If Ireland influenced him, did he influence Ireland? O'Brien's influence in his homeland was not great, probably because Irish workers, even if they were class conscious, tended not to be militant. Most valued community and assumed that labor and capital were reconcilable. Furthermore, O'Brien had fallen away from organized Christianity, including Catholicism. Religion was a primary motor of political and social behavior in Ireland, but O'Brien did not focus on religion in his Irish writings. His secular approach did not find a ready reception in Ireland. Though he did have Irish Catholic friends, he was widely regarded as anti-Catholic, which he denied, while admitting that he might have offended Catholics with some of his remarks. Another charge was that he had betrayed his Irish background. Those opponents of the Union who idolized Daniel O'Connell regarded O'Brien as a turncoat. Having formerly been among their number, he decided that the main trouble was not the British Parliament's legislative control over Ireland but the exploitation of the Irish poor by landlords, priests, and lawyers, for which the remedy was a democratic suffrage, not repeal of the Union.[7] (But this did not mean that the Union itself was satisfactory—O'Brien would later campaign explicitly for repeal alongside manhood suffrage.)

The condition of Ireland affected O'Brien's thinking on land reform.[8] Social problems were traced by O'Brien to political corruption, class power, and the system of landownership. Land was the main source of wealth, and control of the land had to be democratized. Then property laws would be based on popular consent and credit facilities organized by the state so that anyone could rent and cultivate land. In making these points O'Brien had in mind, among other things, the situation in rural Ireland. Rachel O'Higgins thinks that there was a major Irish contribution to Chartism, "a concept of social justice centred on the land rather than on the towns," but that the focus on land damaged the movement. O'Brien was only one of several prominent Chartists who discussed the land, so he was not solely responsible. Nevertheless, the Irish input may have been decisive. The result, according to O'Higgins, was that Chartist proposals for land reform were ill suited to an industrializing society.[9]

This conclusion can be questioned. O'Connor's Land Plan met with wide enthusiasm, and some historians deny that it was unsuited to the times.[10] Later developments probably exacerbated its flaws. Malcolm Chase has shown that political and economic change after the 1840s made it unfashionable.[11] Whatever the pros and cons of the Land Plan, it is not easy to determine the role played in its evolution by Irish conditions. O'Brien, moreover, was an enemy of the plan, preferring his own scheme of nationalization, redistribution, and credit.[12] His principles do not have to be treated as specific to any time or location. He has been hailed as one of the most important advocates of the people's "resumption" of the land, who bridged the gap between platforms of the 1920s and 1930s and those of the late eighteenth century, and who brought in ideas about liberty, sovereignty, and natural rights. Later Irish campaigners were influenced by him, including Michael Davitt, who founded the Irish Land League in 1879, and in his own time O'Brien's program rested upon his observation of the distress of the industrial poor in Britain, including its Irish contingent.[13] O'Brien's awareness of land tenure controversies in Ireland did affect his proposals (it would have been strange had they not), but this did not make his proposals any less valid than they might otherwise have been. As for O'Connor, his Land Plan was to some extent based on Irish experiences, although historians diverge on the details, and it is possible that the Land Plan was shaped less by the Irish situation than by O'Connor's adoption of long-established radical nostrums about personal rights and independence.[14]

The rural and conservative elements noted by Rachel O'Higgins have also been stressed by other observers. Perhaps O'Connor was indeed the Irish landlord who, deep down, remained dubious about radicalism and wished to keep it in check. According to this line of argument, there was tension between the O'Connor formed by rural Ireland and the O'Brien shaped more by "Anglo-Saxon" political and economic developments (radicalism and democracy, free trade and manufacturing).[15] These descriptions are problematic, but they do make plain the complexity of Irishness and the unpredictability of its consequences. O'Brien and O'Connor both drew on their Irish experience, but it led them in different directions.

Irish society, regarded in the nineteenth century and subsequently as conservative, unsophisticated, and unmodern, especially when compared with England, has been reassessed in more recent times. David Lloyd is among those commentators who are dubious about the treatment of the Irish as "victims" of capitalism, colonialism, and modernity. Lloyd suggests that Ireland can be seen as a source of radical and progressive thinking, not simply the setting for a stereotypical backwardness and inability to comprehend or adapt to modern industry and capitalism. Ireland brought forth O'Brien, after all, as well as O'Connor and others who contributed to sustained agitation for reform in Britain and Ireland and elsewhere, and there were nationalist and revolutionary Irish leaders—before and after Chartism—who were patently not of a backward-looking or conventional mind-set. In contemplating the role of the Irish in popular movements, Lloyd notes the paradox of a disorganized peasantry and preindustrial and largely artisanal working class alongside "advanced" and "vanguard" opinions and activities. He queries the portrayal of Ireland as a peripheral colonial economy that remained rural, or a peasant society with local horizons and a settled, "stagnant" population; and he points out that there was more to Irish protest than "subaltern modes of struggle"—violent, nostalgic, inarticulate, spasmodic, reactive. There was an understanding of social and economic change. "Rather than representing a belated political formation," Lloyd concludes, "the Irish working class may be seen to have emerged as embedded at once in the long history of capitalism's becoming and in the no less drawn out process of resistance to that history."[16] This highlights the need to revise former assumptions about the relationship between political radicalism and particular stages of social and economic development, and it further establishes the significance of O'Brien's career. In him and through him, the combination of Irish background and radical program had considerable and lasting effects.

Ireland's importance to O'Brien is evident from the items he published on a range of issues. While he edited the *Poor Man's Guardian*, between 1832 and 1835, he rarely failed to include Irish material in his leading articles, addresses, and other pieces. His comments were wide-ranging, but among the dominant themes were misgovernment in Ireland, the oppression and exploitation of Irish labor, and British elites' insensitivity toward Irish suffering. In August 1833 he ridiculed the "liberality" of Parliament by pointing to the vast sums being wasted in Ireland—money that could do enormous good there were it to be more sensibly disbursed.

> Although we have sometimes impeached the liberality of the "reformed" House of Commons as regards their disposition to remit taxes or to mitigate the penal code, our readers will do us the justice to admit that we never called in question their liberality as to the granting and spending of taxes—especially where those taxes are destined for their own pockets or those of their relatives in the army, navy, commissariat, church, etc.

After hardly any debate at all, a recent Committee of Supply had approved hundreds of thousands of pounds of expenditure in Ireland on such items as inflated official salaries, pointless government inquiries, the publication of useless documents, and the support of erroneous religion and fake education.[17]

A year later, O'Brien was emphasizing Ireland's need for economic justice. Under the heading "Another Bubble for the Benefit of Ireland," he referred to a private speculative arrangement for a "National Commercial and Agricultural Bank of Ireland." A share issue had been announced, with the aim of raising £5 million in capital. Here was "another grand scheme for the welfare of Ireland which will prove, we have no doubt, for the Irish poor, a pompous introduction to nothing." It would not provide employment or elevate the needy, whatever the boasts of its promoters. Talk of plentiful banknotes (easy money) and job creation (lower rates of unemployment) was nonsensical.

> Suppose the people set to work with these paper notes, suppose these notes actually make sails by which the vessel of prosperity is wafted along, of what use will this be to the poor if their employers take away from them just such part of the proceeds of this labour as they choose when they have done? The poor may depend upon it that these new employers, with pockets full of banknotes, will never let them have more than is necessary to keep body and soul together. It is not work that these people want so much as the power of protecting the proceeds of their work when it is done, against the rapacity of masters and the despotism of capital.

In Ireland, O'Brien wrote, the many faced "degradation, starvation, and ruin" at the hands of the few. But change was coming, and the Irish bank scheme and similar ploys were being exposed for what they were.

> The dependence of the unproductive classes on the productive is much greater than that of the productive on the unproductive. The former is essential, the latter artificial; the former intrinsic, the latter relative; and from a knowledge of these facts the productive classes are now progressing into a shape and position which, though at present imperfect and indistinct, will ultimately emancipate them from the ignominious bondage in which they are held.[18]

In the spring of 1835 O'Brien commented on the "Rathcormac massacre" and its aftermath. In county Cork in December 1834, local protesters against tithes had been shot and killed by soldiers deployed to enforce collection. Criminal charges resulted, but they were subsequently dropped (although the authorities did eventually discontinue the sending of military escorts with tithe collectors). O'Brien attacked the British government, the Irish administration, Irish magistrates, and the clergy of the Church of Ireland for the "massacre" and what it represented, robbery and murder. For the Catholic majority in Ireland to be required to support an alien Protestant church was contrary to logic, justice, and Christian ethics, O'Brien declared, and "there is no moral difference in a law that is made by five hundred or a thousand robbers, and that which is made by one only."

> Suppose that our government were an absolute monarchy and that the will of the monarch was the law; and that it was his will that all who resisted payment to a church from which they dissented, and to which they never went, should be shot; we should say that it was a very infamous law; and does it make any difference to the justice and character of such a law whether it is made by one man or by a thousand? Much as we are in the habit of deprecating absolute monarchy, it would be much better to have it with such a law as this, because it would be so much sooner altered. In a free country, a law against which the majority are ranged, as is the case in Ireland, ceases to be law and has no claim on submission, but becomes tyranny of the worst kind because it is not tyranny of one individual will or caprice or whim, but because it pretends to be the voice of the majority, and furnishes the executive with a plea which they would not otherwise possess of putting it in execution. What a wretched villainous law that must be, against which six-sevenths of the people, as in Ireland, rise up.

Multitudes did not react this way to good laws. If they did, society could not exist, for they would be warring against the very values that held society together. "There is a natural impossibility in great numbers ever being unjust and unreasonable," O'Brien argued, "as there is in our guiding the winds or controlling the waves." On the tithe question and on the government of Ireland generally, "Ireland cries for justice." O'Brien continued to make this demand on Ireland's behalf.[19]

Insensitivity to Irish suffering was another of his themes in the *Poor Man's Guardian*. O'Brien contrasted the privileges and comforts of government ministers with the plight of those they should have been helping. "At a time when it was notorious, and proved on oath, that the Irish were living on nettles and bullock's blood, it was gravely proposed to inquire into their condition; and by fellows, too, who had prepared for the task with a regular guttling and guzzling blow-out." O'Brien was particularly scathing about the Tory president of the Board of Trade (1834–35), Alexander Baring, a rich banker, who disputed the available evidence and claimed that Irish suffering was not extensive. "We should like to know from this usurer, what the number has to do with the question. . . . Is hunger the less painful because those who feel it are counted by hundreds and not thousands?"[20]

Ireland featured prominently in a series of addresses of 1836 "To the Radical Reformers of Great Britain and Ireland and to All True Friends of Justice and Humanity." O'Brien suggested that people were becoming apathetic about reform because they had been cheated so often before. Their enemies were ready to take advantage by focusing on relatively unimportant goals so that urgent and necessary changes could be postponed indefinitely. In Ireland this was the design of O'Connell and his followers, who were in league with the British government, a government that was unworthy of confidence not least on account of its Irish policy. It had resorted to coercion in Ireland and would continue to meet proposals for reform there with official inquiries and other delaying tactics. The bigger picture was one of broken promises and dashed hopes. The Irish were even worse off under the Whigs than they had been under previous Tory administrations.[21]

O'Brien subsequently commended William Sharman Crawford, radical MP for Dundalk (1835–37, and subsequently for Rochdale, 1841–52), who had accused O'Connell of political timidity and personal self-interest. Though Crawford was a wealthy landowner, O'Brien commented, he was a friend of the people and he was right to denounce O'Connell as a fraud. O'Connell was doing nothing to help the Irish poor, and Whig proposals on corporations and tithes would do nothing for them either. O'Brien reminded his readers of the "trick" of Catholic emancipation in 1829, when O'Connell had accepted the disfranchisement of the forty-shilling freeholders (which reduced the Irish county electorate from 216,000 to 37,000. O'Connell did not approve of it in public, but he suggested privately that the change would concentrate power in reliable hands). In O'Brien's opinion, this suppression of political rights proved that O'Connell was no champion of liberty. Unless he was stopped he would engage in similar violations in the future. The measures now in contemplation for Ireland, moreover, could only strengthen the propertied and moneyed interests. Who else would benefit if the tithe became part of the rent paid by tenants? Who would take control of local government if the system was reformed along the lines favored by established elites?[22] O'Brien's suspicions about O'Connell did not diminish. He saw O'Connell as a religious dissembler as well as a political traitor.[23]

In *Bronterre's National Reformer* during 1837, O'Brien insisted that tithes must be recognized as public property, and that instead of lightening the burdens on landowners their proceeds should go to relieve the poor. The reform of corporations, he went on, would be of little use unless a majority of the people obtained the municipal vote and the right to serve in local offices. His fervent opposition to the New Poor Law made him object to the extension of similar arrangements to Ireland, and, as noted earlier, he sought to boost support for the anti-poor-law campaign in England by raising the specter of social and economic failure on an Irish scale. In both countries, he contended, the customary right to relief had a better foundation than the right of a landlord to his "conquered estate" or a businessman to "fraud-begotten profits."

> Need I say that a system which, by excluding domiciliary relief, makes imprisonment (that, too, of a most degrading kind) the condition of subsistence, a system which tears asunder all family ties, and which allots but 1s.6d. per week for the support of each inmate (these inmates working hard all the time, mind), need I say that such a system can deserve only reprobation and abhorrence?

O'Brien's remarks on Irish poverty arose in part from his ideas about capital, some of which he owed to Cobbett, who had toured Ireland in 1834. Like Cobbett he identified capital with the land. The land yielded more than could be consumed by the people who worked it, and this excess was the basis of wealth. A barrier to progress in Ireland was the removal of this excess, for it did not stay where it was produced. Irish capital was taken away by the owners of the land that was its source. O'Brien observed a different situation in the United States. There, people on the land tended to stay put and reinvest, with the result that affluence increased through the generations.[24]

O'Brien's frustration mounted as the Irish Poor Law of 1838, the Tithe Commutation Act of 1839, and the Municipal Corporations (Ireland) Act of 1840 brought about some of the circumstances he had warned against. He continued to write and lecture on these matters, dismissing the Irish legislation of the post-1832 "reformed" Parliament as wholly inappropriate.[25] In November 1838 he called on the oppressed of Ireland to support the Charter, to join with their fellow oppressed in Britain to win their rights; and he argued that conditions in Ireland could not be improved without the assistance of British radicals.[26] In August 1842, after speaking engagements across England and Scotland gave him a firsthand acquaintance with the unfortunate condition of the laboring classes, he wrote of "unparalleled" suffering that was "not owing to natural or irremovable causes." It could not be blamed on nature, or God, or anything but "Man's Institutes," and, since it was caused by men, it could also be remedied by men if they adopted the correct measures. O'Brien recommended new laws affecting land, labor, and money, the "great elements of wealth," and declared that nobody needed these more than the people of Ireland.[27]

The prerequisite for the social and economic betterment of Ireland was political reform leading to repeal of the Union (an issue on which he broke with others, including Sharman Crawford, who recommended a federal system). In 1843 O'Brien established a new organ, tellingly titled *Poor Man's Guardian and Repealer's Friend*, in which he discussed the possibility of an inclusive alliance. If Chartists, Complete Suffragists, anti–Corn Law activists, and advocates of self-government for Ireland agreed to combine, he thought, all their goals could be accomplished one by one. The first step was to place government on a representative basis. Other improvements would follow as the transition to democracy proceeded. Self-government for Ireland therefore had to be accompanied by manhood suffrage. O'Brien hoped for assistance from sections of the anti–Corn Law movement, but he did not trust the leaders of the Anti–Corn Law League. They were "money-mongers," factory owners and merchants, bankers and brokers, and they did not respect the rights of labor. In contrast, Chartism and the campaign to repeal the Union were not incompatible.

Although O'Connellites had declared against Chartism, O'Brien insisted that they could not get what they wanted without helping the Chartist cause. Whether intentional or not, their agitation against the Union would contribute to the furthering of democratic principles and the improvement of the material condition of the working classes. Repeal of the Union would not enrich businessmen, fundholders, usurers, mortgagees, and the like at the expense of farmers and laborers (which was the plan of the Anti–Corn Law League). Rather, it would bring peace, plenty, and liberty to an oppressed people. O'Brien denied that self-government for Ireland would mean the separation of that country from Britain. This was just a scare tactic used by those who wanted to block repeal. The truth was that repeal of the Union would result in a closer connection, one determined by choice and interest, because Ireland would have what Britain had: under the imperial crown, management of its own affairs. There was nothing "disloyal" or "unconstitutional" about this (other allegations made by opponents of repeal).

The Union was hardly defensible in any case. Ireland's parliament had only agreed to dissolve itself in 1800 through bullying and bribery. According to O'Brien, the landed aristocracy had wanted the Union in order to go on robbing the Irish people, and the commercial middle classes approved because they saw that the peasantry would be reduced to such straits that many would cross to Britain and take up low-wage employment, thereby increasing the profits of capitalists and entrepreneurs. These Irish workers, entering into competition with the British, pulled down the remuneration for *all* types of labor. O'Brien called upon O'Connell's followers to cease operations against Chartism. In Britain, the Chartists were the only section of the population that favored repeal, and British workers were not indifferent to the fate of the Irish people, for they had a similar experience of hardship. They were not responsible for the misgovernment of Ireland.[28]

O'Brien rejected the "silly assumption that English working men have no sympathy for the wrongs endured by Irishmen." He pointed to such evidence as the continuing circulation of tens of thousands of cheap reprints of the speech from the dock made by Robert Emmet, the Irish republican patriot, at his trial in 1803. Emmet had led an abortive rebellion against British rule, and, after his capture, he was convicted of treason and executed. His speech was admired by succeeding generations, and not only by Irish nationalists, for the dignity and principle behind it impressed many who had grievances against the British state. Emmet was a hero to Chartists, as O'Brien acknowledged. One section of the speech was particularly striking:

> I appeal to the immaculate God—I swear by the Throne of Heaven, before which I must shortly appear—by the blood of the murdered patriots who have gone before me—that my conduct has been, through all this peril, and through all my purposes, governed only by the convictions which I have uttered, and by no other

> view than that of the emancipation of my country from the superinhuman oppression under which she has so long and too patiently travailed; and I confidently and assuredly hope that, wild and chimerical as it may appear, there is still union and strength in Ireland to accomplish this noblest enterprise. Of this I speak with the confidence of intimate knowledge, and with the consolation that appertains to that confidence. Think not, my lords, that I say this for the petty gratification of giving you a transitory uneasiness. A man who never yet raised his voice to assert a lie will not hazard his character with posterity by asserting a falsehood on a subject so important to his country, and on an occasion like this. Yes, my lords, a man who does not wish to have his epitaph written until his country is liberated will not leave a weapon in the power of envy, nor a pretence to impeach the probity which he means to preserve, even in the grave to which tyranny consigns him.

O'Brien was not alone in looking to figures like Emmet for inspiration in the struggles of the 1840s.[29] When the *Northern Star* issued a series of commemorative portraits as a gift to subscribers, Emmet's was among them. Reenactments of Emmet's trial were a perennial favorite among radicals, a reminder of the importance of drama and symbolism to the Chartist movement. Theatrical performance helped to communicate ideas (to those who could not read and write no less than those who could). Robert Hall links this with the Chartist teaching of history and the collective memory that formed around events both near and far. Hall argues that national, ethnic, and generational boundaries were transcended in this effort to bring people together.[30] Writing in March 1884, Robert Gammage vividly remembered the impact of the many cheap editions of Emmet's speech that were read, passed around, and discussed in the Chartist period.[31]

O'Brien focused heavily on Irish issues under such headings as "On the Critical State of Ireland and the Duty of All Good Chartists and Good Repealers—Chartists, be Repealers! Repealers, be Chartists!" and "On the Necessity of all Chartists helping the Repealers to Repeal the Union, and of all Repealers helping the Chartists to make the Charter the basis of our Representative System." As was his wont, O'Brien insisted that a democratic suffrage was the essential requirement. No nation could govern itself and no society could be changed without it. O'Brien also published Irish news. Even in Belfast, he noted in 1843, there was backing for repeal of the Union, but less encouraging were clashes between Catholics and Orangemen. The authorities were sending troops to intervene. O'Brien urged Irish campaigners not to fall into the trap. He claimed that the 1798 Rebellion had been "concocted" by

British agents, though this did not prevent him from printing accounts of "Irish heroism in 1798." He went on to enumerate the "Fruits of the Union," including the "robbery" of Ireland in the form of exports to Britain.[32] O'Connell had initially approved of the People's Charter and was aware that most Chartists sought "justice for Ireland," but he loathed O'Brien and O'Connor on personal as well as political grounds. They had formerly accepted his leadership on Irish issues, and he was offended by their subsequent departure from flattery and obedience. He came to regard them as extremists, and he wanted no rival to challenge his authority in Ireland. Nor could there be any compromise between his vision, of a harmonious society in which landowners took care of a deferential people, and what he saw as O'Brien's wish to destroy landlordism altogether. "Physical force" was not to his liking; his opinion of the French Revolution was the reverse of O'Brien's; and he aimed to control agitation in Ireland in order to influence the British government's Irish policy, which meant not inconveniencing the government while it was dealing with the Chartist challenge. O'Connell did all he could to inhibit Chartism in Ireland and prevent Irish people in Britain from participating in Chartist activities.[33]

Historians disagree about the extent to which the Irish in Britain involved themselves in Chartism. Among the skeptics are J. H. Treble, Andrew Granath, and Martin Mitchell, who posit a lack of interest in Chartism. Treble argues that the vast majority of Irish in Yorkshire, Lancashire, and Cheshire had "little contact" with Chartists, mainly because O'Connell was "for the most part unchallenged" (though there was some concerted action in 1848, after O'Connell's death). In Treble's account, nothing the Chartists could do made much difference—not the engaging of Irish speakers to address Chartist meetings, in the hope of attracting more Irish immigrants, nor the adding of repeal of the Union to the Chartist petition of 1842, something that O'Brien trumpeted in print and on the platform at the time. Granath's study of the Lancashire Irish also suggests insignificant contact with Chartism, and Mitchell shows that the Irish in the west of Scotland, though definitely not apolitical, tended to side with O'Connell.[34] But a much higher level of involvement is indicated by other historians who have studied the lower ranks as well as the leadership of Chartism, and the period as a whole, not just evidence for a Chartist-Irish alliance in 1848. This alliance, it should be noted, was taken seriously by the British government. It represented a threat to the established order and an opportunity for foreign states to take advantage of Britain's embarrassment.[35] O'Connell was the target of sustained criticism from O'Brien, and he was also attacked by the *Northern Star*, as in late 1838 when a meeting was held in Dublin at which

O'Connell not only condemned the leaders of British Chartism as "cut-throats" but also denied a hearing to anyone who took a different view. O'Connell announced that prominent "English radicals" should not be spoken of, for they were no friends to Ireland, and that the meeting had more important business to attend to than to hear excuses on their behalf. There was laughter when he called them "rats and weasels," and he added: "How I delight in that burst of honest enthusiasm; how I love the spirit that is ever evinced by my countrymen." He carried the crowd, and when a bookseller from Liverpool named John Murray tried to raise an objection, O'Connell told him not to interrupt.[36]

Friedrich Engels declared in 1845 that "neither Chartism nor Socialism has had marked success in Ireland," and it is obvious that the Charter never gained in Ireland the popular support it had in Britain. If Chartists in Ireland were small in number, however, they had influence at home and in Britain. They had their own organizations, including the Irish Charter Association, formed in Dublin in 1839. It soon became inactive, but another body, the Irish Universal Suffrage Association, was established in 1841. It faded after three years. Then there was an impressive, if brief, revival in 1848. The IUSA platform combined the six points of the Charter with repeal of the Union and advocated coalition between Chartists and Irish nationalists. This was O'Brien's position too, and he publicized the IUSA and complimented its president, Patrick O'Higgins, a Dublin merchant. Takashi Koseki has pointed out that O'Brien did more than any other prominent Chartist to popularize the notion of a Chartist-Irish alliance on the basis of "from the Charter to repeal," and that the IUSA was more consistent than some Chartists in Britain, in that the latter were willing—unlike the IUSA—to shelve the demand for manhood suffrage in order to conciliate Irish nationalist leaders. Michael Huggins sees less consistency in Irish Chartism, emphasizing its ambivalence on the question of whether the ultimate goal should be national independence or Irish democracy.[37]

This ambivalence might help to explain why Chartism did not grow stronger in Ireland. While O'Connell was alive, Huggins argues, Irish Chartism could formulate no alternative mass platform and tended toward adjunct status in relation to the repeal movement. Irish Chartists' critique of O'Connellite nationalism was weak, and they lacked the will and confidence to go it alone. Yet Huggins also claims that the relevant historiography "has not accorded Irish Chartism the resilience and place it ought to have." For all its flaws, "Chartism had an almost continuous, organized presence in Ireland from 1838 to 1850." O'Connell's dominance was not complete, and there was room for a campaign that stood apart from both the exclusive, confessional O'Connellism and the more romantic and cultural style of nationalism that developed into Young Ireland. It is not easy to reconcile all these opinions, and Huggins further complicates his analysis by declaring that Irish people were indifferent to the Charter and that concerns relating to nation and religion took priority. Even had the Chartists been more robust, it seems, they would not have gained a mass support.[38]

When O'Brien was invited to address a meeting of the London branch of O'Connell's Repeal Association, he accepted with alacrity because he wanted to explain his views and improve relations. Then the London repealers received a directive from Dublin to the effect that the invitation to O'Brien contravened the ban on links with Chartism. The Dublin committee charged that Chartists were out to divide the Irish movement. They were "physical force" men, and some were in the pay of the Tories. Chartists were not to be admitted as members of the Repeal Association. If any had joined, they were to be ejected and their subscriptions returned. Correspondence surrounding this affair appeared in *The Times*, which reported that Dublin's instructions were accepted "without a dissentient voice," although there was "more of sorrow than rejoicing." O'Brien wrote that genuine Chartists would push for repeal *despite* O'Connell, because it was "right and good in itself," but he condemned the Repeal Association's manifesto, which endorsed an Irish legislature elected by household suffrage. Many Chartists at this time decided to enroll as members of repeal bodies in an effort to gain influence over their policy.[39]

O'Brien branded as fallacious O'Connell's stated objection to combination with Chartists, that the latter favored "physical force" while the repeal movement was peaceful. (This point was also made by O'Connor—in correspondence with his and O'Brien's mutual friend Thomas Allsop, for instance, in 1843.)[40] O'Brien cited O'Connell's menacing speeches in Ireland and suggested that anyone making such remarks in England could expect to be arrested. O'Connell *talked* "physical force" even though he pretended to be against it. Nevertheless, Chartists should not hold grudges. Whether or not O'Connell wanted their assistance, they should carry on pressing for Irish independence and "self-government for all classes through the operation of Charter-suffrage." The danger was that O'Connell would plot with the gentry and middle classes. He was no democrat and he probably hoped to exclude the workers from any of the benefits of repeal. By this time O'Brien had also started writing his "Historical Sketch of the Irish Nation." He later claimed that newsagents in Ireland were refusing to sell his publications, perhaps at O'Connell's behest, which meant that he lost revenue and many people were deprived of material they wanted and needed to read.[41]

O'Brien believed that conditions in Ireland were deteriorating in part because of the economic policies of the Tory government appointed in 1841 and led by Peel. The liberalization of trade was not objectionable in theory, but in practice it was harmful because free trade could not operate properly with society organized as it was. Therefore it had to be part of a wider strategy for change, including manhood suffrage and the adjustment of debts and burdens in line with the fall in prices that free trade would bring about. Trade statistics for 1842–43 revealed a sharp increase in imports, which boded ill for domestic agriculture and industry.[42]

Some Chartists did not agree with O'Brien's opinions about Ireland. When the *London Chartist Monthly Magazine* suggested that Ireland could progress with manhood suffrage but with the Union left intact, O'Brien replied that this was based on incomplete knowledge of Irish conditions and a misunderstanding of democracy. He argued that power should not be concentrated but divided and devolved, and he recommended the American model:

> In America there are twenty-six states, enjoying each a separate, independent legislature and executive of its own; yet all are firmly and cordially united under one Congress, which legislates on matters affecting the whole. Now, if twenty-six distinct and independent states, having each its own separate government, can thus live and flourish in harmony together, why should not two states like Britain and Ireland be able to do the same? To be able to do so, all that is required is that, while Ireland legislates exclusively for herself on all matters purely local or Irish, she shall not legislate exclusively or independently on matters which concern England or the empire at large.

An address to the people of Ireland was subsequently issued by the National Association for Promoting the Political and Social Improvement of the People, signed by its secretary, William Lovett, the "moral force" Chartist. The address, which asserted that repealers and Chartists had a common commitment to reason and persuasion rather than intimidation and violence, prioritized manhood suffrage. O'Brien again insisted that it would be better to aim at manhood suffrage in conjunction with repeal of the Union, rather than opt for one ahead of the other. Though repeal without manhood suffrage would be worse than manhood suffrage without repeal, it was wrong not to contend for both.[43]

O'Brien kept his readers up to date with Irish events. He admitted that the Repeal Association was raising plenty of money but held to his line that O'Connell was not to be trusted. "Woe to a party whose destiny depends on the breath of one man, and that man the instrument of a monopolizing class!" The only hope was that "the Irish working classes will have sense and spirit enough to compel Dan and the middle classes to establish Universal Suffrage along with Repeal." O'Brien gave coverage to efforts in some English towns to bring Chartists and repealers together, and to the views on Irish issues expressed by a number of public figures, including Sharman Crawford (who at this time was campaigning for suffrage reform, tenant right, and a federal structure for Britain and Ireland). When O'Connell and Lord Brougham, the former Whig lord chancellor, made speeches that upheld landlord power, O'Brien invoked "a plague on both your houses." O'Brien also commented on the correspondence that first appeared in the O'Connellite *Freeman's Journal* between Patrick O'Higgins of the IUSA and Irish chief secretary Lord Eliot. O'Brien, like O'Higgins, believed that violence and disorder were caused by misgovernment. O'Higgins was an opponent of the Irish Poor Law and had attributed pauperism to high rents, not the shortcomings of the Irish peasant. He opposed emigration schemes because they allowed landowners to avoid responsibility for their tenants, and he denied that "real" radicals (as opposed to the "sham" variety) lacked concern for the problems of Ireland. On all these matters his views accorded with those of O'Brien.[44]

Famine in Ireland and repeal of the Corn Laws led O'Brien to focus more urgently on the land question. He repeated his basic argument about free trade, that it would not benefit the majority unless it was accompanied by other measures. In October 1846 he made the case for free trade in land as well as in the produce of the land. Repealing the Corn Laws was not essential for the relief of Ireland, he asserted, despite what some of its advocates claimed; and the Irish could have no faith in the type of free trade associated with the Anti–Corn Law League, Peel, and the latter's successor as prime minister, Whig leader Lord John Russell. O'Brien also rejected the assumptions that were being made about the Famine—that it was providential, represented a timely lesson for the Irish, and would teach them self-reliance. He wanted "a popular system of landed tenures," with laborers given the chance to work small farms. The land of Ireland, he wrote, could support six times the population of Ireland, if only the system of landholding was reformed. O'Brien pointed to the "freedom of the public lands" in America, where reformers had the good sense to treat the citizenry as the ultimate landlord.

These were themes he developed in his *National Reformer and Manx Weekly Review*, issued from Douglas on the Isle of Man (where O'Brien was based from 1844 to 1847). There was Irish news every week, and comment on the evictions, the "fearful condition" of the country, and the continuing errors of O'Connell. When the organized trades arranged a meeting in Dublin to protest about O'Connell's dictatorial style of leadership, it was reported, he encouraged mob violence against them. O'Brien eagerly published any correspondence or other material that cast O'Connell in an unfavorable light. In December 1846 he accused O'Connell of making a bargain with the Russell government, appointed six months earlier on the fall of Peel, which resembled the Lichfield House Compact of 1835: in return for moderate Irish reforms his movement would not make difficulties for the Whig ministers.[45]

Allegations then began to circulate about arming in Ireland, and O'Brien blamed O'Connell's belligerent rhetoric. He complained that O'Connell had for too long deceived the people of Ireland. Most of them did not know what repeal of the Union was meant to do for them, and O'Connell would not explain because by confusing them he could better manipulate them. "There never was a more palpable humbug than that of calling Chartists 'physical force' men and Dan's Repealers 'moral force' men," thundered O'Brien. "In a word, the fruits of Dan's training are ignorance, despair, and preparations for physical force. Yet Dan rejoices in the title of 'august moral force regenerator.' What a deplorable farce!"[46] Though he found it impossible to refrain from personal remarks, O'Brien devoted most of his attention to constructive reform proposals. Access to the land was central, and he urged the Irish to set about solving the underlying problem: "The rights of property have been guarded by coercion, whilst its duties have been violated with impunity." In his view the Famine made delay unacceptable. He often used items from other newspapers, European and American as well as Irish and British.[47] He assailed the policies and principles that he believed had sentenced Ireland to starvation and allowed self-appointed leaders to practice "duplicity and absurdity" without accountability.[48]

In the late 1840s O'Brien offered his detailed plan for the land, currency, credit, and exchange. While admitting that Irish circumstances differed from those in Britain, he believed that the same methods could be applied in both countries to the general benefit. His premise was that the land had to become public property. This would be the centerpiece in the program issued by the National Reform League in 1849–50, a program that represented O'Brien's mature philosophy, given practical expression in the amalgamation of the Charter with the seven "National Reform" propositions.[49]

O'Brien's proposals for the land contrasted not only with O'Connor's Land Plan but also with other ideas about Irish land, notably those of John Stuart Mill. The quarrel between O'Brien and O'Connor had considerable influence on Mill's thinking. Mill positioned himself between the moderate view to which O'Connor subscribed, that although the distribution of land ought to be altered, the principle of property in land was acceptable, and the more radical view of O'Brien, that land was a social resource and should belong to the people in common. Mill saw merit in the latter claim. Unlike other types of property, he decided, land was not a product of labor, and the argument that all people had the right to what they produced by their labor or accumulated by their abstinence was not relevant. Although a portion of the value of land might be due to labor, this was rarely the labor of the person who owned the land. Mill thought that when private ownership of land did not result in a "positive good," it was neither expedient nor just, but he stopped short of the nationalization proposals of O'Brien. In Ireland he favored alternatives, above all peasant proprietorship.[50]

O'Brien was incensed by remarks in *The Times* in 1847, with some of its correspondents asserting that Ireland's problems had exclusively Irish roots and proved the inferiority of "the Celtic race." O'Brien repeated that the real culprits were those with land and money who kept Ireland in subjection, and the dishonest demagogues who fooled the people. Unfortunately, the truth about Ireland and the way to ensure progress was being hidden. The debate was complicated by erroneous theories and policies (laissez-faire nostrums, emigration schemes, the poor law, moral and religious teachings). If the Irish were given political rights and their own land, O'Brien argued, they would prove themselves the most industrious nation on the face of the earth. As it was, Britain harmed itself through its refusal to improve Ireland. The growing financial crisis that was alarming Britain's landed and moneyed elites and their newspapers could not be separated from the condition of Ireland, and it was to Ireland that one had to look for some of the causes and consequences (such as the drain on bullion that resulted from the establishment of food depots in Ireland, all stocked with imported provisions).[51]

Parliament, to its shame, seemed willing to contemplate only inadequate expedients. O'Brien ridiculed all talk of reclaiming wastelands in Ireland for the use of tenants and laborers. This offered no remedy, he wrote, as anyone who examined the condition of Ireland would realize. Ineffective and ill-chosen contrivances proceeded from the desire of the dominant classes to appear concerned. They just wanted to keep the people quiet. O'Brien continually advanced his proposals on the land, currency, credit, and exchange as the best way forward. The fact that the Irish were starving, even though they produced enough food, he attributed to bad laws. These could easily be changed. When asked by a correspondent about the first steps that should be taken, O'Brien recommended public and voluntary effort to provide the Irish with money and employment. As more evidence of suffering came in, more statistics on evictions and deaths, and more revelations about corruption in Ireland, including the misappropriation of funds by magistrates, jurors, clergymen, farmers, tradesmen, and officials, O'Brien described bolder measures, declaring that this was no time to err on the side of caution.[52]

He discussed Ireland in an international setting and concluded that Irish conditions were not entirely unique, for slack trade, hunger, and political turmoil could also be seen across France, Belgium, Germany, Spain, and Portugal. Even democratic and republican America was not immune, owing to the "scourge of war" (between the United States and Mexico). Confirmation that Ireland's distress would affect others came with testimony from English and Welsh ports of a rising influx of Irish poor.[53]

O'Brien responded to these reports by affirming that the potato blight was not the primary reason for Irish suffering, that what was most needed was land and money reform, and that, since Ireland had enough fertile land for the whole population to be fed, it was possible for every family to have a sufficient portion and support itself without difficulty. "If the potato crop were to fail every year for the next twenty years, or forever, it would matter little or nothing to a people who had all the land to cultivate for themselves, and an honest system of currency and commerce, whereby to effect exchanges of value for value." In O'Connor's Land Plan the assumption was that two acres of land and a £30 cottage would be enough for a family. O'Brien reckoned that Ireland had one and a half million families and sixteen million acres, taking into account those living in towns and engaged in nonagricultural pursuits and the waste lands that could be brought into cultivation. He envisaged farms of twelve acres each; or, allowing for population increase, perhaps two million farms of at least six acres each. "Now (potatoes or no potatoes) who will pretend that six acres of good land would not feed a labourer's family abundantly, and moreover yield him a large surplus for the markets, to be exchanged for clothing, furniture, groceries, and other decent comforts?" About 140,000 Irish arrived in Liverpool in the first fifteen weeks of 1847. What good was the Land Plan, or any such phony reform, to them? Or to the hundreds of thousands who were likely to die in Ireland because they could not leave?[54] When Pope Pius IX assigned a period of prayer for Ireland, O'Brien asked why the Vatican remained silent on the land tenure system, on the merchants who bought up all the food and exported it while the people went hungry, and on the wealthy who refused to relieve their destitute neighbors.[55]

O'Brien also gave coverage to Young Ireland, which had formed its own organization, the Confederation, in rivalry to O'Connell's Repeal Association. The leaders of Young Ireland had decided that O'Connell was too close to the Whig government. Their style of nationalism was rooted in cultural, historical, and educational activities, and they theorized about the viability of "revolutionary" tactics. O'Brien was himself a devotee of "revolutionary" action, though he did not advocate violence. He thought that social and economic change could be accomplished through an extension of political rights and the democratization of lawmaking. Revolutions failed, he maintained, when they were taken over by the propertied and moneyed interests. He did not want this to happen in Ireland. He still believed that Ireland should govern itself, but he hoped that a movement for a democratic suffrage would rise up and "swallow" both the O'Connellites and Young Ireland. On O'Connell's death in May 1847, O'Brien pronounced him a failure.[56]

Social disaster and political polarization in Ireland prompted some nationalists and radicals to take up insurrectionary conspiracy. O'Brien had little sympathy for them, although there was a certain resemblance in ideas—admiration for U.S. institutions, for instance (and in 1848 conspirators in Ireland looked to their countrymen in the United States for support). The strength of separatist and republican sentiment in Ireland is not easy to assess, and there is no scholarly consensus. In fact, as Christine Kinealy points out, "the 1848 rebellion continues to be neglected by Irish historians. At the same time, the influence of Irish radicals on British political developments . . . remains relatively unexplored." O'Brien did not find much to admire in Young Ireland, and when he decided to join one of the Irish bodies in London he chose the Irish Democratic Federation (October 1847). The IDF had broken with the Dublin council of the Confederation because it had not yet approved of fraternization with Chartists.[57]

The Young Ireland revolt coincided with Chartist revival in Britain and the 1848 revolutions in Europe. O'Brien persevered with his own program. In his *Power of the Pence* there were statements about access to the land, without which "free institutions" would be a mockery, and "land limitation," so that nobody would have more than a fair portion of the land, to be determined according to area and population. There was another call for united effort on the part of Chartists and repealers. It was not surprising to find "the ill-governed people of Ireland . . . in the lowest state of degradation and misery," O'Brien reflected, because "it is plain that the character and condition of a people depend upon the government and laws." Where there was no self-government there could be little spirit or energy or enterprise. O'Brien expressed disgust with the trials of Irish political offenders.[58] Questions had been raised about these trials, and O'Brien agreed that they were flawed, but he also commented that violence could not be condoned. He advised the Irish to get knowledge. Out of this would come real change: "The Irish people must be morally, socially, and politically reformed before they can hope to win Ireland for the Irish or to establish their national independence."[59] This remark highlights once again the reservations and awkwardness in O'Brien's attitude.

Ireland needed the O'Brienite nonviolent revolution, plain and simple. Counterrevolution in Europe in 1848–49, with the forces of reactionary conservatism regaining the upper hand against the forces of freedom and enlightenment, disappointed O'Brien but did not discourage him. People everywhere wanted their rights and could not be silenced, he believed, and every government faced a choice: to accept change by legal and peaceful means or to risk the adoption of other methods.

> A parliamentary reform to the full extent of the *People's Charter*, with the necessary social reforms to accompany it, will be the only possible means of averting a general outbreak; and that event will be, itself, a revolution the grandest on record, should it take place. . . . It is with the view to make such revolutions harmless to all classes, and at the same time productive of all the happy consequences anticipated by their authors, I so continuously urge the necessity of studying the laws which ought to govern Land, Credit, Currency, and Exchange.

Justice for Ireland meant justice for every nation. The cause of the people was the same in all places, irrespective of geography, culture, language, and custom.[60]

This point was made by other Chartists in the months before and after the Irish rising of 1848. There was an emphasis on the common interests of Irish nationalists and British radicals and on their shared desire for a more representative form of government and a proper reward for labor. Chartist poets, observes Mike Sanders, "sought through verse to make the aspirations of each side intelligible to the other."

The wish for an alliance did not die, though there was an obvious gap between British and Irish agitators on the subject of violence. There was less restraint on the Irish side. Ian Haywood identifies a "characteristic ambivalence towards violent remedies" in Chartist fiction that dealt with Irish topics. Even when writers did not endorse insurrection, they presented insurrectionists as noble, heroic, and morally superior to their opponents. These writers brought factual material into their stories as well, to illustrate dispossession and hardship, landlord authority, colonial subordination, and the impact of the Famine. Ireland did not lose its potency as "an example of the worst abuses of state power," and Haywood accentuates both the Irish involvement in British radicalism and Ireland's role in generating anger (over the repression there), fear (that the same would happen in Britain unless the Charter was secured), and inspiration (arising from Ireland's struggle for liberty).[61] All three responses were present in London radical circles during the Irish disorders of 1848.[62]

The reception given to Queen Victoria when she visited Ireland in August 1849 was friendly and respectful, which was surprising in view of the repeal agitation, the Famine, and the Young Ireland rising of 1848. Russell's government had ended emergency relief, regarding the Famine as over, but the workhouses were full, and much of Ireland was still starving. Outbreaks of cholera in the spring of 1849 brought many more deaths. The towns visited by the queen, moreover, ought to have been unwelcoming. Cork and Dublin had nationalist town councils, and Belfast was riven by sectarian animosities. Despite all this, her Irish tour gave rise to numerous displays of loyalty. O'Brien wondered why. He concluded that the Irish people had made a distinction between the queen and her ministers. Though they admired her, they would not forgive Russell and his colleagues, or their predecessors in office, for the poverty and oppression which had long been Ireland's lot.[63]

O'Brien's search for explanation has been repeated by modern historians. James Murphy argues that the strength of republican sentiment in nineteenth-century Ireland has been exaggerated. For James Loughlin, the queen's visit offered colorful distraction at a time when nationalism was in disarray and the economy depressed. Loughlin concludes that there was no consistent set of opposition beliefs around which to organize protest. According to the lord lieutenant of Ireland at the time, Lord Clarendon, Queen Victoria's visit was successful because of her refinement and bearing and because the Irish people were grateful for her appearance among them. They considered it a mark of their own worth, making them the equals of Victoria's English and Scottish subjects. They were not the "barbarians" they were sometimes made out to be. Peter Gray notes that the royal visit was marked by an address from the Catholic prelates of Ireland that was less censorious toward the British government than might have been expected. This moderation helps to explain why the visit went so well.[64] Queen Victoria's tour of Ireland could change nothing in the long run, as O'Brien pointed out. He predicted that the Irish poor would not play the government's game and that when excitement about the visit passed away the demand for repeal of the Union and a raft of political, social, and economic reforms would be as strong as before.[65]

The 1848 alliance between Chartism and Young Ireland was but a weak and fleeting coalescence. Interaction remained quite limited in reality, despite the rising ambitions and rhetorical flourishes of those who wanted it most. Historians have often argued that the Famine put an end to the immediate political danger in Ireland, while the relative prosperity of the 1850s in Britain defeated Chartism.[66] O'Brien was not ready to give up the fight, however, and in his post-1848 speeches he was as uncompromising as ever. At one meeting, when speaking about the sovereignty of the people, he declared that Ireland would never know peace and happiness until its people enjoyed the product of their own labor and the land was the property of all. Popular sovereignty would bring radical reform closer, and popular sovereignty could be both an effect and a cause of international working-class solidarity. Ireland would gain much from such a consummation, but in the meantime unrest would continue. Thousands were leaving Ireland each year. Those that remained would not submit to tyranny and exploitation indefinitely.[67]

Sections of O'Brien's "Historical Sketch of the Irish Nation" had appeared in 1843. He was working on a book-length history of Ireland in 1847–48 and persevered with this project thereafter, though as with other writings of his later career it was not published. Ireland was discussed in items that did go to press, including the *Vision of Hell* of 1859 in which O'Brien referred to "divers most cruel and unconstitutional coercion acts to subjugate the small farmers and peasantry of Ireland to the landed proprietors." These acts had formed the basis of Irish policy since 1801 and had empowered an "Anglo-Irish group" of propertied and wealthy families. As usual, O'Brien asserted that Ireland was crying out for a democratic suffrage and new laws on the land, credit, currency, and exchange, just as were Britain, America, and other countries.[68]

Compared to the extent of his Irish coverage in previous years, O'Brien wrote less about Ireland after the rising of 1848, probably because he came to accept the discrepancy between his ideals and Irish realities (and also, in his later career, the outlets for his writing were more limited). There had been no sustained or detailed engagement with Irish journalists or political leaders apart from O'Connell. O'Brien had apparently decided that he could learn little from them. This might be considered a mistake, especially in the case of James Fintan Lalor, who was active in 1848, advocated a radical redefinition of the rights of property, and helped to shape the Irish revolutionary tradition. Lalor, a talented writer for the Young Ireland cause, was much respected by later campaigners. Some of his ideas overlapped with those of O'Brien, but O'Brien preferred to focus on his own agenda. O'Brien might have had a better understanding of Irish politics had he reflected more deeply upon such resources as Lalor's journalism.[69]

Nevertheless, in his heyday O'Brien was one of the most famous and widely read Irishmen involved in reform politics anywhere in the world. He had spent his early years in a district that had been a United Irish stronghold, where there was support for nationalistic causes and armed struggle. His sympathy for his homeland and its people is clear from his writings. He could not separate repeal from manhood suffrage, and he expected these gains to make possible a fundamental shift in Ireland's social and economic condition. Yet material realities seem often to have mattered less than Ireland's usefulness as a discursive construction. O'Brien liked to place Ireland in juxtaposition to England (and sometimes other countries) for purposes of comparison and in order to push his preferred reforms on an intellectual level. When he did so his focus was not on real conditions, or on his personal knowledge of Ireland. He was arguing about ideas. Ireland was no tabula rasa, however, and the relevance of O'Brien's principles was and is debatable. He identified himself with the "sorrow of the land," but his opinions about Ireland, and his assumption that it offered a suitable testing ground for his radical program covering land, currency, credit, and exchange, met with limited favor at a time of national crisis.

CHAPTER 7

# Making and Maintaining Reputation

For Bronterre O'Brien, personal fame and influence and the reorganization of state and society were interconnected aspirations. His career was based on a principled and lasting commitment to reform, but it was also about crafting, communicating, and maintaining an image. This is another reason why it has wider importance. The ways in which O'Brien tried to sustain a reputation as the people's servant illustrate the making of a radical tribune and the progress of radical politics in nineteenth-century Britain. In addition, a study of O'Brien's activity repays consideration because of what it reveals about the presentation and reception of ideas, the interaction of writer and reader, strategies of opinion formation and the protocols of influence available for radical leadership, and how reputation affected and was affected by all these developments.

One of the foremost celebrities of Chartism, especially in its early years, O'Brien had made his name with the *Poor Man's Guardian* and by the late 1830s was a well-known radical leader, but he broke with other leaders during the 1840s and expressed dissatisfaction with the mainstream Chartist movement as it came under the direction of O'Connor. O'Brien was generally overlooked in the memoirs of other Chartists, probably because he quarreled with so many of them, and he published neither a lengthy autobiography (only fragments) nor a magnum opus in which his ideas and activities were laid out systematically and in detail. This failure to do what other public figures accomplished was probably due, as David Stack suggests, to O'Brien's health problems, chronic indebtedness, and relatively early death. But even without these circumstances, Stack goes on, O'Brien's life story—had he written it—would have been incongruous because "nearly all of the many Chartist autobiographies were the work of auto-didactic working men . . . keen to tell a tale of struggle and self-improvement," and O'Brien's "privileged education and slow descent into self-induced poverty would never have accorded with the genre's demands of life as heroic progress."[1] While there is some truth in this assessment, O'Brien's publications, speeches, and life experiences did not place him so far away from Chartist self-chroniclers. He aimed to teach and guide and convince, he knew difficulty and struggle, and in this struggle he was the heroic lead character. Though other Chartist figures have received more attention than O'Brien, he has a claim to be regarded, at his peak, as the most interesting and dynamic of the movement's leaders. It should also be remembered that there was more to O'Brien's career than Chartism. He became famous before the movement established itself and remained active after its decline. What follows in this chapter is a study of leadership viewed through the prism of reputation—for if leaders were really to lead, and exert influence beyond their immediate location and personal circle, they had to build and use reputation.

Having arrived in London from Ireland to study law, O'Brien devoted himself instead to politics and by the mid-1830s was a public figure. In order to remain so, and earn a living, he had to cultivate a reputation. This rested primarily on his relationship with readers. With them he enjoyed a positive rapport, which, though it waxed and waned, never collapsed, despite the fact that none of O'Brien's newspapers proved to be long-lasting or profitable. O'Brien's reputation also rested on personal appearances at large open-air assemblies and in lecture halls and other meeting places. He exemplified the link between oral and print forms of communication in nineteenth-century British political culture. O'Brien's speaking engagements were efforts to use his celebrity and influence, not least in order to help his publications. The core element in his reputation was consistency. O'Brien sought to demonstrate this quality and to prove that he could be trusted. He subordinated other concerns to the need to substantiate his self-description. He was a servant of the people. This was his identity, the image he wanted to project, and it prompted the frequent restatement in his publications that his advice should be heeded because it represented what was best for the people. The problems he experienced led him to dwell on the sacrifices he was making, which in turn fostered a sense of victimhood. He complained that he was not appreciated or assisted as he should have been. He also insisted that his failures were not his fault. Others were to blame. These attitudes grew out of a conjunction of the personal and the political, for he did not sharply distinguish between private and public spheres of activity.

At first, Chartists welcomed and celebrated the guidance of their "schoolmaster." The rise of the *Northern Star* as Chartism's national organ confirmed the inadequacy of O'Brien's papers, but it was partly O'Brien's writing for the *Northern Star* that ensured its success. O'Brien also made other contributions, nurturing working-class pride and developing Chartist communication and language.[2] Opponents of Chartism, such as the "inhabitant householders of Chichester" who sought to deny O'Brien a platform in their town in March 1839, branded him as dangerous and subversive.[3] He repudiated this characterization. Proud of the "schoolmaster" epithet, he went on using it—and liked it to be used by others when addressing or referring to him—long after his separation from the Chartist mainstream. It was part of his identity, and he believed that it gave his remarks more authority. As he went beyond the Charter and developed his broad radical program for social and economic as well as political change, he was desperate to attract the widest possible support. The first step would be a democratic suffrage, which would make possible the new laws that were required for thorough reform of arrangements pertaining to the land, currency, credit, and exchange.

This was the message O'Brien wished to impart, and its reception largely depended on his reputation. Historians have long been interested in reputation and what it reveals about past societies. Some of the components of "honour" and "respect" discussed by Keith Thomas in his study of early modern England had not declined in importance by the nineteenth century. They were flexible, not fixed, but they were observable and they included signs of status and worth. In the formation of reputation, internal qualities and external recognition came together.[4]

The wish to be well regarded (which affected people of all classes) meant that reputation could not be passive but had to be asserted. Criticism was to be withstood, but deciding on the appropriate response took care. Was it more honorable to endure insult and accusation and let them pass, or did one's public credit and self-esteem require counter measures? This points to broader considerations about what a positive reputation demanded. For O'Brien it included recognition by others of his integrity. Public character was linked to private rectitude. O'Brien's debts, and his failure to provide adequately for his family, might have counted against him on this score, and perhaps the awareness that he had fallen down privately made him fight all the more to defend himself publicly. Shame was the opposite of honor, but was it shameful for him to ask for financial help, or would it have been worse not to ask, and to deliver himself and his dependents over to greater suffering? In O'Brien's case, this dilemma reinforced his tendency to blame others for his misfortunes. If he was not responsible, reputation was easier to preserve.

Reputation required adherence to a certain standard of behavior. As with its other elements, however, this was also subjective and flexible. Losing the good opinion of others was to be avoided, but for the man who already had a robust opinion of himself the blow was diminished. The problem for O'Brien was that he lived by his pen. An attack affected not only his personal pride and public name but also his material well-being. The requirement to meet certain standards stemmed from both the fear of losing the respect of others and the conscience-driven, inner conviction that a servant of the people must avoid wrongdoing, and O'Brien appears to have been influenced by each of these stimuli. He was also certain that reputation involved keeping one's word. He hoped that if he did right by his followers, they would do right by him.

Similarities can be noted between O'Brien's attitude and that of other historical figures, especially literary and political figures. All were concerned about reputation, and responded to criticism and exerted themselves to "manage" reputation. Attention was paid to tactics and anticipation—in particular, the process by which a writer and a public sized each other up. Reputation manipulation was part of this and was determined by, and could in turn affect, broader political and cultural changes. Writing style and choice of subject matter were bound to reflect, and might vary as a result of, a writer's determination to prove his talent and his readiness to do what was expected in the role he had cast for himself. The making or unmaking of reputation often depended on the shifting amalgamation of the writer's self-understanding, prevalent literary fashions, and contemporary political and social structures.[5]

A writer's reputation did not necessarily bear a close resemblance to the fixed notions he had about himself, in which case he might worry about how he would be remembered. For those who were politically active there were roles as both exemplar and propagandist. Reputation also rested on one's human appeal. Many readers identified with this or that particular writer. They thought he was like them, with some of the same experiences and sympathies that they had. Yet there could also be disagreements about him, which made him difficult to categorize.[6]

John Rodden has argued that reputations rise or fall depending on access to power and influence, but for a writer much also depends on "the selection, codification, and characterization of responses into key moments, stages, and audiences," the results of which are unpredictable, not least because the writer's work is liable to distortion by friend and foe alike.[7] Therefore, though reputation might proceed from the intrinsic merit of the writings themselves, it is more likely to be a consequence of the negotiated, complicated, tension-ridden interplay of the writer's work, his life and personality, the cultural and institutional arena, and the various settings in which the work is read. The reception of the writings is also contingent and changing. The devotion of a readership might signify writings of real quality, but might also show that readers have magnified features of the work or the writer's personality for their own purposes (meaning that his reputation is to some extent an idealization).

These tendencies also hold good for politicians. Through history, the reputation of political figures has been shaped by partisanship and by philosophical changes. Most leaders have had within them the drive to be regarded as "great men." An elevated status was accorded to them by others and they openly embraced it. Many were available for use by divergent political groups, and their reputations were unstable and unsettled.[8] Francis Place, one of the prominent radicals with whom O'Brien squabbled, gained a name in certain quarters for inconsistency. On some issues he was strident, on others more cautious. To plebeian observers he was too friendly toward the middle classes, but to the latter he was a dangerous agitator. Attitudes toward him were not uniform. The same is true of other political figures. They had disputed reputations. Some lost control over how they were regarded. Some have become the butt of historical myths. Some tried to preempt any such treatment, directly interfering to impose a pattern on scholarship and memory.[9]

Reputation could not be sustained without effort. It emerged from continuous interaction between the person wishing to sustain it and those by whom that person wanted it to be acknowledged. In the words of sociologist Gary Fine: "Reputation becomes a form of social capital or debt that society uses to respond to individuals and that individuals can build upon or squander according to their abilities and choices." Each of Fine's definitions of reputation—objective, functional, and constructed—can be seen to apply to O'Brien. The objective aspect concerns assessment of the person's actions, which are treated as "facts" or "reality." Although this is a matter of interpretation, the underlying assumption is that there is no doubting what the person did. The functional aspect relates to the needs of society and roles that must be filled in society, roles that are expected and normal. In O'Brien's case they included writing and speaking. The constructed aspect arises from political and social goals. Persons wanting prestige and power act on the assumption that establishing a reputation will help.[10]

O'Brien was aware of the social aspects of reputation and the vital importance of self-representation. He was "Bronterre." There was only one Bronterre, and employment of this name is significant not only because of what it meant but also because it created a sense of personal connection between O'Brien, the celebrity, and the people to whom he appealed. They knew him as "Bronterre" and he was part of their world. This is what he wanted. He and his followers could feel that they understood each other and possessed the same motives and values.

O'Brien chose to call himself "Bronterre" because the name encapsulated the image he was seeking. He aspired to be a popular hero and placed himself within a tradition of Irish protest while also drawing upon the radical potential he saw in the early years of the French Revolution. He championed the interests of the poor, oppressed, and disadvantaged. O'Brien's followers were among the very sufferers of exploitation and misgovernment that he was out to rescue, and he was a sufferer too. This is one of the reasons why he idolized Robespierre, with whom he felt a bond personally and politically. He regarded Robespierre as the perfect democrat, and in a different time and place O'Brien intended to walk in Robespierre's shoes. His book on Robespierre, published in 1838, was designed to rehabilitate a much-maligned reformer and encourage British radicals to show the proper reverence for Robespierre's principles. According to O'Brien, no figure in history had suffered more from lies and exaggerations than Robespierre. In commending the latter, O'Brien was also making a plea for himself, another ardent democrat who was liable to be misunderstood.[11]

Reputations have often been contested, and O'Brien was to experience this, much to his cost. In a period of political excitement, social and economic change, and cultural vibrancy, a celebrity could have both positive and negative images. Audiences responded in different ways, in line with different ideas about what was fit and proper in those individuals who made a bid for reputation. Commentators had their own reasons for building someone up or tearing that person down. One of the key developments in O'Brien's career was his rupture with O'Connor, whose sway with the Chartist rank and file O'Brien could not match. They fell out in 1841–42 and openly disagreed on many questions thereafter, and personal jealousy added to their clashes. O'Connor retained his primacy in the movement by undermining others, and O'Connorite Chartists treated O'Brien as a renegade, directly contradicting the assessments made by O'Brien's admirers and the reputation that he wanted for himself. The modern historiography of Chartism has not been unaffected.[12]

Self-interest accounts for the wish for reputation and also the endorsement of or opposition to that reputation. People who are influenced for or against an individual's reputation thereby gain—intentionally or otherwise—a means by which they can define themselves. For O'Brien's supporters and for his opponents, interaction with him influenced the way they thought about themselves, and in evaluating him they also contributed to a wider discursive context. A negative reputation could be confirmed through demonization. To Chartists who sided with O'Connor or with others who happened to quarrel with O'Brien, it was necessary to reduce the latter's importance. He was minimized and resisted. Here is an example of what Gary Fine calls "reputational politics"—a competition for control over how an individual is regarded.[13] O'Brien realized that if he was to succeed in shaping and protecting his own reputation, he and his followers would have to set the agenda.

Originally published in 1854, Gammage's *History of the Chartist Movement* showered O'Brien with compliments. Gammage was a friend and admirer of O'Brien and shared some of his ideas as well as his antipathy toward other prominent Chartists. Gammage was no neutral observer. O'Brien, he asserted, "wielded more of the real democratic mind than any other man in the movement." He was a peerless writer. As an orator he might have been a little less impressive, but he mixed satire, logic, wit, and emotion, and, judged by the effect he had, was highly successful. In Newcastle-upon-Tyne in July 1839, "O'Brien was greeted throughout a long and eloquent address with terrific bursts of cheering." There could be no question of his ability to hold a meeting's attention. "Of all the democratic leaders," Gammage commented, "he was undoubtedly the man with the greatest breadth of mind."[14] Another favorable assessment came from G. W. M. Reynolds, for whose popular publications O'Brien wrote in the early 1850s. Reynolds thought of him as a "prophet," and several of his later works—the *Odes* to Palmerston and Napoleon III and the *Elegy on the Death of Robespierre*—were warmly praised in *Reynolds's Newspaper*.

> Mr. O'Brien does not employ rhyme as a coral rattle, with its silver bells, for the amusement of grown-up babes and sucklings. His verse is the vehicle of the most precious political truths. Its object is the exposure of exalted scoundrelism, and the enunciation of saving principles. These two odes . . . are characterized by that

> lucidity of thought, energy of expression, and raciness of diction of which Mr. O'Brien is so unrivalled a master. . . . These odes cannot but prove acceptable to Mr. O'Brien's numerous admirers, and ought to be extensively circulated amongst the plundered classes.

The ode to "the French usurper" was especially good, "one of the most prodigious achievements in rhyme of which the English language can boast." As for the *Elegy*, it was "unique and wonderful" and equally deserving of wide approbation.

> This fresh production from the pungent pen of Mr. O'Brien is characterized by his usual excellences, fertility of illustration, energy of expression, and marvellous condensation of thought. Mr. O'Brien was the first in England—we believe, in Europe—who had the capacity to perceive, and the courage to proclaim, the great truth that Robespierre was the foremost and the purest of all modern reformers; and that this, and this only, is the reason why his name and memory have been so blackened and defiled by those who have an interest in blinding the working classes as to who are their friends and who are their foes.

Reynolds claimed many post-1848 conversions to O'Brien's ideology and program:

> Some years ago the necessity for social reconstruction was but dimly seen, and the principle but little understood, until the French Revolution of 1848 and its various consequences opened the eyes of the millions throughout Europe. . . . Of the first and foremost teachers of social rights, Mr. O'Brien was assuredly pre-eminent in the country; and now he has the satisfaction of beholding the fruits of his long unrewarded labours, in the amount of proselytism which has at length done homage to his teachings.[15]

Contemporary verdicts on O'Brien as a speaker include that of Flora Tristan, the French utopian, socialist, and feminist, who heard O'Brien in London in 1840. To Tristan, O'Brien was "remarkable for his clear thinking, his lucidity, his self-control, and his knowledge of past events."[16] Writing in the 1880s, but relying on the reminiscences of local people who had been involved in Chartism (and in E. P. Thompson's opinion displaying a mastery of written sources as well as oral traditions), the Yorkshire journalist and historian Frank Peel described O'Brien as "one of the most eloquent of perhaps the most remarkable band of orators that ever stood on a political platform in this country." O'Brien could sway a crowd. He was a "great" speaker whose "ability" and "eloquence" put the lie to the myth that Chartist leaders were simply "violent demagogues" who went in for disturbance and sedition.[17]

In the early years of Chartism, O'Brien's standing was such that any remarks against him were quickly rebuffed by other leaders and by rank-and-file Chartists, whether or not they were personally acquainted with him. During 1841 his name cropped up in a dispute in Manchester over the financial irregularities of R. J. Richardson, the bookseller, trade unionist, and radical organizer who served as a local delegate to the first Chartist Convention and was sentenced to nine months in Lancaster Castle for seditious conspiracy in 1839. Richardson argued that his debts should be paid by the Manchester Chartist Committee, since he had spent the money while serving the Chartist cause, but members of the committee insisted that these were personal debts that had nothing to do with them. As the quarrel intensified, Richardson made various allegations, as did the committee, and these featured increasingly in the Chartist press. In support of its claim that Richardson could not be trusted, the committee placed a statement in the *Northern Star* that not only explained his debts but also condemned him for remarks he had made about O'Brien, "to whose intellectual acquirements and zealous labours we are indebted for many invaluable works and writings."

Richardson had said, "in the presence of parties who are prepared to prove the fact," that O'Brien "was not possessed of two single ideas" and was not the true author of the book on Robespierre but had stolen it from a Frenchman and "palmed it upon the public as an original work of his own." Richardson complained that O'Brien had been paid expenses for speaking at meetings also addressed by Richardson, and yet Richardson had not been paid. The reason for this, according to the Manchester Chartist Committee, was simple: O'Brien had traveled some distance to speak, while Richardson had already been nearby (on personal business). Another of Richardson's offenses was his refusal to sign a petition that called for O'Brien's release from prison, although when Richardson had been in Lancaster Castle he asked to be moved elsewhere on grounds of ill health—"this lover of all that is honourable actually wrote . . . that Mr. O'Brien was as comfortable as if he were in a palace; that prisoners there were much better off than when they were at large."[18]

The Manchester Chartists were ready to defend O'Brien at this time (though largely for their own purposes).[19] In September 1841, at a meeting in Liverpool to mark his release from prison, local Chartist leader William Jones exalted O'Brien and his "gigantic intellect."[20] There were others who did the same, notably Arthur O'Neill, the leader of Christian and "moral force" Chartism in Birmingham. When O'Neill heard that O'Brien wanted to launch a new paper in the spring of 1842, he wrote an appeal, "The Case of Mr. James Bronterre O'Brien," in which he asked that O'Brien be given full backing. The enemies of the people feared nobody more than "our redoubtable Schoolmaster," O'Neill wrote, and his talents and influence were such that the movement *had* to place him in charge of his own newspaper. Chartists could not do without him. He deserved assistance, moreover, as the target of public and private persecution, the full horrors of which were known to only a few. Having suffered so much for the people, it would be wrong for the people not to help him now. O'Neill suggested that some Chartists had forgotten what O'Brien had done for them. They had short memories. They should show their gratitude by ensuring that O'Brien had enough money to make the projected publication a success. If it failed, the people would be disgraced. O'Brien's services would be lost and other men of talent would be discouraged from serving the radical cause in the future. O'Neill recommended that in each Chartist district, local committees should collect money to set up the new paper, and Chartists as individuals or in groups should place orders for the paper, paying a quarter's subscription in advance. "You are morally bound in justice to the great principles you advocate to see that the combined efforts of open enemies and pretended friends do not in this case (as they have in many others) burk the endeavour of Mr. O'Brien to spread sound political knowledge amongst the people."[21] O'Brien was no doubt grateful for this appeal on his behalf, but the Chartist national leadership did not act on O'Neill's suggestion, and although O'Brien went on to conduct several newspapers, he was not freed from financial problems. He appears not to have expected his reputation and influence to suffer despite the admission of financial need (though he sometimes stated otherwise, as in a letter of 1840 to his friend and benefactor Thomas Allsop: "Public support . . . always tends to degrade and injure a public man in the eyes of those he desires to serve").[22]

His closest followers seemed to love him all the more for his misfortunes and his struggle to overcome them. They remained loyal. In his later career, at events to which they flocked in large numbers, O'Brien could not have been treated with greater deference or esteem. In April 1852, for example, when the Eclectic Institution was "crowded to excess" for a celebration of Robespierre's birthday, O'Brien was "rapturously applauded." He was the only living person named in the toasts that followed the speeches: "Prosperity to James Bronterre O'Brien, the consistent and talented advocate of the principles and character of Robespierre."[23]

O'Brien also gained the respect of someone who was not a political ally, Alexander Somerville, a former soldier who became a lecturer for the Anti–Corn Law League and joined in several other reform campaigns as speaker and writer. Somerville was suspicious of Chartism, and years later, looking back, he wrote of O'Connor's dictatorial manner, but he also remembered meeting O'Brien, and he found the latter's *Odes* of the 1850s to be truly remarkable. As he commented in 1860:

> I know nothing in literature like them. If Milton's enthroned Satan had been a reality, and a Chartist with a pen dipped in molten brimstone, he, and only he, might have written, besides him who did write, the scorching anathemas addressed to Louis Napoleon and to some of our British statesmen. In these unique productions, all the dictionaries have been ransacked and exhausted for rhymes that follow in jangling succession, ten, fifteen, or twenty lines rhyming together, comically for a time, until the clanging words become fiery bolts which strike and make the heart quiver as shocks of electricity. They who have not read Bronterre O'Brien have yet to become acquainted with literary genius in one of its weird and eccentric forms.[24]

When some of O'Brien's works were collected, edited, and published as *The Rise, Progress, and Phases of Human Slavery* in 1885, the volume included a "Dedication" to O'Brien written by the radical and republican engraver-cum-writer W. J. Linton. O'Brien, Linton explained, had given himself to "the elucidation of the great reforms needed in the subjects of Land Nationalization, Credit, Currency, and Exchange," and though "frustrated" in his lifetime by "the ceaseless machinations of working class exploiters and landlords," O'Brien could ultimately prevail through the republication of his essential propositions. Clearly, O'Brien was not the only one to believe in his own legend. Linton hailed him as "an eloquent denunciator of the manifold evils of Profit-mongering and Landlordism, whose entire life was devoted to the advocacy of Social Rights."[25]

After his death, the preservation of O'Brien's fame and influence depended upon the efforts of his most faithful followers. Several times during his later years they had set up subscription funds to relieve him and his family. A concerted effort was made around the time of his death to raise money, and a draft biography was put together to this end. A handwritten version survives. It was probably intended to be used as a basis for advertisements and addresses that would be placed in newspapers.

The draft biography was composed at the request of the council of the National Reform League and with the sanction of a public meeting held in the Eclectic Institution in January 1865.

> It has been resolved . . . to address the public on a question deeply affecting the common interests of the industrious orders throughout the kingdom. It respects the life and character of one of the greatest men of modern times, one who has devoted a noble mind and faculties of no common order to the public good. That you may be able to form some idea as to the manner of man he was, we propose to give a short sketch of his history.

The authors were not as well informed about O'Brien's early life as they might have been, which suggests that he had not often spoken with them about it, but they knew of his education and especially his progress at Trinity College, Dublin, "where he studied so assiduously and successfully as to carry off very numerous honours . . . No one had fairer prospects of success in life and his talents and high order of intellect gave promise of future greatness." After arriving in London to complete his training as a lawyer, he changed direction: "Young, impulsive enthusiastic, and fired with a noble ambition to do something for humanity, he voluntarily threw overboard all hopes of preferment in his profession, and entered with heart and soul into the agitation which was then just commencing for Radical reform." The biography then detailed his rise as "Bronterre," the most accomplished political commentator of the age. It related his participation in the campaign against the newspaper stamp and his writing for and editing of a long list of journals. It lauded his books, especially the volume on Robespierre, which effectively redeemed the latter's character. O'Brien would have done more, but "he was stopped by the machinations and persecutions of the eternal enemies of the human race, who dreaded the uplifting of the veil of truth before the eyes of God and man."

Chartism would have been a less impressive movement without O'Brien, but for him it had not been a wholly positive experience.

> At the period of the great Chartist agitation, he was actively engaged throughout England and Scotland, lecturing and addressing large concourses of people, endeavouring to give the movement a healthy tone; and more numerous and enthusiastic audiences were assembled to hear him than were ever known before

> or since. The Government, unfortunately, found means to neutralize all his efforts for good by the help of traitorous leaders stolen from the Chartist ranks; and in the end they succeeded in driving him into comparative obscurity. At the time of this convulsion he was indicted, along with Feargus O'Connor, for sedition and suffered eighteen months' imprisonment in Lancaster Castle for a speech imputed to him but which he declared he never made.

The biography then jumped forward to the foundation of the NRL in 1849 and the launch of its "celebrated" program of reform (the "Seven Propositions"). O'Brien identified the main obstacles to peace, progress, and happiness—"the landlord and profit-monger"—and explained why new laws on the land, currency, credit, and exchange were so urgently necessary. "In all his numerous writings and speeches Mr. O'Brien never ceased advocating and enforcing those great social reform principles which he saw were essential for the people's freedom. He ever contended for *social* rights along with *political* rights on behalf of the entire people."

Reaching the end of his career, though seriously ill and "shut out from all access to the political press by the jealous prescription of the ruling orders," O'Brien persevered. He still gave lectures and speeches. He continued to write, and published the *Odes*, the *Vision of Hell*, and pamphlets on Robespierre. Death did not diminish his importance. It was not his fault that he had not achieved more in his lifetime—but he achieved a great deal in any case, and his legacy would be equally significant.

> In his untiring advocacy of justice for the millions, Mr. O'Brien incurred more obloquy and persecution than perhaps any man of modern times. Had the people for whom he battled but understood and appreciated his efforts on their behalf, different indeed would be their present condition. He devoted himself wholly to the people's cause and was both willing and able if manfully supported in his work to lead them on to victory and freedom.
>
> If the laws and institutions advocated by him were adopted by the nation, there would be no need of a violent revolution, but a change would be effected from the old system to the new with as much facility and by as insensible gradations as in a series of dissolving views where one scene so gradually melts into another that none can say where the new begins or the old ends. Year by year a marked change would be effected in the people's condition until eventually the full and final fruition of happiness and justice would be enjoyed.[26]

This account of O'Brien and his ideas and influence, though by no means a total whitewash, was affirming and inspiring. The draft biography shows how O'Brien wanted to be remembered and how his followers wished to remember him. It was the approved version of his career, and it was a bid to determine the judgment of posterity.

The O'Brienites had access to several press organs in this period. For a time they used the *National Reformer, Secular Advocate, and Freethought Journal*, owned by the atheist and republican Charles Bradlaugh (who, despite disagreeing with O'Brien on certain matters, respected him and had raised money for his support). Their notices in this publication included a description of O'Brien's funeral, which took place (on 31 December 1864) "in the presence of a numerous assemblage of faithful friends."

> The expressions of sorrow at the loss of their revered teacher, of love and devotion to him personally, and for the immutable doctrines he taught, their account of his principles, persecutions, sacrifices, and sufferings, above all of his unflinching and heroic struggle, extending over a period of thirty-five years, for the political and social rights of the masses, were heartfelt and impressive.

Another notice was placed on behalf of a memorial committee, established by the council of the NRL in 1865 and tasked with the raising of money for O'Brien's widow and family (Gammage, who had a medical practice in Sunderland, served as treasurer of the memorial fund for the North of England). This notice was a shorter version of the aforementioned draft. As became the usual practice, in announcing the proposed memorial fund the opportunity was taken to summarize O'Brien's career, pay homage to him, and thereby police his reputation. Mention was made of his early rise as a reformer, his work at the *Poor Man's Guardian*, and platform appearances with Henry Hunt. These activities were but the beginning for the people's servant.

> As a writer for the press, and as an unrivalled orator, the name of Bronterre O'Brien has sent a thrill of hope through the hearts of thousands. Choosing the difficult and thorny path of agitator for the rights and interests of the industrious orders, he has thrown a flood of light on the great questions of a National Currency and National Exchange; and the still more important question of Land Reform has found in him an able and zealous exponent. Whatever differences of opinion may

> prevail as to his views on these and other important points, or however men may differ as to the wisdom of his policy on all occasions, none can refuse him their meed of praise and admiration for his undaunted courage, perseverance, and singleness of purpose, in energetically advocating what he deemed indispensably necessary for the public weal.

O'Brien, "during a lifetime of privation and penury, devoted his rare talents and acquirements to the public service . . . spotless and incorruptible . . . unallured by the blandishments of wealth, unmoved by the terrors of power or the clamours of the populace." He was the model of consistency and perseverance. He carried on, "through good reports and evil reports," and never put his own welfare before the cause of the people. With his mind and ability, he might have had "a splendid fortune and a high position in society." Instead, "he voluntarily renounced all worldly advantages for the sake of consecrating himself to a high and noble mission—that of the instruction and melioration of the condition of his fellow-creatures."[27]

This message was repeated at meetings and in the press over the following years, mainly in conjunction with trade union, internationalist, and radical campaigning. In February 1867, a large meeting in the Eclectic Institution, chaired by Gammage, celebrated O'Brien's birthday. Speakers—who included T. E. Bowkett and the French exile Joseph Collet—referred to O'Brien's role and importance (he was "their best teacher and greatest benefactor"), his "noble" character and "honour and integrity," his many sacrifices, his principles that were impossible to refute, his love of justice, his earnest and profound thought, and his "excellent" writing. The occasion was also marked by eulogistic poems about O'Brien, which were subsequently published along with a report of the meeting and letters from Mazzini and Blanc, who had both been invited but were unable to attend. Two years later, eleven O'Brienites signed a letter to the *Bee-hive* newspaper in which they responded to a recent article on Ernest Jones, the most important figure in late Chartism and an advocate of socialist and internationalist goals, who had died a few weeks previously. These men wrote to remind readers of O'Brien's ideas and activities and to prevent him from being marginalized or demoted in the collective radical consciousness.

> Without the least desire to detract from the merit due to Ernest Jones, we believe the public career of Bronterre O'Brien will bear comparison with any man who has appeared in the political and social arena during the last forty years, for public virtue, unswerving fidelity, and enlightened views upon national reform. As an act of

> justice to his illustrious memory, the undersigned disciples and personal friends beg of you space for the insertion of the following facts in connection with his public life, which will aid in placing his true character before your readers and establish his claims to remembrance and the gratitude of all reformers.

There followed yet another summary of O'Brien's career and accomplishments, and in the concluding remarks it was stated that his followers had "pledged themselves over his tomb to do their utmost . . . to make known his doctrines and labours as a beacon light to guide the people and an example to follow by those who would make themselves worthy of the love and veneration of the good and true."[28] Loyalty to O'Brien and commitment to his vision led some O'Brienites to leave their homes and start afresh in America, where they tried to show the world that it was possible to live in conformity with O'Brien's teachings on social equality and economic justice.[29]

For all the positive comments about O'Brien, however, there were public figures who did not have a good word to say about him. Early in his career he was condemned by veteran radicals Richard Carlile and Francis Place. O'Brien had come into contact with Carlile in London in 1830 when he joined in the agitation for parliamentary reform. As journalists they both fought the "war of the unstamped," and at the end of the 1830s they sometimes shared a platform at Chartist meetings. But O'Brien did not share Carlile's secularist and atheistic views, and the gap between them widened as Carlile adopted elements of orthodox liberal political economy under the influence of Place. O'Brien and Place had little in common personally or politically. Place later described O'Brien's *Operative* as "a strange paper from a three parts insane and savage man." He and Carlile dismissed O'Brien as a rabble-rousing enemy of property. In *An Address to that Portion of the People of Great Britain and Ireland calling themselves Reformers*, published in 1839, Carlile attacked O'Brien as one of the "wild and extravagant" men whose pretensions to leadership had to be quashed. O'Connor was another—"I dislike the sound of these Irish O's in connection with the question of English Reform . . . The temper of an Irishman is best suited to the state of Ireland." Carlile considered O'Brien an obstacle to the public good and "not solid and steady enough, not sufficiently philosophical, for the necessities of English Reform," and he objected specifically to O'Brien's belief that a democratic suffrage was the prerequisite for thorough social and economic change. Carlile argued in 1839 that winning the vote should not be the priority because it would do nothing for the people in the existing condition of state and society. He thought that the restoration of the land to the people should come first, while O'Brien maintained that it could only come after—because it would be made possible by—the shift to a more representative form of government. Place was unconcerned about the unequal division of land and, accepting the Malthusian teaching about population outstripping resources, thought that a land policy based on "equality" would deter effort and increase indolence. Carlile and Place clearly disagreed with O'Brien on principles. They were also resentful because they saw their own role in reform politics diminishing as they were supplanted by other leaders.[30]

O'Brien's reputation might have suffered from their negative remarks, but he was skilled in self-defense. During 1836, for instance, Place wrote against O'Brien's articles on the New Poor Law, trade unions, factory regulation, church and local government reform, and coercion in Ireland. He clashed with O'Brien about the causes of popular distress and the way to alleviate it. Place argued that although O'Brien wished to help the laboring poor, his ideas and proposals were flawed. O'Brien responded by assuring the workers that he would always tell them the truth. Place claimed that he was out to mislead them and that he was attacking the wrong targets. These were fatuous assertions from someone who cared nothing for the masses. Place seemed only to worry about the problems faced by shopkeepers, tradesmen, and the commercial middle classes, and maintained that in many cases they were no better off than wage laborers. O'Brien agreed that some of them were in difficulty—but most of them were not, for they had capital and property and therefore power over others. They used this power to enrich themselves, and they opposed fundamental change because they benefited from the existing order. Place had approved of a reduction in working hours, but this was not because he really wished to stop exploitation. Rather, he thought that excessive working hours created unemployment (productivity was kept up by demanding more from each worker, not by hiring more workers). Would Place use this argument in relation to shopkeepers and businessmen? If they kept their stores and offices open too long, would they not take customers away from other stores and offices? To O'Brien, Place's position was unhelpful and inconsistent. Place was not tackling root problems of inequality and injustice, of which overwork was but one result. A system in which laborers had to work long hours and still struggled to support themselves and their families was unpardonable.[31]

O'Brien also defended his name and opinions against Carlile. When he had a disagreement with another leader, he often made it known that he was ready to meet his opponent for debate in front of an audience. In most cases his challenge was not taken up, which O'Brien could then use as a form of vindication. In September 1838 it was Carlile who failed to respond, and O'Brien placed a notice in the *Northern Star* to make this clear. He also reissued the challenge. Though Carlile had not complied with the conditions previously suggested for a public debate, O'Brien explained, it was not too late. If Carlile would contact O'Brien the necessary arrangements could still be made.[32]

O'Brien's reputation was affected by the acrimonious disputes in which he engaged with other prominent figures. The rift with O'Connor altered his standing among Chartists. After hailing him as "schoolmaster," hero, and champion, the *Northern Star* and its writers and many of its correspondents became unforgiving critics of O'Brien. Some had formerly been among his staunchest supporters. One such was John Campbell, the Irish-born weaver who became a Chartist leader in Manchester and secretary of the National Charter Association. At the end of 1842 he wrote to the *Northern Star* on behalf of himself and other officeholders in the movement who had been castigated by O'Brien as corrupt and dishonorable self-seekers. Campbell confessed that he had once respected O'Brien, but that had passed. "No man will deny you possess talents in a superior degree; the only regret is that you should so prostitute them as to render them either useless or injurious," Campbell wrote. "A bad man must always resort, as you have done, either to surmise falsehoods or else to invent and fabricate the most palpable lies." O'Brien now had nothing to offer but "lame and contemptible" writings and "ungentlemanly," "vindictive," and "cowardly" deeds. In March 1845 the *Northern Star* accused O'Brien of "tergiversations, inconsistencies, and downright apostasy" and declared him to be governed by "malignant and disappointed envy." A few months later O'Connor used the front page to denounce O'Brien for his "folly." Utterly "disgraced" as a journalist and as a man, O'Brien was known to be not a friend but the worst enemy of the people. In November 1848, presenting his recent speaking tour of Scotland in the best possible light, O'Connor congratulated himself that though his enemies had done their utmost to spoil his reception, the whole enterprise had been "glorious." Naturally, O'Brien was among the plotters. He had "pulled the wires that worked the puppets."[33]

O'Brien was also assailed in verse. In September 1842 the *Northern Star* included "A New Chartist Song" by the popular lecturer and poet E. P. Mead. A former naval officer who had taken up O'Connorite politics and was active in and around Birmingham at this time, Mead ridiculed and rejected leaders who had fallen out with O'Connor, and their versions of Chartism, and in particular O'Brien and comments he had made in the *British Statesman.*

> Then cheer up, my hearties, and quit ye like men,
> And rally round Feargus, again and again,
> In spite of the *Statesman* and heartless Bronterre,
> Who's as crazy, by Jove! as a very March hare.
> I trust your contempt for O'Brien, like mine,
> Will only to Feargus your hearts more incline.[34]

While the quarrel with O'Connor was the most damaging to O'Brien's livelihood and peace of mind, he broke with many others during his career. He became a firm friend of Henry Hetherington, addressing meetings with him and writing for and editing the *Poor Man's Guardian* and other Hetherington titles, and standing up with Hetherington to the official persecution to which the radical unstamped was subjected. Nevertheless, by the end of 1836 they were at odds. O'Brien was disappointed by the moderation of the London Working Men's Association, to which Hetherington adhered, and he was writing for other publications, in rivalry with those of Hetherington. Later, when O'Brien was editing the *Operative*, that paper was attacked by the *Charter*, the LWMA's organ, for being too militant. There was also a personal grievance, for O'Brien believed that Hetherington owed him money. Although Hetherington campaigned for the Charter and O'Brien was willing to collaborate on shared goals, they were no longer close. After Hetherington's death O'Brien publicly impugned his atheism.[35]

O'Brien's association in the mid-1830s with Cambridgeshire landowner and utopian Tory James Bernard, owner (briefly) of the *London Mercury* when O'Brien was its editor, foundered on a disagreement about landlords and farmers. Bernard thought of them as allies of the working class, but O'Brien denied that the interests of property could be reconciled with those of labor unless social and economic reforms followed the democratization of the system of government.[36]

Another notable falling out was that between O'Brien and William Carpenter, for whose *Political Letters* O'Brien began writing in early 1831. Committed to radical causes, and brazenly evading the stamp regulations by issuing each *Letter* as a separate publication, the two men worked well together for a time, and later they were fellow Chartists. Though Carpenter was editor of the *Charter* during 1839, when it was an unwelcome competitor for patrons to O'Brien's *Operative*, the personal relationship between O'Brien and Carpenter was not broken. They jointly launched the *Southern Star* in 1840. Soon O'Brien was in prison, however, and he quarreled with Carpenter about money. O'Brien expected that some of the profits of the *Southern Star* would go toward the upkeep of his wife and children while he was incarcerated, but in the absence of evidence that a precise agreement was made it is not clear that Carpenter broke his word. What is clear is that O'Brien objected to Carpenter's application to Thomas Allsop, among others, for financial backing for the *Southern Star*. O'Brien told Allsop that he had not known in advance of Carpenter's intentions. He did not approve of what Carpenter had done. He was embarrassed (Carpenter approached individuals to whom O'Brien already owed money), and he hoped that nobody would connect him with such "villainy," but he confessed that he feared they would.[37]

Money was also important in the quarrel between O'Brien and Ernest Jones in 1854. Jones had risen to a position of ascendancy in the National Charter Association, and his *People's Paper* was now the main Chartist organ. He shared some of O'Brien's ideas, had offered him column space in the *People's Paper*, addressed meetings with him, and joined with Gammage in an effort to raise money for O'Brien in 1852. Gammage had subsequently turned against Jones and lost a paid position in the NCA. He proposed that O'Brien should be joint editor of the *People's Paper* as a way of undermining Jones and securing a regular income for O'Brien. The original prospectus for the *People's Paper* did provide for the election of a coeditor by the Chartist body, but Jones resisted, for he was far from affluent himself (he was indebted to the wealthy stockbroker Allsop just as O'Brien was), and he had conducted the paper alone for two years without taking any payment. Accused of an intrigue to hijack the paper, O'Brien responded by insisting that he knew of no such plan, that he had not asked to be joint editor, and that nobody in the National Reform League had made any move to this end. Among Chartists, however, Jones was able to garner sympathy at O'Brien's expense. He included numerous letters in the *People's Paper* that took his side and opposed a change in editorial arrangements, and there were various unsavory claims and counterclaims about who did what and who said what in whose hearing. Gammage declared that he had only spoken of O'Brien as joint editor after the proposal had been made by others. O'Brien rejected an allegation made in print by Jones that he had refused to write for the *People's Paper* unless he received a share of the profits that Jones wanted to devote to the people's movement. O'Brien also referred to times when Jones did not include material offered by him despite previously agreeing to do so.[38]

Judging by the memoirs of other leading Chartists, O'Brien was not important. Though Gammage wrote of him more favorably and at greater length than most of the other leaders, Gammage, as noted, was not impartial. The Newcastle radical and temperance campaigner Robert Lowery was quite frequently in O'Brien's company in the late 1830s.[39] Lowery published autobiographical chapters in 1856–57—some eighty thousand words in all—and provided fascinating insights into early Chartism. He referred to O'Brien only twice. He and O'Brien addressed meetings together in Scotland in 1839, and they were appointed by the first Chartist Convention to go to Ireland—but O'Brien chose not to go because, Lowery claimed, he knew he would not get a hearing. The suggestion here was that O'Brien lacked courage.[40]

O'Brien features hardly at all in such works as *The Life of Thomas Cooper, Written by Himself* (1872) and *The Life and Struggles of William Lovett* (1877). Cooper, who rose to prominence as a radical leader in Leicester, remained loyal to O'Connor when O'Brien went his own way in the early 1840s, though he later apologized and admitted that O'Brien had deserved better at the hands of his fellow Chartists. It was probably Cooper who persuaded the poet E. P. Mead to attack O'Brien in 1842.[41] (Both Cooper and Lovett became enemies of O'Connor, so they had that in common with O'Brien.) In his autobiography Cooper referred to O'Brien only twice (his breach with O'Connor, his willingness to join the Complete Suffrage Union).[42] O'Brien had come to know Lovett when they both campaigned for reform in the early 1830s in London, and they were important figures in early Chartism, but O'Brien's suspicion of the London Working Men's Association extended to Lovett because he was its leader. He was also close to Place. In 1839 O'Brien argued that Lovett should not be secretary of the Chartist Convention because the secretary ought to be a consensus figure and the LWMA was not entirely trusted by the laboring masses, especially in the industrial towns of the North (partly a reflection of the tension in early Chartism between "moral force" and "physical force"). In 1842 Lovett, like O'Brien, approved of the Complete Suffrage Union. The two did agree on certain political and religious topics, though they were never on friendly terms. In 1853 Lovett objected to the use of premises he owned—the National Hall in Holborn—for a celebration of Robespierre's birthday chaired by O'Brien.[43] In Lovett's autobiography O'Brien is mentioned only four times (his editorship of the *Poor Man's Guardian*, his remarks at the Chartist Convention of 1839 about the people's right to arm, his motion to dissolve the convention when it had finished its deliberations, and his trial in 1840).[44]

More than thirty years after O'Brien's death, Linton (who had written the "Dedication" of 1885) remembered him as "perhaps the cleverest man of our party, and a forcible speaker," yet had nothing further to add.[45] Linton's one-time colleague William Edwin Adams acknowledged O'Brien only as a figure in decline. This "tribune of the people in the palmy period of Chartism" was a quarrelsome misfit who became "a social and almost intellectual wreck." His ideas on political reform, the land, and currency "made him an authority among a small school of Chartists," and he retained a personal following into the 1850s, but by then he was merely "a loafer in Fleet Street." Adams wrote: "It was there that I used to see him towards the close of his career—shabby, snuffy, beery. A good speaker even to the last, he was in demand at . . . debating halls of the Metropolis. For opening a discussion in a pothouse, he was rewarded with five shillings and his night's liquor."[46] Drink and politics went together, meeting places were also drinking places, and the remarks of Adams were still doing the rounds among historians more than a hundred years after O'Brien's death.[47] But in fairness to O'Brien, Adams only knew him when he was past his prime, and it was probably debt and illness that made him appear "shabby," not alcoholism. (Audiences would hardly have gathered to hear him speak had he been a drunkard, and known as such.) In any case, O'Brien did not care what other *leaders* thought of him. He broke with them and condemned them in his papers. His reputation depended much more on his standing among the radical body, and beyond.

Reputation is connected to forms of communication.[48] The primary forms of communication for O'Brien were correspondence, lectures and speeches, and above all print. O'Brien prioritized his relationship with his readers. After the *Poor Man's Guardian* folded at the end of 1835, he found other outlets. A series of "Bronterre's Letters" appeared during 1836. O'Brien made a personal request for support. He clearly believed that his name counted for something. His letters, he explained, would fulfill the pledge he had previously made to his readers—that he would never abandon them—and he trusted them not to abandon him. His letters would be signed "Bronterre . . . the name under which I first drew attention as a public writer." As "Bronterre," O'Brien intended "to inspire my readers with some confidence in my integrity" and to communicate "as a man would write who desired to make his readers his friends."[49]

In January 1837 O'Brien launched *Bronterre's National Reformer*. It only lasted eleven weeks, but he initially had high hopes. The first number included an address that mixed biographical detail with political purpose. O'Brien assumed that by telling people about his life and experiences, they would be more willing to trust him. He described his arrival in London as a trainee lawyer nearly eight years before, and his decision to devote himself to radical causes. "I found the law was all fiction and rascality, and that radical reform was all truth and matter of dire necessity." Now that he had his own paper he was determined to make the most of it. The stamp regulations meant that he could not include "news or occurrences" without paying a tax, which would increase the price of *Bronterre's National Reformer* and limit its circulation. The government made allowances for publications that supported its policies, O'Brien went on, but he could expect no such indulgence. Therefore, he had made an arrangement with the editor of the *London Mercury*, John Bell, to write about current affairs for that paper. He could fill *Bronterre's National Reformer* with ideas that were "applicable in all times and places." He asked readers to send him information on the condition of the working classes, the activities of trade unions, and the strength of the "democratic party" in different parts of the country. O'Brien also addressed his readers' concerns, and his own, in the correspondence section of *Bronterre's National Reformer*. He wanted an ongoing debate in order for the publication to be useful.[50]

The major development in metropolitan radicalism in the early months of 1837 was the initiative headed by the London Working Men's Association for a People's Charter. *Bronterre's National Reformer* backed the six points and welcomed the decision to put together a mass petition for what was in effect "a new parliamentary constitution" that would place representation on its proper basis. O'Brien appealed to his readers, again relying upon an established relationship: "My friends, I hope you will not fail to do your duty, by giving the petition and petitioners all the support in your power."[51]

*Bronterre's National Reformer* ceased publication in the spring of 1837. O'Brien's book on Robespierre appeared in the following year. It began with a statement to "my friends and fellow-labourers"—that is, "the radical and social reformers of Britain and Ireland." As well as being designed to do justice to Robespierre and stimulate support for democratic change, the book was meant to prepare the way for other writings that O'Brien had in progress.[52] He was announcing that his relationship with his readers would continue. Over time the relationship would not infrequently be interrupted, as when his papers failed, but he repeatedly restored it with new publications. This meant that his communication with them could carry on. He simply took up where he had left off.

O'Brien was associated with several newspapers in the late 1830s and early 1840s, but to his mind the most promising avenue opened in the summer of 1842 when he became editor and co-owner of the *British Statesman*. He altered its price and size twice, hoping to boost circulation, but at the end of 1842 the *British Statesman* had to be sold.

In the first number of O'Brien's *British Statesman* there was an address "To the Unenfranchised Millions, Their Friends of the Middle Classes, and More Particularly to the Subscribers of the O'Brien Press." O'Brien confirmed that he would have full independence as editor and that he would make his paper a force for "genuine democracy," and he called upon his readers to play their part. If they backed the *British Statesman* they would be backing him, for he was "liable to sink or swim with the fortunes of the paper." The following week, the whole of the front page was given over to statements from O'Brien. Three pages were devoted to the "Progress of the Movement" (O'Brien gave most space to Chartist activities and the Complete Suffrage Union), and letters of congratulation to O'Brien upon his return as a newspaper proprietor covered more than two and a half columns.[53]

Chartists should build alliances, O'Brien argued. The premise was that he knew what was best for the people. His hope was that the people would understand and respond in the manner prescribed. Yet the people did not buy the *British Statesman* in sufficient numbers, and O'Brien was unable to save it.[54] He had edited the *British Statesman* for less than seven months. He made hardly any money from it, and when it was sold he was not in good health. His next paper, the *Poor Man's Guardian and Repealer's Friend* of 1843, lasted only thirteen weeks. As before, O'Brien began with confidence. His morale was soon undermined by personal, political, and financial circumstances, and he looked to "all my old friends, disciples, and supporters in town and country."[55] He asked for help to raise money. He was still respected—his correspondents called him "Citizen Editor" and "My Dear Schoolmaster"—but he could not easily translate this into a secure livelihood.[56]

After the demise of the *Poor Man's Guardian and Repealer's Friend*, O'Brien thought of emigration to the United States. A lecture tour and donations from friends would, he thought, provide enough for himself and his family to make the journey. He subsequently decided upon a different course of action: he would set up on the Isle of Man, to take advantage of its freedom from postage charges and newspaper taxes. From October 1844 he occupied rooms in Duke Street, Douglas, and established a library, a printing and stationery business, and a paper, the *National Reformer*. The latter failed, but then he relaunched it as the *National Reformer and Manx Weekly Review* in October 1846.[57]

Each week the *National Reformer and Manx Weekly Review* offered long editorials, three to four pages of correspondence between O'Brien and his readers, and plenty of domestic and foreign news along with reviews and comment. On the letters pages he carried on detailed discussions (some of which became quarrels), and in his editorials he told "all true Chartists" what they should be thinking and doing.[58] Once again, however, he was unable to sustain his relationship with readers in a financially viable way. The paper failed in May 1847. O'Brien went back to London. He showed remarkable resilience in these years. With each failure he decided that if he tried again he would be successful. He was convinced that people needed him. He could not allow himself to be separated from them.

In November 1848 he reentered the newspaper business with his *Power of the Pence*, resuming contact with "friends and readers."[59] The *Power of the Pence* lasted for five months. He was soon in print again. The *Social Reformer*, edited by "Bronterre O'Brien and Friends," began to appear in August 1849. His correspondents were glad to have him back and hoped that the new paper would sell enough copies to survive. They wanted what O'Brien wanted—"a revolution of the mind," as one of them put it.[60] This is indicative of the continuing rapport between O'Brien and his public. Despite all that had happened, and all the time that had passed, O'Brien's followers still regarded him as one of their own, as their champion and mouthpiece. On this basis he could be both the servant and hero he wanted to be. He had created a reputation. Nevertheless, even among Chartists he had only minority appeal. Reputation did not bring the levels of influence and income that O'Brien had expected.

His combative nature and difficult relationships with other leaders contributed to this disappointment. Though he did not find it impossible to work as part of a team, from the mid-1840s he rarely did so, and if he was shunned by others he also *chose* to act alone. This could be regarded as a strength, for he cared about his independence and integrity and was determined to stick to his own program. It could be considered a weakness, though, because he opened himself up to charges that he was selfish and argumentative. In August 1851, for example, discussions began for a broad-based organization that would bring together elements from the O'Brienite, Owenite, internationalist, Chartist, and middle-class reform camps. Eventually the National Charter and Social Reform Union was established. O'Brien's National Reform League committed itself to the new initiative, but then O'Brien changed his mind, finding that the NCSRU was too divided on key questions to make real advances. The NRL contingent withdrew. O'Brien advised that the NCSRU should allow itself to be guided by the people. He favored a wide coalition but doubted that prevalent political and social conditions were conducive, and he was frustrated by the lack of agreement on aims and methods among the groups involved in the NCSRU. The main reason given by the NRL for withdrawing was a concern to prevent disunity in Chartism by staying focused on the six points. Yet when the NCSRU issued a manifesto, there was nothing in it to which O'Brien and his body could have taken exception (the Charter, land nationalization, a free press, free education, better employment of labor, and a just distribution of wealth). O'Brien's critics did not understand or approve of his refusal to help the NCSRU. He seemed stubborn and antagonistic, unable and unwilling to be a team player.[61]

This impression was reinforced even by commentators who respected O'Brien, helped him out financially, and adopted some of his principles. In the *Reasoner* during 1852, radical and secularist George Jacob Holyoake took issue with O'Brien's constant refrain that nobody in the reform press was brave enough to tell the truth. Wherever O'Brien went he said the same thing, Holyoake reported, and his self-centeredness was becoming tiresome. He usually attended meetings with "a tail," a number of followers who "call for him in season and out of season."

> When Mr. O'Brien had a paper, he of course told the *whole* truth, but it was soon seen that other papers told more, for upon many points Mr. O'Brien has very narrow views. Yet many people believe what he thus confidently asserts, and will continue to believe it unless someone takes the liberty, as we do now, of denying respectfully but emphatically the truth of what he so alleges.

Holyoake thought that O'Brien's "egotistic dogmatism" limited his usefulness and influence.

> Mr. O'Brien complains that no public men take up his doctrines on Land, Currency, and Exchange. How can he expect anybody to agree with him who agrees with nobody but himself? Mr. O'Brien has become a sort of perambulatory dissenter, attending every meeting and disagreeing with everything and everybody.

A correspondent, "L'ami de la liberté," wrote to the *Reasoner* to object to Holyoake's remarks.

> I ask you to point out to me even one among the some 400 newspapers of this kingdom that devotes itself to the elucidation of the equal rights—social, political, and moral—of the universal family of man. I admit that a few of them do

> occasionally touch upon some of these rights; but I distinctly aver that none of them ever continuously, systematically, or *earnestly* advocate them. Which among the "respectable" press (you know that your own paper, and the *Northern Star* and a few others, are not "respectable" in the *genteel* sense of the word), which of them dare denounce landlordism, profit-mongering, and usury, as the true causes of all the social, and the greater part of even the physical and moral, evil in the world?
>
> You complain that Mr. O'Brien goes about to public meetings with a "tail," who call for him in season and out of season. If by "tail" you mean a clique acting concertedly for the sake of obtruding Mr. O'Brien upon public notice, I emphatically deny that any such "tail" exists. The fact is that a number of the working classes have been imbued with the true theory of human rights, as taught by Mr. O'Brien; and it is not to be wondered at if they are anxious that their favourite teacher should be heard, or that they should sometimes protest against the false doctrines too often instilled into the public ear by *ignorant misleaders* or *false friends* of the people.
>
> You call Mr. O'Brien a perambulatory dissenter, who goes about disagreeing with everybody and with everything. Now, so far as my experience goes, I never knew a public man more ready than he is to accord to every man his due. It is true that he will never submit to a compromise with error for the sake of temporary applause or to promote personal interests.

Holyoake responded by pointing to the discrepancy between O'Brien's position, that no newspaper dared to tell the truth, and the correspondent's admission that "a few" in fact did. He rejected the correspondent's statement about the "tail" of O'Brienites, and he repeated that O'Brien was too inflexible.

> That Mr. O'Brien will not submit to compromise, is no more than is true of many persons and papers that he denounces. The misfortune is that Mr. O'Brien . . . considers everything a compromise which does not meet his views, and hurls serious accusations at his brother reformers—making the fraternity of democracy a bear-garden of imputations.[62]

In an age when orality mattered as much to radical leaders as communication through print, O'Brien was an active public speaker. His personal appearances were meant to enhance his fame and generate support for his publications. Matthew Bevis, in exploring the union of platform and print, and performance and reputation, has emphasized that radical leaders had to "carry the crowd." Orality flourished alongside the growth of the market for print. The vocal and the written were equally important, and written texts shaped speech just as platform rhetoric and the rhythms of the spoken word influenced writing.[63] Carrying the crowd was essential to radical leaders' efforts to win approval for their ideas, to broaden political participation through oratory and ritual, and to make extraparliamentary politics matter no less than deliberations inside Parliament. Owen Ashton includes O'Brien among the Chartist leaders who became "personalities" through their oratory, a development to which command of language, impressive bearing, and memorable dress and mannerisms all contributed. O'Brien was still able to carry the crowd at the end of his career.[64]

When O'Brien was conducting the *British Statesman* he tried to help it with personal appearances. His lecturing and writing were connected. In July 1842 he mentioned that he had spoken at more than 150 meetings since his release from prison in September 1841. He would go on seeking to enlighten the public, he added, both as speaker and writer.[65] In 1843, when the *Poor Man's Guardian and Repealer's Friend* was facing collapse, O'Brien solicited speaking engagements in an effort to raise money. He hoped for audiences in and around London.[66] Personal appearances were also offered when he was based on the Isle of Man, as part of O'Brien's strategy to make the *National Reformer and Manx Weekly Review* pay its way. In December 1846 he announced that he would be traveling to London. He stopped en route to speak in Liverpool and Manchester (assistants carried on the paper in his absence, and he sent material to them for inclusion). He wrote that he was willing to attend any meetings that could be arranged, especially in London: "All I require is a day's notice; and that the meetings or lectures shall be attended by men who are in earnest in desiring to do some real good for the country." Concern was mounting about the land, currency, credit, and exchange, and O'Brien wanted to give his opinions in person as well as in the press.[67] He lectured in London in February 1847 while continuing to seek financial support for the *National Reformer and Manx Weekly Review*.[68] After London he addressed meetings in Manchester, Edinburgh, and Glasgow. These went well and showed that "our doctrines are finding support."[69]

While conducting the *Power of the Pence* O'Brien again offered personal appearances. He knew well enough by now that his paper would not last unless he promoted it effectively. He made plans to speak on political reform, national prosperity, socialism, the land, and credit and exchange at venues in London, Leicester, Manchester, Glasgow, and any other towns from which he received invitations, during the spring of 1849. To begin with, he took the chair every Monday evening at "The Wheatsheaf," Hand Court, Holborn, and every Friday evening at the Scientific and Literary Institute, John Street, Fitzrovia. He promised "friendly discussions . . . on all the engrossing questions of the day."[70]

O'Brien combined his writing for the *Social Reformer* with activities at the Eclectic Institution. He provided "improving" classes and lectures at different locations, including the John Street Institute and his office in Hollywell Street, Strand.[71] The *Social Reformer* publicized events that were organized to raise money for "the Eclectic Club," and the club made good any weekly losses on the paper. By October 1849 O'Brien had a regular Sunday night speaking engagement in Newman Street, Fitzrovia, not far from the John Street Institute.[72]

O'Brien's personal appearances underpinned his reputation. As fund-raising exercises they were not successful, for he did not make much money either for himself or for his papers. They preserved a relationship and instructed minds, however, and had he not gone on lecture tours or convened political meetings or associated himself with particular clubs and venues, it would have been more difficult for him to sustain his reputation. Able still to attract an audience in his later years, his self-image as servant of the people remained intact.

Though O'Brien was a fine orator, print was a more important medium for him because he could reach more people in a paper than he could through personal appearances. The character he wished to establish rested squarely on claims to integrity and consistency. In the first of "Bronterre's Letters" of 1836, O'Brien declared that in everything he had written since taking up radical causes he had never deviated from his stated principles. He was not writing for individual aggrandizement or with seditious purposes. He wrote only to explain the "erroneous and atrocious" condition of British society and to spread knowledge, so that people would be better able to understand problems and apply remedies.[73] These purposes were also in his mind when he published his annotated translation of *Buonarroti's History of Babeuf's Conspiracy*. Under the "particular arrangement" made for this publication in 1836, none of the money from sales went to O'Brien. Therefore, if he recommended it as "a good textbook for all genuine Radicals" there could be no question as to his motives; and he wanted readers to notice the harmony between the doctrines that had been advanced by the *Poor Man's Guardian*, those elaborated in the notes in *Buonarroti's History*, and those that O'Brien was now expounding in his letters.[74] He prided himself on his record.

O'Brien believed that his influence would decrease if he allowed doubts to arise about his integrity. He moved to dispel any suggestion of error or inconsistency, as when he justified his support for a file-smiths' strike in Sheffield even though he disagreed with their effort to restrict entry to the trade. The employers had all the advantages, he wrote. They had powerful friends, plenty of money, and the ability to hold out longer than the workers. The workers wanted higher wages. In return, employers demanded that a limit on apprentices be removed. With a larger labor pool, O'Brien stressed, employers would in future find it easier to alter wages and conditions to suit themselves. The workers were right to resist. If they did not strike today, they might face pauperization tomorrow.

> The attempt to limit the number of workmen and apprentices to be taken by the masters, I consider to be, *in the abstract*, unjust, but being a minor injustice, consequent upon and rendered necessary by a major injustice on the part of the masters, and of the laws the masters help to make, I for that reason support and defend it. . . . Nor am I inconsistent in this. My object being to put down injustice, I am necessarily led to drive at the aggressive injustice first, which renders the minor ones necessary; and that point settled, I am then ready to drive at the inferior and secondary ones.[75]

O'Brien continued to base appeals on his own good name. In *Bronterre's National Reformer* he stood on his record.[76] In the *Life and Character of Robespierre* there were further statements about his consistency. Half way through the book he included a notice to readers that referred to his many previous attacks on the aristocracy and the professional and commercial middle classes, the propertied and moneyed oppressors of the people who used their political power, social status, and economic ascendancy to block reforms. "In all my preceding observations on the upper and middle orders . . . I wish to be distinctly understood, as not including in my censure the *individuals* of those orders who are *friendly* to the emancipation of the labouring classes." Furthermore, "in all cases where I speak fiercely of the upper and middle classes, I mean my denunciations to apply to the *knowing* and *willing* oppressors only—never to the unwilling, ignorant, or thoughtless." O'Brien preferred not to break up the flow of his arguments by constantly restating this proviso. He had made the same point in other writings, so his readers already knew what he thought without having to be reminded.[77] This assumed bond of familiarity and trust was very important to O'Brien's self-image as the servant of the people.

Later, in the *British Statesman*, O'Brien decided that he ought once again to explain his position regarding a merger with middle-class reformers. Clearly this was a matter upon which he was sensitive. He urged the people to receive as allies "the honest and sensible portion" of the middle classes, but he was not suggesting that democrats should yield. Middle-class reformers had to shift toward them, not the other way round. O'Brien offered advice along these lines to "our old and dear friends the Working Classes."[78]

Although, as he often did, O'Brien was presenting his personal desires in an objective guise, the cooperation he favored had much to commend it. O'Brien was breaking from mainstream Chartism in the early 1840s, however, and many within the movement no longer wished to follow his lead. The divergence was illustrated in the *British Statesman*, which carried material against O'Connor's *Northern Star* and gave space to the factional in-fighting between Chartist groups and leaders.[79]

O'Brien was at the center of some of this disputation and could be as abusive and unforgiving as anyone involved. In August 1842 he wrote that O'Connor and the *Northern Star* had done all they could to destroy the *British Statesman*. They had lied about O'Brien and accused him of inconsistency, but if Chartists reflected for a moment they would realize that it was O'Connor, not O'Brien, who frequently changed his position on public questions. O'Brien was praised and O'Connor condemned in correspondence from numerous Chartists that was published in the *British Statesman*. O'Brien also released a *Vindication*, in which he replied to allegations made against him in the *Northern Star*.[80]

Consistency was an attribute, and a selling point, that O'Brien prized for himself and his newspapers. Yet the preservation of consistency seemed a thankless task. By the time of his involvement with the *National Reformer and Manx Weekly Review*, in the spring of 1847, O'Brien was expressing anger and resentment. For all his consistency, and self-sacrifice, he had not received much help to make a success of his papers:

> Were I to accept an appointment tomorrow at ten or twelve guineas a week, on a metropolitan Whig or Tory paper (and time was when I could have got the larger sum), the great bulk of the Chartist body (yourselves included) would call me renegade, apostate, traitor, turncoat. There is no name, however opprobrious, they would think too bad for me. Yet, for being true and faithful to your interests for sixteen long years, to the deep injury of myself and my family, they would appear to have no better reward for me than the prospect of being doomed to fill a most arduous and responsible situation for life, not only without pay but attended with

> positive and ruinous loss. In truth, but for my own personal and non-political friends, I should have been dead and buried long ago.[81]

O'Brien had to face facts. The advantages that accrued from reinforcing and making use of his reputation had been diminishing. He believed that he still had an important role to play, and others thought so too, but doubts were creeping in, and to O'Brien's self-conception as servant and hero was added another component—victim.

As early as 1832 O'Brien displayed a tendency toward self-pity, though this was done privately in a letter to Robert Owen. By taking up political journalism and reform agitation, O'Brien was conscious that he had cut himself off from family and friends who disagreed with his choice. He suggested to Owen that no servant of the people could expect an easy life, not least because prevailing social and political conditions were so obscene, so overwhelming, that they inevitably affected personal relationships.

> I cannot conclude these remarks without expressing my deep regret that my avocations in life have been hitherto such as to preclude the possibility of my taking an active part in so glorious a work without risking my prospects in life, and what I regard still more, the friendship and esteem of almost all those I love. Indeed, the part I have taken already, although confined to private circles, has done me serious injury. It is truly mortifying to think that a man is doomed by the present unnatural system to suffer persecution and neglect just in proportion to the extent of his wishes to benefit mankind.[82]

Notwithstanding the victimhood complex, for most of his career O'Brien wore the mantle of people's servant with self-assurance. In "Bronterre's Letters" he made no secret of his belief that he was peculiarly fitted to guide and instruct. He had the best ideas and the necessary talents.[83] On occasion he also congratulated writers who were laboring in the same field as himself. He identified by name Augustus Beaumont, the American who arrived in London in 1835, wrote for the *Radical*, and joined the London Working Men's Association before relocating to Newcastle-upon-Tyne and editing the *Northern Liberator*.[84] Beaumont's creed overlapped with O'Brien's—"an equal opportunity to every man of obtaining all the advantages of society; no one having a monopoly, and each exclusively enjoying the produce of his own industry and intellect"—and O'Brien reprinted some of Beaumont's material from the *Radical*. At the same time, he was quick to make clear who was the principal and who the subordinate in this common radical endeavor: "I thank my stars that Bronterre has at last got one hand to assist him."[85]

O'Brien sought to develop a sense of intimacy and familiarity with his public. He directly addressed "the working classes" time and again, using personal language to plead with, encourage, and advise them. Late in 1838 he referred to growing excitement about the prospect of war and issued one of his most impassioned appeals. He denied that war would be appropriate or necessary—not to defend India from Russia, nor to put down the Canadian rebellion, nor to prevent France from challenging British economic interests in the Mediterranean and South America. The working classes must decide, O'Brien declared, for there could be no war without their concurrence, and he urged them to cast off old assumptions and think clearly about what he was telling them.

> In case a war be got up by the aristocracy and shopocracy of this country, *will you, the Working Classes, fight for them*? If you stupidly say "yes, yes," as your fathers did in the late war, I shall forever despair of you. If you vehemently exclaim "NO! NO!" and "NEVER!" I shall have hopes of your speedy regeneration.[86]

In *Bronterre's National Reformer* O'Brien asserted that the progress of his paper would benefit the people. If it was successful, the people would be successful. He identified himself and his paper with the people's welfare and the fate of radical reform. He seized upon any increase in readership, any sign that his ideas were winning approval, any sales in a town that had not previously taken his work.[87] Since he was their servant and guide, O'Brien reasoned, the people should follow his advice and purchase and read his publications.[88] O'Brien had no doubt that he should be recognized and rewarded for his services.[89]

He was equally adamant that his newspapers failed through no fault of his own. The reasons were to be found in the ill will of others and in the evils of the newspaper business. As the people's servant, O'Brien was obliged to carry on. He belonged to them, and their duty was to support him. In O'Brien's makeup there was a will to serve and a readiness to put principle before profit, but there was also egomania. O'Brien held that his personal circumstances were of *public* importance and that reformers should *care* about what happened to him. His setbacks were a reflection on them, just as his victories would be their victories.

During the 1840s O'Brien became increasingly frustrated. It was galling, he confessed, to find his ideas being taken more seriously, even by political opponents, at a time when his ability to exploit this opportunity was diminished by lack of funds. In 1847 he pointed to the impact of his advocacy of currency reform (in the *National Reformer and Manx Weekly Review*) on the Conservative *Morning Post* ("Though we are acknowledged only under the vague title of an '*Isle of Man journal*' . . . we feel abundantly content with having, in our obscurity, supplied this text . . . Verily, we are progressing!").[90] He struck a similarly celebratory tone when he saw the Whig *Liverpool Mercury* discussing matters it would have shunned just a few years earlier, including currency reform.[91] But what good was all this if O'Brien's newspapers kept running out of money?

O'Brien's sense of grievance grew rapidly. He felt unappreciated. He vented his resentment when *Bronterre's National Reformer* came to an abrupt end, its last issue appearing on 18 March 1837. O'Brien did not admit to any personal shortcoming. Instead, he tried to explain why his paper had not gained the patronage it merited. The work was sound, he concluded, but the response to it inadequate. "Little do the working classes know what a man has to contend against, whose soul yearns to serve and save them."[92] Was a life of noble self-sacrifice for the sake of an ungrateful populace to be O'Brien's destiny? This would prey on his mind in the following years.

One of the purposes of his book on Robespierre was to increase anticipation for other writings O'Brien had in progress, "which I should have completed long ago, had it not been for the pecuniary disabilities to which my politics have hitherto condemned me." He wanted financial assistance in the form of sales. If people ignored this, they would not only sentence O'Brien to hardship but would also sentence themselves to further years of misgovernment. O'Brien urged his readers not to allow their champion to be cut down, as Robespierre had been cut down.[93]

Among the obstacles facing the authentic radical tribune was the lack of access to effective networks of communication and information, for these were mostly controlled by his adversaries. O'Brien's indignation came to the fore in this area. In the Robespierre book he claimed that all efforts to establish a democratic organ in London had failed owing to the limits imposed by the government and the domination of the press by wealthy elites.

> The press is, from top to bottom, one crawling mass of corruption, in the hands of unprincipled speculators, sold, body and soul, if such devils can have souls, to the ruling classes. What, from the state of the law, and what, from the infernal combinations of proprietors, printers, publishers, and news-vendors, the establishment of an honest poor man's press is next to impossible.[94]

This was illustrated again in October 1842, when O'Brien appealed for money to continue the *British Statesman.*[95] Messages of support flooded in, and various schemes were mooted to place the *British Statesman* on a better footing. O'Brien believed that no radical leader was more deserving of support than he was. He described himself as "a man who (whatever his enemies may pretend) has dared and suffered more than any other man living for our common principles, and who, although the name of his calumniators and persecutors is Legion, has never yet been able to get one of them to meet him before the Public."[96] Time ran out for the *British Statesman,* much to O'Brien's chagrin: "I am destroying my health and my happiness in the attempt to do what other people ought to do for their own sakes with or without me."[97]

Despair turned into renewed gusto when O'Brien returned with the *Poor Man's Guardian and Repealer's Friend* of 1843, but within weeks he received a warning from a correspondent in Edinburgh, describing opposition to the paper in that town, which prompted the following statement:

> Every mean and clandestine effort is being resorted to, to destroy the *Guardian* by preventing its circulation; but we shall see our beloved wife and four infant children starved to death before we surrender our right to defend the plenitude of the poor man's claims to his legitimate share of every advantage of the social state. . . . For this it is that our destruction is equally sought by the Government and the traitors in our own party.

O'Brien informed his "friends and readers" that "I have done my best for you, but under existing circumstances I cannot do a tithe of a tithe of what I desire." A correspondent in Salford expressed regret that the paper was not being marketed more energetically, and O'Brien agreed, pointing to the lack of money for posters and advertisements. Revelations surfaced about agents who were refusing to sell the paper, apparently in obedience to leaders to whom O'Brien had given offense. "Conspiracy," he complained, was always perpetrated against radicals who told the truth and refused to bow to factions.[98]

O'Brien imagined that his enemies were mocking him. They would probably make much of the failure of yet another of his papers, but they never explained *why* these failures happened. In every case, O'Brien insisted, the problem was lack of money (and not worth). The *British Statesman* had been financially insecure before O'Brien took charge of it, and would have folded had he not agreed to edit it and take on part-ownership. Earlier papers had not had sufficient capital and credit and had faced competition from other radical organs. A few had failed only after O'Brien had ceased to be associated with them. He had increased the circulation of every paper he had written for or edited, but this was a fact that his enemies liked to keep quiet, as was the fact that many papers failed each year—most of which had more money and backing than O'Brien's ever enjoyed. Criticism from O'Connor was particularly unjust. When O'Brien joined the *British Statesman*, it cost 5d. and sold twelve hundred copies a week. Under O'Brien its sales passed twenty-six hundred a week, at the higher price of 6d. O'Connor was claiming that it failed because of O'Brien, but it really failed because of the debt O'Brien had inherited when he took over and because O'Connor and his followers attacked it, knowing that O'Brien wished to be independent and would not yield to them. O'Brien hoped that by making all this absolutely clear he could correct false impressions.[99]

When the *National Reformer and Manx Weekly Review* ran into difficulties, O'Brien appealed again to "brother reformers and working men and women. . . . All I ask, for the present, is some indulgence and consideration in return for all the sacrifices I have made."[100] He trusted that he would not be abandoned by his "subscribers, readers, and friends" and "all who feel sincerely desirous to establish the political and social rights of the unrepresented and oppressed classes." O'Brien was not asking for a handout. Unwilling to take advantage of those he was trying to serve, he preferred to provide copies of his paper or advertising space as repayment for the sums advanced to him. If the paper failed, it would not be his fault, nor that of his loyal readers, "but the people's generally, who would neither support my paper nor start one of their own."[101]

One Yorkshire Chartist, John Kennedy of Ripon, wrote to wish O'Brien good luck and to condole with him on the level of aid he had received. O'Brien took the opportunity to highlight the spread of ideas he had long been promoting, and to attack other Chartist leaders, men who had either opposed him or not done enough to help him. He claimed that his principles would have gained many more adherents had it not been for Feargus O'Connor, Henry Vincent, William Lovett, Peter Murray McDouall, James Leach, Thomas Cooper, Ernest Jones, R. J. Richardson, Matthew Fletcher, "and all the other old and new chiefs of the popular party." Their cowardice and selfishness had prevented them from joining with O'Brien and taking up a truly radical program. Instead, they had been "nibbling, like mice in a cheese, at sectional abuses, or trying to feather their own nests, through the medium of ephemeral political speculations, which are all destined to end in smoke and in disappointment and stink."[102]

The *National Reformer and Manx Weekly Review* could not be saved, and whatever satisfaction it gave O'Brien to blame others and to feel that his talents and services had not been properly acknowledged, its demise in May 1847 marked another disappointment. In his next publication, the *Power of the Pence*, old frustrations and animosities resurfaced. Early in 1849 he published an editorial titled "Liberty of the Press." The condition of the press in Britain was mortifying, he wrote. Much depended on the social context. In a healthy social order with enlightened public opinion, an effective press helped to preserve the best features of the existing society, but in a corrupt society the press tended to reflect the errors sanctioned by a contaminated public opinion. O'Brien took this personally. He asserted, in addition, that the *National Reformer and Manx Weekly Review* had failed in part because of official persecution. The paper had made headway, and was covering its costs, when the government decided to lay postage charges upon O'Brien, even though the Isle of Man was traditionally excluded from such charges and no other publication that came from the island was targeted in this manner. O'Brien resented both the financial demands that were made of those who wished to conduct newspapers, and the cutthroat rivalry in the newspaper business, "the trade." He had been subjected to each of these inappropriate and unnecessary afflictions. In Britain, it appeared, only the middle and upper classes could set up newspapers that made money. If the workers had one that paid its way, the government would close it down.[103]

In the *Social Reformer* O'Brien reemphasized his sacrifices for the people and his need for assistance. The *Social Reformer* ceased to appear in October 1849.[104] O'Brien thought he had been let down again by those who should have given him more backing. His reversal was also a blow to them and to the causes they all believed in. Their enemies had enjoyed another triumph. This was no reason to give up, but it did highlight the lack of appreciation accorded to O'Brien for his labors, and even more the circumstances (especially in the political system and newspaper business) that worked against honest radicals of O'Brien's ilk. O'Brien continued to claim that he was sacrificing himself for something bigger. He retained a dominant self-image, a concern for reputation, and a strong sense of grievance.

There is a current of complaint in O'Brien's letters to his friend Mathews. During 1856, 1857, and 1858, O'Brien wrote of his efforts to serve the people, the recognition to which his labors entitled him, but which he had not received, and the ongoing consequences in terms of lack of money to advertise and print. He kept hoping that "the democrats" would assist him and "my friends" would arrange loans or gifts, so that he could worry less about his family and focus on radical reform. Sometimes

O'Brien expressed confidence that his prospects were improving, but even in the good times he was frustrated because he wanted to do more and was prevented.[105] He made this point many times to another correspondent, Thomas Allsop, from the mid-1840s and into the 1860s. If he could just obtain a modest amount to live on, he thought, he would be better placed to raise money to cover publishing costs. He could thereby overcome the persecution of "the middle classes," be an even more effective people's champion, and repair the damage that had been done to his "public name."[106] If he was not active, visible, and valued, O'Brien realized, it would be impossible for him to maintain reputation, to contribute as he wished to reform debates, and to correct misunderstandings—or lies—about himself and his ideas.

O'Brien was sensitive about his reputation to the end of his days. Then, as in earlier years, he was still seeking recognition and support.[107] He continued to write and lecture, which kept his name before the public, and one of the reasons he went to Tiverton in the spring of 1857 to stand against Lord Palmerston in the general election was to sustain his own celebrity status. A publication of 1859 included remarks "To Many Enquiring Old Friends Whom I Cannot Answer By Private Letter." O'Brien explained why he had not reprinted earlier articles, or finished the full biography of Robespierre he had commenced in the 1830s, or written "the larger and more important works I promised the public twenty-two years ago," including a "philosophical history of England," a "real history of the French Revolution," and a "philosophical review of the life and times of Oliver Cromwell."

> Voluminous and elaborate works, requiring great research, profound thought, and the exercise of the gravest judgment, as well as of the higher faculties of the mind in the way of critical analysis and disquisition, ought not to be lightly undertaken. Such works can come only from men in circumstances sufficiently easy to ensure to them personal safety, mental composure, and diligent application to the work on hand, undistracted by every-day cares and anxieties, merely to subsist a family from hand to mouth. I need say no more. Had the Chartists of 1839 kept their word with me, I could have kept mine with them.[108]

Since his release from prison in 1841 he had known poverty and debt. Yet he would have enjoyed an income of £1,500 a year from writing and lecturing,

> had it not been for the dark and malignant combination by which the middle classes have closed the public press against me, shut me out of every literary and

> scientific institution in the kingdom, as a lecturer, and, latterly, all but banished me from the public platform, through the agency of hired or deluded mobs, headed by ex-Chartist renegades and ex-socialist imposters, who have made their peace with the middle classes to escape starvation and be let live an easy life.[109]

This combination of forces against him gave O'Brien a ready-made explanation for all his disappointments over the years. He was a casualty in the conflict between moneyed and propertied elites on one side, and the productive laboring masses on the other. Servant of the people, O'Brien merged the personal and the political to the extent that there was no distinction between individual wants and the public interest. His career was bound up with the fate of radicalism. He became the central figure in the drama. What happened to him became evidence of the corruption of state and society.

O'Brien's experiences raise questions about the limits and potential of extra-parliamentary political leadership in Britain during the Chartist era. No leader could lead without the appropriate reputation. On reputation depended influence, status, treatment by others, and self-understanding. How was reputation to be built, sustained, and employed if not through the principal means of radical communication and mobilization—the platform and especially print? Leaders had to capture and command the attention of their supporters, and if influence was to be expanded, and reputation perpetuated, they probably had to reach beyond their core support base as well. O'Brien's career provides a useful case study. In his fixation with reputation; in his constant exertion to preserve it through demonstrations of consistency, principle, usefulness, intellect, and devotion; in his appeal to the workers and call for cross-class political alliances; in the image he sought to project and the explanations he offered when things did not go his way: in all these respects, O'Brien's thoughts and actions cast light on the gains made by radicalism in the early and mid-nineteenth century and on some of the reasons why it could advance no further at that time.

O'Brien placed responsibility for his problems on others and on unfavorable circumstances. Convinced that his services should be recognized and rewarded, he found ways of interpreting failure that kept intact his self-understanding, and this made him bold and resilient when it came to creating and defending reputation. O'Brien's career also reveals a great deal about the content and purchase of radical politics in his day, especially in relation to the presentation of ideas and the interaction of writer and reader; it offers insight into methods of opinion formation and the nature and amount of influence available to radical leaders; and it clearly establishes the importance of reputation. O'Brien's celebrity as servant of the people proved to be both asset and burden.

# Notes

### Introduction

1. Antony Taylor, "Commemoration, Memorialization, and Social Memory in Post-Chartist Radicalism: The 1885 Halifax Chartist Reunion in Context," in *The Chartist Legacy*, ed. Owen Ashton, Robert Fyson, and Stephen Roberts (Rendlesham, 1999), 271–72, 276–77.
2. See John Saville, introduction to Theodore Rothstein, *From Chartism to Labourism: Historical Sketches of the English Working Class Movement* (London, 1983), xxii–xxiii, xxvi.
3. Rothstein, *From Chartism to Labourism*, 53, 91, 100–106, 349.
4. Rothstein, *From Chartism to Labourism*, 22–24, 48–49, 52, 80, 101.
5. Malcolm Chase, *The Chartists: Perspectives and Legacies* (London, 2015), 20–21, 174. See also Dorothy Thompson, *The Dignity of Chartism: Essays by Dorothy Thompson*, ed. Stephen Roberts (London, 2015), 194.
6. Edward Porritt, review of "Columbia Studies" of 1916, *American Historical Review* 22 (1917): 649–52; F. C. Mather, review of F. F. Rosenblatt, *The Chartist Movement in Its Social and Political Aspects* (London, 1967), *Economic History Review* 22 (1969): 147–48; Gregory Claeys, *Citizens and Saints: Politics and Anti-politics in Early British Socialism* (Cambridge, 1989), 209–10.
7. Dorothy Thompson, *Outsiders: Class, Gender, and Nation* (London, 1993), 28, 32; Asa Briggs, introduction to G. D. H. Cole, *Chartist Portraits* (New York, 1965), xi; Graham

Wallas, "O'Brien, James [Bronterre]," *Dictionary of National Biography*, vol. 41, ed. Sidney Lee (London, 1895), 315–16.

8. London School of Economics, Wallas Papers, 1/48/10–11, 29–31, Beer to Wallas, 12 Oct., 11 Nov. 1911.
9. Mark Hovell, *The Chartist Movement* (Manchester, 1959), 23, 32, 40, 95–96, 125, 150, 167–68, 188, 197, 215, 236–38, 240, 245, 267, 275, 297, 304.
10. Julius West, *A History of the Chartist Movement* (New York, 1968), 43, 70–72, 87–88, 95, 195, 217, 226, 245, 282.
11. Reg Groves, *But We Shall Rise Again: A Narrative History of Chartism* (London, 1938), 25–26, 118, 121, 202–3, 210.
12. Alfred Plummer, *Bronterre: A Political Biography of Bronterre O'Brien, 1804–1864* (Toronto, 1971); Alfred Plummer, "The Place of Bronterre O'Brien in the Working-Class Movement," *Economic History Review* 2 (1929): 61–80; *Lives of Victorian Political Figures II*, vol. 4: *James Bronterre O'Brien*, ed. David Stack (London, 2007), xxi–xxiv, 109, 144, 174; Thomas Kemnitz, "Recent Work on the Chartist Movement," *Newsletter: European Labour and Working-Class History* 2 (1972): 25–27; "A Radical in His Time," *Times Literary Supplement*, 20 Aug. 1971 (a review of Plummer's *Bronterre*); Cole, *Chartist Portraits*, xvi; Chase, *The Chartists: Perspectives and Legacies*, 21; Ray Faherty, "Bronterre O'Brien's Correspondence with Thomas Allsop: New Evidence on the Decline of a Chartist Leader," *Newsletter: European Labour and Working Class History* 8 (1975): 28–33. Eagerness to consult newly available sources led Rachel O'Higgins, then working on a study of the Irish influence in Chartism, to write direct to the vendors of the Allsop letters in 1967. This was the first body of previously unknown material relating to O'Brien that had emerged in many years. London School of Economics, Allsop Collection, Misc.525/1, Rachel O'Higgins to Francis Edwards Ltd., and the reply, 2 and 10 Oct. 1967.
13. See especially Ben Maw, "Bronterre O'Brien's Class Analysis: The Formative Phase, 1832–1836," *History of Political Thought* 28 (2007): 253–89; and Ben Maw, "The Democratic Anti-Capitalism of Bronterre O'Brien," *Journal of Political Ideologies* 13 (2008): 201–26.
14. Asa Briggs, "National Bearings," in *Chartist Studies*, ed. Asa Briggs (London, 1959), 296, 301; and Asa Briggs, introduction to Cole, *Chartist Portraits*, vii–viii.
15. F. C. Mather, *Public Order in the Age of the Chartists* (Manchester, 1959), 7, 16.
16. F. C. Mather, review of *An Anthology of Chartist Literature*, ed. Yuri Kovalev (London, 1957), *Victorian Studies* 2 (1958): 178–80; John Saville, introduction to R. G. Gammage, *History of the Chartist Movement, 1837–1854* (New York, 1969), 18–19.
17. W. H. Maehl, introduction to R. G. Gammage, *Reminiscences of a Chartist* (Manchester,

1983), 14–16.

18. Dorothy Thompson, *The Chartists: Popular Politics in the Industrial Revolution* (New York, 1984), 37–38, 49–50, 55–56, 101–5, 129, 131, 305–6; Dorothy Thompson, *Dignity of Chartism*, 51–52, 127–31; Dorothy Thompson, "Ireland and the Irish in English Radicalism before 1850," in *The Chartist Experience: Studies in Working-Class Radicalism and Culture, 1830–1860*, ed. James Epstein and Dorothy Thompson (London, 1982), 129–30; *National Reformer and Manx Weekly Review*, 22 Mar. 1847.
19. See *The People's Charter: Democratic Agitation in Early Victorian Britain*, ed. Stephen Roberts (London, 2003), 14–15; Miles Taylor, *Ernest Jones, Chartism, and the Romance of Politics, 1819–1869* (Oxford, 2003), 138; Maehl, introduction to Gammage, *Reminiscences of a Chartist*, 16–17; G. D. H. Cole, *A History of Socialist Thought* (5 vols., London, 1953–61), 1: 153.
20. Thompson, *The Chartists*, 101–2; Eileen Yeo, "Some Practices and Problems of Chartist Democracy," in Epstein and Thompson, *Chartist Experience*, 350; Malcolm Chase, *Chartism: A New History* (Manchester, 2007), 145; Maehl, introduction to Gammage, *Reminiscences of a Chartist*, 14; J. B. O'Brien, *The Life and Character of Maximilian Robespierre* (London, 1838), 284.
21. See Martin Lawn's review of Alec Ellis, *Educating Our Masters: Influences on the Growth of Literacy in Victorian Working Class Children* (Brookfield, Vt., 1985), *History of Education Quarterly* 26 (1986): 614–17. Lawn thinks that Ellis pays insufficient attention to working-class self-education as a (sometimes informal, noninstitutional) group activity.
22. Nicholas Rogers, "Class and Popular Education in Nineteenth-Century Britain," *History of Education Quarterly* 19 (1979): 482; and for arguments about the usefulness, or otherwise, of fiction, see Paul Murphy, "'Imagination Flaps Its Sportive Wings': Views of Fiction in British Working-Class Periodicals, 1816–1858," *Victorian Studies* 32 (1989): 339–64.
23. *Poor Man's Guardian*, 20 Sept. 1834.
24. Patricia Hollis, *The Pauper Press: A Study in Working-Class Radicalism of the 1830s* (Oxford, 1970), 10, 20–21, 23, 143–44; Iorwerth Prothero, *Artisans and Politics in Early Nineteenth-Century London: John Gast and His Times* (London, 1981), 298.
25. Hollis, *Pauper Press*, 275.
26. National Cooperative Archive, Manchester, Robert Owen Papers, GB1499, ROC/15/3/1, O'Brien to Owen, 27 May 1832.
27. Hollis, *Pauper Press*, 275–80.
28. Paul Pickering, *Chartism and the Chartists in Manchester and Salford* (Basingstoke, 1995), 160.
29. Edward Royle and James Walvin, *English Radicals and Reformers, 1760–1848* (Lexington,

Ky., 1982), 149. Royle had earlier highlighted O'Brien's "socialist analysis" as part of the eclectic radicalism of the 1820s and 1830s, which brought together various political, religious, social, and economic elements. Despite the importance of O'Brien's writing in the *Poor Man's Guardian*, however, and his ongoing activities into the 1850s, when his works were still read and he lectured regularly at socialist and secularist venues, Royle wonders about his impact, not least because of the unchanging, conservative sentiment that continued to grip some of those venues. See Edward Royle, *Victorian Infidels* (Manchester, 1974), 43, 140, 207, 215.

30. Hollis, *Pauper Press*, 106.
31. Faherty, "O'Brien's Correspondence with Thomas Allsop," 28–33; Stack, *Bronterre O'Brien*, xxii–xxiv, 109, 144, 174.
32. Thomas Kemnitz, "Chartist Newspaper Editors," *Victorian Periodicals Newsletter* 5 (1972): 4.
33. J. T. Ward, *Chartism* (New York, 1973), 54, 71, 108, 150–51, 220–21, 244.
34. A. R. Schoyen, *The Chartist Challenge: A Portrait of George Julian Harney* (New York, 1958), 14, 16, 59, 78–79, 84, 109–10, 122.
35. Ward, *Chartism*, 150–51, 159, 244; Henry Weisser, review of Ward's *Chartism*, *American Historical Review* 80 (1975): 643–44.
36. Gary Entz, *Llewellyn Castle: A Workers' Cooperative on the Great Plains* (Lincoln, Nebr., 2013), 33–34, 36–38.
37. Maw, "Democratic Anti-Capitalism," 201, 210–11, 215–19.
38. Gwynne Lewis, "Robespierre through the Chartist Looking-Glass," in *Robespierre*, ed. Colin Haydon and William Doyle (Cambridge, 1999), 196–97, 200, 203, 208, 210.
39. C. C. Barfoot and Theo D'haen, "Tropes of Revolution: Introduction," in *Tropes of Revolution: Writers' Reactions to Real and Imagined Revolutions, 1789–1989*, ed. C. C. Barfoot and Theo D'haen (Amsterdam, 1991), 7–8; Joanna Innes, Mark Philp, and Robert Saunders, "The Rise of Democratic Discourse in the Reform Era: Britain in the 1830s and 1840s," in *Re-imagining Democracy in the Age of Revolutions*, ed. Joanna Innes and Mark Philp (Oxford, 2013), 120–21; Henry Weisser, "Chartist Internationalism, 1845–1848," *Historical Journal* 14 (1971): 58–59.
40. David Jones, *Chartism and the Chartists* (London, 1975), 37–40, 64, 186–87; Stack, *Bronterre O'Brien*, xxix; Royle and Walvin, *English Radicals*, 169–70; Thompson, *The Chartists*, 105; V. G. Kiernan, *Poets, Politics, and the People* (London, 1989), 152–53, 156–60, 165–66, 175; D. F. Schafer, "James Bronterre O'Brien: A Working-Class Radical, 1831–1842" (MA thesis, University of Oklahoma, 1967), 100; Andrew Messner, "Land, Leadership, Culture, and Emigration: Some Problems in Chartist Historiography," *Historical Journal*

42 (1999): 1097–98, 1107. John Garrard has also noted working-class radicalism's reliance on leaders, like O'Brien, who were not from working-class backgrounds. Garrard adds: "To achieve acceptance at a time of intense class antagonism, such men had to identify their lives with those they led, and often partially to detach themselves from their origins." John Garrard, *Democratization in Britain: Elites, Civil Society, and Reform since 1800* (Basingstoke, 2002), 205. To the extent that O'Brien was recognized at the time as aloof and condescending, his influence would have been limited. It is not clear that many workers regarded him in this way, however, and of course in his lifestyle and experiences he had much in common with them.

41. Thompson, *Outsiders*, 28, 30, 32, 39–41, 58; Briggs, introduction to Cole, *Chartist Portraits*, ix, xi.
42. Carl Brand, review of Theodore Rothstein, *From Chartism to Labourism: Historical Sketches of the English Working-Class Movement* (New York, 1929), *American Historical Review* 35 (1930): 914–15; Chase, *The Chartists: Perspectives and Legacies*, 16–17, 20–21.
43. Cole, *Chartist Portraits*, 239–42, 256–57, 261, 265–67.
44. Cole did think enough of O'Brien to include him in the first volume of *A History of Socialist Thought*, published in 1953. This volume, dealing with "The Forerunners, 1789–1850," has O'Brien listed among fifty-four "Principal Characters," and O'Brien is mentioned several times in a chapter on Chartism. But Cole's overall verdict is hostile. O'Brien gave up "revolutionary ideas" after 1841, and "nothing" came of his post-1848 proposals until the 1880s; though he "survived to count for something after 1848," he "might have counted for a great deal more if he had been able to keep off the drink." Chartism produced no socialist theory of its own, and despite O'Brien's "intellectual claims," he "did little beyond echoing other men's ideas" (Cole apparently means the ideas of Robert Owen, Louis Blanc, and Karl Marx). This is hardly a fair estimation of O'Brien's contribution, and Cole can be challenged on specifics too—as with his claim that O'Brien favored "a working-class uprising against the rich" and then switched to nonviolence, and retreated to a policy of gradual, compensated, parliamentary transfer of land after having advocated a more aggressive confiscation of property. All this obscures both the complexity of and the consistencies in O'Brien's thought. See Cole, *A History of Socialist Thought*, 1: 142, 148, 150, 153–57.
45. Hollis, *Pauper Press*, viii, 100, 203–4, 207, 210.
46. Hollis, *Pauper Press*, 218–58, 286–90, 293, 299, 302.
47. Noel Thompson, *The Market and Its Critics: Socialist Political Economy in Nineteenth-Century Britain* (London, 1988), 121–25, 179–81; Peter Gurney, "'Rejoicing in Potatoes': The Politics of Consumption in England during the 'Hungry Forties,'" *Past and Present*

203 (2009): 101–2, 136; E. P. Thompson, "The Moral Economy of the English Crowd in the Eighteenth Century," *Past and Present* 50 (1971): 76–136; E. P. Thompson, *Customs in Common: Studies in Traditional Popular Culture* (London, 1991), 337; Sharon Bolton and Knut Laaser, "Work, Employment, and Society through the Lens of Moral Economy," *Work, Employment, and Society* 27 (2013): 511–12; Peter Linebaugh, "Commonists of the World Unite!" *Radical History Review* 56 (1993): 61–62.

48. E. P. Thompson, *The Making of the English Working Class* (London, 1991), 800, 883, 903–5.
49. Plummer, *Bronterre*, 25; and Plummer, "O'Brien in the Working-Class Movement," 61–80.
50. Plummer, *Bronterre*, 37, 73, 80, 139–40, 158.
51. Plummer, *Bronterre*, 247–50, 253–54, 256–58.
52. Stack, *Bronterre O'Brien*, xxxi, 231–32; Logie Barrow, "The Homerton Social Democratic Club, 1881–1882," *History Workshop* 5 (1978): 188–99; Stan Newens, "Thomas Edward Bowkett: Nineteenth-Century Pioneer of the Working-Class Movement in East London," *History Workshop* 9 (1980): 143–48; Andrew Whitehead, "Dan Chatterton and His 'Atheistic Communistic Scorcher,'" *History Workshop* 25 (1988): 83–99; Stan Shipley, *Club Life and Socialism in Mid-Victorian London* (London, 1983), chs. 1–3; Janet McCalman, "Respectability and Working-Class Politics in Late Victorian London," *Historical Studies* 19 (1980): 120–22; Noel Thompson, *The Real Rights of Man: Political Economies for the Working Class, 1775–1850* (London, 1998), 125–28, 133–34; E. Eldon Barry, *Nationalization in British Politics* (Stanford, Calif., 1965), 49–50, 54–57, 90–91, 109; Gregory Claeys, *Machinery, Money, and the Millennium: From Moral Economy to Socialism, 1815–1860* (Princeton, N.J., 1987), 158, 163, 217; Henry Collins and Chimen Abramsky, *Karl Marx and the British Labour Movement: Years of the First International* (London, 1965), 24, 73, 128–29, 249, 252; Mark Bevir, *The Making of British Socialism* (Princeton, N.J., 2011), 17–18, 107, 111–15, 119–21.
53. Shipley, *Club Life and Socialism*, ch. 1 and appendix 2; Mark Lause, "The American Radicals and Organized Marxism: The Initial Experience, 1869–1874," *Labor History* 33 (1992): 63–64, 79; Lewis Feuer, "The Influence of the American Communist Colonies on Engels and Marx," *Western Political Quarterly* 19 (1966): 460–62; Andrew Whitehead, "The *New World* and the O'Brienite Colony in Kansas," *Bulletin of the Society for the Study of Labour History* 53 (1988): 40–43; Entz, *Llewellyn Castle*, 135–39, 217.
54. Miles Taylor, *The Decline of British Radicalism, 1847–1860* (Oxford, 1995), 37–38, 99, 104–7, 109, 113–14, 122, 255–56.
55. Robert Saunders, *Democracy and the Vote in British Politics, 1832–1867* (Farnham, 2011), 4–9, 13, 28–31, 33, 37.
56. Bernard Moss, "Republican Socialism and the Making of the Working Class in Britain,

France, and the United States," *Comparative Studies in Society and History* 35 (1993): 409–10.

57. McCalman, "Respectability and Working-Class Politics," 108–9, 111, 119–22.
58. Hollis, *Pauper Press*, 299–300; Edward Royle, *Revolutionary Britannia? Reflections on the Threat of Revolution in Britain, 1789–1848* (Manchester, 2000), 142; Samuel Bernstein, "Babeuf and Babouvism" (parts 1 and 2), *Science and Society* 2 (1937–38): 192; Samuel Bernstein, "From Utopianism to Marxism," *Science and Society* 14 (1949–50): 63; Samuel Bernstein, "Buonarroti's Classic History of Babouvism," *Science and Society* 21 (1957): 346–52; and Samuel Bernstein, "Some Recent Historical Literature: From the Enlightenment to the Commune," *Science and Society* 22 (1958): 343–45.
59. David Thomson, *The Babeuf Plot: The Making of a Republican Legend* (London, 1947), 63; U. G. Weatherly, "Babeuf's Place in the History of Socialism," *Publications of the American Economic Association*, 3rd ser., 8 (1907): 113–24; K. D. Tönnesson, "The Babouvists: From Utopian to Practical Socialism," *Past and Present* 22 (1962): 60–76; V. G. Simkhovitch, "Marxism versus Socialism," *Political Science Quarterly* 24 (1909): 641–66; Richard Widdicombe, "Early Histories of Utopian Thought," *Utopian Studies* 3 (1992): 35.
60. See "Book Notes," *Science and Society* 30 (1966): 124.
61. See reviews of Edouard Dolléans, *Le Chartisme, 1830–1845* (Paris, 1913) by J. H. Clapham, *English Historical Review* 29 (1914): 389–90; and Walter Hall, *American Historical Review*, 20 (1915): 406–7.
62. Joel Wiener, "The Press and the Working Class, 1815–1840," *Victorian Periodicals Newsletter* 4 (1971): 1–4; Richard Ashcraft, "Liberal Political Theory and Working-Class Radicalism in Nineteenth-Century England," *Political Theory* 21 (1993): 259–61, 263, 270.
63. See Desmond Morton, review of H. S. Foxwell, *Bibliography of the English Socialist School* (London, 1976), *Victorian Periodicals Newsletter* 11 (1978): 139; Christiane Eisenberg, "Variations in Socialism: The Rise of a Political Labour Movement in Britain and Germany," *Diplomacy and Statecraft* 8 (1997): 124–38; E. A. Kosminski, "Russian Work on English Economic History," *Economic History Review* 1 (1928): 230.
64. H. J. Laski, "Introduction to the *Communist Manifesto*," *Social Scientist* 27 (1999): 61, 78; Max Morris, "Chartism and the British Working Class Movement," *Science and Society* 12 (1948): 405–6, 416–17.
65. Morris underlined O'Brien's contribution to political theory in general, and independent working-class perspectives in particular. "Bronterre O'Brien, above all, was feeling his way to a scientific analysis of the capitalist state, and to an understanding of the political, legal, and cultural implications of capitalist property relations. Unlike Marx, however, he was not able to develop a coherent theory of the system." See *From Cobbett to the*

*Chartists, 1815–1848: Extracts from Contemporary Sources*, ed. Max Morris (London, 1951), 20–21, 131.

66. Kenneth Morgan, review of Kristine O'Connor, *Joan Maynard: Passionate Socialist* (London, 2003), *English Historical Review* 119 (2004): 576–77.
67. "Honouring the Memory of Bronterre O'Brien: The Address by Arthur Scargill at the 1996 Commemoration in Abney Park Cemetery," Race Mathews Papers, MS9967, Box 140, State Library of Victoria, Melbourne, Australia.
68. Paul Sweezy, "Origins of Present-Day Socialism," *Science and Society* 12 (1948): 76–77, 79; Gareth Stedman Jones, "Some Notes on Karl Marx and the English Labour Movement," *History Workshop* 18 (1984): 129–30; Stack, *Bronterre O'Brien*, 226; Entz, *Llewellyn Castle*, 57–60; Henry Collins, "The English Branches of the First International," in *Essays in Labour History*, ed. Asa Briggs and John Saville (London, 1960), 247, 257, 259–60, 263, 266–67, 274. Collins argues that the O'Brienites—with their "characteristic blend of physical force Chartism, producers' cooperation, and land and currency reform"—played an important role in the development of socialist thought in the 1870s.
69. Ralph Fox, "Marx, Engels, and Lenin on the British Workers' Movement," *Bulletin of the Marx Memorial Library* 118 (1986–87): 9–10; Mark Bevir, "Marxism and British Socialism," *The European Legacy: Toward New Paradigms* 1 (1996): 545–49; Maw, "O'Brien's Class Analysis," 285–89; Wiener, "Press and the Working Class," 1–4.
70. Joel Wiener, *The War of the Unstamped: The Movement to Repeal the British Newspaper Tax, 1830–1836* (Ithaca, N.Y., 1969), 122, 210, 221.
71. "For the centre of gravity of the materialist conception of history lies in the fact that it sees in the *classes* of society the instruments of the historical process, and to O'Brien belongs the honour of having been one of the very few thinkers who realized this before Marx." During the 1830s O'Brien was "foremost among those who most clearly and consistently brought an understanding of class antagonisms and of the resulting class struggles to bear upon the treatment of the questions of the day." Rothstein, *From Chartism to Labourism*, 100, 105.
72. Thompson, *Real Rights of Man*, 14, 56–57, 111–12, 114, 117, 120–22; Claeys, *Machinery, Money, and the Millennium*, 158–60.
73. Claeys, *Citizens and Saints*, 175, 190, 239–46, 260, 271–72, 317, 319–20.
74. Schafer, "James Bronterre O'Brien," 1, 13, 100; Robert Iverson, "Babouvism and James Bronterre O'Brien: A Study of the Role of Continental Radicalism in the Development of British Socialism" (MA thesis, State University of Iowa, 1949), 61, 70, 179.
75. The early part of Pelling's book is devoted to the "socialist revival" of the 1880s, but there is a statement about the survival of "remnants of Chartism" and a suggestion that

there had been a gradual increase in socialist strength before the 1880s, making the "revival" less of a "great turning-point" than it might appear. Henry Pelling, *The Origins of the Labour Party, 1880–1900* (Oxford, 1965), 5, 7, 13–37. See also Mira Stern's review of Pelling's book in *Science and Society* 19 (1955): 79–80.

76. H. M. Hyndman, "Socialism in England," *North American Review* 143 (1886): 228; Sidney Webb, "Socialism in England," *Publications of the American Economic Association* 4 (1889): 19; Taylor, "Commemoration, Memorialization, and Social Memory," 271–72, 276–77; Logie Barrow and Ian Bullock, *Democratic Ideas and the British Labour Movement, 1880–1914* (Cambridge, 1996), 11–12; Barry, *Nationalization*, 46, 63, 71, 136–37; J. F. C. Harrison, *Robert Owen and the Owenites in Britain and America: The Quest for the New Moral World* (London, 1959), 249; Mark Bevir, "The British Social Democratic Federation, 1880–1885: From O'Brienism to Marxism," *International Review of Social History* 37 (1992): 207–29; Mark Bevir, "Republicanism, Socialism, and Democracy in Britain: The Origins of the Radical Left," *Journal of Social History* 34 (2000): 352–56; Paul Fox and H. Scott Gordon, "The Early Fabians: Economists and Reformers," *Canadian Journal of Economics and Political Science* 17 (1951): 309; Paul Thompson, "Fabian Socialism," *Past and Present* 25 (1963): 89; Fox, "Marx, Engels, and Lenin," 11–13; Iverson, "Babouvism," 181–82; Entz, *Llewellyn Castle*, 178–206, 216, 219–23.
77. Laura Mayhall, review of Barrow and Bullock, *Democratic Ideas*, *Social History* 23 (1998): 119–22.
78. See E. C. K. Gonner's review of W. J. Linton, *The English Republic*, ed. Kineton Parkes (London, 1891), *English Historical Review* 7 (1892): 800–802.
79. C. R. Fay, review of Cole, *Chartist Portraits*, *Economic Journal* 52 (1942): 66–69.
80. Wallace Douglas, review of the first edition (1948) of Morris, *From Cobbett to the Chartists*, *Science and Society* 13 (1948–49): 90–92; and for an introduction to some different strands in Chartism—political, social, collectivist, communitarian, cultural, and others—see Ian Haywood, *The Literature of Struggle: An Anthology of Chartist Fiction* (Aldershot, 1995).
81. Gammage, *Reminiscences of a Chartist*, 24, 39, 75.
82. On the context see Barry, *Nationalization*, 63; Claeys, *Machinery, Money, and the Millennium*, 163; Iverson, "Babouvism," 161, 181; David Martin, "The Agricultural Interest and Its Critics, 1840–1914," in *Agriculture and Politics in England, 1815–1939*, ed. J. R. Wordie (Basingstoke, 2000), 128–48; Stedman Jones, "Some Notes on Karl Marx," 129; Clyde Reeves, "Henry George's Speaking in the Land Reform Movements: The West Coast 'Training Phase,'" *American Journal of Economics and Sociology* 24 (1965): 54; Robert Home, "Peri-Urban Informal Housing Development in Victorian England: The

Contribution of Freehold Land Societies," *Planning Perspectives* 25 (2010): 366–67; Entz, *Llewellyn Castle*, 179–80, 183–85.

83. Stack, *Bronterre O'Brien*, xxx–xxxii, 179–80, 226, 232.
84. Entz, *Llewellyn Castle*, 21–23, 48.
85. E.g., Babeuf, one of O'Brien's heroes of the French Revolution, should be seen as a facilitator of practical, not utopian, forms of socialism according to Weatherly, "Babeuf's Place," 113–24.
86. Barry, *Nationalization*, 28, 31–34.
87. Miles Taylor, "O'Brien, James [Bronterre]," *Oxford Dictionary of National Biography* (Oxford, 2004), online edition, May 2009; Thomas Horne, *Property Rights and Poverty: Political Argument in Britain, 1605–1834* (Chapel Hill, N.C., 1990), 246–47; Chase, *Chartism: A New History*, 338, 349.
88. These statements are taken from reviews of Plummer's *Bronterre*: by Joseph D'Oronzio, *American Historical Review* 78 (1973): 103–4; by W. H. Maehl, *Journal of Modern History* 44 (1972): 596–98; and by Patricia Hollis, *Victorian Studies* 16 (1972): 237–40.
89. See "A Radical in His Time," *Times Literary Supplement*, 20 Aug. 1971; also Stack, *Bronterre O'Brien*, xxi–xxii; and Kemnitz, "Recent Work," 25–27.
90. David Stack, "A Question of Character: The Reputation of Bronterre O'Brien in the Chartist Movement," paper delivered at Chartism Day, a conference at the University of Sheffield, 16 June 2007, as reported in the *Society for the Study of Labour History Newsletter* 6 (2007): 10–11.
91. Stack, *Bronterre O'Brien*, xix, 179, 220.
92. Gammage, *Reminiscences of a Chartist*, 23–24, 30, 42.

## CHAPTER 1. RISE OF THE "SCHOOLMASTER"

1. *Bronterre's National Reformer*, 7 Jan. 1837; Gammage, *Chartist Movement*, 71–72; Plummer, *Bronterre*, 15–34; Bernard Canavan, "The Edgeworths of Edgeworthstown: A Rediscovered Heritage," *History Workshop Journal* 43 (1997): 240–48; Cole, *Chartist Portraits*, 242–43; Taylor, "O'Brien, James"; Thompson, "Ireland and the Irish," 129; Peter Brock, "Polish Democrats and English Radicals, 1832–1862: A Chapter in the History of Anglo-Polish Relations," *Journal of Modern History* 25 (1953): 143; Collins and Abramsky, *Marx and the British Labour Movement*, 4; Hollis, *Pauper Press*, 313; Prothero, *Artisans and Politics*, 275; Stack, *Bronterre O'Brien*, xii–xiv, xxviii, xli, 1–2, 17.
2. *Dictionary of Nineteenth-Century Journalism in Great Britain and Ireland*, ed. Laurel Brake and Marysa Demoor (Gent, 2009), 97, 466; Plummer, *Bronterre*, 37, 43–45, 48–49,

52–53, 56–57; Chase, *Chartism: A New History*, 14–16; Stack, *Bronterre O'Brien*, xiv–xv, xli, 1–2, 17–18; Cole, *Chartist Portraits*, 239, 241–43, 246; Thompson, *The Chartists*, 14, 17, 23, 29, 31–32, 35–36, 42; J. T. Ward, *The Factory Movement, 1830–1855* (London, 1962), 175, 179–80; Wiener, *War of the Unstamped*, 89–90, 120, 146, 166, 168, 213–14, 221–22, 269–70; Groves, *But We Shall Rise Again*, 25; Asa Briggs, "The Local Background of Chartism," in Briggs, *Chartist Studies*, 18; Asa Briggs, introduction to the 1965 edition of Cole, *Chartist Portraits*, xi; Asa Briggs, "The Language of 'Class' in Early Nineteenth-Century England," in Briggs and Saville, *Essays in Labour History*, 68–69; Gammage, *Chartist Movement*, 72–73, 76; Jones, *Chartism and the Chartists*, 37–38; Ward, *Chartism*, 54, 64–66, 69–71, 77–78, 150; Royle and Walvin, *English Radicals*, 149.

3. Plummer, *Bronterre*, 73–76, 84–88, 139–40, 152, 165–67, 176–77; Kemnitz, "Chartist Newspaper Editors," 1–2, 4–5; Alexander Wilson, "Chartism in Glasgow," in Briggs, *Chartist Studies*, 272; Jones, *Chartism and the Chartists*, 97, 99–100; Gammage, *Chartist Movement*, 206; Ward, *Chartism*, 77–78, 107–8, 144, 150–51; Dorothy Thompson, *The Early Chartists* (Columbia, S.C., 1971), 44, 57–61; Thompson, *The Chartists*, 37–38, 42, 49–50, 268–69; Chase, *Chartism: A New History*, 16, 44, 236, 241; Malcolm Chase, "Building Identity, Building Circulation: Engraved Portraiture and the *Northern Star*," in *Papers for the People: A Study of the Chartist Press*, ed. Joan Allen and Owen Ashton (London, 2005), 25, 35, 37; Hollis, *Pauper Press*, 108, 291; Stack, *Bronterre O'Brien*, xv–xviii, xix, xli–xliv, 18, 61–62, 71–72, 88, 109–10, 131–32, 173–74, 180, 192, 219, 226; Cole, *Chartist Portraits*, 244, 246, 248–50, 254, 259.
4. *Bronterre's National Reformer*, 7 Jan. 1837.
5. *Operative*, 11 Nov. 1838.
6. *Northern Star*, 27 Jan. 1838.
7. Thompson, *Outsiders*, 52–53; Joel Wiener, review of Paul Murphy, *Towards a Working-Class Canon: Literary Criticism in British Working-Class Periodicals, 1816–1858* (Columbus, Ohio, 1994), *Albion* 27 (1995): 689–90; Ian Haywood, *The Revolution in Popular Literature: Print, Politics, and the People, 1790–1860* (Cambridge, 2004), 143–46.
8. Paul Pickering, "Class without Words: Symbolic Communication in the Chartist Movement," *Past and Present* 112 (1986): 144–46, 152.
9. Stack, *Bronterre O'Brien*, 72; Brake and Demoor, *Nineteenth-Century Journalism*, 466.
10. Hollis, *Pauper Press*, 253–57, 266.
11. *Poor Man's Guardian*, 2 Nov. 1833; Hollis, *Pauper Press*, 257–58.
12. British Library, General Reference Collection, "Bronterre's Letters," 1836, nos. 1, 5–6; *Bronterre's National Reformer*, 14 Jan., 11 Feb. 1837; *Midland Representative and Birmingham Herald*, 18 Feb. 1832; *Poor Man's Guardian*, 26 May 1832, 29 Aug. 1835; *Power*

*of the Pence*, 16 Dec. 1848; Jones, *Chartism and the Chartists*, 139; Hollis, *Pauper Press*, 266; Derek Fraser, "The Agitation for Parliamentary Reform," in *Popular Movements, 1830–1850*, ed. J. T. Ward (Basingstoke, 1970), 51; Morris, *From Cobbett to the Chartists*, 25, 131–33, 137–39, 144, 169–70; Rothstein, *From Chartism to Labourism*, 22–24, 98–99; Prothero, *Artisans and Politics*, 283–84, 388; Groves, *But We Shall Rise Again*, 25–26.

13. *Manchester and Salford Advertiser*, 25 May 1839; *Poor Man's Guardian*, 26 May 1832, 3 Jan. 1835; *Twopenny Dispatch*, 10 Sept. 1836; "Bronterre's Letters," 1836, no. 9; O'Brien, *Robespierre*, 311–12; *Poor Man's Guardian and Repealer's Friend*, 1843, no. 8; Royle and Walvin, *English Radicals*, 151; Thompson, *The Chartists*, 14, 17, 23, 29, 31–32, 35–36; Thompson, "Ireland and the Irish," 126, 128; M. E. Rose, "The Anti-Poor Law Agitation," in Ward, *Popular Movements*, 81; Jones, *Chartism and the Chartists*, 60; Ward, *Chartism*, 54, 69–71, 77–78.
14. O'Brien, *Robespierre*, 280.
15. *British Statesman*, 25 June 1842; *Hansard Parliamentary Debates*, 3rd ser., 64 (1842): 551–615.
16. Dror Wahrman, *Imagining the Middle Class: The Political Representation of Class in Britain, 1780–1840* (Cambridge, 1995).
17. Alexander Wilson, "Chartism," in Ward, *Popular Movements*, 119; D. S. Gadian, "Class Consciousness in Oldham and Other North West Industrial Towns, 1830–1850," *Historical Journal* 21 (1978): 167; R. A. Sykes, "Some Aspects of Working-Class Consciousness in Oldham, 1830–1842," *Historical Journal* 23 (1980): 178.
18. "Bronterre's Letters," 1836, no. 7; *Bronterre's National Reformer*, 14, 21, 28 Jan., 25 Feb. 1837; O'Brien, *Robespierre*, 255, 279, 306, 313; *British Statesman*, 7 Jan. 1843; *Poor Man's Guardian and Repealer's Friend*, 1843, nos. 5, 7, 8; *National Reformer and Manx Weekly Review*, 10 Oct. 1846, 16 Jan., 20, 27 Feb., 22 May 1847; *Power of the Pence*, 23 Dec. 1848, 13, 20 Jan., 24 Mar. 1849; *Social Reformer*, 6, 20 Oct. 1849; Norman Gash, "After Waterloo: British Society and the Legacy of the Napoleonic Wars," *Transactions of the Royal Historical Society*, 5th ser., 28 (1978): 153–54; Hollis, *Pauper Press*, 211–13.
19. Plummer, *Bronterre*, 74–77, 80, 83–84, 87–88, 92–93, 113, 130; Cole, *Chartist Portraits*, 248–49; Thompson, "Ireland and the Irish," 140–41; Thompson, *Outsiders*, 109–12, 116, 124, 126–27; Jones, *Chartism and the Chartists*, 83, 88–89, 114; Iorwerth Prothero, "William Benbow and the Concept of the 'General Strike,'" *Past and Present* 63 (1974): 139; Chase, *Chartism: A New History*, 161; T. M. Parsinnen, "Association, Convention, and Anti-Parliament in British Radical Politics, 1771–1848," *English Historical Review* 88 (1973): 528, 530; Robert Hall, "Hearts and Minds: The Politics of Everyday Life and Chartism, 1832–1840," *Labour History Review* 74 (2009): 30, 35, 39; James Huzel, *The Popularization*

*of Malthus in Early Nineteenth-Century England* (Aldershot, 2006), 165–67, 180, 183, 186, 190–97.

20. "Bronterre's Letters," 1836, nos. 1, 4–5, 7, 9, 11, 14–15; *Bronterre's National Reformer*, 7, 14, 28 Jan., 4, 18, 25 Feb., 11, 18 Mar. 1837; O'Brien, *Robespierre*, 279–80, 311–12; *British Statesman*, 19 June, 23 July, 6 Aug., 24 Sept. 1842, 7 Jan. 1843; *Poor Man's Guardian and Repealer's Friend*, 1843, nos. 1, 5, 7, 11, 12; *National Reformer and Manx Weekly Review*, 10, 31 Oct., 7 Nov., 5 Dec. 1846, 6, 27 Feb., 13 Mar. 1847; *Power of the Pence*, 10, 17 Feb., 24 Mar. 1849; *Social Reformer*, 25 Aug., 22, 29 Sept., 20 Oct. 1849.
21. Plummer, *Bronterre*, 31–33, 35, 37, 40–42; Hollis, *Pauper Press*, 266; Jones, *Chartism and the Chartists*, 37–38; Ralph Miliband, "The Politics of Robert Owen," *Journal of the History of Ideas* 15 (1954): 237; Schoyen, *Chartist Challenge*, 12–13; Harrison, *Robert Owen and the Owenites*, 215, 259; Stack, *Bronterre O'Brien*, 2, 122, 144, 174, 219.
22. Angus McLaren, "Contraception and the Working Classes: The Social Ideology of the English Birth Control Movement in Its Early Years," *Comparative Studies in Society and History* 18 (1976): 246; James Field, "The Early Propagandist Movement in English Population Theory," *American Economic Review* 1 (1911): 223; Stack, *Bronterre O'Brien*, 25–26, 48, 226. McLaren's *Birth Control in Nineteenth-Century England* (London, 1978) points to a division within popular radicalism for and against birth control.
23. There is material relating to Finch, Rigby, and Pare in the Owen Papers, GB1499, ROC. On Campbell see W. H. Fraser, *Alexander Campbell and the Search for Socialism* (Manchester, 1996); and W. H. Fraser, "Owenite Socialism in Scotland," *Scottish Economic and Social History* 16 (1996): 60–91.
24. Owen Papers, ROC/2/31/3, J. B. Bernard to Robert Owen, 10 May 1837.
25. E.g., J. B. O'Brien, *Buonarroti's History of Babeuf's Conspiracy for Equality* (London, 1836), 213.
26. Allsop Collection, Misc.525/1/9, O'Brien to Thomas Allsop, 27 June 1855.
27. *Northern Star*, 1 July 1843.
28. *Midland Representative and Birmingham Herald*, 18 Feb. 1832; *Destructive*, 2 Feb., 9 Mar. 1833; Clive Behagg, "An Alliance with the Middle Class: The Birmingham Political Union and Early Chartism," in Epstein and Thompson, *Chartist Experience*, 63; Thompson, *Making of the English Working Class*, 896–97.
29. Owen Papers, ROC/15/3/1, O'Brien to Owen, 27 May 1832.
30. British Library, Add. MS 46,344, John Burns Papers, LXIV, ff. 1–2, Owen to Allsop, 20 Nov. 1832. Allsop appears to have become an enthusiast for Owenism at about the same time as O'Brien, and from the early 1830s he helped to raise funds for the movement, spread its message, sought positions for individual Owenites, asked to accompany Owen on

speaking tours, and even gently rebuked Owen when he thought the latter was taking on too much work or becoming too extreme in his views. See Owen Papers, ROC/1/24/1–7, Allsop to Owen, 14 Sept. 1830, 7, 13 Jan. 1832, 17 Mar. 1837, 3 Feb., 2 Aug. 1838, 7 Mar. 1840.

31. Owen Papers, ROC/15/3/1, O'Brien to Owen, 27 May 1832.
32. Gregory Claeys, "John Adolphus Etzler, Technological Utopianism, and British Socialism: The Tropical Emigration Society's Venezuelan Mission and Its Social Context, 1833–1848," *English Historical Review* 101 (1986): 357–58, 364; Frank Manuel, "Toward a Psychological History of Utopias," *Daedalus* 94 (1965): 298.
33. *Power of the Pence*, 3 Mar. 1849.
34. *Poor Man's Guardian*, 7 Dec. 1833.
35. Jacqueline Ariouat, "Rethinking Partisanship in the Conduct of the Chartist Trials, 1839–1848," *Albion* 29 (1997): 596–621.
36. *Northern Star*, 11, 18, 25 Aug. 1838.
37. O'Brien, *Robespierre*, 152–54.
38. E.g., *British Statesman*, 25 June, 2, 9, 16, 23, 30 July, 6, 13, 20, 27 Aug., 3, 10, 17, 24 Sept., 1, 8, 15, 22, 29 Oct., 5, 12, 19, 26 Nov., 10, 17 Dec. 1842; *Poor Man's Guardian and Repealer's Friend*, 1843, nos. 1–13.
39. *Social Reformer*, 1 Sept. 1849.
40. J. B. O'Brien, *An Elegy on the Death of Robespierre* (London, 1857), 14–15; and J. B. O'Brien, *A Dissertation and Elegy on the Life and Death of the Immortal Maximilian Robespierre* (London, 1859), 20–22.
41. Gareth Stedman Jones, "The Language of Chartism," in Epstein and Thompson, *Chartist Experience*, 3–58; David Lloyd and Paul Thomas, "Culture and Society or 'Culture and the State'?" *Social Text* 30 (1992): 43, 49–50.
42. *Bronterre's National Reformer*, 7 Jan. 1837; *Manchester and Salford Advertiser*, 29 July 1837; O'Brien, *Robespierre*, 283, 286–87, 351; *British Statesman*, 9 July, 1, 29 Oct. 1842; *Poor Man's Guardian and Repealer's Friend*, 1843, nos. 1, 2, 4, 8, 13.
43. Plummer, *Bronterre*, 94, 113, 117–18, 141, 160–63; Robert Hall, *Voices of the People: Democracy and Chartist Political Identity, 1830–1870* (Monmouth, 2007), 49, 51; Ward, *Chartism*, 153; Jones, *Chartism and the Chartists*, 125, 127; Royle, *Revolutionary Britannia*, 114; Chase, *Chartism: A New History*, 63, 86, 272; Royle and Walvin, *English Radicals*, 177–78; W. H. Fraser, "The Chartist Press in Scotland," in Allen and Ashton, *Papers for the People*, 92–93; Gammage, *Chartist Movement*, 103–4; Pickering, *Chartism and the Chartists in Manchester and Salford*, 161–62.
44. "Bronterre O'Brien's Address to the Electors and Non-Electors of Newcastle-upon-Tyne, written in H. M. Prison, Lancaster Castle, in June 1841." The address is reproduced in

Plummer, *Bronterre*, 264–66. See also Ward, *Chartism*, 151; Gammage, *Chartist Movement*, 194; Cole, *Chartist Portraits*, 255–57; Stack, *Bronterre O'Brien*, xliv, 121. On the Corn Law question, Malcolm Chase rightly points out that there were some protectionists within the Chartist movement, but he erroneously names O'Brien among them. Chase, *Chartism: A New History*, 272. See also Ward, *Factory Movement*, 195, 241, 302.

45. Plummer, *Bronterre*, 158.
46. Ward, *Chartism*, 77–78, 104–5, 107–8; Wilson, "Chartism in Glasgow," 262, 269; Jennifer Bennett, "The London Democratic Association, 1837–1841: A Study in London Radicalism," in Epstein and Thompson, *Chartist Experience*, 105–6; Schoyen, *Chartist Challenge*, 15–26; David Goodway, *London Chartism, 1838–1848* (Cambridge, 1982), 22–23, 25, 31; Groves, *But We Shall Rise Again*, 37–38, 41–42, 44–45, 47; Prothero, *Artisans and Politics*, 317–19, 322, 392–93; Royle, *Revolutionary Britannia*, 94; Plummer, *Bronterre*, 80–82; Stack, *Bronterre O'Brien*, xvi, 18, 72.
47. *Northern Star*, 27 Apr. 1839.
48. Allsop Collection, Misc.525/1/1, O'Brien to Allsop, 29 Nov. 1836.
49. Ward, *Chartism*, 104–5, 107–8, 113–14, 117, 119, 122–25, 128, 130–31, 137; Hollis, *Pauper Press*, 124, 131, 133, 135, 148; Plummer, *Bronterre*, 94–97, 99–100, 111–15, 118–22, 129–33, 141–51; Cole, *Chartist Portraits*, 247–54; Thomas Kemnitz, "The Chartist Convention of 1839," *Albion* 10 (1978): 152–70; Prothero, "William Benbow," 134–71; Parsinnen, "Association, Convention, and Anti-Parliament," 519–20, 526, 528–29; Morris, *From Cobbett to the Chartists*, 155; Chase, *Chartism: A New History*, 35, 63, 75–76, 86–87, 161; Gammage, *Chartist Movement*, 149, 174, 153, 178–79; Thompson, *Early Chartists*, 198; Thompson, *The Chartists*, 95; Stack, *Bronterre O'Brien*, xvi–xvii, xlii–xliv, 87–88, 109–10; Schoyen, *Chartist Challenge*, ch. 3.
50. The authorities placed him under close surveillance and began to check his mail in August 1839. Mather, *Public Order*, 221.
51. British Library, General Reference Collection, handbills: "The People's Charter!" (26 Mar. 1839); "The Chartists!" (26 Mar. 1839); and "To George Irving, Esq., Mayor of the City of Chichester" (28 Mar. 1839).
52. *Manchester and Salford Advertiser*, 11 Dec. 1841; Donald Read, "Chartism in Manchester," in Briggs, *Chartist Studies*, 49; Chase, *Chartism: A New History*, 107–8; Thompson, *Outsiders*, 61–4; E. C. K. Gonner, "The Early History of Chartism, 1836–1839," *English Historical Review* 4 (1889): 636, 642.
53. *Leeds Times*, 25 May 1839; J. F. C. Harrison, "Chartism in Leicester"; and J. F. C. Harrison, "Chartism in Leeds," both in Briggs, *Chartist Studies*, 77–78, 131; W. H. Fraser, *Chartism in Scotland* (Pontypool, 2010), 44–45, 52, 56–59, 66; Fraser, "Chartist Press in Scotland," 87;

Alexander Wilson, *The Chartist Movement in Scotland* (Manchester, 1970), 54, 72–73, 76–78, 170.

54. Fraser, *Chartism in Scotland*, 217.
55. Gammage, *Chartist Movement*, 90; Briggs, "National Bearings," 301; Fraser, "Chartist Press in Scotland," 95–96; Jones, *Chartism and the Chartists*, 83; Chase, *Chartism: A New History*, 102; Iorwerth Prothero, "Chartism in London," *Past and Present* 44 (1969): 97–98, 101.
56. Gammage, *Reminiscences of a Chartist*, 64.
57. Gammage, *Chartist Movement*, 111–14, 118–21, 135–37; Cole, *Chartist Portraits*, 248–53; Jones, *Chartism and the Chartists*, 83, 88–89; Chase, *Chartism: A New History*, 161; Ward, *Chartism*, 117, 119, 122–25; Brian Harrison and Patricia Hollis, "Chartism, Liberalism, and the Life of Robert Lowery," *English Historical Review* 82 (1967): 508; Parsinnen, "Association, Convention, and Anti-Parliament," 524, 526–29; Wiener, *War of the Unstamped*, 216–17, 230–31, 276; Mather, *Public Order*, 229; Thompson, *Early Chartists*, 21, 213; Goodway, *London Chartism*, 31.
58. Prothero, "William Benbow," 138–39, 163; Parsinnen, "Association, Convention, and Anti-Parliament," 527–29; Chase, *Chartism: A New History*, 75–76; Ward, *Chartism*, 113–14; Thompson, *The Chartists*, 62–63, 73.
59. *Bronterre's National Reformer*, 4 Feb. 1837.
60. John Plotz, "Crowd Power: Chartism, Carlyle, and the Victorian Public Sphere," *Representations* 70 (2000): 87–88.
61. W. H. Maehl, "Chartist Disturbances in Northeastern England, 1839," *International Review of Social History* 8 (1963): 397–98, 400–403; Stack, *Bronterre O'Brien*, 87–88; Stephen Roberts, *The Chartist Prisoners: The Radical Lives of Thomas Cooper and Arthur O'Neill* (Oxford, 2008), 24–28.
62. J. T. Coleridge, "My Recollections of the Circuit," *American Law Register* 9 (1861): 273–74.
63. Owen Papers, ROC/6/6/16, John Finch to Robert Owen, 8 Apr. 1840.
64. Allsop Collection, Misc.525/1/2–4, O'Brien to Allsop, 17, 23 June, 4 Aug. 1840.
65. Allsop Collection, Misc.525/1/2, O'Brien to Allsop, 17 June 1840.
66. Allsop Collection, Misc.525/1/3, O'Brien to Allsop, 23 June 1840; and for Smith's account see *Southern Star*, 12 July 1840.
67. Allsop Collection, Misc.525/2/22, O'Connor to Allsop, 26 Apr. 1840.
68. Plummer, *Bronterre*, 152–55, 159, 162–63; Stack, *Bronterre O'Brien*, xvi–xvii, xx–xxi, xxvii, xliv, 110, 121, 226; Gammage, *Chartist Movement*, 192–94; Cole, *Chartist Portraits*, 255; Thompson, *The Chartists*, 272; Ward, *Chartism*, 150; Groves, *But We Shall Rise Again*, 117; Schoyen, *Chartist Challenge*, 107; Chase, *The Chartists: Perspectives and Legacies*, 134. Chase has argued that the quarrel between O'Brien and O'Connor about the 1841 general

election has diverted historians' attention away from what the Chartists actually achieved at that election. They made an effort to contest at least thirty constituencies (though only nine of their candidates proceeded to the polls). Electoral activity was probably more important to the movement than some scholars have appreciated. See Malcolm Chase, "'Labour's Candidates': Chartist Challenges at the Parliamentary Polls, 1839–1860," *Labour History Review* 74 (2009): 65, 69–70, 77.

69. An accomplished orator, Jones became the subject of official attention and was sentenced to six months in prison for sedition after addressing a meeting in Leicester. He later spent time in the United States before returning to his hometown. Gammage, *Chartist Movement*, 210–11, 229–31, 402, 405; and Gammage, *Reminiscences of a Chartist*, 57.
70. *Chartism: Authentic Report of the Speech of Mr. William Jones upon Responding to the Toast of "The People's Charter, and May It Soon Become the Law of the Land," at a Soirée Held in Liverpool on 27 September 1841, in Celebration of the Release of James Bronterre O'Brien and Feargus O'Connor from Their Dungeons* (Liverpool, 1841), 13–16.
71. E.g., Paul Pickering, "Betrayal and Exile: A Forgotten Chartist Experience," in *Unrespectable Radicals? Popular Politics in the Age of Reform*, ed. Michael Davis and Paul Pickering (Aldershot, 2008), 202–3.
72. Gammage, *Reminiscences of a Chartist*, 57–58.
73. Plummer, *Bronterre*, 164, 167–76; Hollis, *Pauper Press*, 304–5; Stack, *Bronterre O'Brien*, xviii, xxii–xxiv, xliv, 121–22, 131–32, 143–44, 173; Briggs, introduction to Cole, *Chartist Portraits*, x–xii; Gammage, *Chartist Movement*, 203–6; Stedman Jones, "Language of Chartism," 27–28; Prothero, "William Benbow," 144–45, 162; Thompson, *The Chartists*, 102, 267–69; Ward, *Chartism*, 144, 150–51, 157, 159, 166; Groves, *But We Shall Rise Again*, 121, 125; Jones, *Chartism and the Chartists*, 37–38, 73–74, 151; Chase, *Chartism: A New History*, 198, 200, 203, 206–7, 236, 238, 255–56; Cole, *Chartist Portraits*, 257–59.

### Chapter 2. Radical and Outsider

1. *British Statesman*, 25 June, 2, 9, 16, 23 July, 13, 20 Aug., 3, 17, 24 Sept., 1, 15, 22 Oct., 5, 19, 26 Nov., 10 Dec. 1842; *Poor Man's Guardian and Repealer's Friend*, 1843, no. 1.
2. *British Statesman*, 26 Nov. 1842.
3. Alexander Wilson, "The Suffrage Movement," in *Pressure from Without in Early Victorian England*, ed. Patricia Hollis (London, 1974), 85–86, 89.
4. *Mr. O'Brien's Vindication of His Conduct at the Late Birmingham Conference; Containing His "Blackguard Letter" to the Editor of the "Star," Which That Personage Suppressed; Also, His Letter to the "British Statesman"; Spirited Defence of Him by Mr. McGregor of Edinburgh;*

*Vincent's Portrait of a Demagogue; Etc., Etc.* (Birmingham, 1842), 23.

5. *Mr. O'Brien's Vindication*, 3–4, 19–20.
6. *Northern Star*, 4 June, 16 July, 3, 10, 17 Sept. 1842.
7. *Northern Star*, 17 Sept. 1842.
8. E.g., *Bronterre's National Reformer*, 28 Jan., 11 Feb. 1837.
9. *British Statesman*, 19, 25 June, 6, 13, 27 Aug., 10 Sept., 1, 15 Oct., 5, 12, 26 Nov., 10 Dec. 1842.
10. Gammage, *Chartist Movement*, 203–5, 267–69. Having denounced traitors to the Chartist cause as "devils," O'Brien came to be regarded by many Chartists as a traitor. As Paul Pickering has pointed out, not all so-called traitors acted upon selfish motives. Some were prompted by loyalty to the movement, which they thought was being ruined by its recognized leaders (especially O'Connor)—they were acting on a higher call to protect the movement. See Pickering, "Betrayal and Exile," 205–6.
11. Pickering, *Chartism and the Chartists in Manchester and Salford*, 51; Stephen Roberts, *Radical Politicians and Poets in Early Victorian Britain* (Lewiston, N.Y., 1993), 19, 81, 111; Wilson, *Chartist Movement in Scotland*, 212; Fraser, *Chartism in Scotland*, 100, 143, 161; Gammage, *Reminiscences of a Chartist*, 59, 73. Dorothy Thompson relates that Halifax Chartists responded to O'Brien's attack on O'Connor by removing O'Brien's portrait from their meeting place. She sees in the quarrel between the two leaders much personal vanity on both sides, but for her, the telling point is that the vast majority of Chartists sided with O'Connor, not O'Brien. They did not want to be sidetracked into other activities or fringe ideologies and preferred to stick with the mainstream movement and its acknowledged, established leadership. Thompson, *Dignity of Chartism*, 52, 102, 127–28, 134.
12. *Poor Man's Guardian and Repealer's Friend*, 1843, nos. 1–2, 7–13; *National Reformer and Manx Weekly Review*, 3, 17, 24 Oct., 19 Dec. 1846, 9 Jan., 17 Apr., 1, 15, 22 May 1847; *Power of the Pence*, 31 Mar. 1849; *Social Reformer*, 25 Aug., 22 Sept. 1849.
13. Allsop Collection, Misc.525/1/5, O'Brien to Allsop, 4 Sept. 1847.
14. Allsop Collection, Misc.525/2, O'Connor to Allsop, especially nos. 10 and 21, undated, (1847?).
15. Allsop Collection, Misc.525/3/3, 9, 11, Oastler to Allsop, 20 July 1846, 29 July 1847, 15 Dec. 1850.
16. Allsop Collection, Misc.525/1/15, O'Brien to Allsop, 7 Aug. 1847; see also the letters at 525/1/16–18.
17. Allsop Collection, Misc.525/1/19–22, O'Brien to Allsop, Aug.–Sept. 1847.
18. People's History Museum, Manchester, Labour History Archive, LP/OB, O'Brien Papers, OB.1, O'Brien to Mathews, undated (1843?).

19. Stack, *Bronterre O'Brien*, xviii, xliv, 173–74; Chase, *Chartism: A New History*, 236; Plummer, *Bronterre*, 177–79; Jones, *Chartism and the Chartists*, 101; Cole, *Chartist Portraits*, 260; Robert Fyson, "Bronterre O'Brien: A Chartist in the Isle of Man, 1844–1847," *Isle of Man Natural History and Antiquarian Society Proceedings* 10 (1998): 393–400.
20. John Belchem, "The Neglected 'Unstamped': The Manx Pauper Press of the 1840s," *Albion* 24 (1992): 613–14.
21. Allsop Collection, Misc.525/1/6–7, O'Brien to Allsop, 10 Nov., 8 Dec. 1847.
22. Henry Weisser, "Chartism in 1848: Reflections on a Non-revolution," *Albion* 13 (1981): 22; Gammage, *Chartist Movement*, 301–2, 312; Schoyen, *Chartist Challenge*, 162–63.
23. Owen Papers, ROC/1/24/16, Allsop to Owen, 12 Apr. 1848.
24. Thompson, *The Chartists*, 324; Stack, *Bronterre O'Brien*, xvi–xvii, xix–xxi, xxvii, xlv–xlvi, 110, 179–80, 219, 226, 231; Ward, *Chartism*, 204–6, 220–22; Jones, *Chartism and the Chartists*, 151, 162, 166; John Belchem, "1848: Feargus O'Connor and the Collapse of the Mass Platform," in Epstein and Thompson, *Chartist Experience*, 281; Edward Royle, "The *Cause of the People*, the People's Charter Union, and 'Moral Force' Chartism in 1848," in Allen and Ashton, *Papers for the People*, 147–49, 158–59; Parsinnen, "Association, Convention, and Anti-Parliament," 531; Harrison and Hollis, "Robert Lowery," 518; Anne Humpherys, "G. W. M. Reynolds: Popular Literature and Popular Politics," *Victorian Periodicals Review* 16 (1983): 79, 86; Haywood, *Revolution in Popular Literature*, ch. 7; Chase, *Chartism: A New History*, 289, 302, 335–36, 338; Cole, *Chartist Portraits*, 260–61, 263–65; Plummer, *Bronterre*, 189–94, 198–207.
25. E.g., *Social Reformer*, 11 Aug., 1, 15, 29 Sept., 6, 13, 20 Oct. 1849; O'Brien, *Elegy*, 2; and O'Brien, *Dissertation and Elegy*, 31.
26. Rothstein, *From Chartism to Labourism*, 151.
27. Gammage, *Reminiscences of a Chartist*, 26, 28, 34.
28. *Northern Star*, 16 Mar. 1850.
29. *Northern Star*, 16 Mar. 1850.
30. Wilson, *Chartist Movement in Scotland*, 245, 248; Fraser, *Chartism in Scotland*, 169–70.
31. *Northern Star*, 25 Oct. 1851.
32. *Northern Star*, 20 Dec. 1851.
33. John Saville, *1848: The British State and the Chartist Movement* (Cambridge, 1987), 119; Robert Saunders, "Chartism from Above: British Elites and the Interpretation of Chartism," *Historical Research* 81 (2008): 478–79, 482; Mike Sanders, *The Poetry of Chartism: Aesthetics, Politics, History* (Cambridge, 2009), 166–68, 176–77, 183–84; Margot Finn, *After Chartism: Class and Nation in English Radical Politics, 1848–1874* (Cambridge, 1993), 85–87; Robert Fyson, "Late Chartism in the Potteries, 1848–1858," *Labour History*

*Review* 74 (2009): 111–29; Haywood, *Literature of Struggle*, 14–15; and Haywood, *Revolution in Popular Literature*, 221.

34. John Belchem, "Chartism and the Trades, 1848–1850," *English Historical Review* 98 (1983): 586–87.
35. Weisser, "Chartist Internationalism," 49–66; Margot Finn, "'A Vent Which Has Conveyed Our Principles': English Radical Patriotism in the Aftermath of 1848," *Journal of Modern History* 64 (1992): 644, 650, 655, 657–59; Gregory Claeys, "Mazzini, Kossuth, and British Radicalism, 1848–1854," *Journal of British Studies* 28 (1989): 251–52, 257; Stack, *Bronterre O'Brien*, xlv, 180, 220; Rothstein, *From Chartism to Labourism*, 146, 154, 157, 160, 163, 165, 176–77, 179.
36. David Nicholls, "The English Middle Class and the Ideological Significance of Radicalism, 1760–1886," *Journal of British Studies* 24 (1985): 426–28; Prothero, "William Benbow," 144–45, 162; Parsinnen, "Association, Convention, and Anti-Parliament," 519–20; Richard Hendrix, "Popular Humor and the *Black Dwarf*," *Journal of British Studies* 16 (1976): 109.
37. *Operative*, 18 Nov. 1838.
38. James Epstein, "The Constitutional Idiom: Radical Reasoning, Rhetoric, and Action in Early Nineteenth-Century England," *Journal of Social History* 23 (1990): 557–58, 569.
39. Plummer, *Bronterre*, 179–83; Stedman Jones, "Language of Chartism," 32, 34; Cole, *Chartist Portraits*, 256–57.
40. Plummer, *Bronterre*, 180, 185–89; Stack, *Bronterre O'Brien*, xviii, 144; Joy MacAskill, "The Chartist Land Plan," in Briggs, *Chartist Studies*, 305, 307, 315, 340; Ward, *Chartism*, 170, 180; Ward, *Factory Movement*, 309; Gammage, *Chartist Movement*, 267–69, 272–74; Cole, *Chartist Portraits*, 259–60; Jones, *Chartism and the Chartists*, 131; Rothstein, *From Chartism to Labourism*, 53, 79–80; Fraser, *Chartism in Scotland*, 143; Schoyen, *Chartist Challenge*, 149; Roberts, *Radical Politicians*, 94; Stedman Jones, "Language of Chartism," 43.
41. *National Reformer and Manx Weekly Review*, 9 Jan., 17 Apr., 15, 22 May 1847; Stedman Jones, "Language of Chartism," 42–43; Chase, *Chartism: A New History*, 272; Gregory Claeys, "The Triumph of Class-Conscious Reformism in British Radicalism, 1790–1860," *Historical Journal* 26 (1983): 979.
42. Gurney, "'Rejoicing in Potatoes,'" 101–2, 136.
43. *Bronterre's National Reformer*, 14, 21, 28 Jan., 25 Feb. 1837; O'Brien, *Robespierre*, 278–79; *British Statesman*, 9, 16, 23 July, 6, 27 Aug., 17, 24 Sept., 1, 15 Oct. 1842.
44. *British Statesman*, 29 Oct. 1842, 7 Jan. 1843; *Poor Man's Guardian and Repealer's Friend*, 1843, nos. 1–2, 5–7, 9; *National Reformer and Manx Weekly Review*, 3, 31 Oct., 7, 14, 21, 28 Nov., 19 Dec. 1846, 17 Apr., 1, 8 May 1847.

45. *Power of the Pence*, 25 Nov., 30 Dec. 1848, 20 Jan., 24 Feb. 1849; *Social Reformer*, 18, 25 Aug., 1, 8, 22 Sept., 6 Oct. 1849.
46. J. B. O'Brien, "The Rise, Progress, and Phases of Human Slavery: How It Came into the World, and How It Shall Be Made to Go Out," reprinted in *The Chartist Movement in Britain, 1838–1850*, ed. Gregory Claeys (6 vols., London, 2001), 6: 299–442. The "Human Slavery" essays were, thinks Dorothy Thompson, "among some of the best Chartist writing on non-immediate questions"—which reflects her recognition of O'Brien's strengths but also her belief that he had ceased to be a true Chartist and was only on the margins of the movement by the late 1840s. She also points to the context for O'Brien's essays, the post-1848 "unscrambling of the coalition that had been Chartism." Thompson, *Dignity of Chartism*, 136.
47. Plummer, *Bronterre*, 194–97; Stack, *Bronterre O'Brien*, xix, xlv, 144, 174, 219, 232; Stedman Jones, "Language of Chartism," 32, 34; Cole, *Chartist Portraits*, 261–62.
48. Plummer, *Bronterre*, 207–10.
49. "Bronterre's Letters," 1836, nos. 1, 9, 14; *Bronterre's National Reformer*, 7, 14, 28 Jan., 4, 11, 25 Feb., 4 Mar. 1837; O'Brien, *Robespierre*, 276, 281, 284, 287, 469, 519–21; *Poor Man's Guardian and Repealer's Friend*, 1843, nos. 2–3, 6–12; *National Reformer and Manx Weekly Review*, 3 Oct. 1846, 27 Feb., 20 Mar., 3, 24 Apr., 8, 22 May 1847; *Power of the Pence*, 16, 30 Dec. 1848, 17 Feb., 17, 24 Mar., 7, 14 Apr. 1849; *Social Reformer*, 11, 18, 25 Aug., 1, 8, 15, 22, 29 Sept., 6, 13, 20 Oct. 1849; Stack, *Bronterre O'Brien*, xiii; Plummer, *Bronterre*, 210–15; Harrison and Hollis, "Robert Lowery," 528.
50. Iverson, "Babouvism," 125–35.
51. "Bronterre's Letters," 1836, no. 14; *Bronterre's National Reformer*, 7, 14 Jan., 11 Feb. 1837; O'Brien, *Bronterre*, 287; *Poor Man's Guardian and Repealer's Friend*, 1843, nos. 6, 9; *National Reformer and Manx Weekly Review*, 20 Mar., 8, 22 May 1847.
52. Eileen Yeo, "Christianity in Chartist Struggle, 1838–1842," *Past and Present* 91 (1981): 110–12, 126–27; Hollis, *Pauper Press*, 281.
53. *Social Reformer*, 1, 8 Sept., 20 Oct. 1849.
54. O'Brien Papers, OB.18: O'Brien's inscribed copy of John Finch, *Chartist Bible: The Seven Seals Broke Open, or the Bible of the Reformation Restored* (London, 1853).
55. British Library, General Reference Collection, J. B. O'Brien, *A Vision of Hell: or, Peep into the Realms Below, Alias Lord Overgrown's Dream, Describing His Lordship's Fancied Reunion with the Late Sir Robert Peel in the Regions Below* (London, 1859), 2.
56. Harrison and Hollis, "Robert Lowery," 505, 522, 526.
57. *Observer*, 16 Mar. 1857; *Manchester Guardian*, 30 Mar. 1857. Though he does not discuss O'Brien's visit to Tiverton in 1857, Malcolm Chase lists the constituency as one of those

in which Chartist candidates had the chance to do well. Chartism could make advances electorally, Chase points out, where electorates were not so "popular," owing to the effects of the £10 borough franchise. In expanding industrial towns most workers lived in low-quality housing and did not meet the £10 qualification, but in small country towns the housing was better and it was often overvalued for rating purposes. In places like Tiverton, therefore, Chartism could appeal to a large section of the local electorate. See Chase, "'Labour's Candidates,'" 78–79.

58. O'Brien Papers, OB.4, O'Brien to Mathews, 31 Mar. 1857.
59. O'Brien Papers, OB.4, O'Brien to Mathews, 31 Mar. 1857.
60. Plummer, *Bronterre*, 216–46; Jones, *Chartism and the Chartists*, 111, 171–72, 180–82, 185; Belchem, "Chartism and the Trades," 558–87; Cole, *Chartist Portraits*, 263–65; Ward, *Chartism*, 222–26, 231–32; Chase, *Chartism: A New History*, 336, 338, 356; Stack, *Bronterre O'Brien*, xx–xxi, xlvi, 180, 191–92.
61. O'Brien Papers, OB.2–4, O'Brien to Mathews, 6 Mar., 23 Sept. 1856, 31 Mar. 1857.
62. Allsop Collection, Misc.525/1/9, O'Brien to Allsop, 27 June 1855.
63. Allsop Collection, M539, O'Brien to Allsop, 14 Feb. 1854, and Misc.525/1/23, O'Brien to Allsop, undated, 1855.
64. O'Brien Papers, OB.6–8, O'Brien to Mathews, 17 Nov., 23 Dec. 1857, 20 Mar. 1858.
65. O'Brien Papers, OB.9, O'Brien to Mathews, 24 Mar. 1858. Thomas Allsop helped Jones financially for many years; e.g., Owen Papers, ROC/1/24/27, Allsop to Owen, 22 Apr. 1854.
66. Allsop Collection, Misc.525/1/10–14, O'Brien to Allsop, 22, 26 Sept., 1, 11 Oct., 3 Dec. 1862.
67. Allsop Collection, Misc.525/1/11–12, 14, O'Brien to Allsop, 26 Sept., 1 Oct., 3 Dec. 1862.
68. O'Brien Papers, OB.2–3, O'Brien to Mathews, 6 Mar., 23 Sept. 1856.
69. O'Brien Papers, OB.5–6, O'Brien to Mathews, 19 Sept., 17 Nov. 1857.
70. O'Brien Papers, OB.5–9, O'Brien to Mathews, 19 Sept., 17 Nov., 23 Dec. 1857, 20, 24 Mar. 1858.
71. Allsop Collection, Misc.525/1/12, O'Brien to Allsop, 1 Oct. 1862.

### Chapter 3. A Concept of Revolution

1. Chase, *Chartism: A New History*, 1, 30, 36, 41, 67, 69, 77–79, 83, 109, 137, 141, 149–50, 170.
2. Stedman Jones, "Language of Chartism," 3–4, 8, 12–16, 22–23, 39, 40–42, 44.
3. Claeys, *Citizens and Saints*, 226, 269.
4. Maehl, "Chartist Disturbances," 389–414; R. N. Soffer, "Attitudes and Allegiances in the Unskilled North, 1830–1850," *International Review of Social History* 10 (1965): 429–54.
5. Paul Pickering, "'And Your Petitioners, Etc.': Chartist Petitioning in Popular Politics, 1838–1848," *English Historical Review* 116 (2001): 368–88; Paul Pickering, "'The Hearts

of the Millions': Chartism and Popular Monarchism in the 1840s," *History* 88 (2003): 227–48. See also Robert Poole, "French Revolution or Peasants' Revolt? Petitioners and Rebels in England from the Blanketeers to the Chartists," *Labour History Review* 74 (2009): 19–20, 22. For some of O'Brien's remarks on these matters, see *Operative*, 4 Nov. 1838, 27 Jan., 24 Mar., 28 Apr., 5, 19 May 1839.

6. Haywood, *Revolution in Popular Literature*, 1–2, 5–6, 131–32, 139–52, 221.
7. Haywood, *Literature of Struggle*, 2, 13–17.
8. Sanders, *Poetry of Chartism*, 1–5, 7, 90. Music was another cultural form (and still understudied) that was "an integral part of Chartist political activities." Meetings and processions usually included music, and this music can reveal much about the experience and appeal of popular radicalism and the pride, independence, and sense of identity that shaped the Chartist movement. Chartism had a sound as well as a language and a visual appearance. See Kate Bowan and Paul Pickering, "'Songs for the Millions': Chartist Music and Popular Aural Tradition," *Labour History Review* 74 (2009): 44–63.
9. Sanders, *Poetry of Chartism*, 126–28, 166–68, 176–77, 182–86, 196, 201, 206–7.
10. Saunders, "Chartism from Above," 463–84.
11. John Morrow, *Thomas Carlyle* (London, 2006), 75–76, 78, 80–83, 85–95, 98–100, 102–3.
12. Mark Cumming, "Carlyle's Seagreen Robespierre and the Perilous Delights of Picturesque History," in Haydon and Doyle, *Robespierre*, 177–93.
13. Plotz, "Crowd Power," 87–114.
14. Ian Haywood, "George W. M. Reynolds and 'The Trafalgar Square Revolution': Radicalism, the Carnivalesque, and Popular Culture in Mid-Victorian England," *Journal of Victorian Culture* 7 (2002): 23–59.
15. Chase, *Chartism: A New History*, 77–78.
16. *Chartist Circular*, 25 Jan., 1 Feb., 9, 30 May, 5 Dec. 1840, 27 Feb., 29 May 1841.
17. *Chartist Circular*, 5, 12 Dec. 1840.
18. *Chartist Circular*, 3 Apr., 1 May 1841.
19. *Northern Star*, 6 Apr., 18 May 1839.
20. *Northern Star*, 16 Nov., 21 Dec. 1839, 4 Jan. 1840.
21. *Northern Star*, 24 Sept. 1842.
22. Chase, *Chartism: A New History*, 68–69; Innes, Philp, and Saunders, "Democratic Discourse," 126.
23. Rob Breton, "Violence and the Radical Imagination," *Victorian Periodicals Review* 44 (2011): 24–41.
24. *Reynolds's Political Instructor*, 4 May 1850.
25. *Poor Man's Guardian*, 2 Nov. 1833; and see also Hollis, *Pauper Press*, 253–58; Garrard,

*Democratization*, 11; Peter Gurney, "Exclusive Dealing in the Chartist Movement," *Labour History Review* 74 (2009): 93. O'Brien thought that the ballot, if introduced without manhood suffrage, would hinder the cause of reform by reducing the pressure that could be exerted upon voters through such means as exclusive dealing.

26. Hollis, *Pauper Press*, 275, 299–300; O'Brien, *Buonarroti's History*, 66; Schafer, "James Bronterre O'Brien," 14.
27. On his supposed drift into "moderation," see Stack, *Bronterre O'Brien*, xvii, xix, 87–88, 110, 131–32; Maw, "Democratic Anti-Capitalism," 201, 215–17, 219; Schafer, "James Bronterre O'Brien," 11, 78, 92–98.
28. E.g., *Poor Man's Guardian*, 12 Dec. 1835; *Operative*, 11 Nov., 30 Dec. 1838.
29. *Operative*, 30 Dec. 1838.
30. Innes, Philp, and Saunders, "Democratic Discourse," 123; Schafer, "James Bronterre O'Brien," 20–21, 27–28, 40, 42–44, 72–76, 78, 82–83, 86; and handbills: "The People's Charter!" (26 Mar. 1839), "The Chartists!" (26 Mar. 1839), and "To George Irving, Esq., Mayor of the City of Chichester" (28 Mar. 1839).
31. *London Mercury*, 18 June 1837.
32. *Poor Man's Guardian*, 30 July 1831, 11 Feb., 4 Aug., 13 Oct. 1832.
33. *Poor Man's Guardian*, 11 Feb. 1832.
34. *Poor Man's Guardian*, 4 July, 17 Oct., 12 Dec. 1835.
35. Benoît Agnes, "A Chartist Singularity? Mobilizing to Promote Democratic Petitions in Britain and France, 1838–1848," *Labour History Review* 78 (2013): 51–66.
36. Pamela Pilbeam, "The Insurrectionary Tradition in France, 1835–1848," *Modern and Contemporary France* 1 (1993): 253–64.
37. Claeys, *Machinery, Money, and the Millennium*, xxiv, 110–11, 135, 158–59, 163; Maw, "Democratic Anti-Capitalism," 201–26.
38. Maw, "O'Brien's Class Analysis," 253–89.
39. Owen Papers, ROC/15/3/1, O'Brien to Owen, 27 May 1832, ROC/1/24/4, Allsop to Owen, 17 Mar. 1837; John Burns Papers, LXIV, ff. 1–2, Owen to Allsop, 20 Nov. 1832; *Northern Star*, 1 July 1843; Claeys, *Citizens and Saints*, 183, 189, 193, 195, 198, 219, 242–43, 260, 263, 272, 277, 286–87; Stack, *Bronterre O'Brien*, 2, 122, 174. Many Chartists adopted Owenite ideas to the extent that they set up their own shops as a consumers' self-defense initiative. Exclusive dealing was a related activity. "Chartists took up the weapon of political shopping and shopkeeping because they were exploited as consumers as well as producers." Gurney, "Exclusive Dealing," 106. See also Edward Royle, "Chartists and Owenites: Many Parts but One Body," *Labour History Review* 65 (2000): 2–21, which argues that divisions between the two groups have often been exaggerated. For an

example of mixing at local level see Malcolm Chase, "Chartism, 1838–1858: Responses in Two Teesside Towns," in Roberts, *People's Charter*, 163.

40. E.g., *Poor Man's Guardian*, 1 Dec. 1832, 26 Jan., 2 Feb., 23 Mar. 1833, 3 May 1834, 28 Mar. 1835; *Bronterre's National Reformer*, 15 Jan. 1837; *London Mercury*, 25 Dec. 1836, 12 Mar. 1837; *Operative*, 25 Nov. 1838.
41. *Operative*, 18 Nov. 1838; "Bronterre's Letters," 1836, no. 1; O'Brien, *Robespierre*, 259–60; *British Statesman*, 15 May, 25 June, 9 July, 27 Aug. 1842; *Poor Man's Guardian and Repealer's Friend*, 1843, nos. 1, 11; *National Reformer and Manx Weekly Review*, 25 May 1847.
42. Epstein, "Constitutional Idiom," 557–58, 569; Jones, *Chartism and the Chartists*, 37–40, 64, 186–87; Stack, *Bronterre O'Brien*, xxix; Royle and Walvin, *English Radicals*, 169–70; Thompson, *The Chartists*, 105; Prothero, *Artisans and Politics*, 333–34; Hollis, *Pauper Press*, viii, 100, 203–4, 207, 210, 218–58, 286–90, 293, 299, 302; Messner, "Land, Leadership, Culture, and Emigration," 1098–99, 1106–7; Morris, *From Cobbett to the Chartists*, 30, 74, 161–62, 235.
43. E.g., Harrison and Hollis, "Robert Lowery," 505, 522, 526; Garrard, *Democratization*, 213. Much to O'Brien's disgust, many Chartists accepted orthodox political economy. In later times they would swell the ranks of Victorian Liberalism and give it a more popular character. It is possible that old Chartists did not have to compromise in this respect, but rather that "liberalism" itself changed to accommodate radical energy and ideas. Robert Hall, "Chartism Remembered: William Aitken, Liberalism, and the Politics of Memory," in Roberts, *People's Charter*, 174–94.
44. *Operative*, 17 Mar. 1839. See also "Bronterre's Letters," 1836, nos. 1, 5–6, 9; *Bronterre's National Reformer*, 11 Feb. 1837; O'Brien, *Robespierre*, 276–88, 311–12, 352–53; *British Statesman*, 25 June, 9 July 1842; *Poor Man's Guardian and Repealer's Friend*, 1843, no. 8; *Power of the Pence*, 16 Dec. 1848.
45. *Bronterre's National Reformer*, 15 Jan. 1837.
46. Stedman Jones, "Language of Chartism," 16–17.
47. *Poor Man's Guardian*, 19 Oct. 1833.
48. *Bronterre's National Reformer*, 7 Jan. 1837.
49. Plummer, *Bronterre*, 31–33, 35, 37, 40–42; Hollis, *Pauper Press*, 266; Jones, *Chartism and the Chartists*, 37–38; Miliband, "Robert Owen," 237; Stack, *Bronterre O'Brien*, 2, 122, 144, 174, 219. For further remarks by O'Brien on the Owenite refusal to engage in political activity, see *Poor Man's Guardian*, 7 Dec. 1833; "Bronterre's Letters," 1836, no. 7; *Bronterre's National Reformer*, 4 Mar. 1837; *British Statesman*, 5 June 1842; *Poor Man's Guardian and Repealer's Friend*, 1843, nos. 3, 7–8; *National Reformer and Manx Weekly Review*, 3, 24 Oct.,

5, 19, 26 Dec. 1846, 30 Jan., 6 Mar. 1847; *Power of the Pence*, 27 Jan., 24 Feb., 3 Mar. 1849; *Social Reformer*, 18 Aug., 1 Sept., 6 Oct. 1849.

50. Plummer, *Bronterre*, 179–83; Stedman Jones, "Language of Chartism," 32, 34; Cole, *Chartist Portraits*, 256–57; Stack, *Bronterre O'Brien*, xvi, xlii, 61, 72; Barry, *Nationalization*, 23–29, 31, 34–39, 90–91, 109, 165; T. M. Parsinnen, "Thomas Spence and the Origins of English Land Nationalization," *Journal of the History of Ideas* 34 (1973): 135–41.

51. Ashcraft, "Liberal Political Theory," 249–72. For some of O'Brien's clearest statements on the land question, see "Bronterre's Letters," 1836, nos. 1, 7; *Bronterre's National Reformer*, 7, 28 Jan., 25 Feb., 18 Mar. 1837; O'Brien, *Robespierre*, 13–14, 280, 303–6, 313, 519–21; *British Statesman*, 6 Aug. 1842; *Poor Man's Guardian and Repealer's Friend*, 1843, nos. 1, 3–8, 10–11, 13; *National Reformer and Manx Weekly Review*, 3, 10, 17, 24 Oct., 14, 21 Nov., 5, 19 Dec. 1846, 2, 9, 16, 23 Jan., 6, 13, 20 Feb., 6, 27 Mar., 3, 10, 17 Apr., 1, 8, 15 May 1847; *Power of the Pence*, 23, 30 Dec. 1848, 6, 20, 27 Jan., 3, 10 Feb., 3, 24 Mar., 14 Apr. 1849; *Social Reformer*, 25 Aug., 1, 22 Sept., 6, 13, 20 Oct. 1849; O'Brien, *Dissertation and Elegy*, 4–5, 21–22.

52. *Poor Man's Guardian and Repealer's Friend*, 1843, nos. 7–8; *National Reformer and Manx Weekly Review*, 17, 24 Oct., 19 Dec. 1846, 9 Jan., 17 Apr., 1, 15, 22 May 1847; *Power of the Pence*, 31 Mar. 1849; *Social Reformer*, 25 Aug. 1849.

53. Michael J. Turner, "Ireland and Irishness in the Political Thought of Bronterre O'Brien," *Irish Historical Studies* 39 (2014): 40–57.

54. Michael J. Turner, "Chartism, Bronterre O'Brien, and the 'Luminous Political Example of America,'" *History* 97 (2012): 43–69.

55. O'Brien, *Buonarroti's History*; O'Brien, *Robespierre*, 3–12, 15, 17, 21–22, 24, 41–45, 83–96, 217, 219–22, 256–57, 274, 276, 280–82, 303–4, 307–10, 313, 350–53, 468–70, 519–22; O'Brien, *Elegy*, 2, 14–15; O'Brien, *Dissertation and Elegy*, 4–5, 7–15, 20–22, 32, 34, 36; "Bronterre's Letters," 1836, nos. 2, 5–7, 9; *Bronterre's National Reformer*, 11 Mar. 1837; *Power of the Pence*, 18 Nov., 16 Dec. 1848, 17, 24 Mar., 7 Apr. 1849; *Social Reformer*, 18 Aug., 1 Sept. 1849. See also *French Utopias: An Anthology of Ideal Societies*, ed. Frank and Fritzie Manuel (New York, 1971), 245–58; Plummer, *Bronterre*, 59–72; Stack, *Bronterre O'Brien*, xv, xli–xlii, 179–80; Gammage, *Chartist Movement*, 73–75; Jones, *Chartism and the Chartists*, 37; Cole, *Chartist Portraits*, 245–46; Moss, "Republican Socialism," 408–9; James Epstein and David Karr, "Playing at Revolution: British 'Jacobin' Performance," *Journal of Modern History* 79 (2007): 501; John Dinwiddy, "English Radicals and the French Revolution, 1800–1850," in *The French Revolution and the Creation of Modern Political Culture*, ed. François Furet and Mona Onouf (Oxford, 1989), 447–66; Bert Hoselitz, review of A. G. Garrone, *Buonarroti e Babeuf* (Turin, 1948) and *Buonarroti e i rivoluzionari dell 'Ottocento*

(Milan, 1951), *Journal of Modern History* 26 (1954): 188–89.

56. "Bronterre's Letters," 1836, no. 2.
57. "Bronterre's Letters," 1836, nos. 7, 9.
58. "Bronterre's Letters," 1836, no. 5.
59. "Bronterre's Letters," 1836, nos. 5–6.
60. Roger Magraw, *France 1815–1914: The Bourgeois Century* (New York, 1986), part 2; Hugh Collingham, *The July Monarchy* (London, 1988); John Gunn, *When the French Tried to Be British: Party, Opposition, and the Quest for Civil Disagreement, 1814–1848* (Montreal, 2009); Jill Harsin, *Barricades: The War of the Streets in Revolutionary Paris, 1830–1848* (New York, 2002), ch. 3; Sarah Maza, *The Myth of the French Bourgeoisie* (Cambridge, Mass., 2003), chs. 5–6; David Pinkney, *Decisive Years in France, 1840–1847* (Princeton, N.J., 1986); and David Pinkney, "The Crowd in the French Revolution of 1830," *American Historical Review* 70 (1964): 1–17.
61. *Bronterre's National Reformer*, 11 Mar. 1837.
62. O'Brien, *Robespierre*, 3–5.
63. O'Brien, *Robespierre*, 217.
64. O'Brien, *Robespierre*, 219–22, 251–57.
65. For examples see Georges Lefebvre, *The Coming of the French Revolution* (Princeton, N.J., 2005), first published in 1939; and Albert Soboul, *A Short History of the French Revolution, 1789–1799* (Berkeley, Calif., 1977). Among the most important revisionist works to have challenged this approach are Alfred Cobban, *The Social Interpretation of the French Revolution* (Cambridge, 1964), and François Furet, *Interpreting the French Revolution* (Cambridge, 1981).
66. Plummer, *Bronterre*, 247–50, 253–54, 256–58; Stack, *Bronterre O'Brien*, xxxi, 226, 231–32; Barrow, "Homerton Social Democratic Club," 188–99; Newens, "Thomas Edward Bowkett," 143–48; Whitehead, "Dan Chatterton," 83–99; Hollis, *Pauper Press*, 299–300; Royle, *Revolutionary Britannia*, 142; reviews of Dolléans, *Le Chartisme*, by Clapham, 389–90, and by Hall, 406–7; Wiener, "Press and the Working Class," 1–4; Ashcraft, "Liberal Political Theory," 259–61, 263, 270; Morton, review of Foxwell, *Bibliography of the English Socialist School*, 139; Stedman Jones, "Some Notes on Karl Marx," 129–30.
67. Lewis, "Robespierre through the Chartist Looking-Glass," 205–6, 210–11; Michael J. Turner, "Revolutionary Connection: Maximilian Robespierre and Bronterre O'Brien," *The Historian* 75 (2013): 237–61; Bernard Porter, *The Refugee Question in Mid-Victorian Politics* (Cambridge, 1979), ch. 2.
68. Samuel Hollander, "Marx and Engels on Constitutional Reform versus Revolution," *Theoria* 57 (2010): 51–91; Neil Harding, "Marx, Engels, and the *Manifesto*: Working Class,

Party, and Proletariat," *Journal of Political Ideologies* 3 (1998): 13–44.

69. O'Brien, *Robespierre*, 276–85.
70. O'Brien, *Robespierre*, 303–11.
71. O'Brien, *Robespierre*, 468–70.
72. *Poor Man's Guardian and Repealer's Friend*, 1843, no. 5.
73. *Poor Man's Guardian and Repealer's Friend*, 1843, nos. 8, 11.
74. O'Brien became frustrated as he was sidelined by other Chartist leaders and his own reform program did not make the progress he had expected. Faherty, "O'Brien's Correspondence with Allsop," 28–33. One possibility that arises from Faherty's account is that there were personal and ideological factors that limited the appeal of O'Brien's concept of revolution.
75. Claeys, *Citizens and Saints*, 296–97.
76. Linda Colley, *Britons: Forging the Nation, 1707–1837* (London, 1992), 284–85, 306–8, 311–12, 365–66, 368, 370–72.
77. Jonathan Parry, *The Politics of Patriotism: English Liberalism, National Identity, and Europe, 1830–1886* (Cambridge, 2006); Saunders, *Democracy and the Vote*, 131–59.
78. Maurizio Isabella, *Risorgimento in Exile: Italian Émigrés and the Liberal International in the Post-Napoleonic Era* (Oxford, 2009), 9–11, 122–27, 145–46, 149, 210–11.
79. Barfoot and D'haen, "Tropes of Revolution," 7.
80. Lewis, "Robespierre through the Chartist Looking-Glass," 195–96, 199–200, 202–3; Iverson, "Babouvism," 3, 5, 14–48, 61–66, 70–73, 99–113; Bernstein, "Babeuf and Babouvism" (parts 1 and 2), 29–57, 166–94.
81. Iverson, "Babouvism," 99–100, 103, 106–9, 152–53, 169–72, 177–78; Lewis, "Robespierre through the Chartist Looking-Glass," 201, 206–7; Prothero, "William Benbow," 134–71; R. B. Rose, "Babeuf, Dictatorship, and Democracy," *Historical Studies* 15 (1972): 223–36.
82. Stack, *Bronterre O'Brien*, xv, xlii, 179–80; Iorwerth Prothero, "Chartists and Political Refugees," in *Exiles from European Revolutions: Refugees in Mid-Victorian England*, ed. Sabine Freitag (Oxford, 2003), 212–13, 216–18, 220–21, 228; Schafer, "James Bronterre O'Brien," 9, 15–16, 45–51; Finn, *After Chartism*, 83; Epstein and Karr, "Playing at Revolution," 495–98, 500–501, 506–7, 512; Innes, Philp, and Saunders, "Democratic Discourse," 117, 120–21, 127; Lewis, "Robespierre through the Chartist Looking-Glass," 194–211; Schoyen, *Chartist Challenge*, 12, 28, 33, 144, 184, 194, 197, 207.
83. *Northern Star*, 27 Apr. 1839. The convention did not accept Joseph Williams as a delegate.
84. Allsop Collection, Misc.525/1/7, O'Brien to Allsop, 8 Dec. 1847.
85. Owen Papers, ROC/1/24/9, Allsop to Owen, 31 July 1847.
86. *Power of the Pence*, 18, 25 Nov., 9 Dec. 1848.

87. *Power of the Pence*, 16 Dec. 1848, 17, 24 Mar. 1849.

88. *Power of the Pence*, 7 Apr. 1849; *Social Reformer*, 18, 25 Aug, 1 Sept. 1849.

89. Finn, "'A Vent Which Has Conveyed Our Principles,'" 644, 650, 655, 657–59; Claeys, "Mazzini, Kossuth, and British Radicalism," 251–52, 257.

90. *Northern Star*, 25 Oct. 1851.

91. E.g., *Social Reformer*, 11, 18 Aug. 1849.

92. T. C. Jones, "French Republican Exiles in Britain, 1848–1870" (PhD thesis, University of Cambridge, 2010), 2, 18–19, 36–37, 68–70, 81–82, 84, 109–10, 117, 127–30; Claeys, *Citizens and Saints*, 269–70, 317; Fabrice Bensimon, "The French Exiles and the British," in Freitag, *Exiles*, 89–91, 96–98; Finn, *After Chartism*, 68–69, 84–85, 90, 114, 116, 118, 120–21, 176, 191, 203–4; Porter, *Refugee Question*, 2, 14, 17, 23, 27, 31, 39, 51, 84, 87, 90.

93. Claeys, *Citizens and Saints*, 306; Finn, *After Chartism*, 162, 170; Maurizio Isabella, "Italian Exiles and British Politics before and after 1848," in Freitag, *Exiles*, 72, 76–77; Jones, "French Republican Exiles," 77, 110, 120.

94. Sylvie Aprile, "Voices of Exile: French Newspapers in England," in Freitag, *Exiles*, 153–54, 156; Salvo Mastellone, "Mazzini's International League in the Light of the London Democratic Manifestos, 1837–1850," *Studia Politica* 3 (2006): 525–32.

95. Bensimon, "French Exiles," 96.

96. Claeys, *Citizens and Saints*, 297–98; Ansgar Reiss, "Home Alone? Reflections on Political Exiles Returning to Their Native Countries," in Freitag, *Exiles*, 307–9.

97. Jones, "French Republican Exiles," 120–21.

98. Finn, *After Chartism*, 68–69, 75–77, 79, 90–91, 104, 155–56, 162, 170, 229; Jones, "French Republican Exiles," 166–69, 175–76, 201, 212–14.

99. Lewis, "Robespierre through the Chartist Looking-Glass," 195, 208–9.

100. Marc Mulholland, "'Its Patrimony, Its Unique Wealth!' Labour-Power, Working-Class Consciousness, and Crisis," *Critique: Journal of Socialist Theory* 38 (2010): 375–417.

101. Jones, "French Republican Exiles," 94, 96, 98–99, 102.

102. *New World of Politics, Arts, Literature, and Sciences* 1 (July 1849): 22–24.

103. *New World of Politics, Arts, Literature, and Sciences* 3 (Oct. 1849): 95–96.

104. Louis Blanc, *1848: Historical Revelations Inscribed to Lord Normanby* (London, 1858), v–x, 53–62.

105. *Working Man*, 1 Mar. 1867.

106. Owen Papers, ROC/17/17/110, James Rigby to Robert Owen, 30 Apr. 1856.

107. Owen Papers, ROC/1/24/13–16, 18–23, 25, Allsop to Owen, 30 Mar., 5, 6, 12, 27, 29 Apr., 3, 5, 9, 22 May, 5 Sept. 1848.

108. Stack, *Bronterre O'Brien*, 180; Jones, "French Republican Exiles," 101, 248–49.

109. Alexandre Ledru-Rollin, *The Decline of England* (London, 1850), 4–5, 276, 278–79, 319, 321–24, 326; and for context see Bensimon, "French Exiles," 89, 91, 97–98; Sabine Freitag, introduction to Freitag, *Exiles*, 5–6; Aprile, "Voices of Exile," 150, 155–56, 160; Reiss, "Home Alone," 303–4, 306–8; Finn, *After Chartism*, 87–89, 90, 118, 120, 129–30, 162, 176; Porter, *Refugee Question*, 14–15, 17, 24, 26–27, 29, 31, 36–39, 61, 67, 76, 87, 110, 130, 144, 154, 170, 203; Jones, "French Republican Exiles," 12–13, 19–21, 30, 37–38, 40–41, 48–50, 80, 109, 111, 115–16, 118–19, 128–30, 132, 153, 194–95.
110. Prothero, "Chartists and Political Refugees," 209–12, 215–16, 218–25.
111. Weisser, "Chartist Internationalism," 49–66; Messner, "Land, Leadership, Culture, and Emigration," 1104–6. Historians disagree about the extent and importance of internationalism: e.g., Finn, *After Chartism*, 121; Taylor, *Decline of British Radicalism*, 112.
112. Finn, *After Chartism*, 83, 97, 120, 122–24, 134–35, 150–51, 191–92, 286.
113. Collet joined O'Brien's National Reform League and edited several publications, including the *Working Man*. Jones, "French Republican Exiles," 47, 124, 149, 180–81, 184–85, 190, 193, 223.
114. *Power of the Pence*, 18 Nov. 1848; *Social Reformer*, 29 Sept. 1849; *Reynolds's Political Instructor*, 5 Jan. 1850; Finn, *After Chartism*, 84–87, 116.
115. *Social Reformer*, 25 Aug., 1, 8, 22 Sept. 1849.
116. *Social Reformer*, 29 Sept., 6, 20 Oct. 1849.
117. *Social Reformer*, 25 Aug. 1849.
118. J. B. O'Brien, *Ode to Lord Palmerston* (London, 1856) and *An Ode to Louis Napoleon Bonaparte* (London, 1857). See also O'Brien Papers, OB.2–3, O'Brien to Mathews, 6 Mar., 23 Sept. 1856.
119. Sanders, *Poetry of Chartism*, 166–68, 173–77, 180–201; Belchem, "Chartism and the Trades," 586–87; Haywood, *Literature of Struggle*, 14–15; Finn, *After Chartism*, 84–87.
120. *Northern Star*, 3 Feb., 3 Mar. 1849.
121. *Northern Star*, 8 June 1850.
122. E.g., *Northern Star*, 5, 12 Apr. 1851.
123. *Northern Star*, 20 Dec. 1851; and for context see Jonathan Parry, "The Impact of Napoleon III on British Politics, 1851–1880," *Transactions of the Royal Historical Society*, 6th ser., 11 (2001): 147–75.
124. Allsop Collection, M539, O'Brien to Allsop, 14 Feb. 1854, and Misc.525/1/23, O'Brien to Allsop, undated, 1855; Jones, *Chartism and the Chartists*, 162; Cole, *Chartist Portraits*, 265; Stack, *Bronterre O'Brien*, xx, xlvi; Plummer, *Bronterre*, 228–32; Schoyen, *Chartist Challenge*, 238; Collins and Abramsky, *Marx and the British Labour Movement*, 10.
125. Owen Papers, ROC/1/24/28, Allsop to Owen, 23 Dec. 1855.

126. O'Brien Papers, OB.4–7, 9, O'Brien to Mathews, 31 Mar., 19 Sept., 17 Nov., 23 Dec. 1857, 24 Mar. 1858.
127. O'Brien, *Ode to Louis Napoleon Bonaparte*; Finn, *After Chartism*, 180–87; David Brown, *Palmerston* (New Haven, Conn., 2010), 409–11; Porter, *Refugee Question*, ch. 6; Owen Papers, ROC/1/22/6–7, Anna Allsop to Owen, 25 Mar., 28 June 1858.
128. E.g., Allsop Collection, Misc.525/1/11, O'Brien to Allsop, 26 Sept. 1862.
129. Brock, "Polish Democrats," 143; Prothero, "Chartists and Political Refugees," 214–16; *Northern Star*, 5, 12 Apr. 1851.

### Chapter 4. "National Reform"

1. *National Reformer and Manx Weekly Review*, 16 Jan. 1847.
2. *Social Reformer*, 20 Oct. 1849.
3. *Reynolds's Political Instructor*, 29 Dec. 1849.
4. Stedman Jones, "Language of Chartism," 3–4, 12–17, 23, 30–31, 53; Hollis, *Pauper Press*, 4, 45, 247–49.
5. Claeys, *Citizens and Saints*, 215–16.
6. Stack, *Bronterre O'Brien*, xxviii–xxix.
7. Briggs, "National Bearings," 296; Saville, introduction to the 1969 edition of Gammage, *Chartist Movement*, 18–19.
8. Claeys, *Machinery, Money, and the Millennium*, 158.
9. Hollis, *Pauper Press*, 106, 275, 278.
10. Claeys, *Citizens and Saints*, 314; Barry, *Nationalization*, 90–91, 109, 165.
11. Innes, Philp, and Saunders, "Democratic Discourse," 114, 117–18, 120–21, 123; Schafer, "James Bronterre O'Brien," 2–3, 7, 31–33.
12. *Hansard Parliamentary Debates*, 3rd ser., 63 (1842): 46–47, and 99 (1848): 941.
13. Saunders, *Democracy and the Vote*, 3–13.
14. Thompson, *Market and Its Critics*, 124–25; D'Oronzio, review of Plummer, *Bronterre*, 103–4; Belchem, "Neglected 'Unstamped,'" 613–14.
15. Stedman Jones, "Language of Chartism," 17–18, 21, 30–32, 34; Claeys, *Machinery, Money, and the Millennium*, xxiv, 110–11, 135, 158–60, 163; Noel Thompson, *The People's Science: The Popular Political Economy of Exploitation and Crisis, 1816–1834* (Cambridge, 1984), ch. 3; Thompson, *Market and Its Critics*, 20; Malcolm Chase, *The People's Farm: English Radical Agrarianism, 1775–1840* (Oxford, 1988), 2, 121–23, 164–65; Parsinnen, "Thomas Spence," 135–41; Parsinnen, "Association, Convention, and Anti-Parliament," 519–20; Maw, "Democratic Anti-Capitalism," 201–26; Bernstein, "From Utopianism to Marxism," 63; Stack, *Bronterre O'Brien*, 2, 122; Ashcraft, "Liberal Political Theory," 260–61; Jones,

*Chartism and the Chartists*, 37–38, 186–87; Royle and Walvin, *English Radicals*, 149; Morris, "Chartism and the British Working-Class Movement," 405–9, 416–17; Morris, *From Cobbett to the Chartists*, 74; Lloyd and Thomas, "Culture and Society," 43, 49–50; Bevir, "Republicanism, Socialism, and Democracy," 352–53.

16. Thompson, *Real Rights of Man*, vii, 1–19, 29; David Martin, "Land Reform," in Hollis, *Pressure from Without*, 134–35; Barry, *Nationalization*, 23–27.
17. Martin, "Land Reform," 136–37; Stack, *Bronterre O'Brien*, 2; Thompson, *Real Rights of Man*, 20–29, 45–49, 53–58.
18. Owen Papers, ROC/15/3/1, O'Brien to Owen, 27 May 1832; Martin, "Land Reform," 135–36; Barry, *Nationalization*, 27–29; Ben Maw, "Robert Owen's Unintended Legacy: Class Conflict," in *Robert Owen and His Legacy*, ed. Noel Thompson and Chris Williams (Cardiff, 2011), 155–73. Though a leading Owenite wrote in 1840 that O'Brien was "entirely with us," this was an exaggeration. Another of Owen's correspondents had turned against O'Brien and his followers—a "mad party"—by the 1850s. Owen Papers, ROC/6/6/16, John Finch to Owen, 8 Apr. 1840, and ROC/17/17/110, James Rigby to Owen, 30 Apr. 1856.
19. Thompson, *Real Rights of Man*, ch. 6.
20. Thompson, *Real Rights of Man*, ch. 8.
21. Maw, "O'Brien's Class Analysis," 253–89.
22. *Poor Man's Guardian and Repealer's Friend*, 1843, no. 8.
23. Stedman Jones, "Language of Chartism," 46; Gash, "After Waterloo," 154; Yeo, "Christianity in Chartist Struggle," 110–12, 126–27; Theodore Koditschek, *Class Formation and Urban-Industrial Society: Bradford, 1750–1850* (Cambridge, 1990), 504–5; Robert Hall, "Creating a People's History: Political Identity and History in Chartism, 1832–1848," in Ashton, Fyson, and Roberts, *Chartist Legacy*, 245–47.
24. Hollis, *Pauper Press*, 203–4, 207, 210, 286–89, 299; Nicholls, "English Middle Class," 426–28; Schafer, "James Bronterre O'Brien," 15–16; Iverson, "Babouvism," chs. 3–4; Clapham's review of Dolléans, *Le Chartisme*, 389–90; Feargus D'Arcy, "Irish Trade Unions before Congress," *History Ireland* 2 (1994): 25–30.
25. Ashcraft, "Liberal Political Theory," 251–52, 259–61, 263; Barry, *Nationalization*, 25; Martin, "Land Reform," 134–35; Bernstein, "Some Recent Historical Literature," 343–45.
26. Horne, *Property Rights*, ch. 6.
27. *Poor Man's Guardian*, 23 May 1835; Horne, *Property Rights*, 250–51; and see also Eric Roark, *Removing the Commons: A Lockean Left-Libertarian Approach to the Just Use and Appropriation of Natural Resources* (Lanham, Md., 2013).
28. Claeys, *Citizens and Saints*, 183, 189, 193, 195, 198, 219, 242–43, 260, 263, 272, 277, 286–87; Stack, *Bronterre O'Brien*, 2, 122, 174; Saville, introduction to Gammage, *Chartist Movement*,

18–19; Hendrix, "Popular Humor," 109; Briggs, introduction to Cole, *Chartist Portraits*, xi.

29. Prothero, "William Benbow," 144–45, 162; Prothero, "Chartism in London," 97–98, 101; David Large, "William Lovett," in Hollis, *Pressure from Without*, 109–11, 117; Harrison and Hollis, "Robert Lowery," 522, 526; Stedman Jones, "Language of Chartism," 3–58; Epstein, "Constitutional Idiom," 553–74.
30. H. T. Dickinson, "The Debate on the Rights of Man in Britain: From the Levellers to the Chartists," *Valahian Journal of Historical Studies* 15 (2011): 11–41; Koditschek, *Class Formation*, 484–86, 490–96, 505–15.
31. David Worrall, "Kinship, Generation, and Community: The Transmission of Political Ideology in Radical Plebeian Print Culture," *Studies in Romanticism* 43 (2004): 283–95; Craig Calhoun, *The Question of Class Struggle: Social Foundations of Popular Radicalism during the Industrial Revolution* (Chicago, 1982).
32. *Poor Man's Guardian*, 13 Apr., 30 Nov. 1833, 22 Mar., 11 Oct. 1834, 28 Mar. 1835.
33. *Reynolds's Political Instructor*, 6, 27 Apr. 1850.
34. Claeys, *Citizens and Saints*, 184–85, 188–93, 209–10; Morris, *From Cobbett to the Chartists*, 190; Schafer, "James Bronterre O'Brien," ch. 2; Miliband, "Robert Owen," 237; Margaret Escott, "Robert Owen as Politician and Parliamentarian," in Thompson and Williams, *Robert Owen*, 143. The point is made in Harrison, *Robert Owen and the Owenites*, 236, 248, that interest in communitarianism faded in Britain after the mid-1840s because of economic conditions and Owenism's institutional weaknesses, but also because it was merged with other programs, not least O'Brien's "democratic politics." The NRL represents, in part, O'Brien's wish to adapt and reconstruct Owenism (and of course he had long been urging that Owenites and Chartists should join together in one movement).
35. *Poor Man's Guardian*, 1, 15 Dec. 1832, 26 Jan., 2 Feb., 23 Mar., 22 June, 2, 30 Nov., 7 Dec. 1833, 22 Mar., 14 June, 26 July, 23 Aug., 20 Sept., 11, 18 Oct., 4 Nov. 1834, 28 Mar. 1835.
36. *Poor Man's Guardian*, 15 Dec. 1832, 7 June 1834; *National Reformer and Manx Weekly Review*, 26 Oct. 1846.
37. Royle, *Revolutionary Britannia*, 93; Martin, "Land Reform," 134–37, 147; Hollis, *Pauper Press*, 212–13. See also Christopher Hill, *Puritanism and Revolution* (London, 1965), 99–120, on the changing applications of the "Norman Yoke" theory from the late eighteenth to the mid-nineteenth centuries. Hill argues that O'Brien gradually discarded it to focus on a more clearly socialist program.
38. Maw, "O'Brien's Class Analysis," 262–63, 265.
39. Hollis, *Pauper Press*, viii, 211, 223–24; Wiener, "Press and the Working Class," 1–4; Stack, *Bronterre O'Brien*, xii–xiii, 17; O'Brien, *Buonarroti's History*, 217–22.

40. Gammage, *Chartist Movement*, 111–12, 114, 119–20, 136.
41. Stack, *Bronterre O'Brien*, 144, 174; Asa Briggs, "Thomas Attwood and the Economic Background of the Birmingham Political Union," *Cambridge Historical Journal* 9 (1948): 190, 216.
42. *Northern Star*, 15 Aug. 1838.
43. Maw, "O'Brien's Class Analysis," 269–70; Thompson, *Market and Its Critics*, 40–44.
44. O'Brien, *Robespierre*, 254–55.
45. *The Opinions of William Cobbett*, ed. James Grande, John Stevenson, and Richard Thomas (Farnham, 2013), chs. 2, 4, 6, 12; *The Collected Social and Political Writings of William Cobbett*, ed. Noel Thompson and David Eastwood (17 vols., London, 1998), 1: xxix, xxxiii–xxxv; Morris, *From Cobbett to the Chartists*, 243.
46. Matthew Roberts, "'The Feast of the Gridiron Is at Hand': Chartism, Cobbett, and Currency," in *William Cobbett, Romanticism, and the Enlightenment*, ed. James Grande and John Stevenson (London, 2015), 107–21.
47. According to Cole, *History of Socialist Thought*, 1: 114, in its well-developed, post-1848 form, O'Brien was "probably" the first to put together a plan for finance and production that could be applied to British conditions.
48. *Manchester and Salford Advertiser*, 25 May 1839.
49. Stack, *Bronterre O'Brien*, xlvi, 144, 219. The Peelite version of "distributive economic justice" and "market-distributed entitlements" offended many on the political Right as well as the Left. Tory protectionists wanted a different approach to trade and money—one that was more conservative socially and constitutionally—and their concern about local markets and credit, and indeed local freedoms, led them to frame arguments that resembled O'Brien's, although the motivations were different. See David Eastwood, "Tories and Markets: Britain, 1800–1850," in *Markets in Historical Context: Ideas and Politics in the Modern World*, ed. Mark Bevir and Frank Trentmann (Cambridge, 2004), 70–89.
50. O'Brien Papers, OB.13, "To the Social and Political Reformers of Great Britain," handwritten, 1865.
51. Those who had "cringed" to Peel and Overstone on earth now "cursed" them in hell. O'Brien, *Vision of Hell*, 12.
52. *Northern Star*, 29 Mar. 1845.
53. *Northern Star*, 29 Mar. 1845.
54. Maw, "Democratic Anti-Capitalism," 201, 204.
55. Claeys, *Machinery, Money, and the Millennium*, 159.
56. *Poor Man's Guardian*, 2, 23 Feb., 23 Nov. 1833, 1, 22 Mar., 26 July 1834; *Destructive*, 24 Aug.

1833; *Bronterre's National Reformer,* 7 Jan. 1837.

57. Claeys, *Citizens and Saints,* 220–22, 227–31.
58. *Poor Man's Guardian,* 1, 29 Sept. 1832, 7 Dec. 1833, 28 Mar. 1835; "Bronterre's Letters," 1836, no. 7; *Bronterre's National Reformer,* 4 Mar. 1837; *British Statesman,* 5 June 1842; *Poor Man's Guardian and Repealer's Friend,* 1843, nos. 3, 7–8; *National Reformer and Manx Weekly Review,* 3, 24 Oct., 5, 19, 26 Dec. 1846, 30 Jan., 6 Mar. 1847; *Power of the Pence,* 27 Jan., 24 Feb., 3 Mar. 1849; *Social Reformer,* 18 Aug., 1 Sept., 6 Oct. 1849.
59. *Southern Star,* 9 Feb. 1840; *Power of the Pence,* 27 Jan. 1849.
60. *Chartist Circular,* 3 Apr., 1 May 1841.
61. *Poor Man's Guardian,* 1 Dec. 1832, 26 Jan., 2 Feb., 23 Mar. 1833, 3 May 1834, 28 Mar. 1835; *Bronterre's National Reformer,* 15 Jan. 1837; *London Mercury,* 25 Dec. 1836, 12 Mar. 1837; *Operative,* 25 Nov. 1838.
62. *Poor Man's Guardian,* 21, 28 Mar. 1835.
63. *Poor Man's Guardian,* 28 Mar. 1835; *Bronterre's National Reformer,* 7 Jan., 25 Feb. 1837; *Northern Star,* 13, 20 Nov. 1841; *National Reformer and Manx Weekly Review,* 16 Jan. 1847.
64. Malcolm Chase, "Out of Radicalism: The Mid-Victorian Freehold Land Movement," *English Historical Review* 106 (1991): 323; Martin, "Land Reform," 150–52; Barry, *Nationalization,* 34, 36–38; Home, "Peri-urban Housing," 366–67.
65. *Operative,* 18 Nov. 1838.
66. Bevir, *Making of British Socialism,* 107–10.
67. *Northern Star,* 16 June 1838.
68. *Operative,* 25 Nov. 1838.
69. Taylor, *Decline of British Radicalism,* 100.
70. Iverson, "Babouvism," 5, 10–11, 16–22, 24, 28–29; R. B. Rose, *Gracchus Babeuf: The First Revolutionary Communist* (Stanford, Calif., 1978), 329; Maw, "O'Brien's Class Analysis," 261, 267; Briggs, "National Bearings," 301–2.
71. Bernstein, "Buonarroti's Classic History of Babouvism," 346–52. Rose, *Gracchus Babeuf,* 2, argues that despite O'Brien's translation, Babouvism was "virtually forgotten" until the early twentieth century. But see Thomson, *Babeuf Plot,* 59, 63; Simkhovitch, "Marxism versus Socialism," 651; Weatherly, "Babeuf's Place," 113–24; Bernstein, "Babeuf and Babouvism," 192; Tönnesson, "The Babouvists," 71; Cole, *History of Socialist Thought,* 1: 19. O'Brien's publication of Buonarroti in November 1836 is included in a list of "important dates in the first years of Chartism" in Thompson, *Early Chartists,* 37; and in Collins and Abramsky, *Marx and the British Labour Movement,* 5, it is stated that O'Brien's book "transmitted to the internationally minded section of the Chartist movement the socialist ideas of revolutionary France." These ideas were still important to the British

Left, thanks to O'Brien, after the Second World War, according to Morris, *From Cobbett to the Chartists*, 30.

72. Ian Birchall, *The Spectre of Babeuf* (Basingstoke, 1997).
73. Rose, "Babeuf, Dictatorship, and Democracy," 223–36; Pilbeam, "Insurrectionary Tradition," 254–55.
74. O'Brien, *Buonarroti's History*, 213, 220.
75. O'Brien, *Buonarroti's History*, 214–20; Chase, *People's Farm*, 125–26; Stack, *Bronterre O'Brien*, 25–46; Iverson, "Babouvism," 79–84, 89–90, 95–98, 114–15, 138–39, 184–94; Pilbeam, "Insurrectionary Tradition," 253–64; Moss, "Republican Socialism," 409.
76. Turner, "Chartism, Bronterre O'Brien, and the 'Luminous Political Example of America,'" 43–69; Claeys, *Citizens and Saints*, 292–96; Maw, "Democratic Anti-Capitalism," 209; Royden Harrison, "British Labour and American Slavery," *Science and Society* 25 (1961): 310.
77. *Poor Man's Guardian*, 9, 16, 23 May 1835. See also Turner, "Ireland and Irishness," 40–57; Schafer, "James Bronterre O'Brien," 27–29; Rachel O'Higgins, "The Irish Influence in the Chartist Movement," *Past and Present* 20 (1960): 93–94.
78. Reeve Huston, "Multiple Crossings: Thomas Ainge Devyr and Transatlantic Land Reform," in *Transatlantic Rebels: Agrarian Radicalism in Comparative Context*, ed. Thomas Summerhill and James Scott (East Lansing, Mich., 2004), 137–66; Stack, *Bronterre O'Brien*, xliii, 87; Jamie Bronstein, *Land Reform and Working-Class Experience in Britain and the United States, 1800–1862* (Stanford, Calif., 1999), 108–9.
79. *London Mercury*, 7 May 1837.
80. *British Statesman*, 23 July 1842; *Poor Man's Guardian and Repealer's Friend*, 1843, nos. 3, 5–6; *National Reformer and Manx Weekly Review*, 6 Mar., 3, 10, 17 Oct., 14, 21, 28 Nov., 5 Dec. 1846; *Power of the Pence*, 2, 16, 23, 30 Dec. 1848, 6 Jan., 3, 10, 17 Feb., 3, 24, 31 Mar., 7, 14 Apr. 1849; *Social Reformer*, 11 Aug., 1, 15 Sept., 6, 13, 20 Oct. 1849.
81. G. D. Lillibridge, *Beacon of Freedom: The Impact of American Democracy upon Great Britain, 1830–1870* (Philadelphia, 1955), 70–71; Jamie Bronstein, "Land Reform and Political Traditions in Nineteenth-Century Britain and the United States," in *Critiques of Capital in Modern America and Britain: Transatlantic Exchanges 1800 to the Present Day*, ed. Mark Bevir and Frank Trentmann (Basingstoke, 2002), 35, 38; Entz, *Llewellyn Castle*, 112–13, 118, 125, 133, 135, 138, 141, 146, 150, 152, 154–55, 167–68, 173–76, 217.
82. Bronstein, *Land Reform and Working-Class Experience*, 88, 107, 109, 135. The availability of land in parts of the British Empire, specifically the white colonies of settlement, proved a powerful draw to many Chartists. There was considerable emigration to Australia and New Zealand, for instance, as well as to the United States. Though the acquiring of land

in the colonies was not as straightforward as incoming Chartists might have imagined, they were determined to make the effort, particularly as the Land Plan at home ran into financial and legal problems. "The colonies of settlement emerged," Paul Pickering writes, "as a place where the passion for the land could be easily translated into a vision of independent yeomanry democracy." Pickering, "Betrayal and Exile," 211.

83. Jamie Bronstein, "The Homestead and the Garden Plot: Cultural Pressures on Land Reform in Nineteenth-Century Britain and the United States," *The European Legacy: Toward New Paradigms* 6 (2001): 166–67.
84. Gregory Claeys, "Lewis Masquerier and the Later Development of American Owenism, 1835–1845," *Labor History* 29 (1988): 237.
85. O'Brien, "Human Slavery," 299–442. See also Stack, *Bronterre O'Brien*, xix, xlv; Cole, *Chartist Portraits*, 261–62; Iverson, "Babouvism," 114–25, 151; Thomas Haskell, "Capitalism and the Origins of the Humanitarian Sensibility," *American Historical Review* 90 (1985): 350.
86. Lewis, "Robespierre through the Chartist Looking-Glass," 204, argues that O'Brien exaggerated Robespierre's commitment to democracy.
87. *Poor Man's Guardian*, 31 Aug. 1833, 15 Nov. 1834; *Operative*, 25 Nov. 1838.
88. Richard Whatmore, "The Politics of Political Economy in France from Rousseau to Constant," in Bevir and Trentmann, *Markets in Historical Context*, 46–69.
89. Mulholland, "'Its Patrimony, Its Unique Wealth,'" 375–417.
90. Soffer, "Attitudes and Allegiances," 451–54; Kiernan, *Poets, Politics, and the People*, 160–61; Messner, "Land, Leadership, Culture, and Emigration," 1094, 1096–97; Martin, "Land Reform," 132–33; Jeremy Burchardt, "Land, Labour, and Politics: Parliament and Allotment Provision, 1830–1870," in Wordie, *Agriculture and Politics*, 98–127.
91. Douglas, review of Morris, *From Cobbett to the Chartists*, 90–92; Moss, "Republican Socialism," 408–10.
92. John Rule and Roger Wells, *Crime, Protest, and Popular Politics in Southern England, 1740–1850* (London, 1997), 59, 119, 129, 149.
93. Eisenberg, "Variations in Socialism," 134.
94. Chase, *Chartism: A New History*, 145–46, 167–68, 247–60, 271–72, 274–75, 277–79, 290–92, 327–33; MacAskill, "Chartist Land Plan," 305, 307; Martin, "Land Reform," 149–50; Barry, *Nationalization*, 31, 38–39; Allsop Collection, Misc.525/3/11, Oastler to Allsop, 15 Dec. 1850.
95. Richard Cobden to C. P. Villiers, 12 Nov. 1842, in *The Letters of Richard Cobden*, ed. Anthony Howe (3 vols., Oxford, 2007, 2010, 2015), 1: 301–2.
96. Allsop Collection, Misc.525/2/28, O'Connor to Allsop, undated, 1843. Five years earlier

than this, R. S. C. Bainbridge, one of Owen's followers in Newcastle-upon-Tyne, thought of O'Connor as anything but an antisocialist following a meeting in the town at which the latter spoke. In a letter to Owen, Bainbridge wrote that O'Connor was "your steadfast friend" for "three fourths of his speech was pure and undefiled Owenism." Owen Papers, ROC/2/1/1, Bainbridge to Owen, 10 Feb. 1838.

97. *National Reformer and Manx Weekly Review*, 17 Apr., 7 Nov., 19 Dec. 1846, 9 Jan., 14 May 1847; Faherty, "O'Brien's Correspondence with Thomas Allsop," 30; MacAskill, "Chartist Land Plan," 315, 340; Stack, *Bronterre O'Brien*, xxii–xxiii, xxviii, 144; Iverson, "Babouvism," 75–76; Ward, *Chartism*, 178, 180; Jones, *Chartism and the Chartists*, 131; Cole, *Chartist Portraits*, 259; Claeys, "Triumph of Class-Conscious Reformism," 979; Martin, "Land Reform," 148–49; Barry, *Nationalization*, 34–35; Gammage, *Chartist Movement*, 267–69; Bronstein, *Land Reform and Working-Class Experience*, 107–8, 110.

98. Paul Barker, "Nowadays: The Chartist Model Town of O'Connorville," *New Statesman*, 25 July 1997, 54.

99. Thompson, *The Chartists*, 305–6; James Epstein, *The Lion of Freedom: Feargus O'Connor and the Chartist Movement, 1832–1842* (London, 1982), 251. There is also a favorable verdict in W. H. G. Armytage, "The Chartist Land Colonies, 1846–1848," *Agricultural History* 32 (1958): 87–96.

100. Malcolm Chase, "'Wholesome Object Lessons': The Chartist Land Plan in Retrospect," *English Historical Review* 118 (2003): 62.

101. Claeys, "Triumph of Class-Conscious Reformism," 979; Hall's review of Dolléans, *Le Chartisme*, 406–7.

102. *Manchester Guardian*, 6 Sept. 1845.

103. *Poor Man's Guardian and Repealer's Friend*, 1843, no. 8.

104. Chase, *People's Farm*, 171, 183, 188; Maw, "Democratic Anti-Capitalism," 211–12; Plummer, "O'Brien in the Working-Class Movement," 61–80; Cole, *Chartist Portraits*, 257, 266; Schafer, "James Bronterre O'Brien," 19. While emphasizing the role of O'Brien (and Spence) in advocating and explaining the people's "resumption" of the land, Barry's *Nationalization* usefully points out that in the British context "nationalization"—state ownership acquired by parliamentary means—was not necessarily the same as "socialism"—public ownership of all important means of production, distribution, and exchange.

105. Malcolm Chase, "Chartism and the Land: 'The Mighty People's Question,'" in *The Land Question in Britain, 1750–1950*, ed. Matthew Cragoe and Paul Readman (Basingstoke, 2010), 57–73. The Land Plan's ties with other initiatives—especially building and freehold land societies—has also been stressed in Angus Macintyre, review of A. M.

Hadfield, *The Chartist Land Company* (Newton Abbot, 1970), *Economic History Review* 24 (1971): 301–2.

106. Chase, "Chartism and the Land," 63, 67–68.
107. *National Reformer and Manx Weekly Review*, 14, 21, 28 Nov., 5, 12, 19 Dec. 1846, 2, 9, 16, 23 Jan., 6, 20 Feb., 6, 13, 27 Mar., 3, 24 Apr., 1, 15 May 1847. On Bowkett see Newens, "Thomas Edward Bowkett," 143–48.
108. *Reynolds's Weekly Newspaper*, 30 June 1850.
109. Humpherys, "G. W. M. Reynolds," 86; Haywood, "George W. M. Reynolds," 27.
110. Iverson, "Babouvism," 153–66, 195–202; Jones, *Chartism and the Chartists*, 171–72; Stack, *Bronterre O'Brien*, xix; Barry, *Nationalization*, 39.
111. Owen Papers, ROC/1/24/13–15, 23, Allsop to Owen, 30 Mar., 5, 6 Apr., 22 May 1848.
112. *Northern Star*, 8 Dec. 1849.
113. *Power of the Pence*, 23, 30 Dec. 1848, 6 Jan. 1849.
114. *Power of the Pence*, 20 Jan., 10 Mar. 1849; and for context see Anthony Howe, "The 'Manchester School' and the Landlords: The Failure of Land Reform in Early Victorian Britain," in Cragoe and Readman, *Land Question*, 74–91.
115. *Power of the Pence*, 3, 10 Feb., 24 Mar. 1849.
116. Allsop Collection, Misc.525/1/7, O'Brien to Allsop, 8 Dec. 1847.
117. Allsop Collection, Misc.525/1/9, O'Brien to Allsop, 27 June 1855; O'Brien Papers, OB.4–9, O'Brien to Mathews, 31 Mar., 19 Sept., 17 Nov., 23 Dec. 1857, 20, 24 Mar. 1858.
118. O'Brien, *Vision of Hell*, 6–7, 9.
119. Allsop Collection, Misc.525/1/10, 12, O'Brien to Allsop, 22 Sept., 1 Oct. 1862.
120. O'Brien Papers, OB.13, "To the Social and Political Reformers of Great Britain."
121. Ursula Vogel, "The Land Question: A Liberal Theory of Communal Property," *History Workshop* 27 (1989): 106–35.
122. Martin, "Agricultural Interest," 128–48; Home, "Peri-urban Housing," 366–67; Thompson, *Real Rights of Man*, 14, 120–22; Entz, *Llewellyn Castle*, 179–80, 183–84, 186–90, 221–23; Reeves, "Henry George's Speaking," 54.
123. Vogel, "Land Question," 106, 114–15, 119–20, 126; Martin, "Land Reform," 141, 145; John Medearis, "Labor, Democracy, Utility, and Mill's Critique of Private Property," *American Journal of Political Science* 49 (2005): 143–44; Gregory Claeys, "Justice, Independence, and Industrial Democracy: The Development of John Stuart Mill's Views on Socialism," *Journal of Politics* 49 (1987): 142; and Gregory Claeys, review of Mark Francis, *Herbert Spencer and the Invention of Modern Life* (Ithaca, N.Y., 2007), *International Review of Social History* 54 (2009): 292–94.
124. Vogel, "Land Question," 109–11; Martin, "Land Reform," 153–56.

125. Howe, "'Manchester School' and the Landlords," 74–91.
126. Matthew Cragoe and Paul Readman, introduction to Cragoe and Readman, *Land Question*, 1–18.
127. Harold Perkin, "Land Reform and Class Conflict in Victorian Britain," in *The Victorians and Social Protest*, ed. John Butt and I. F. Clarke (Newton Abbot, 1973), 177–217.
128. Thompson, *Real Rights of Man*, ch. 9.
129. Schafer, "James Bronterre O'Brien," 50, 59, 62, 68.
130. Maw, "Democratic Anti-Capitalism," 209.
131. Finn, *After Chartism*, 231; Barrow, "Homerton Social Democratic Club," 188–90; Shipley, *Club Life and Socialism*, 1–20, 24–25, 28, 34, 46–47, 50–51, 56, 67, 71–76, 80–83; Whitehead, "The *New World* and the O'Brienite Colony," 40–43; Entz, *Llewellyn Castle*, 209–26; Barrow and Bullock, *Democratic Ideas*, 11–12; Bevir, "British Social Democratic Federation," 207–29; Bevir, *Making of British Socialism*, 17–18, 107, 110–15, 119–21; Thompson, "Fabian Socialism," 86–89; Fox, "Marx, Engels, and Lenin," 9–15; Sweezy, "Origins of Present-Day Socialism," 76–77, 79; Lause, "American Radicals," 63–64, 79.

## Chapter 5. America's Democratic Promise

1. Stedman Jones, "Language of Chartism," 12–13.
2. Royle, *Revolutionary Britannia*, 94; Henry Weisser, *British Working-Class Movements and Europe, 1815–1848* (Manchester, 1975), 87–88; Joan Hugman, "'A Small Drop of Ink': Tyneside Chartism and the *Northern Liberator*," in Ashton, Fyson, and Roberts, *Chartist Legacy*, 24–47.
3. O'Brien, *Robespierre*, 23; "Bronterre's Letters," 1836, nos. 7, 10.
4. Ward, *Chartism*, 141, 247.
5. Chase, *Chartism: A New History*, 1, 82, 143, 268.
6. *Chartism: Authentic Report of the Speech of Mr. William Jones*, 15.
7. Jones, *Chartism and the Chartists*, 160.
8. Chase, *Chartism: A New History*, 287.
9. Chase, *Chartism: A New History*, 92; Ward, *Chartism*, 135, 236–41; Royle, *Revolutionary Britannia*, 112; Wilson, "Chartism in Glasgow," 281; Briggs, "National Bearings," 292; Thompson, *The Chartists*, 160–62, 168, 197, 212, 220; John Charlton, *The Chartists: The First National Workers' Movement* (London, 1997), 83; Jones, *Chartism and the Chartists*, 28, 116–17, 167–68, 182, 186.
10. Fraser, "Chartist Press in Scotland," 92.
11. *Chartist Circular*, 18 Apr., 8, 15 Aug. 1840, 20 Jan., 13 Mar. 1841.
12. Glenn Airey, "Feargus O'Connor, Ernest Jones, and *The Labourer*," in Allen and Ashton,

*Papers for the People*, 119; Royle, "The *Cause of the People*," 153.

13. Jones, *Chartism and the Chartists*, 96, 187.
14. Howard Temperley, *Britain and America since Independence* (Basingstoke, 2002), 44.
15. *The Charter*, 20 Oct. 1839.
16. *Northern Star*, 2 Aug. 1845.
17. Denis Paz, "Chartist Lecturers and the Culture of Victorian Lecturing," conference paper, Consortium on the Revolutionary Era, Huntsville, Ala., 2008. I am grateful to Professor Paz for a copy of his paper.
18. Lillibridge, *Beacon of Freedom*, 41, 48.
19. Jamie Bronstein, "From the Land of Liberty to Land Monopoly: The United States in a Chartist Context," in Ashton, Fyson, and Roberts, *Chartist Legacy*, 147–70; Gregory Claeys, "The Example of America as a Warning to England? The Transformation of America in British Radicalism and Socialism, 1790–1850," in *Learning and Living: Essays in Honour of J. F. C. Harrison*, ed. Malcolm Chase and Ian Dyck (Aldershot, 1996), 66–80.
20. Ray Boston, *British Chartists in America, 1839–1900* (Manchester, 1971), 13, 17, 19–20.
21. Robert Saunders, "'Let America Be the Test': Democracy and Reform in Britain, 1832–1867," in *The American Experiment and the Idea of Democracy in British Culture, 1776–1914*, ed. Ella Dzelzainis and Ruth Livesey (Farnham, 2013), 79–85, 89.
22. Boston, *Chartists in America*, 6–7, 14–17. Australia and New Zealand were also attractive destinations, and many Chartists went there believing that they could have the life they had wanted in Britain, complete with political rights and economic security. As Paul Pickering puts it, "Chartism was one of Britain's most successful, if unheralded, exports. A recognition of this globalization from below underscores the need for a transnational approach to nineteenth-century labour history." Pickering, "Betrayal and Exile," 207–12. See also Messner, "Land, Leadership, Culture, and Emigration," 1094, 1100–1104.
23. James Epstein, "'America' in the Victorian Cultural Imagination," in *Anglo-American Attitudes: From Revolution to Partnership*, ed. Frank Leventhal and Roland Quinault (Aldershot, 2000), 115–16.
24. O'Brien, *Robespierre*, 129; *British Statesman*, 16 July, 5 Nov. 1842; *National Reformer and Manx Weekly Review*, 26 Dec. 1846; *Power of the Pence*, 11 Nov. 1848, 7, 14 Apr. 1849; Plummer, *Bronterre*, 29, 69, 77–78, 124, 148, 164–65; *Poor Man's Guardian and Repealer's Friend*, 1843, no.13; Allsop Collection, Misc.525/1/9–12, O'Brien to Allsop, 27 June 1855, 22, 26 Sept., 1 Oct. 1862.
25. *British Statesman*, 23 July 1842; *Poor Man's Guardian and Repealer's Friend*, 1843, nos. 3–7, 13; *National Reformer and Manx Weekly Review*, 6, 13, 20 Feb., 6, 13, 20, 27 Mar., 3, 10, 17, 24 Apr., 8, 22, 29 May 1847; *Power of the Pence*, 3 Mar. 1849; Claeys, "John Adolphus Etzler,"

357–58, 364; Joel Nydahl, introduction to *The Collected Works of John Adolphus Etzler, 1833–1844* (Delmar, N.Y., 1977), vii–xxxi; Manuel, "Toward a Psychological History," 298; Chase, *People's Farm*, 141; Malcolm Chase, "Exporting the Owenite Utopia: Thomas Powell and the Tropical Emigration Society," in Thompson and Williams, *Robert Owen*, 201, 203.

26. *Social Reformer*, 11 Aug., 1, 15 Sept., 6, 13 Oct. 1849; Wilbur Shepperson, "Some Plans for British Immigration to Texas in 1849 and 1850," *Southwestern Historical Quarterly* 63 (1960): 439–49.
27. E.g., Feuer, "American Communist Colonies," 456–74.
28. Lillibridge, *Beacon of Freedom*, 43–45.
29. Owen went to the United States in 1824. He started a settlement at New Harmony, Indiana, in line with his ideas about cooperation, mutuality, independence, and social reorganization. Owen returned to Britain in 1830 at a time when his principles were gathering more support. These principles continued to be influential in America as well as Britain. Royle and Walvin, *English Radicals*, 137–38, 187.
30. O'Brien, *Buonarroti's History*, 213–15.
31. *London Mercury*, 7 May 1837; Hollis, *Pauper Press*, 280.
32. O'Brien, *Buonarroti's History*, 219; *British Statesman*, 23 July 1842; *Poor Man's Guardian and Repealer's Friend*, 1843, nos. 3, 5–6; *National Reformer and Manx Weekly Review*, 21 Nov. 1846.
33. Malcolm Chase, "From Millennium to Anniversary: The Concept of Jubilee in Late Eighteenth- and Nineteenth-Century England," *Past and Present* 129 (1990): 132–47; Reeves, "Henry George's Speaking," 54.
34. Huston, "Multiple Crossings," 151–53, 155–60; Claeys, "Lewis Masquerier," 231, 233, 237; Lillibridge, *Beacon of Freedom*, 69–71.
35. Lause, "American Radicals," 63–64. See also Henry Collins, review of Samuel Bernstein, *The First International in America* (New York, 1962), *Science and Society* 27 (1963), 338–41.
36. Bronstein, *Land Reform and Working-Class Experience*, 88. Bronstein erroneously states that O'Brien visited America in 1845 (282 n. 117)—an impossibility in view of his financial circumstances.
37. *British Statesman*, 16 July, 5 Nov. 1842.
38. *National Reformer and Manx Weekly Review*, 26 Dec. 1846.
39. Bronstein, "Land Reform and Political Traditions," 35, 38.
40. *British Statesman*, 16, 23, 30 July, 27 Aug., 8, 15 Oct., 5 Nov., 3 Dec. 1842.
41. E.g., *National Reformer and Manx Weekly Review*, 12, 26 Dec. 1846.
42. *Power of the Pence*, 17 Feb. 1849.
43. *Power of the Pence*, 16, 23 Dec. 1848, 17 Feb., 24 Mar., 7, 14 Apr. 1849.

44. *Power of the Pence*, 11, 25 Nov., 23, 30 Dec., 1848, 6 Jan., 10 Feb., 24 Mar., 14 Apr. 1849.
45. F. M. Trollope, *Domestic Manners of the Americans* (London, 1832); Thomas Hamilton, *Men and Manners in America* (Edinburgh, 1833); Frederick Marryat, *A Diary in America, with Remarks upon Its Institutions* (London, 1839); Charles Dickens, *American Notes for General Circulation* (London, 1842); Charles Lyell, *Travels in North America in the Years 1841–1842* (London, 1845).
46. James Stuart, *Three Years in North America* (Edinburgh, 1833); Harriet Martineau, *Society in America* (London, 1837); J. S. Buckingham, *America: Historical, Statistic, and Descriptive* (London, 1841); George Warburton, *Hochelaga: Or, England in the New World* (London, 1846).
47. "The Testimony of European Writers on America" appeared in *Power of the Pence*, 17 Feb. 1849.
48. Allan Nevins, *America through British Eyes* (New York, 1948), 79–102, 205–6.
49. *Power of the Pence*, 11, 25 Nov., 30 Dec. 1848, 6 Jan., 24, 31 Mar. 1849.
50. *Power of the Pence*, 16, 23 Dec. 1848, 17, 24 Feb., 14 Apr. 1849.
51. *Power of the Pence*, 3 Mar. 1849.
52. *Power of the Pence*, 2, 16, 23, 30 Dec. 1848, 6 Jan., 3, 10, 17 Feb., 24, 31 Mar., 7, 14 Apr. 1849.
53. *Poor Man's Guardian*, 2 Feb. 1833.
54. Simon Morgan, "America, Protectionism, and Democracy in British Free Trade Debates, 1815–1861," in Dzelzainis and Livesey, *American Experiment*, 93, 95.
55. *Power of the Pence*, 13, 20 Jan., 10, 24 Feb., 3, 10, 17 Mar. 1849.
56. *National Reformer and Manx Weekly Review*, 10 Oct., 5, 12 Dec. 1846, 15 May 1847; *British Statesman*, 27 Aug., 5 Nov. 1842.
57. *Power of the Pence*, 25 Nov., 30 Dec. 1848, 24 Mar. 1849.
58. *Power of the Pence*, 10 Feb., 3 Mar. 1849.
59. *Power of the Pence*, 30 Dec. 1848.
60. *British Statesman*, 8 Oct., 19 Nov., 3 Dec. 1842; *National Reformer and Manx Weekly Review*, 10, 17 Oct., 12, 26 Dec. 1846, 24 Apr., 22 May 1847.
61. *British Statesman*, 19 June, 30 July, 27 Aug., 8, 15 Oct. 1842; *National Reformer and Manx Weekly Review*, 24 Oct. 1846.
62. *British Statesman*, 9 July, 29 Oct. 1842; *National Reformer and Manx Weekly Review*, 3 Oct. 1846, 16, 30 Jan., 13 Feb., 24 Apr. 1847.
63. *Power of the Pence*, 16, 30 Dec. 1848, 17 Feb., 14 Apr. 1849; Royle, "The *Cause of the People*," 162; Harrison, "British Labour and American Slavery," 310.
64. Royle and Walvin, *English Radicals*, 186; Iain McCalman, "Anti-slavery and Ultra-radicalism in Early Nineteenth-Century England: The Case of Robert Wedderburn,"

*Slavery and Abolition* 7 (1986): 99–117.

65. Adam Smith, "Victorian Radicalism and the Idea of America: *Reynolds's Newspaper*, 1850–1900," in Dzelzainis and Livesey, *American Experiment*, 137–39, 143.
66. Haskell, "Capitalism and the Origins of the Humanitarian Sensibility," 350; Chase, *Chartism: A New History*, 306–7; Messner, "Land, Leadership, Culture, and Emigration," 1109.
67. Catherine Gallagher, *The Body Economic: Life, Death, and Sensation in Political Economy and the Victorian Novel* (Princeton, N.J., 2006); David Roediger, *The Wages of Whiteness: Race and the Making of the American Working Class* (London, 1991).
68. Ira Katznelson, "Working-Class Formation and the State: Nineteenth-Century England in American Perspective," in *Britain and America: Studies in Comparative History, 1760–1970*, ed. David Englander (London, 1997), 171–95.
69. Douglas Lorimer, *Colour, Class, and the Victorians: English Attitudes to the Negro in the Mid-Nineteenth Century* (New York, 1978), 31, 68, 177, 211.
70. On these points see *Black Victorians / Black Victoriana*, ed. G. H. Gerzina (New Brunswick, N.J., 2003).
71. Thomas Murphy, *A Land without Castles: The Changing Image of America in Europe, 1780–1830* (Lanham, Md., 2001), 210–11.
72. Morgan, "America, Protection, and Democracy," 100–101; Richard Huzzey, "British Liberties, American Emancipation, and the Democracy of Race," in Dzelzainis and Livesey, *American Experiment*, 121, 123–25, 128.
73. *Northern Star*, 6 Mar. 1847.
74. *Power of the Pence*, 3 Mar. 1849.
75. O'Brien, "Human Slavery," 357.
76. Nevins, *America through British Eyes*, 14, 16, 22–23, 88–90, 95–96, 101, 208–9, 213, 216.
77. Seymour Drescher, *The Mighty Experiment: Free Labor versus Slavery in British Emancipation* (New York, 2004), 151–53, 166, 173; Royle and Walvin, *English Radicals*, 34–35, 186; J. P. Greene, "Introduction: Empire and Liberty," in *Exclusionary Empire: English Liberty Overseas, 1600–1900*, ed. J. P. Greene (New York, 2010), 13; and P. S. Onuf, "Federalism, Democracy, and Liberty in the New American Nation," in Greene, *Exclusionary Empire*, 136, 154–58.
78. Drescher, *Mighty Experiment*, 106–10, 114, 129, 161–63, 171–73, 188–89, 217–18, 221.
79. Ward, *Chartism*, 247; Drescher, *Mighty Experiment*, 161, 166, 181, 219.
80. *Northern Star*, 12 Feb. 1848, 23 Mar. 1850.
81. Drescher, *Mighty Experiment*, 51, 121, 123, 127, 130, 136, 144, 153, 157, 159–60, 162, 194.
82. Andrew Heath, "'The Producers on One Side and the Capitalists on the Other': Labor

Reform, Slavery, and the Career of a Transatlantic Radical," *American Nineteenth Century History* 13 (2012): 199–227; Harrison, *Robert Owen and the Owenites*, 249.

83. *Social Reformer*, 11 Aug., 1, 15 Sept., 6, 13, 20 Oct. 1849.
84. O'Brien, "Human Slavery," 403–7.
85. O'Brien Papers, OB.6–7, O'Brien to Mathews, 17 Nov., 23 Dec. 1857.
86. O'Brien Papers, OB.7–9, O'Brien to Mathews, 23 Dec. 1857, 20, 24 Mar. 1858.
87. Plummer, *Bronterre*, 202, 222, 258, 270–71, 274, 276; Collins, review of Bernstein's *First International in America*, 338–41; Charlton, *Chartists*, 75, 83.
88. *Power of the Pence*, 11 Nov., 9, 16, 23 Dec. 1848, 20 Jan., 3, 17 Feb., 7, 14 Apr. 1849.
89. *Power of the Pence*, 11 Nov. 1848.
90. Shepperson, "Some Plans for British Immigration," 439–49; Ward, *Chartism*, 238; *Social Reformer*, 11 Aug., 1, 15 Sept., 6, 13 Oct. 1849.
91. Whitehead, "The *New World* and the O'Brienite Colony," 40–43; Entz, *Llewellyn Castle*, 1–5, 13, 19–20, 22–23, 62–68, 79–81, 120–33, 136–37, 142–43, 154–66; Shipley, *Club Life and Socialism*, 80–83.
92. Entz, *Llewellyn Castle*, xiii–xv, 11–12, 18, 214–24.

### Chapter 6. The Irish Dimension

1. *Oxford Companion to Irish History*, ed. Sean Connolly (Oxford, 1998), 85; Thompson, "Ireland and the Irish," 129; Paul Pickering, *Feargus O'Connor: A Political Life* (Monmouth, 2008), 81, 107; Timothy Keane, "'Ireland's Wrongs as England's Grievance': Representations of Ireland in English Radical Discourse, 1824–1850" (PhD thesis, National University of Ireland, Galway, 2010), iii, 1–2, 22, 145–47, 152–53, 160–61, 178–80, 248; Takashi Koseki, "Chartism and Irish Nationalism, 1839–1848: Bronterre O'Brien, the London Irish, and Attempts at a Chartist-Irish Alliance" (MPhil thesis, University of Birmingham, 1988). I would like to thank Dr. Keane for sending me a copy of his thesis. There appears to be only one surviving copy of Dr. Koseki's thesis, his own, and I am grateful to him for allowing me to borrow it.
2. *Bronterre's National Reformer*, 7 Jan. 1837; Gammage, *Chartist Movement*, 71–72; Plummer, *Bronterre*, 15–34; Canavan, "The Edgeworths," 240–48; Cole, *Chartist Portraits*, 242–43; Hollis, *Pauper Press*, 313; Stack, *Bronterre O'Brien*, xii–xiv, xxviii, xli, 1–2, 17.
3. O'Brien stated in a letter of May 1832 that he planned to visit Ireland for "a week or two" (Owen Papers, ROC/15/3/1, O'Brien to Owen, 27 May 1832) but it is not clear that he did so.
4. Faherty, "O'Brien's Correspondence with Thomas Allsop," 28–33.
5. Graham Davis, *The Irish in Britain, 1815–1914* (Dublin, 1991), 166–69, 189; Francis Hearn,

*Domination, Legitimation, and Resistance: The Incorporation of the Nineteenth-Century English Working Class* (Westport, Conn., 1978), 215–16; Eric Strauss, *Irish Nationalism and British Democracy* (New York, 1951), 127–31.

6. *Bronterre's National Reformer*, 4 Feb. 1837.
7. Thompson, *Outsiders*, 109, 111–12, 126–27; D'Arcy, "Irish Trade Unions," 25–30; Christine Kinealy, "Politics in Ireland," in *A Companion to Nineteenth-Century Britain*, ed. Chris Williams (Oxford, 2007), 478–79; Joseph Clayton, "Irish Catholics and the British Labour Movement," *Studies: An Irish Quarterly Review*, 14 (1925): 284–94; Hollis, *Pauper Press*, 117, 121, 279; Stack, *Bronterre O'Brien*, xi; Michael Huggins, "Democracy or Nationalism? The Problems of the Chartist Press in Ireland," in Allen and Ashton, *Papers for the People*, 129–34, 136, 142–43.
8. Contemporary debate about land reform often focused on Ireland. E.g., Martin, "Agricultural Interest," 128–48. See also Christine Kinealy, "Economy and Society in Ireland," in Williams, *Nineteenth-Century Britain*, 493, 495, 497; Peter Gray, *Famine, Land, and Politics: British Government and Irish Society, 1843–1850* (Dublin, 1999), 5–16; T. A. Jackson, *Ireland Her Own: An Outline History of the Irish Struggle* (London, 1976), 228, 235, 244–45, 261–65; K. T. Hoppen, *Ireland since 1800: Conflict and Conformity* (London, 1996), 19, 21, 29, 36–50; Roy Foster, *Modern Ireland, 1600–1972* (London, 1989), 331–37, 342–44; Strauss, *Irish Nationalism*, 74–79, 81–83, 86–7, 101–3, 106, 129–30, 133–37, 140–41, 161; Davis, *Irish in Britain*, 162–63, 165–67; K. B. Nowlan, "O'Connell and Irish Nationalism," in *Daniel O'Connell: Portrait of a Radical*, ed. K. B. Nowlan and M. R. O'Connell (New York, 1985), 12, 15.
9. O'Higgins, "Irish Influence," 90, 93–94.
10. Thompson, *The Chartists*, 305–6; Armytage, "Chartist Land Colonies," 87–96.
11. Chase, "'Wholesome Object Lessons,'" 59–85. See also Chase, "Chartism and the Land," 57–73.
12. E.g., *Poor Man's Guardian and Repealer's Friend*, 1843, nos. 7–8; *National Reformer and Manx Weekly Review*, 17, 24 Oct., 19 Dec. 1846, 9 Jan., 17 Apr., 1, 15, 22 May 1847; *Power of the Pence*, 31 Mar. 1849; *Social Reformer*, 25 Aug. 1849. See also Pickering, *Feargus O'Connor*, 102, 107–8; Keane, "'Ireland's Wrongs,'" 142–43.
13. Barry, *Nationalization*, 23–29, 31, 34–39, 90–91, 109, 165; Parsinnen, "Thomas Spence," 135–41; Ashcraft, "Liberal Political Theory," 249–72; Strauss, *Irish Nationalism*, 129, 161.
14. O'Higgins, "Irish Influence," 93–94; Davis, *Irish in Britain*, 165; Strauss, *Irish Nationalism*, 129–30.
15. See John Hooker's review of Élie Halévy, *A History of the English People, 1841–1852* (New York, 1948), *Catholic Historical Review* 35 (1949): 191–92.

16. David Lloyd, "The Subaltern in Motion: Subalternity, the Popular, and Irish Working-Class History," *Postcolonial Studies* 8 (2005): 431–32.
17. *Poor Man's Guardian*, 31 Aug. 1833.
18. *Poor Man's Guardian*, 16 Aug. 1834.
19. *Poor Man's Guardian*, 14 Mar. 1835.
20. *Poor Man's Guardian*, 14 Mar. 1835.
21. "Bronterre's Letters," 1836, nos. 4, 9.
22. "Bronterre's Letters," 1836, no. 14; Hoppen, *Ireland since 1800*, 18; Oliver MacDonagh, *The Emancipationist: Daniel O'Connell, 1830–1847* (New York, 1989), ch. 1.
23. "Bronterre's Letters," 1836, no. 14. O'Brien was a vigorous contributor on the negative side, but O'Connell's contemporary and subsequent reputation offers a record of interpretive twists and turns, often related to the course of political and social change in and beyond Ireland.
24. *Bronterre's National Reformer*, 7, 15 Jan., 4, 18, 25 Feb., 18 Mar. 1837.
25. E.g., O'Brien, *Robespierre*, 312.
26. *Operative*, 4 Nov. 1838.
27. *British Statesman*, 6 Aug. 1842.
28. *Poor Man's Guardian and Repealer's Friend*, 1843, no. 1.
29. *Poor Man's Guardian and Repealer's Friend*, 1843, no. 4.
30. Hall, "Creating a People's History," 245–46.
31. Gammage, *Reminiscences of a Chartist*, 38–39.
32. *Poor Man's Guardian and Repealer's Friend*, 1843, nos. 2–4.
33. Thompson, *Outsiders*, 109, 112–13, 116–19, 124, 136–38, 150, 153, 157–58, 161; Dorothy Thompson, "The Chartists in 1848," in *These Fissured Isles: Ireland, Scotland, and the Making of Modern Britain, 1798–1848*, ed. Terry Brotherstone, Anna Clark, and Kevin Whelan (Edinburgh, 2005), 172–73; Nowlan, "O'Connell," 12–14; Koseki, "Chartism and Irish Nationalism," ch. 2; Takashi Koseki, *Patrick O'Higgins and Irish Chartism* (Hosei University, Ireland-Japan Papers No. 2, 1990), 10–11 (I am grateful to Dr. Koseki for a copy of his paper on O'Higgins); Jackson, *Ireland Her Own*, 227–28, 235; L. H. Lees, *Exiles of Erin: Irish Migrants in Victorian London* (Ithaca, N.Y., 1979), 226–27; Strauss, *Irish Nationalism*, 102, 104; William Lowe, "The Chartists and the Irish Confederates: Lancashire, 1848," *Irish Historical Studies* 24 (1984): 174; O'Higgins, "Irish Influence," 86–87, 92; J. H. Treble, "O'Connor, O'Connell, and the Attitudes of Irish Immigrants towards Chartism in the North of England, 1838–1848," in Butt and Clarke, *Victorians and Social Protest*, 37–40, 42–43, 47–48, 56–58, 60–61; Davis, *Irish in Britain*, 175, 187–88; Ruth-Ann Harris, "The Failure of Republicanism among Irish Migrants to Britain,

1800–1840," *Eire-Ireland* 21 (1986): 125–26; Martin Mitchell, "The Catholic Irish and Chartism in the West of Scotland," in Brotherstone, Clark, and Whelan, *These Fissured Isles*, 179–80; Pickering, *Feargus O'Connor*, 29–30, 34, 49–51, 53–54; Christine Kinealy, *Repeal and Revolution: Ireland in 1848* (Manchester, 2009), 42–44, 104.

34. Treble, "O'Connor, O'Connell, and Irish Immigrants," 33–35, 56–58; Andrew Granath, "The Irish in Mid Nineteenth-Century Lancashire, 1830–1881" (MA thesis, University of Lancaster, 1975), ch. 4; Mitchell, "Catholic Irish and Chartism," 178–94.
35. Koseki, "Chartism and Irish Nationalism," 3–6, 9–10, 15, 22, 24–30, 49, 108–21, 130–64; Kinealy, *Repeal and Revolution*, 7, 43, 104, 147–49, 151–52; Strauss, *Irish Nationalism*, 72, 126–31; Roger Swift, "The Historiography of the Irish in Nineteenth-Century Britain," in *The Irish in the New Communities*, ed. Patrick O'Sullivan (London, 1992), 66–67, 69–70; Jackson, *Ireland Her Own*, 231–32, 249, 252, 254; Gray, *Famine, Land, and Politics*, 303–4; Lees, *Exiles of Erin*, 226–29, 237, 239; Davis, *Irish in Britain*, 161–62, 164–65, 169–75, 178–80, 183, 188–89; Hearn, *Domination, Legitimation, and Resistance*, 215–17; O'Higgins, "Irish Influence," 83, 85, 89–94; John Belchem, "English Working-Class Radicalism and the Irish, 1815–1850," in *The Irish in the Victorian City*, ed. Roger Swift and Sheridan Gilley (London, 1985), 85–93; Iain McCalman, "'Erin go Bragh': The Irish in British Popular Radicalism, 1790–1840," in *Irish-Australian Studies: Papers Delivered at the Fifth Irish-Australian Conference*, ed. Oliver MacDonagh and W. F. Mandle (Canberra, 1989), 169, 171, 174, 179–81; Lowe, "Chartists and Irish Confederates," 172, 174–87, 196; Pickering, *Chartism and the Chartists in Manchester and Salford*, 93–97; Frank Neal, *Sectarian Violence: The Liverpool Experience, 1819–1914* (Manchester, 1988), 115–21; Bernard Reaney, "Irish Chartists in Britain and Ireland: Rescuing the Rank and File," *Saothar* 10 (1984): 94–97; Harris, "Failure of Republicanism," 122–27, 133, 136; Thompson, *Outsiders*, 103–6, 108–11, 113–16, 120–23, 125–28, 135–40, 148, 155–56, 158–61; G. J. Billy, *Palmerston's Foreign Policy: 1848* (New York, 1993), 55–83.
36. *Northern Star*, 22 Dec. 1838.
37. Friedrich Engels, *The Condition of the Working Class in England*, ed. David McLellan (Oxford, 1999), 280; Koseki, "Chartism and Irish Nationalism," 10–11, 30, 89, 91–100, 108–13, 164; Koseki, *Patrick O'Higgins*, 1–3, 5–9, 12–15, 18–27, 29, 30–32; Kinealy, *Repeal and Revolution*, 44–45; Pickering, *Feargus O'Connor*, 19, 81, 143–47; Thompson, *Outsiders*, 119, 121–22, 145, 151–54, 158; Hearn, *Domination, Legitimation, and Resistance*, 212; O'Higgins, "Irish Influence," 87–89; Reaney, "Irish Chartists," 94, 97–101; Huggins, "Democracy or Nationalism," 129, 134–37, 139–40.
38. Huggins, "Democracy or Nationalism," 130, 136, 142–43.
39. *The Times*, 6 June 1843; *Poor Man's Guardian and Repealer's Friend*, 1843, nos. 2–3;

Thompson, *Outsiders*, 124; Lees, *Exiles of Erin*, 226–27; Koseki, *Patrick O'Higgins*, 11; Goodway, *London Chartism*, 62.

40. O'Connor wrote that a refusal to pay rents, following public remarks by O'Connell, would lead to violence in Ireland, and that he himself—O'Connor—would not have encouraged such behavior (and indeed had ruled it out as part of the Chartist campaign in Britain). Yet "lovers of peace, law, and order" persisted in thinking him a "destructive" and O'Connell somehow less dangerous. "You will mark my words that the Repeal agitation will not pass over without blows. Is it not shocking to witness the invitations to French rascals to come amongst the Irish to settle their disputes? I know of no other circumstances that would induce me to take up a musket, but I certainly would do it to meet Froggy on British or Irish ground." Allsop Collection, Misc.525/2/28, O'Connor to Allsop, undated, 1843.
41. *Poor Man's Guardian and Repealer's Friend*, 1843, nos. 4–9.
42. *Poor Man's Guardian and Repealer's Friend*, 1843, no. 5.
43. *Poor Man's Guardian and Repealer's Friend*, 1843, nos. 8, 10.
44. *Poor Man's Guardian and Repealer's Friend*, 1843, nos. 10, 13; *Freeman's Journal*, 23 Jan., 9, 15, 31 Mar., 20, 24, 29 July 1843; *Northern Star*, 29 July 1843.
45. *National Reformer and Manx Weekly Review*, 3, 10, 17, 24, 31 Oct., 14 Nov., 5, 19 Dec. 1846; Gray, *Famine, Land, and Politics*, 111, 119–20; Terry Brotherstone and Liz Leicester, "Chartism, the Great Hunger, and the 'Hugest Question,'" in Brotherstone, Clark, and Whelan, *These Fissured Isles*, 202–3, 206–14.
46. *National Reformer and Manx Weekly Review*, 19 Dec. 1846.
47. *National Reformer and Manx Weekly Review*, 24 Oct., 21, 28 Nov., 5, 26 Dec. 1846, 2, 9, 16 Jan., 6, 13, 20, 27 Feb., 6, 13, 20, 27 Mar., 3, 10, 24 Apr., 1, 29 May 1847.
48. *National Reformer and Manx Weekly Review*, 19 Dec. 1846, 9 Jan. 1847.
49. *National Reformer and Manx Weekly Review*, 16 Jan. 1847; *Reynolds's Political Instructor*, 29 Dec. 1849.
50. Medearis, "Labor, Democracy, Utility," 143–44; Claeys, "Justice, Independence, and Industrial Democracy," 142; R. N. Lebow, "J. S. Mill and the Irish Land Question," in *John Stuart Mill on Ireland*, ed. R. N. Lebow (Philadelphia, 1979), 3–22; David Martin, *John Stuart Mill and the Land Question* (Hull, 1981), 22–24; Martin, "Agricultural Interest," 134–36; Lynn Zastoupil, "Moral Government: J. S. Mill on Ireland," *Historical Journal* 26 (1983): 707–17; E. D. Steele, "J. S. Mill and the Irish Question: The Principle of Political Economy, 1848–1865," *Historical Journal* 13 (1970): 216–36; Bruce Kinzer, "J. S. Mill and Irish Land: A Reassessment," *Historical Journal* 27 (1984): 111–27.
51. *The Times*, 1, 4, 11 Jan. 1847; *National Reformer and Manx Weekly Review*, 23, 30 Jan. 1847.

52. *National Reformer and Manx Weekly Review*, 13, 27 Feb., 6 Mar. 1847.
53. *National Reformer and Manx Weekly Review*, 24 Apr., 8 May 1847.
54. *National Reformer and Manx Weekly Review*, 1 May 1847. O'Brien's claim that bad laws rather than the potato blight lay behind Ireland's predicament resembles more recent verdicts, although this remains contested ground.
55. *National Reformer and Manx Weekly Review*, 8 May 1847.
56. *National Reformer and Manx Weekly Review*, 31 Oct., 7, 21, 28 Nov., 5, 12, 19 Dec. 1846, 2, 30 Jan., 29 May 1847.
57. Huggins, "Democracy or Nationalism," 134, 137, 142; Thompson, "Ireland and the Irish," 135; Thompson, "The Chartists in 1848," 170, 174–77; Royle, *Revolutionary Britannia*, 128–29, 133; Kinealy, "Politics in Ireland," 481; Kinealy, *Repeal and Revolution*, 7, 105, 140, 147–52, 164, 279, 290–91; Lees, *Exiles of Erin*, 227–28; Pickering, *Feargus O'Connor*, 132–34, 137.
58. *Power of the Pence*, 11 Nov., 16, 23 Dec. 1848, 20 Jan., 3 Feb., 31 Mar., 7 Apr. 1849.
59. *Social Reformer*, 1, 8, 15 Sept. 1849.
60. *Power of the Pence*, 14 Apr. 1849.
61. Sanders, *Poetry of Chartism*, 170–72; Haywood, *Literature of Struggle*, 10–13.
62. In Thomas Allsop's household there was, above all, deep pessimism—a feeling that "something dreadful will happen there"—and Allsop himself looked upon Ireland "in the most dismal light." Owen Papers, ROC/1/22/3, 5, Anna Allsop to Owen, 20 July 1848 and undated 1848.
63. *Social Reformer*, 11 Aug. 1849.
64. James Loughlin, "Allegiance and Illusion: Queen Victoria's Irish Visit of 1849," *History* 87 (2002): 491–513; James Murphy, *Abject Loyalty: Nationalism and Monarchy in Ireland during the Reign of Queen Victoria* (Washington, D.C., 2001), ch. 3; Sean Connolly, "Queen Victoria in Ireland, August 1849: A Sidelight on the Development of Nationalism and Unionism," Irish History Resources, Queen's University Belfast, 2008; Gray, *Famine, Land, and Politics*, 219–22.
65. *Social Reformer*, 1, 8, 15 Sept. 1849.
66. E.g., Tadhg O'Ceallaigh, review of *Leaders and Workers: Irish Leaders and Thinkers of the Labour Movement*, ed. John Boyle (Cork, 1968), in *Studia Hibernica* 7 (1969): 220–21.
67. *Northern Star*, 3 Mar. 1849.
68. Allsop Collection, Misc.525/1/7, O'Brien to Allsop, 8 Dec. 1847; O'Brien, *Vision of Hell*, 2, 7–8.
69. On Lalor and Irish land, see *James Fintan Lalor: Collected Writings*, ed. John Kelly (Poole,

1997); David Buckley, *James Fintan Lalor: Radical* (Cork, 1990); Philip Bull, *Land, Politics, and Nationalism: A Study of the Irish Land Question* (New York, 1996).

### Chapter 7. Making and Maintaining Reputation

1. Stack, *Bronterre O'Brien*, xxi.
2. Murphy, *Towards a Working-Class Canon*, 49, 54, 79–80, 112, 144, 175, 178; Pickering, "Class without Words," 144–46, 152.
3. "To George Irving, Esq., Mayor of the City of Chichester," 28 Mar. 1839 (handbill).
4. Keith Thomas, *The Ends of Life: Roads to Fulfillment in Early Modern England* (Oxford, 2009), ch. 5.
5. David Womersley, *Gibbon and the "Watchmen of the Holy City": The Historian and His Reputation, 1776–1815* (Oxford, 2002), 1–5, 7–8, 364–66; Christopher Whatley, "'It Is Said That Burns Was a Radical': Contest, Concession, and the Political Legacy of Robert Burns, c.1796–1859," *Journal of British Studies* 50 (2011): 639–66; Edgar Shannon, *Tennyson and the Reviewers: A Study of His Literary Reputation and of the Influence of the Critics upon His Poetry, 1827–1851* (Cambridge, Mass., 1952), vii–viii, 26, 31, 33–35, 88, 90–92, 95, 163–66; Gary Fine and Jeanne Barker-Nunn, "Herman Melville and the Demise of Literary Reputation," in Gary Fine, *Difficult Reputations* (Chicago, 2001), 211, 228–29.
6. John Rodden, *Scenes from an Afterlife: The Legacy of George Orwell* (Wilmington, Del., 2003), 163–64, 166–67, 172, 251–60; Gordon Beadle, "George Orwell and the Victorian Radical Tradition," *Albion* 7 (1975): 287–99.
7. John Rodden, *The Politics of Literary Reputation: The Making and Claiming of "St. George" Orwell* (New York, 1989), xii, 69.
8. Robert McDonald, "Thomas Jefferson's Changing Reputation as Author of the Declaration of Independence: The First Fifty Years," *Journal of the Early Republic* 19 (1999): 169–95; Jeffrey Pasley, "Politics and the Misadventures of Thomas Jefferson's Modern Reputation: A Review Essay," *Journal of Southern History* 72 (2006): 871–908.
9. Gregory Claeys, "Whigs, Liberals, and Radicals," *Historical Journal* 33 (1990): 741–43; David Stack, "The Death of John Stuart Mill," *Historical Journal* 54 (2011): 167–90; Philip Williamson, "Baldwin's Reputation: Politics and History, 1937–1967," *Historical Journal* 47 (2004): 127–68; Patrick Murray, "Obsessive Historian: Eamon de Valera and the Policing of His Reputation," *Proceedings of the Royal Irish Academy* 101, section C (2001): 37–65.
10. Gary Fine, "Constructing Difficult Reputations," in Fine, *Difficult Reputations*, 2, 7–8.
11. O'Brien, *Robespierre*, 3–5. On O'Brien's self-image see also Stack, *Bronterre O'Brien*, xii–xiv, xxviii, xli.

12. E.g., Dorothy Thompson's emphasis on O'Brien's personal and political weaknesses and her sympathetic treatment of O'Connor. Thompson, *The Chartists*, 37–38, 49–50, 55–56, 101–5, 129, 131, 305–6.
13. Fine, "Constructing Difficult Reputations," 24–25.
14. Gammage, *Chartist Movement*, 71, 75–77, 137.
15. *Reynolds's Weekly Newspaper*, 30 June 1850; *Reynolds's Newspaper* 27 July 1856, 14 Sept. 1857. ("Weekly" was dropped from the title in 1851. This Sunday broadsheet replaced the more polemical *Reynolds's Political Instructor*, which had appeared from 1849 to 1850.)
16. *Flora Tristan's London Journal, 1840*, translated by Dennis Palmer and Giselle Pincetl (Boston, Mass., 1980), 49.
17. Frank Peel, *The Risings of the Luddites, Chartists, and Plug-Drawers* (London, 1968), 316, 318; and E. P. Thompson, introduction to Peel, *The Risings of the Luddites*, vii–xv. Peel's book was first published in 1880, with further editions in 1888 and 1895. Though Peel thought that Chartism had declined in 1848 because of the "absurd" Kennington Common affair, he considered the most important cause to be repeal of the Corn Laws, which made for "wonderfully changed" conditions. Free trade benefited working people (see 348–49 in Peel's book): "They gradually acquired a position and comforts to which as a body they had hitherto been strangers, and with increasing prosperity the old hatred for the classes above them in the social scale was moderated or died out, and ultimately constitutional agitation took the place of the physical force methods with which they had so long been familiar." Modern scholars have shown up as too narrow and limited the assumption that Chartism resulted only from social divisions and economic hardship.
18. *Northern Star*, 14 Aug. 1841.
19. Manchester leaders engaged in "a succession of disputes" with the difficult Richardson—see Pickering, *Chartism and the Chartists in Manchester and Salford*, 202–4—and there is a sense in which his enemies automatically became their friends.
20. *Chartism: Authentic Report of the Speech of Mr. William Jones*, 16.
21. *Northern Star*, 9 Apr. 1842.
22. Allsop Collection, Misc.525/1/4, O'Brien to Allsop, 4 Aug. 1840.
23. *Northern Star*, 10 Apr. 1852.
24. Alexander Somerville, *Conservative Science of Nations, Preliminary Instalment* (Montreal, 1860), 217.
25. "Dedication" by "Spartacus," in O'Brien, "Human Slavery," 301. Impressed by O'Brien's social and economic ideas, which greatly influenced his own, Linton appears to have begun joining O'Brien at meetings and on the platform at the time of the European and Irish disorders of 1848. F. B. Smith, *Radical Artisan: William James Linton, 1812–1897*

(Manchester, 1973), 24, 32, 68, 77, 123.

26. O'Brien Papers, OB.13, "To the Social and Political Reformers of Great Britain."

27. *National Reformer, Secular Advocate, and Freethought Journal*, 8 Jan., 19 Feb. 1865. According to the memorial fund accounts, dating from January to October 1865, a total of £52 11s. 4d. was raised and disbursed. Apart from payments to O'Brien's wife and to the fund's secretary and collectors, the money was spent on funeral expenses, books, stamps, paper, printing, the hiring of a hall, musicians for a raffle, and the framing of a portrait. O'Brien Papers, OB.14, "The O'Brien Fund."

28. *Working Man*, 1 Mar. 1867; *Bee-hive*, 13 Feb. 1869.

29. Whitehead, "The *New World* and the O'Brienite Colony," 40–43; Entz, *Llewellyn Castle*, ch. 1. The Chartist leader John Campbell, whose career in radical politics owed much initially to O'Brien's help, did not try to live according to O'Brien's ideas when he settled in the United States. As seen above in ch. 5, though he still adhered to some of these ideas he also adopted an overtly racist perspective in the American context.

30. Stack, *Bronterre O'Brien*, 25–26, 46–48, 57; Plummer, *Bronterre*, 27–28, 49, 78, 85, 89, 121, 215; Chase, *People's Farm*, 124–25, 130–33; Horne, *Property Rights*, 247; David Nicholls, review of Dudley Miles, *Francis Place, 1771–1854* (New York, 1988), *Victorian Studies* 33 (1989): 183–84; Gregory Claeys, "Whigs, Liberals, and Radicals," 741–43; Thompson, *Making of the English Working Class*, 508, 799–800, 883; Briggs, introduction to Cole, *Chartist Portraits*, xi; Ward, *Factory Movement*, 194; Thompson, *Outsiders*, 28, 32.

31. E.g., "Bronterre's Letters," 1836, nos. 9, 15.

32. *Northern Star*, 22 Sept. 1838.

33. *Northern Star*, 12 Nov. 1842, 29 Mar., 10 May 1845, 4 Nov. 1848. O'Brien's version of events was, of course, rather different: e.g., Allsop Collection, Misc.525/1/5, 15, 19, O'Brien to Allsop, 7, 31 Aug., 4 Sept. 1847. On O'Brien's breach with his former protégé Campbell, see also Paul Pickering, "Chartism and the 'Trade of Agitation' in Early Victorian Britain," in Roberts, *People's Charter*, 34.

34. *Northern Star*, 17 Sept. 1842.

35. Plummer, *Bronterre*, 29, 31, 43, 50, 53–57, 82, 88, 131, 137, 190, 215, 247; Stack, *Bronterre O'Brien*, xv, 18; Wiener, *War of the Unstamped*, 168; Goodway, *London Chartism*, 22–23, 25, 31; Allsop Collection, Misc.525/1/1, O'Brien to Allsop, 29 Nov. 1836.

36. Gregory Claeys, "A Utopian Tory Revolutionary at Cambridge: The Political Ideas and Schemes of James Bernard, 1834–1839," *Historical Journal* 25 (1982): 583–603; Stack, *Bronterre O'Brien*, xvi, xlii, 61, 72; Plummer, *Bronterre*, 80–84.

37. Plummer, *Bronterre*, 33, 44, 50, 78, 137, 140, 143, 148, 152; Goodway, *London Chartism*, 34; Stack, *Bronterre O'Brien*, 17–18, 72; Cole, *Chartist Portraits*, 254; Allsop Collection,

Misc.525/1/2–3, O'Brien to Allsop, 17, 23 June 1840.

38. *People's Paper*, 31 Dec. 1853, 21, 28 Jan., 4, 11 Feb. 1854; Owen Papers, ROC/1/24/27, Allsop to Owen, 22 Apr. 1854; Stack, *Bronterre O'Brien*, 191–92; Plummer, *Bronterre*, 188, 190, 202, 204, 224, 226–28; Ward, *Chartism*, 225–26, 231–32; Cole, *Chartist Portraits*, 264.
39. Plummer, *Bronterre*, 89, 111, 116, 147–48.
40. *Robert Lowery: Radical and Chartist*, ed. Brian Harrison and Patricia Hollis (London, 1979), 136, 144.
41. Plummer, *Bronterre*, 174–75; Stephen Roberts, "Thomas Cooper in Leicester, 1840–1843," in Roberts, *People's Charter*, 141–42; Roberts, *Chartist Prisoners*, 74, 79, 82, 89; Gammage, *Chartist Movement*, 203–5, 213, 272–73, 404–10.
42. Thomas Cooper, *The Life of Thomas Cooper, Written by Himself* (London, 1872), 179, 220.
43. Plummer, *Bronterre*, 31, 43, 53, 59, 77, 79, 88–89, 96, 99, 119, 168–69, 174, 176, 215, 225; Stack, *Bronterre O'Brien*, xvi, xviii, 72, Wilson, "Suffrage Movement," 85–86, 89; Large, "William Lovett," 109–10, 111, 117.
44. William Lovett, *The Life and Struggles of William Lovett, in His Pursuit of Bread, Knowledge and Freedom; with Some Short Account of the Different Associations He Belonged to and of the Opinions He Entertained* (London, 1876), 59, 205, 225, 238.
45. W. J. Linton, *Memories* (London, 1895), 42.
46. W. E. Adams, *Memoirs of a Social Atom* (2 vols., London, 1903), 1: 159, 204, 210, 235, 2: 316–17.
47. E.g., Brian Harrison, *Drink and the Victorians: The Temperance Question in England, 1815–1872* (Pittsburgh, Pa., 1971), 53. See also Schoyen, *Chartist Challenge*, 271.
48. Fine, "Constructing Difficult Reputations," 3.
49. "Bronterre's Letters," 1836, nos. 1–2, 5–7, 15.
50. *Bronterre's National Reformer*, 7, 15, 28 Jan., 11, 18 Feb., 18 Mar. 1837.
51. *Bronterre's National Reformer*, 11, 25 Feb., 4 Mar. 1837.
52. O'Brien, *Robespierre*, 3–4, 15–16.
53. *British Statesman*, 25 June, 2 July 1842.
54. *British Statesman*, 3, 10, 17 Dec. 1842.
55. *Poor Man's Guardian and Repealer's Friend*, 1843, nos. 1–2.
56. *Poor Man's Guardian and Repealer's Friend*, 1843, nos. 2–7, 9–11, 13.
57. Stack, *Bronterre O'Brien*, xviii, xliv, 173–74; Chase, *Chartism: A New History*, 236; Plummer, *Bronterre*, 177–79; Jones, *Chartism and the Chartists*, 101; Cole, *Chartist Portraits*, 260; Fyson, "Bronterre O'Brien: A Chartist in the Isle of Man," 393–400; Belchem, "Neglected 'Unstamped,'" 613–14.
58. *National Reformer and Manx Weekly Review*, 10, 17, 31 Oct., 14 Nov., 12 Dec. 1846.

59. *Power of the Pence*, 11 Nov. 1848.
60. *Social Reformer*, 11, 18 Aug., 1, 29 Sept. 1849.
61. Claeys, *Citizens and Saints*, 276–83; Ward, *Chartism*, 222–26; Chase, *Chartism: A New History*, 335–36.
62. *Reasoner and Theological Examiner*, 12 (1852): 258–59, 306–7.
63. Matthew Bevis, "Volumes of Noise," *Victorian Literature and Culture* 31 (2003): 577–91; Messner, "Land, Leadership, Culture, and Emigration," 1099–1100; Malcolm Chase, "Digital Chartists: Online Resources for the Study of Chartism," *Journal of Victorian Culture* 14 (2009): 298, 300; Cris Yelland, "Speech and Writing in the *Northern Star*," *Labour History Review* 65 (2000): 22–40; Maehl, introduction to Gammage, *Reminiscences of a Chartist*, 14–15.
64. Owen Ashton, "Orators and Oratory in the Chartist Movement, 1840–1848," in Ashton, Fyson, and Roberts, *Chartist Legacy*, 52–54, 70.
65. *British Statesman*, 30 July, 6, 20 Aug. 1842.
66. *Poor Man's Guardian and Repealer's Friend*, 1843, nos. 4–7, 9–11, 13.
67. *National Reformer and Manx Weekly Review*, 12 Dec. 1846, 2, 9, 16 Jan. 1847.
68. *National Reformer and Manx Weekly Review*, 6 Feb. 1847.
69. *National Reformer and Manx Weekly Review*, 3, 10 Apr. 1847.
70. *Power of the Pence*, 24 Feb., 3 Mar., 14 Apr. 1849.
71. *Social Reformer*, 11, 18 Aug., 1, 29 Sept. 1849.
72. *Social Reformer*, 15 Sept., 6, 20 Oct. 1849.
73. "Bronterre's Letters," 1836, no. 1.
74. "Bronterre's Letters," 1836, nos. 5–7, 15; O'Brien, *Buonarroti's History*, xiii–xxiv.
75. "Bronterre's Letters," 1836, no. 11.
76. *Bronterre's National Reformer*, 11, 25 Feb., 4 Mar. 1837.
77. O'Brien, *Robespierre*, 259–60.
78. *British Statesman*, 9 July 1842.
79. E.g., *British Statesman*, 25 June, 16, 23, 30 July 1842.
80. *British Statesman*, 13, 27 Aug., 10 Sept., 12 Nov. 1842; *Northern Star*, 9 July, 13 Aug., 3, 10, 17 Sept., 12 Nov. 1842.
81. *National Reformer and Manx Weekly Review*, 6, 13 Mar. 1847.
82. Owen Papers, ROC/15/3/1, O'Brien to Owen, 27 May 1832.
83. "Bronterre's Letters," 1836, nos. 1–2, 5–7, 15.
84. W. H. Maehl, "Augustus Hardin Beaumont: Anglo-American Radical (1798–1838)," *International Review of Social History* 14 (1969): 237–50; Royle, *Revolutionary Britannia*, 94; Weisser, *British Working-Class Movements*, 87–88; Hugman, "'A Small Drop of Ink,'"

24–47.

85. "Bronterre's Letters," 1836, nos. 7, 10.
86. *Operative*, 11 Nov. 1838.
87. *Bronterre's National Reformer*, 7, 15, 28 Jan., 11, 18 Feb., 18 Mar. 1837.
88. O'Brien, *Robespierre*, 3–4, 15–16.
89. *British Statesman*, 30 July, 6, 20 Aug. 1842.
90. *National Reformer and Manx Weekly Review*, 13, 20, 27 Feb., 6 Mar. 1847; *Morning Post*, 9 Feb. 1847.
91. *National Reformer and Manx Weekly Review*, 3, 10 Apr. 1847; *Liverpool Mercury*, 13, 20, 27 Mar., 3 Apr. 1847.
92. *Bronterre's National Reformer*, 18 Mar. 1837.
93. O'Brien, *Robespierre*, 3–4, 15–16.
94. O'Brien, *Robespierre*, 285.
95. *British Statesman*, 15, 22 Oct. 1842.
96. *British Statesman*, 22, 29 Oct., 5, 12, 19, 26 Nov. 1842.
97. *British Statesman*, 3, 10, 17 Dec. 1842.
98. *Poor Man's Guardian and Repealer's Friend*, 1843, nos. 4–7, 9–11, 13.
99. *Poor Man's Guardian and Repealer's Friend*, 1843, no. 13.
100. *National Reformer and Manx Weekly Review*, 3 Oct. 1846, 6 Feb. 1847.
101. *National Reformer and Manx Weekly Review*, 6, 13 Mar., 3, 10 Apr. 1847.
102. *National Reformer and Manx Weekly Review*, 24 Apr. 1847.
103. *Power of the Pence*, 6 Jan. 1849.
104. *Social Reformer*, 11, 18 Aug., 1, 15, 29 Sept., 6, 20 Oct. 1849.
105. O'Brien Papers, OB.2–3, 6–9, O'Brien to Mathews, 6 Mar., 23 Sept. 1856, 17 Nov., 23 Dec. 1857, 20, 24 Mar. 1858.
106. Allsop Collection, Misc.525/1/6–7, 9–14, O'Brien to Allsop, 10 Nov., 8 Dec. 1847, 27 June 1855, 22, 26 Sept., 1, 11 Oct., 3 Dec. 1862.
107. O'Brien, *Elegy*, 2, 16; and O'Brien, *Dissertation and Elegy*, 93–94.
108. O'Brien, *Dissertation and Elegy*, 2.
109. O'Brien, *Dissertation and Elegy*, 5.

# Bibliography

### Archives

#### British Library, London


General Reference Collection, "Bronterre's Letters," 1836

General Reference Collection, O'Brien, J. Bronterre, *A Vision of Hell: or, Peep into the Realms Below, Alias Lord Overgrown's Dream, Describing His Lordship's Fancied Reunion with the Late Sir Robert Peel in the Regions Below* (London, 1859)

General Reference Collection, handbills: "The People's Charter!" (26 Mar. 1839); "The Chartists!" (26 Mar. 1839); and "To George Irving, Esq., Mayor of the City of Chichester" (28 Mar. 1839)

Add. MS 46,344, John Burns Papers


#### London School of Economics


Allsop Collection

Wallas Papers


#### National Cooperative Archive, Manchester


Robert Owen Papers

### People's History Museum, Manchester

Labour History Archive, O'Brien Papers

### State Library of Victoria, Melbourne, Australia

Race Mathews Papers (Box 140), "Honouring the Memory of Bronterre O'Brien: The Address by Arthur Scargill at the 1996 Commemoration in Abney Park Cemetery"

### Contemporary Newspapers and Periodicals

*Bee-hive*

*British Statesman*

*Bronterre's National Reformer*

*The Charter*

*Chartist Circular*

*Destructive*

*Freeman's Journal*

*Leeds Times*

*Liverpool Mercury*

*London Mercury*

*Manchester and Salford Advertiser*

*Manchester Guardian*

*Midland Representative and Birmingham Herald*

*Morning Post*

*National Reformer and Manx Weekly Review*

*National Reformer, Secular Advocate, and Freethought Journal*

*New World of Politics, Arts, Literature, and Sciences*

*Northern Star*

*Observer*

*Operative*

*People's Paper*

*Poor Man's Guardian*

*Poor Man's Guardian and Repealer's Friend*

*Power of the Pence*

*Reasoner and Theological Examiner*

*Reynolds's Newspaper*

*Reynolds's Political Instructor*

*Reynolds's Weekly Newspaper*

*Social Reformer*
*Southern Star*
*The Times*
*Twopenny Dispatch*
*Working Man*

### Published Primary Sources

Adams, W. E., *Memoirs of a Social Atom* (2 vols., London, 1903).

Blanc, Louis, *1848: Historical Revelations Inscribed to Lord Normanby* (London, 1858).

Buckingham, J. S., *America: Historical, Statistic, and Descriptive* (London, 1841).

*Chartism: Authentic Report of the Speech of Mr. William Jones upon Responding to the Toast of "The People's Charter, and May It Soon Become the Law of the Land," at a Soirée Held in Liverpool on 27 September 1841, in Celebration of the Release of James Bronterre O'Brien and Feargus O'Connor from Their Dungeons* (Liverpool, 1841).

Claeys, Gregory, ed., *The Chartist Movement in Britain, 1838–1850* (6 vols., London, 2001).

Cobbett, William, *The Collected Social and Political Writings of William Cobbett*, ed. Noel Thompson and David Eastwood (London, 1998).

Cobden, Richard, *The Letters of Richard Cobden*, ed. Anthony Howe (3 vols., Oxford, 2007, 2010, 2015).

Coleridge, J. T., "My Recollections of the Circuit," *American Law Register* 9 (1861): 257–84.

Cooper, Thomas, *The Life of Thomas Cooper, Written by Himself* (London, 1872).

Dickens, Charles, *American Notes for General Circulation* (London, 1842).

Engels, Friedrich, *The Condition of the Working Class in England*, ed. David McLellan (Oxford, 1999).

Finch, John, *Chartist Bible: The Seven Seals Broke Open, or the Bible of the Reformation Restored* (London, 1853).

Gammage, R. G., *History of the Chartist Movement, 1837–1854* (New York, 1969).

———, *Reminiscences of a Chartist* (Manchester, 1983).

Hamilton, Thomas, *Men and Manners in America* (Edinburgh, 1833).

*Hansard Parliamentary Debates*, 3rd series.

Hyndman, H. M., "Socialism in England," *North American Review* 143 (1886): 225–36.

Ledru-Rollin, Alexandre, *The Decline of England* (London, 1850).

Linton, W. J., *Memories* (London, 1895).

Lovett, William, *The Life and Struggles of William Lovett, in His Pursuit of Bread, Knowledge and Freedom; with Some Short Account of the Different Associations He Belonged to and of the Opinions He Entertained* (London, 1876).

Lowery, Robert, *Robert Lowery: Radical and Chartist*, ed. Brian Harrison and Patricia Hollis (London, 1979).

Lyell, Charles, *Travels in North America in the Years 1841–1842* (London, 1845).

Manuel, Frank, and Fritzie Manuel, eds., *French Utopias: An Anthology of Ideal Societies* (New York, 1971).

Marryat, Frederick, *A Diary in America, with Remarks upon Its Institutions* (London, 1839).

Martineau, Harriet, *Society in America* (London, 1837).

Morris, Max, ed., *From Cobbett to the Chartists, 1815–1848: Extracts from Contemporary Sources* (London, 1951).

O'Brien, J. Bronterre, *Buonarroti's History of Babeuf's Conspiracy for Equality* (London, 1836).

———, *A Dissertation and Elegy on the Life and Death of the Immortal Maximilian Robespierre* (London, 1859).

———, *An Elegy on the Death of Robespierre* (London, 1857).

———, *The Life and Character of Maximilian Robespierre* (London, 1838).

———, *Mr. O'Brien's Vindication of His Conduct at the Late Birmingham Conference; Containing His "Blackguard Letter" to the Editor of the "Star," Which That Personage Suppressed; Also, His Letter to the "British Statesman"; Spirited Defence of Him by Mr. McGregor, of Edinburgh; Vincent's Portrait of a Demagogue; Etc., Etc.* (Birmingham, 1842).

———, *Ode to Lord Palmerston* (London, 1856).

———, *An Ode to Louis Napoleon Bonaparte* (London, 1857).

———, "The Rise, Progress, and Phases of Human Slavery: How It Came into the World, and How It Shall be Made to Go Out," reprinted in Claeys, *The Chartist Movement in Britain*, 6: 299–442.

Palmer, Dennis, and Giselle Pincetl, translators, *Flora Tristan's London Journal, 1840* (Boston, Mass., 1980).

Peel, Frank, *The Risings of the Luddites, Chartists, and Plug-Drawers* (London, 1968).

Somerville, Alexander, *Conservative Science of Nations, Preliminary Instalment* (Montreal, 1860).

Stack, David, ed., *Lives of Victorian Political Figures II*, vol. 4: *James Bronterre O'Brien* (London, 2007).

Stuart, James, *Three Years in North America* (Edinburgh, 1833).

Thompson, Dorothy, *The Early Chartists* (Columbia, S.C., 1971).

Trollope, F. M., *Domestic Manners of the Americans* (London, 1832).

Warburton, George, *Hochelaga: Or, England in the New World* (London, 1846).

Webb, Sidney, "Socialism in England," *Publications of the American Economic Association* 4 (1889): 7–73.

### Secondary Sources: Books

Allen, Joan, and Owen Ashton, eds., *Papers for the People: A Study of the Chartist Press* (London, 2005).

Ashton, Owen, Robert Fyson, and Stephen Roberts, eds., *The Chartist Legacy* (Rendlesham, 1999).

Barfoot, C. C., and Theo D'haen, eds., *Tropes of Revolution: Writers' Reactions to Real and Imagined Revolutions, 1789–1989* (Amsterdam, 1991).

Barrow, Logie, and Ian Bullock, *Democratic Ideas and the British Labour Movement, 1880–1914* (Cambridge, 1996).

Barry, E. Eldon, *Nationalization in British Politics* (Stanford, Calif., 1965).

Bevir, Mark, *The Making of British Socialism* (Princeton, N.J., 2011).

Bevir, Mark, and Frank Trentmann, eds., *Critiques of Capital in Modern America and Britain: Transatlantic Exchanges 1800 to the Present Day* (Basingstoke, 2002).

———, eds., *Markets in Historical Context: Ideas and Politics in the Modern World* (Cambridge, 2004).

Billy, G. J., *Palmerston's Foreign Policy: 1848* (New York, 1993).

Birchall, Ian, *The Spectre of Babeuf* (Basingstoke, 1997).

Boston, Ray, *British Chartists in America, 1839–1900* (Manchester, 1971).

Brake, Laurel, and Marysa Demoor, eds., *Dictionary of Nineteenth-Century Journalism in Great Britain and Ireland* (Gent, 2009).

Briggs, Asa, ed., *Chartist Studies* (London, 1959).

Briggs, Asa, and John Saville, eds., *Essays in Labour History* (London, 1960).

Bronstein, Jamie, *Land Reform and Working-Class Experience in Britain and the United States, 1800–1862* (Stanford, Calif., 1999).

Brotherstone, Terry, Anna Clark, and Kevin Whelan, eds., *These Fissured Isles: Ireland, Scotland, and the Making of Modern Britain, 1798–1848* (Edinburgh, 2005).

Brown, David, *Palmerston* (New Haven, Conn., 2010).

Buckley, David, *James Fintan Lalor: Radical* (Cork, 1990).

Bull, Philip, *Land, Politics, and Nationalism: A Study of the Irish Land Question* (New York, 1996).

Butt, John, and I. F. Clarke, eds., *The Victorians and Social Protest* (Newton Abbot, 1973).

Calhoun, Craig, *The Question of Class Struggle: Social Foundations of Popular Radicalism during the Industrial Revolution* (Chicago, 1982).

Charlton, John, *The Chartists: The First National Workers' Movement* (London, 1997).

Chase, Malcolm, *Chartism: A New History* (Manchester, 2007).

———, *The Chartists: Perspectives and Legacies* (London, 2015).

———, *The People's Farm: English Radical Agrarianism, 1775–1840* (Oxford, 1988).

Chase, Malcolm, and Ian Dyck, eds., *Learning and Living: Essays in Honour of J. F. C. Harrison* (Aldershot, 1996).

Claeys, Gregory, *Citizens and Saints: Politics and Anti-Politics in Early British Socialism* (Cambridge, 1989).

———, *Machinery, Money, and the Millennium: From Moral Economy to Socialism, 1815–1860* (Princeton, N.J., 1987).

Cobban, Alfred, *The Social Interpretation of the French Revolution* (Cambridge, 1964).

Cole, G. D. H., *Chartist Portraits* (New York, 1965).

———. *A History of Socialist Thought* (5 vols., London, 1953–61).

Colley, Linda, *Britons: Forging the Nation, 1707–1837* (London, 1992).

Collingham, Hugh, *The July Monarchy* (London, 1988).

Collins, Henry, and Chimen Abramsky, *Karl Marx and the British Labour Movement: Years of the First International* (London, 1965).

Connolly, Sean, ed., *Oxford Companion to Irish History* (Oxford, 1998).

Cragoe, Matthew, and Paul Readman, eds., *The Land Question in Britain, 1750–1950* (Basingstoke, 2010).

Davis, Graham, *The Irish in Britain, 1815–1914* (Dublin, 1991).

Davis, Michael, and Paul Pickering, eds., *Unrespectable Radicals? Popular Politics in the Age of Reform* (Aldershot, 2008).

Drescher, Seymour, *The Mighty Experiment: Free Labor versus Slavery in British Emancipation* (New York, 2004).

Dzelzainis, Ella, and Ruth Livesey, eds., *The American Experiment and the Idea of Democracy in British Culture, 1776–1914* (Farnham, 2013).

Englander, David, ed., *Britain and America: Studies in Comparative History, 1760–1970* (London, 1997).

Entz, Gary, *Llewellyn Castle: A Workers' Cooperative on the Great Plains* (Lincoln, Nebr., 2013).

Epstein, James, *The Lion of Freedom: Feargus O'Connor and the Chartist Movement, 1832–1842* (London, 1982).

Epstein, James, and Dorothy Thompson, eds., *The Chartist Experience: Studies in Working-Class Radicalism and Culture, 1830–1860* (London, 1982).

Fine, Gary, *Difficult Reputations* (Chicago, 2001).

Finn, Margot, *After Chartism: Class and Nation in English Radical Politics, 1848–1874* (Cambridge, 1993).

Foster, Roy, *Modern Ireland, 1600–1972* (London, 1989).

Fraser, W. H., *Alexander Campbell and the Search for Socialism* (Manchester, 1996).

———, *Chartism in Scotland* (Pontypool, 2010).

Freitag, Sabine, ed., *Exiles from European Revolutions: Refugees in Mid-Victorian England* (Oxford, 2003).

Furet, François, *Interpreting the French Revolution* (Cambridge, 1981).

Furet, François, and Mona Onouf, eds., *The French Revolution and the Creation of Modern Political Culture* (Oxford, 1989).

Gallagher, Catherine, *The Body Economic: Life, Death, and Sensation in Political Economy and the Victorian Novel* (Princeton, N.J., 2006).

Garrard, John, *Democratization in Britain: Elites, Civil Society, and Reform since 1800* (Basingstoke, 2000).

Gerzina, G. H., ed., *Black Victorians/Black Victoriana* (New Brunswick, N.J., 2003).

Goodway, David, *London Chartism, 1838–1848* (Cambridge, 1982).

Grande, James, and John Stevenson, eds., *William Cobbett, Romanticism, and the Enlightenment* (London, 2015).

Grande, James, and John Stevenson and Richard Thomas, eds., *The Opinions of William Cobbett* (Farnham, 2013).

Gray, Peter, *Famine, Land, and Politics: British Government and Irish Society, 1843–1850* (Dublin, 1999).

Greene, J. P., ed., *Exclusionary Empire: English Liberty Overseas, 1600–1900* (New York, 2010).

Groves, Reg, *But We Shall Rise Again: A Narrative History of Chartism* (London, 1938).

Gunn, John, *When the French Tried to Be British: Party, Opposition, and the Quest for Civil Disagreement, 1814–1848* (Montreal, 2009).

Hall, Robert, *Voices of the People: Democracy and Chartist Political Identity, 1830–1870* (Monmouth, 2007).

Harrison, Brian, *Drink and the Victorians: The Temperance Question in England, 1815–1872* (Pittsburgh, Pa., 1971).

Harrison, J. F. C., *Robert Owen and the Owenites in Britain and America: The Quest for the New Moral World* (London, 1969).

Harsin, Jill, *Barricades: The War of the Streets in Revolutionary Paris, 1830–1848* (New York, 2002).

Haydon, Colin, and William Doyle, eds., *Robespierre* (Cambridge, 1999).

Haywood, Ian, *The Literature of Struggle: An Anthology of Chartist Fiction* (Aldershot, 1995).

———, *The Revolution in Popular Literature: Print, Politics, and the People, 1790–1860* (Cambridge, 2004).

Hearn, Francis, *Domination, Legitimation, and Resistance: The Incorporation of the Nineteenth-Century English Working Class* (Westport, Conn., 1978).

Hill, Christopher, *Puritanism and Revolution* (London, 1965).

Hollis, Patricia, *The Pauper Press: A Study in Working-Class Radicalism of the 1830s* (Oxford, 1970).

———, ed., *Pressure from Without in Early Victorian England* (London, 1974).

Hoppen, K. T., *Ireland since 1800: Conflict and Conformity* (London, 1996).

Horne, Thomas, *Property Rights and Poverty: Political Argument in Britain, 1605–1834* (Chapel Hill, N.C., 1990).

Hovell, Mark, *The Chartist Movement* (Manchester, 1959).

Huzel, James, *The Popularization of Malthus in Early Nineteenth-Century England* (Aldershot, 2006).

Innes, Joanna, and Mark Philp, eds., *Re-Imagining Democracy in the Age of Revolutions* (Oxford, 2013).

Isabella, Maurizio, *Risorgimento in Exile: Italian Émigrés and the Liberal International in the Post-Napoleonic Era* (Oxford, 2009).

Jackson, T. A., *Ireland Her Own: An Outline History of the Irish Struggle* (London, 1976).

Jones, David, *Chartism and the Chartists* (London, 1975).

Kelly, John, ed., *James Fintan Lalor: Collected Writings* (Poole, 1997).

Kiernan, V. G., *Poets, Politics, and the People* (London, 1989).

Kinealy, Christine, *Repeal and Revolution: Ireland in 1848* (Manchester, 2009).

Koditschek, Theodore, *Class Formation and Urban-Industrial Society: Bradford, 1750–1850* (Cambridge, 1990).

Koseki, Takashi, *Patrick O'Higgins and Irish Chartism* (Hosei University, Ireland-Japan Papers No. 2, 1990).

Lebow, R. N., ed., *John Stuart Mill on Ireland* (Philadelphia, 1979).

Lees, L. H., *Exiles of Erin: Irish Migrants in Victorian London* (Ithaca, N.Y., 1979).

Lefebvre, Georges, *The Coming of the French Revolution* (Princeton, N.J., 2005).

Leventhal, Frank, and Roland Quinault, eds., *Anglo-American Attitudes: From Revolution to Partnership* (Aldershot, 2000).

Lillibridge, G. D., *Beacon of Freedom: The Impact of American Democracy upon Great Britain, 1830–1870* (Philadelphia, 1955).

Lorimer, Douglas, *Colour, Class, and the Victorians: English Attitudes to the Negro in the Mid-Nineteenth Century* (New York, 1978).

MacDonagh, Oliver, *The Emancipationist: Daniel O'Connell, 1830–1847* (New York, 1989).

MacDonagh, Oliver, and W. F. Mandle, eds., *Irish-Australian Studies: Papers Delivered at the Fifth Irish-Australian Conference* (Canberra, 1989).

Magraw, Roger, *France 1815–1914: The Bourgeois Century* (New York, 1986).

Martin, David, *John Stuart Mill and the Land Question* (Hull, 1981).

Mather, F. C., *Public Order in the Age of the Chartists* (Manchester, 1959).

Maza, Sarah, *The Myth of the French Bourgeoisie* (Cambridge, Mass., 2003).

McLaren, Angus, *Birth Control in Nineteenth-Century England* (London, 1978).

Morrow, John, *Thomas Carlyle* (London, 2006).

Murphy, James, *Abject Loyalty: Nationalism and Monarchy in Ireland during the Reign of Queen Victoria* (Washington, D.C., 2001).

Murphy, Paul, *Towards a Working-Class Canon: Literary Criticism in British Working-Class Periodicals, 1816–1858* (Columbus, Ohio, 1994).

Murphy, Thomas, *A Land without Castles: The Changing Image of America in Europe, 1780–1830* (Lanham, Md., 2001).

Neal, Frank, *Sectarian Violence: The Liverpool Experience, 1819–1914* (Manchester, 1988).

Nevins, Allan, *America through British Eyes* (New York, 1948).

Nowlan, K. B., and M. R. O'Connell, eds., *Daniel O'Connell: Portrait of a Radical* (New York, 1985).

O'Sullivan, Patrick, ed., *The Irish in the New Communities* (London, 1992).

Parry, Jonathan, *The Politics of Patriotism: English Liberalism, National Identity, and Europe, 1830–1886* (Cambridge, 2006).

Pelling, Henry, *The Origins of the Labour Party, 1880–1900* (Oxford, 1965).

Pickering, Paul, *Chartism and the Chartists in Manchester and Salford* (Basingstoke, 1995).

———, *Feargus O'Connor: A Political Life* (Monmouth, 2008).

Pinkney, David, *Decisive Years in France, 1840–1847* (Princeton, N.J., 1986).

Plummer, Alfred, *Bronterre: A Political Biography of Bronterre O'Brien, 1804–1864* (Toronto, 1971).

Porter, Bernard, *The Refugee Question in Mid-Victorian Politics* (Cambridge, 1979).

Prothero, Iorwerth, *Artisans and Politics in Early Nineteenth-Century London: John Gast and His Times* (London, 1981).

Roark, Eric, *Removing the Commons: A Lockean Left-Libertarian Approach to the Just Use and Appropriation of Natural Resources* (Lanham, Md., 2013).

Roberts, Stephen, *The Chartist Prisoners: The Radical Lives of Thomas Cooper and Arthur O'Neill* (Oxford, 2008).

———, *Radical Politicians and Poets in Early Victorian Britain* (Lewiston, N.Y., 1993).

———, ed., *The People's Charter: Democratic Agitation in Early Victorian Britain* (London, 2003).

Rodden, John, *The Politics of Literary Reputation: The Making and Claiming of "St. George" Orwell* (New York, 1989).

———, *Scenes from an Afterlife: The Legacy of George Orwell* (Wilmington, Del., 2003).

Roediger, David, *The Wages of Whiteness: Race and the Making of the American Working Class* (London, 1991).

Rose, R. B., *Gracchus Babeuf: The First Revolutionary Communist* (Stanford, Calif., 1978).

Rothstein, Theodore, *From Chartism to Labourism: Historical Sketches of the English Working Class Movement* (London, 1983).

Royle, Edward, *Revolutionary Britannia? Reflections on the Threat of Revolution in Britain, 1789–1848* (Manchester, 2000).

———, *Victorian Infidels* (Manchester, 1974).

Royle, Edward, and James Walvin, *English Radicals and Reformers, 1760–1848* (Lexington, Ky., 1982).

Rule, John, and Roger Wells, *Crime, Protest, and Popular Politics in Southern England, 1740–1850* (London, 1997).

Sanders, Mike, *The Poetry of Chartism: Aesthetics, Politics, History* (Cambridge, 2009).

Saunders, Robert, *Democracy and the Vote in British Politics, 1832–1867* (Farnham, 2011).

Saville, John, *1848: The British State and the Chartist Movement* (Cambridge, 1987).

Schoyen, A. R., *The Chartist Challenge: A Portrait of George Julian Harney* (New York, 1958).

Shannon, Edgar, *Tennyson and the Reviewers: A Study of His Literary Reputation and of the Influence of the Critics upon His Poetry, 1827–1851* (Cambridge, Mass., 1952).

Shipley, Stan, *Club Life and Socialism in Mid-Victorian London* (London, 1983).

Smith, F. B., *Radical Artisan: William James Linton, 1812–1897* (Manchester, 1973).

Soboul, Albert, *A Short History of the French Revolution, 1789–1799* (Berkeley, Calif., 1977).

Strauss, Eric, *Irish Nationalism and British Democracy* (New York, 1951).

Summerhill, Thomas, and James Scott, eds., *Transatlantic Rebels: Agrarian Radicalism in Comparative Context* (East Lansing, Mich., 2004).

Swift, Roger, and Sheridan Gilley, eds., *The Irish in the Victorian City* (London, 1985).

Taylor, Miles, *The Decline of British Radicalism, 1847–1860* (Oxford, 1995).

———, *Ernest Jones, Chartism, and the Romance of Politics, 1819–1869* (Oxford, 2003).

Temperley, Howard, *Britain and America since Independence* (Basingstoke, 2002).

Thomas, Keith, *The Ends of Life: Roads to Fulfillment in Early Modern England* (Oxford, 2009).

Thompson, Dorothy, *The Chartists: Popular Politics in the Industrial Revolution* (New York, 1984).

———, *The Dignity of Chartism: Essays by Dorothy Thompson*, ed. Stephen Roberts (London, 2015).

———, *Outsiders: Class, Gender, and Nation* (London, 1993).

Thompson, E. P., *Customs in Common: Studies in Traditional Popular Culture* (London, 1991).

———, *The Making of the English Working Class* (London, 1991).

Thompson, Noel, *The Market and Its Critics: Socialist Political Economy in Nineteenth-Century Britain* (London, 1988).

———, *The People's Science: The Popular Political Economy of Exploitation and Crisis, 1816–1834* (Cambridge, 1984).

———, *The Real Rights of Man: Political Economies for the Working Class, 1775–1850* (London, 1998).

Thompson, Noel, and Chris Williams, eds., *Robert Owen and His Legacy* (Cardiff, 2011).

Thomson, David, *The Babeuf Plot: The Making of a Republican Legend* (London, 1947).

Wahrman, Dror, *Imagining the Middle Class: The Political Representation of Class in Britain, 1780–1840* (Cambridge, 1995).

Ward, J. T., *Chartism* (New York, 1973).

———, *The Factory Movement, 1830–1855* (London, 1962).

———, ed., *Popular Movements, 1830–1850* (Basingstoke, 1970).

Weisser, Henry, *British Working-Class Movements and Europe, 1815–1848* (Manchester, 1975).

West, Julius, *A History of the Chartist Movement* (New York, 1968).

Wiener, Joel, *The War of the Unstamped: The Movement to Repeal the British Newspaper Tax, 1830–1836* (Ithaca, N.Y., 1969).

Williams, Chris, ed., *A Companion to Nineteenth-Century Britain* (Oxford, 2007).

Wilson, Alexander, *The Chartist Movement in Scotland* (Manchester, 1970).

Womersley, David, *Gibbon and the "Watchmen of the Holy City": The Historian and His Reputation, 1776–1815* (Oxford, 2002).

Wordie, J. R., ed., *Agriculture and Politics in England, 1815–1939* (Basingstoke, 2000).

### Secondary Sources: Articles, Essays, Reviews

Agnes, Benoît, "A Chartist Singularity? Mobilizing to Promote Democratic Petitions in Britain and France, 1838–1848," *Labour History Review* 78 (2013): 51–66.

Airey, Glenn, "Feargus O'Connor, Ernest Jones, and *The Labourer*," in Allen and Owen, *Papers for the People*, 106–28.

Aprile, Sylvie, "Voices of Exile: French Newspapers in England," in Freitag, *Exiles*, 149–63.

Ariouat, Jacqueline, "Rethinking Partisanship in the Conduct of the Chartist Trials, 1839–1848," *Albion* 29 (1997): 596–621.

Armytage, W. H. G., "The Chartist Land Colonies, 1846–1848," *Agricultural History* 32 (1958): 87–96.

Ashcraft, Richard, "Liberal Political Theory and Working-Class Radicalism in Nineteenth-Century England," *Political Theory* 21 (1993): 249–72.

Ashton, Owen, "Orators and Oratory in the Chartist Movement, 1840–1848," in Ashton, Fyson, and Roberts, *Chartist Legacy*, 48–79.

Barfoot, C. C., and Theo D'haen, "Tropes of Revolution: Introduction," in Barfoot and D'haen, *Tropes of Revolution*, 7–9.

Barker, Paul, "Nowadays: The Chartist Model Town of O'Connorville," *New Statesman* 25 July 1997, 54.

Barrow, Logie, "The Homerton Social Democratic Club, 1881–1882," *History Workshop* 5 (1978): 188–99.

Beadle, Gordon, "George Orwell and the Victorian Radical Tradition," *Albion* 7 (1975): 287–99.

Behagg, Clive, "An Alliance with the Middle Class: The Birmingham Political Union and Early Chartism," in Epstein and Thompson, *Chartist Experience*, 59–86.

Belchem, John, "1848: Feargus O'Connor and the Collapse of the Mass Platform," in Epstein and Thompson, *Chartist Experience*, 269–310.

———, "Chartism and the Trades, 1848–1850," *English Historical Review* 98 (1983): 558–87.

———, "English Working-Class Radicalism and the Irish, 1815–1850," in Swift and Gilley, *Irish in the Victorian City*, 85–97.

———, "The Neglected 'Unstamped': The Manx Pauper Press of the 1840s," *Albion* 24 (1992): 605–16.

Bennett, Jennifer, "The London Democratic Association, 1837–1841: A Study in London Radicalism," in Epstein and Thompson, *Chartist Experience*, 87–119.

Bensimon, Fabrice, "The French Exiles and the British," in Freitag, *Exiles*, 88–102.

Bernstein, Samuel, "Babeuf and Babouvism" (parts 1 and 2), *Science and Society* 2 (1937–38): 29–57, 166–94.

———, "Buonarroti's Classic History of Babouvism," *Science and Society* 21 (1957): 346–52.

———, "From Utopianism to Marxism," *Science and Society* 14 (1949–50): 58–67.

———, "Some Recent Historical Literature: From the Enlightenment to the Commune," *Science and Society* 22 (1958): 330–55.

Bevir, Mark, "The British Social Democratic Federation, 1880–1885: From O'Brienism to Marxism," *International Review of Social History* 37 (1992): 207–29.

———, "Marxism and British Socialism," *The European Legacy: Toward New Paradigms* 1 (1996): 545–49.

———, "Republicanism, Socialism, and Democracy in Britain: The Origins of the Radical Left," *Journal of Social History* 34 (2000): 351–68.

Bevis, Matthew, "Volumes of Noise," *Victorian Literature and Culture* 31 (2003): 577–91.

Bolton, Sharon, and Knut Laaser, "Work, Employment, and Society through the Lens of Moral Economy," *Work, Employment, and Society* 27 (2013): 508–25.

"Book Notes," *Science and Society* 30 (1966): 124.

Bowan, Kate, and Paul Pickering, "'Songs for the Millions': Chartist Music and Popular Aural Tradition," *Labour History Review* 74 (2009): 44–63.

Brand, Carl, review of Theodore Rothstein, *From Chartism to Labourism: Historical Sketches of the English Working-Class Movement* (New York, 1929), in *American Historical Review* 35 (1930): 914–15.

Breton, Rob, "Violence and the Radical Imagination," *Victorian Periodicals Review* 44 (2011): 24–41.

Briggs, Asa, introduction to the 1965 edition of Cole, *Chartist Portraits*, vii–xv.

———, "The Language of 'Class' in Early Nineteenth-Century England," in Briggs and Saville, *Essays in Labour History*, 43–73.

———, "The Local Background of Chartism," in Briggs, *Chartist Studies*, 1–28.

———, "National Bearings," in Briggs, *Chartist Studies*, 288–303.

———, "Thomas Attwood and the Economic Background of the Birmingham Political Union," *Cambridge Historical Journal* 9 (1948): 190–216.

Brock, Peter, "Polish Democrats and English Radicals, 1832–1862: A Chapter in the History of Anglo-Polish Relations," *Journal of Modern History* 25 (1953): 139–56.

Bronstein, Jamie, "From the Land of Liberty to Land Monopoly: The United States in a Chartist Context," in Ashton, Fyson, and Roberts, *Chartist Legacy*, 147–70.

———, "The Homestead and the Garden Plot: Cultural Pressures on Land Reform in Nineteenth-Century Britain and the United States," *The European Legacy: Toward New Paradigms* 6 (2001): 159–75.

———, "Land Reform and Political Traditions in Nineteenth-Century Britain and the United States," in Bevir and Trentmann, *Critiques of Capital*, 26–48.

Brotherstone, Terry, and Liz Leicester, "Chartism, the Great Hunger, and the 'Hugest Question,'" in Brotherstone, Clark, and Whelan *These Fissured Isles*, 195–215.

Burchardt, Jeremy, "Land, Labour, and Politics: Parliament and Allotment Provision, 1830–1870," in Wordie, *Agriculture and Politics*, 98–127.

Canavan, Bernard, "The Edgeworths of Edgeworthstown: A Rediscovered Heritage," *History Workshop Journal* 43 (1997): 240–48.

Chase, Malcolm, "Building Identity, Building Circulation: Engraved Portraiture and the *Northern Star*," in Allen and Ashton, *Papers for the People*, 25–53.

———, "Chartism, 1838–1858: Responses in Two Teesside Towns," in Roberts, *People's Charter*, 152–73.

———, "Chartism and the Land: 'The Mighty People's Question,'" in Cragoe and Readman, *Land Question*, 57–73.

———, "Digital Chartists: Online Resources for the Study of Chartism," *Journal of Victorian*

*Culture* 14 (2009): 294–301.

———, "Exporting the Owenite Utopia: Thomas Powell and the Tropical Emigration Society," in Thompson and Williams, *Robert Owen*, 197–218.

———, "From Millennium to Anniversary: The Concept of Jubilee in Late Eighteenth- and Nineteenth-Century England," *Past and Present* 129 (1990): 132–47.

———, "'Labour's Candidates': Chartist Challenges at the Parliamentary Polls, 1839–1860," *Labour History Review* 74 (2009): 64–89.

———, "Out of Radicalism: The Mid-Victorian Freehold Land Movement," *English Historical Review* 106 (1991): 319–45.

———, "'Wholesome Object Lessons': The Chartist Land Plan in Retrospect," *English Historical Review* 118 (2003): 59–85.

Claeys, Gregory, "The Example of America as a Warning to England? The Transformation of America in British Radicalism and Socialism, 1790–1850," in Chase and Dyck, *Learning and Living*, 66–80.

———, "John Adolphus Etzler, Technological Utopianism, and British Socialism: The Tropical Emigration Society's Venezuelan Mission and Its Social Context, 1833–1848," *English Historical Review* 101 (1986): 351–75.

———, "Justice, Independence, and Industrial Democracy: The Development of John Stuart Mill's Views on Socialism," *Journal of Politics* 49 (1987): 122–47.

———, "Lewis Masquerier and the Later Development of American Owenism, 1835–1845," *Labor History* 29 (1988): 230–40.

———, "Mazzini, Kossuth, and British Radicalism, 1848–1854," *Journal of British Studies* 28 (1989): 225–61.

———, "The Triumph of Class-Conscious Reformism in British Radicalism, 1790–1860," *Historical Journal* 26 (1983): 969–85.

———, "A Utopian Tory Revolutionary at Cambridge: The Political Ideas and Schemes of James Bernard, 1834–1839," *Historical Journal* 25 (1982): 583–603.

———, "Whigs, Liberals, and Radicals," *Historical Journal* 33 (1990): 737–45.

———, review of Mark Francis, *Herbert Spencer and the Invention of Modern Life* (Ithaca, N.Y., 2007), in *International Review of Social History* 54 (2009): 292–94.

Clapham, J. H., review of Edouard Dolléans, *Le Chartisme, 1830–1845* (Paris, 1913), in *English Historical Review* 29 (1914): 389–90.

Clayton, Joseph, "Irish Catholics and the British Labour Movement," *Studies: An Irish Quarterly Review* 14 (1925): 284–94.

Collins, Henry, "The English Branches of the First International," in Briggs and Saville, *Essays in Labour History*, 242–75.

———, review of Samuel Bernstein, *The First International in America* (New York, 1962), in *Science and Society* 27 (1963): 338–41.

Connolly, Sean, "Queen Victoria in Ireland, August 1849: A Sidelight on the Development of Nationalism and Unionism," Irish History Resources, Queen's University Belfast, 2008.

Cragoe, Matthew, and Paul Readman, introduction to Cragoe and Readman, *Land Question*, 1–18.

Cumming, Mark, "Carlyle's Seagreen Robespierre and the Perilous Delights of Picturesque History," in Haydon and Doyle, *Robespierre*, 177–93.

D'Arcy, Feargus, "Irish Trade Unions before Congress," *History Ireland* 2 (1994): 25–30.

Dickinson, H. T., "The Debate on the Rights of Man in Britain: From the Levellers to the Chartists," *Valahian Journal of Historical Studies* 15 (2011): 11–41.

Dinwiddy, John, "English Radicals and the French Revolution, 1800–1850," in Furet and Onouf, *French Revolution*, 447–66.

D'Oronzio, Joseph, review of Plummer, *Bronterre*, in *American Historical Review* 78 (1973): 103–4.

Douglas, Wallace, review of *From Cobbett to the Chartists: Extracts from Contemporary Sources*, ed. Max Morris (London, 1948), in *Science and Society* 13 (1948–49): 90–92.

Eastwood, David, "Tories and Markets: Britain, 1800–1850," in Bevir and Trentmann, *Markets in Historical Context*, 70–89.

Eisenberg, Christiane, "Variations in Socialism: The Rise of a Political Labour Movement in Britain and Germany," *Diplomacy and Statecraft* 8 (1997): 124–38.

Epstein, James, "'America' in the Victorian Cultural Imagination," in Leventhal and Quinault, *Anglo-American Attitudes*, 107–23.

———, "The Constitutional Idiom: Radical Reasoning, Rhetoric, and Action in Early Nineteenth-Century England, *Journal of Social History* 23 (1990): 553–74.

Epstein, James, and David Karr, "Playing at Revolution: British 'Jacobin' Performance," *Journal of Modern History* 79 (2007): 495–530.

Escott, Margaret, "Robert Owen as Politician and Parliamentarian," in Thompson and Williams, *Robert Owen*, 129–54.

Faherty, Ray, "Bronterre O'Brien's Correspondence with Thomas Allsop: New Evidence on the Decline of a Chartist Leader," *Newsletter: European Labour and Working Class History* 8 (1975): 28–33.

Fay, C. R., review of Cole, *Chartist Portraits*, in *Economic Journal* 52 (1942): 66–69.

Feuer, Lewis, "The Influence of the American Communist Colonies on Engels and Marx," *Western Political Quarterly* 19 (1966): 456–74.

Field, James, "The Early Propagandist Movement in English Population Theory," *American*

*Economic Review* 1 (1911): 207–36.

Fine, Gary, "Constructing Difficult Reputations," in Fine, *Difficult Reputations*, 1–31.

Fine, Gary, and Jeanne Barker-Nunn, "Herman Melville and the Demise of Literary Reputation," in Fine, *Difficult Reputations*, 210–31.

Finn, Margot, "'A Vent Which Has Conveyed Our Principles': English Radical Patriotism in the Aftermath of 1848," *Journal of Modern History* 64 (1992): 637–59.

Fox, Paul, and H. Scott Gordon, "The Early Fabians: Economists and Reformers," *Canadian Journal of Economics and Political Science* 17 (1951): 307–19.

Fox, Ralph, "Marx, Engels, and Lenin on the British Workers' Movement," *Bulletin of the Marx Memorial Library* 118 (1986–87): 9–15.

Fraser, Derek, "The Agitation for Parliamentary Reform," in Ward, *Popular Movements*, 31–53.

Fraser, W. H., "The Chartist Press in Scotland," in Allen and Ashton, *Papers for the People*, 82–105.

———, "Owenite Socialism in Scotland," *Scottish Economic and Social History* 16 (1996): 60–91.

Freitag, Sabine, introduction to Freitag, *Exiles*, 1–16.

Fyson, Robert, "Bronterre O'Brien: A Chartist in the Isle of Man, 1844–1847," *Isle of Man Natural History and Antiquarian Society Proceedings* 10 (1998): 393–400.

———, "Late Chartism in the Potteries, 1848–1858," *Labour History Review* 74 (2009): 111–29.

Gadian, D. S., "Class Consciousness in Oldham and Other North West Industrial Towns, 1830–1850," *Historical Journal* 21 (1978): 161–72.

Gash, Norman, "After Waterloo: British Society and the Legacy of the Napoleonic Wars," *Transactions of the Royal Historical Society*, 5th ser., 28 (1978): 145–57.

Gonner, E. C. K., "The Early History of Chartism, 1836–1839," *English Historical Review* 4 (1889): 625–44.

———, review of W. J. Linton, *The English Republic*, ed. Kineton Parkes (London, 1891), in *English Historical Review* 7 (1892): 800–802.

Greene, J. P., "Introduction: Empire and Liberty," in Greene, *Exclusionary Empire*, 1–24.

Gurney, Peter, "Exclusive Dealing in the Chartist Movement," *Labour History Review* 74 (2009): 90–110.

———, "'Rejoicing in Potatoes': The Politics of Consumption in England during the 'Hungry Forties,'" *Past and Present* 203 (2009): 99–136.

Hall, Robert, "Chartism Remembered: William Aitken, Liberalism, and the Politics of Memory," in Roberts, *People's Charter*, 174–94.

———, "Creating a People's History: Political Identity and History in Chartism, 1832–1848," in Ashton, Fyson, and Roberts, *Chartist Legacy*, 232–54.

———, "Hearts and Minds: The Politics of Everyday Life and Chartism, 1832–1840," *Labour History Review* 74 (2009): 27–43.

Hall, Walter, review of Edouard Dolléans, *Le Chartisme, 1830–1845* (Paris, 1913), in *American Historical Review* 20 (1915): 406–7.

Harding, Neil, "Marx, Engels, and the *Manifesto*: Working Class, Party, and Proletariat," *Journal of Political Ideologies* 3 (1998): 13–44.

Harris, Ruth-Ann, "The Failure of Republicanism among Irish Migrants to Britain, 1800–1840," *Eire-Ireland* 21 (1986): 122–36.

Harrison, Brian, and Patricia Hollis, "Chartism, Liberalism, and the Life of Robert Lowery," *English Historical Review* 82 (1967): 503–35.

Harrison, J. F. C., "Chartism in Leeds," in Briggs, *Chartist Studies*, 65–98.

———, "Chartism in Leicester," in Briggs, *Chartist Studies*, 99–146.

Harrison, Royden, "British Labour and American Slavery," *Science and Society* 25 (1961): 291–319.

Haskell, Thomas, "Capitalism and the Origins of the Humanitarian Sensibility," *American Historical Review* 90 (1985): 339–61.

Haywood, Ian, "George W. M. Reynolds and 'The Trafalgar Square Revolution': Radicalism, the Carnivalesque, and Popular Culture in Mid-Victorian England," *Journal of Victorian Culture* 7 (2002): 23–59.

Heath, Andrew, "'The Producers on One Side and the Capitalists on the Other': Labor Reform, Slavery, and the Career of a Transatlantic Radical," *American Nineteenth Century History* 13 (2012): 199–227.

Hendrix, Richard, "Popular Humor and the *Black Dwarf*," *Journal of British Studies* 16 (1976): 108–28.

Hollander, Samuel, "Marx and Engels on Constitutional Reform versus Revolution," *Theoria* 57 (2010): 51–91.

Hollis, Patricia, review of Plummer, *Bronterre*, in *Victorian Studies* 16 (1972): 237–40.

Home, Robert, "Peri-Urban Informal Housing Development in Victorian England: The Contribution of Freehold Land Societies," *Planning Perspectives* 25 (2010): 365–73.

Hooker, John, review of Élie Halévy, *A History of the English People, 1841–1852* (New York, 1948), in *Catholic Historical Review* 35 (1949): 191–92.

Hoselitz, Bert, review of A. G. Garrone, *Buonarroti e Babeuf* (Turin, 1948) and *Buonarroti e i rivoluzionari dell 'Ottocento* (Milan, 1951), in *Journal of Modern History* 26 (1954): 188–90.

Howe, Anthony, "The 'Manchester School' and the Landlords: The Failure of Land Reform in Early Victorian Britain," in Cragoe and Readman, *Land Question*, 74–91.

Huggins, Michael, "Democracy or Nationalism? The Problems of the Chartist Press in Ireland," in Allen and Ashton, *Papers for the People*, 129–45.

Hugman, Joan, "'A Small Drop of Ink': Tyneside Chartism and the *Northern Liberator*," in Ashton, Fyson, and Roberts, *Chartist Legacy*, 24–47.

Humpherys, Anne, "G. W. M. Reynolds: Popular Literature and Popular Politics," *Victorian Periodicals Review* 16 (1983): 79–89.

Huston, Reeve, "Multiple Crossings: Thomas Ainge Devyr and Transatlantic Land Reform," in Summerhill and Scott, *Transatlantic Rebels*, 137–66.

Huzzey, Richard, "British Liberties, American Emancipation, and the Democracy of Race," in Dzelzainis and Livesey, *American Experiment*, 121–34.

Innes, Joanna, Mark Philp, and Robert Saunders, "The Rise of Democratic Discourse in the Reform Era: Britain in the 1830s and 1840s," in Innes and Philp, *Re-Imagining Democracy*, 114–28.

Isabella, Maurizio, "Italian Exiles and British Politics before and after 1848," in Freitag, *Exiles*, 59–87.

Katznelson, Ira, "Working-Class Formation and the State: Nineteenth-Century England in American Perspective," in Englander, *Britain and America*, 171–95.

Kemnitz, Thomas, "The Chartist Convention of 1839," *Albion* 10 (1978): 152–70.

———, "Chartist Newspaper Editors," *Victorian Periodicals Newsletter* 5 (1972): 1–11.

———, "Recent Work on the Chartist Movement," *Newsletter: European Labour and Working-Class History* 2 (1972): 25–27.

Kinealy, Christine, "Economy and Society in Ireland," in Williams, *Nineteenth-Century Britain*, 489–503.

———, "Politics in Ireland," in Williams, *Nineteenth-Century Britain*, 473–88.

Kinzer, Bruce, "J. S. Mill and Irish Land: A Reassessment," *Historical Journal* 27 (1984): 111–27.

Kosminski, E. A., "Russian Work on English Economic History," *Economic History Review* 1 (1928): 208–33.

Large, David, "William Lovett," in Hollis, *Pressure from Without*, 105–30.

Laski, H. J., "Introduction to the *Communist Manifesto*," *Social Scientist* 27 (1999): 49–111.

Lause, Mark, "The American Radicals and Organized Marxism: The Initial Experience, 1869–1874," *Labor History* 33 (1992): 55–80.

Lawn, Martin, review of Alec Ellis, *Educating Our Masters: Influences on the Growth of Literacy in Victorian Working Class Children* (Brookfield, Vt., 1985), in *History of Education Quarterly* 26 (1986): 614–17.

Lebow, R. N., "J. S. Mill and the Irish Land Question," in Lebow, *Mill on Ireland*, 3–22.

Lewis, Gwynne, "Robespierre through the Chartist Looking-Glass," in Haydon and Doyle, *Robespierre*, 194–211.

Linebaugh, Peter, "Commonists of the World Unite!" *Radical History Review* 56 (1993): 59–67.

Lloyd, David, "The Subaltern in Motion: Subalternity, the Popular, and Irish Working-Class History," *Postcolonial Studies* 8 (2005): 421–37.

Lloyd, David, and Paul Thomas, "Culture and Society or 'Culture and the State'?" *Social Text* 30 (1992): 27–56.

Loughlin, James, "Allegiance and Illusion: Queen Victoria's Irish Visit of 1849," *History* 87 (2002): 491–513.

Lowe, William, "The Chartists and the Irish Confederates: Lancashire, 1848," *Irish Historical Studies* 24 (1984): 172–96.

MacAskill, Joy, "The Chartist Land Plan," in Briggs, *Chartist Studies*, 304–41.

Macintyre, Angus, review of A. M. Hadfield, *The Chartist Land Company* (Newton Abbot, 1970), in *Economic History Review* 24 (1971): 301–2.

Maehl, W. H., "Augustus Hardin Beaumont: Anglo-American Radical (1798–1838)," *International Review of Social History* 14 (1969): 237–50.

———, "Chartist Disturbances in Northeastern England, 1839," *International Review of Social History* 8 (1963): 389–414.

———, introduction to Gammage, *Reminiscences of a Chartist*, 7–19.

———, review of Plummer, *Bronterre*, in *Journal of Modern History* 44 (1972): 596–98.

Manuel, Frank, "Toward a Psychological History of Utopias," *Daedalus* 94 (1965): 293–322.

Martin, David, "The Agricultural Interest and Its Critics, 1840–1914," in Wordie, *Agriculture and Politics*, 128–48.

———, "Land Reform," in Hollis, *Pressure from Without*, 131–58.

Mastellone, Salvo, "Mazzini's International League in the Light of the London Democratic Manifestos, 1837–1850," *Studia Politica* 3 (2006): 525–32.

Mather, F. C., review of F. F. Rosenblatt, *The Chartist Movement in Its Social and Political Aspects* (London, 1967), in *Economic History Review* 22 (1969): 147–48.

———, review of *An Anthology of Chartist Literature*, ed. Yuri Kovalev (London, 1957), in *Victorian Studies* 2 (1958): 178–80.

Maw, Ben, "Bronterre O'Brien's Class Analysis: The Formative Phase, 1832–1836," *History of Political Thought* 28 (2007): 253–89.

———, "The Democratic Anti-Capitalism of Bronterre O'Brien," *Journal of Political Ideologies* 13 (2008): 201–26.

———, "Robert Owen's Unintended Legacy: Class Conflict," in Thompson and Williams, *Robert Owen*, 155–73.

Mayhall, Laura, review of Barrow and Bullock, *Democratic Ideas*, in *Social History* 23 (1998): 119–22.

McCalman, Iain, "Anti-Slavery and Ultra-Radicalism in Early Nineteenth-Century England: The

Case of Robert Wedderburn," *Slavery and Abolition* 7 (1986): 99–117.

———, "'Erin go Bragh': The Irish in British Popular Radicalism, 1790–1840," in MacDonagh and Mandle, *Irish-Australian Studies*, 168–84.

McCalman, Janet, "Respectability and Working-Class Politics in Late Victorian London," *Historical Studies* 19 (1980): 108–24.

McDonald, Robert, "Thomas Jefferson's Changing Reputation as Author of the Declaration of Independence: The First Fifty Years," *Journal of the Early Republic* 19 (1999): 169–95.

McLaren, Angus, "Contraception and the Working Classes: The Social Ideology of the English Birth Control Movement in Its Early Years," *Comparative Studies in Society and History* 18 (1976): 236–51.

Medearis, John, "Labor, Democracy, Utility, and Mill's Critique of Private Property," *American Journal of Political Science* 49 (2005): 135–49.

Messner, Andrew, "Land, Leadership, Culture, and Emigration: Some Problems in Chartist Historiography," *Historical Journal* 42 (1999): 1093–109.

Miliband, Ralph, "The Politics of Robert Owen," *Journal of the History of Ideas* 15 (1954): 233–45.

Mitchell, Martin, "The Catholic Irish and Chartism in the West of Scotland," in Brotherstone, Clark, and Whelan, *These Fissured Isles*, 178–94.

Morgan, Kenneth, review of Kristine O'Connor, *Joan Maynard: Passionate Socialist* (London, 2003), in *English Historical Review* 119 (2004): 576–77.

Morgan, Simon, "America, Protectionism, and Democracy in British Free Trade Debates, 1815–1861," in Dzelzainis and Livesey, *American Experiment*, 93–106.

Morris, Max, "Chartism and the British Working-Class Movement," *Science and Society* 12 (1948): 400–417.

Morton, Desmond, review of H. S. Foxwell, *Bibliography of the English Socialist School* (London, 1976), in *Victorian Periodicals Newsletter* 11 (1978): 139.

Moss, Bernard, "Republican Socialism and the Making of the Working Class in Britain, France, and the United States," *Comparative Studies in Society and History* 35 (1993): 390–413.

Mulholland, Marc, "'Its Patrimony, Its Unique Wealth!' Labour-Power, Working-Class Consciousness, and Crisis," *Critique: Journal of Socialist Theory* 38 (2010): 375–417.

Murphy, Paul, "'Imagination Flaps Its Sportive Wings': Views of Fiction in British Working-Class Periodicals, 1816–1858," *Victorian Studies* 32 (1989): 339–64.

Murray, Patrick, "Obsessive Historian: Eamon de Valera and the Policing of His Reputation," *Proceedings of the Royal Irish Academy* 101, section C (2001): 37–65.

Newens, Stan, "Thomas Edward Bowkett: Nineteenth-Century Pioneer of the Working-Class Movement in East London," *History Workshop* 9 (1980): 143–48.

Nicholls, David, "The English Middle Class and the Ideological Significance of Radicalism, 1760–1886," *Journal of British Studies* 24 (1985): 415–33.

———, review of Dudley Miles, *Francis Place, 1771–1854* (New York, 1988), in *Victorian Studies* 33 (1989): 183–84.

Nowlan, K. B., "O'Connell and Irish Nationalism," in Nowlan and O'Connell, *Daniel O'Connell*, 9–18.

Nydahl, Joel, introduction to *The Collected Works of John Adolphus Etzler, 1833–1844* (Delmar, N.Y., 1977), vii–xxxi.

O'Ceallaigh, Tadhg, review of *Leaders and Workers: Irish Leaders and Thinkers of the Labour Movement*, ed. John Boyle (Cork, 1968), in *Studia Hibernica* 7 (1969): 220–21.

O'Higgins, Rachel, "The Irish Influence in the Chartist Movement," *Past and Present* 20 (1960): 83–96.

Onuf, P. S., "Federalism, Democracy, and Liberty in the New American Nation," in Greene, *Exclusionary Empire*, 132–59.

Parry, Jonathan, "The Impact of Napoleon III on British Politics, 1851–1880," *Transactions of the Royal Historical Society*, 6th ser., 11 (2001): 147–75.

Parsinnen, T. M., "Association, Convention, and Anti-Parliament in British Radical Politics, 1771–1848," *English Historical Review* 88 (1973): 504–33.

———, "Thomas Spence and the Origins of English Land Nationalization," *Journal of the History of Ideas* 34 (1973): 135–41.

Pasley, Jeffrey, "Politics and the Misadventures of Thomas Jefferson's Modern Reputation: A Review Essay," *Journal of Southern History* 72 (2006): 871–908.

Perkin, Harold, "Land Reform and Class Conflict in Victorian Britain," in Butt and Clarke, *Victorians and Social Protest*, 177–217.

Pickering, Paul, "'And Your Petitioners, Etc.': Chartist Petitioning in Popular Politics, 1838–1848," *English Historical Review* 116 (2001): 368–88.

———, "Betrayal and Exile: A Forgotten Chartist Experience," in Davis and Pickering, *Unrespectable Radicals? Popular Politics in the Age of Reform*, 201–17.

———, "Chartism and the 'Trade of Agitation' in Early Victorian Britain," in Roberts, *People's Charter*, 19–34.

———, "Class without Words: Symbolic Communication in the Chartist Movement," *Past and Present* 112 (1986): 144–62.

———, "'The Hearts of the Millions': Chartism and Popular Monarchism in the 1840s," *History* 88 (2003): 227–48.

Pilbeam, Pamela, "The Insurrectionary Tradition in France, 1835–1848," *Modern and Contemporary France* 1 (1993): 253–64.

Pinkney, David, "The Crowd in the French Revolution of 1830," *American Historical Review* 70 (1964): 1–17.

Plotz, John, "Crowd Power: Chartism, Carlyle, and the Victorian Public Sphere," *Representations* 70 (2000): 87–114.

Plummer, Alfred, "The Place of Bronterre O'Brien in the Working-Class Movement," *Economic History Review* 2 (1929): 61–80.

Poole, Robert, "French Revolution or Peasants' Revolt? Petitioners and Rebels in England from the Blanketeers to the Chartists," *Labour History Review* 74 (2009): 6–26.

Porritt, Edward, review of "Columbia Studies" of 1916, in *American Historical Review* 22 (1917): 649–52.

Prothero, Iorwerth, "Chartism in London," *Past and Present* 44 (1969): 76–105.

———, "Chartists and Political Refugees," in Freitag, *Exiles*, 209–33.

———, "William Benbow and the Concept of the 'General Strike,'" *Past and Present* 63 (1974): 134–71.

"A Radical in His Time," *Times Literary Supplement*, 20 Aug. 1971 (a review of Plummer's *Bronterre*), 992.

Read, Donald, "Chartism in Manchester," in Briggs, *Chartist Studies*, 29–64.

Reaney, Bernard, "Irish Chartists in Britain and Ireland: Rescuing the Rank and File," *Saothar* 10 (1984): 94–103.

Reeves, Clyde, "Henry George's Speaking in the Land Reform Movements: The West Coast 'Training Phase,'" *American Journal of Economics and Sociology* 24 (1965): 51–68.

Reiss, Ansgar, "Home Alone? Reflections on Political Exiles Returning to Their Native Countries," in Freitag, *Exiles*, 297–318.

Roberts, Matthew, "'The Feast of the Gridiron Is at Hand': Chartism, Cobbett, and Currency," in Grande and Stevenson, *Cobbett, Romanticism, and the Enlightenment*, 107–21.

Roberts, Stephen, "Thomas Cooper in Leicester, 1840–1843," in Roberts, *People's Charter*, 133–51.

Rogers, Nicholas, "Class and Popular Education in Nineteenth-Century Britain," *History of Education Quarterly* 19 (1979): 477–84.

Rose, M. E., "The Anti-Poor Law Agitation," in Ward, *Popular Movements*, 78–94.

Rose, R. B., "Babeuf, Dictatorship, and Democracy," *Historical Studies* 15 (1972): 223–36.

Royle, Edward, "The *Cause of the People*, the People's Charter Union, and 'Moral Force' Chartism in 1848," in Allen and Ashton, *Papers for the People*, 146–67.

———, "Chartists and Owenites: Many Parts but One Body," *Labour History Review* 65 (2000): 2–21.

Saunders, Robert, "Chartism from Above: British Elites and the Interpretation of Chartism,"

*Historical Research* 81 (2008): 463–84.

———, "'Let America Be the Test': Democracy and Reform in Britain, 1832–1867," in Dzelzainis and Livesey, *American Experiment*, 79–91.

Saville, John, introduction to the 1969 edition of Gammage, *Chartist Movement*, 5–66.

———, introduction to the 1983 edition of Rothstein, *From Chartism to Labourism*, v–xxvi.

Shepperson, Wilbur, "Some Plans for British Immigration to Texas in 1849 and 1850," *Southwestern Historical Quarterly* 63 (1960): 439–49.

Simkhovitch, V. G., "Marxism versus Socialism," *Political Science Quarterly* 24 (1909): 641–66.

Smith, Adam, "Victorian Radicalism and the Idea of America: *Reynolds's Newspaper*, 1850–1900," in Dzelzainis and Livesey, *American Experiment*, 135–46.

Soffer, R. N., "Attitudes and Allegiances in the Unskilled North, 1830–1850," *International Review of Social History* 10 (1965): 429–54.

Stack, David, "The Death of John Stuart Mill," *Historical Journal* 54 (2011): 167–90.

Stedman Jones, Gareth, "The Language of Chartism," in Epstein and Thompson, *Chartist Experience*, 3–58.

———, "Some Notes on Karl Marx and the English Labour Movement," *History Workshop* 18 (1984): 124–37.

Steele, E. D., "J. S. Mill and the Irish Question: The Principle of Political Economy, 1848–1865," *Historical Journal* 13 (1970): 216–36.

Stern, Mira, review of Henry Pelling, *The Origins of the Labour Party, 1880–1900* (New York, 1954), in *Science and Society* 19 (1955): 79–80.

Sweezy, Paul, "Origins of Present-Day Socialism," *Science and Society* 12 (1948): 65–81.

Swift, Roger, "The Historiography of the Irish in Nineteenth-Century Britain," in O'Sullivan, *Irish in the New Communities*, 52–81.

Sykes, R. A., "Some Aspects of Working-Class Consciousness in Oldham, 1830–1842," *Historical Journal* 23 (1980): 167–79.

Taylor, Antony, "Commemoration, Memorialization, and Social Memory in Post-Chartist Radicalism: The 1885 Halifax Chartist Reunion in Context," in Ashton, Fyson, and Roberts, *Chartist Legacy*, 255–85.

Taylor, Miles, "O'Brien, James [Bronterre O'Brien]," *Oxford Dictionary of National Biography* (Oxford, 2004), online edition, May 2009.

Thompson, Dorothy, "The Chartists in 1848," in Brotherstone, Clark, and Whelan, *These Fissured Isles*, 165–76.

———, "Ireland and the Irish in English Radicalism before 1850," in Epstein and Thompson, *Chartist Experience*, 120–51.

Thompson, E. P., "The Moral Economy of the English Crowd in the Eighteenth Century," *Past and Present* 50 (1971): 76–136.

———, introduction to the 1968 edition of Peel, *The Risings of the Luddites, Chartists, and Plug-Drawers*, vii–xv.

Thompson, Paul, "Fabian Socialism," *Past and Present* 25 (1963): 86–89.

Tönnesson, K. D., "The Babouvists: From Utopian to Practical Socialism," *Past and Present* 22 (1962): 60–76.

Treble, J. H., "O'Connor, O'Connell, and the Attitudes of Irish Immigrants towards Chartism in the North of England, 1838–1848," in Butt and Clarke, *Victorians and Social Protest*, 33–70.

Turner, Michael J., "Chartism, Bronterre O'Brien, and the 'Luminous Political Example of America,'" *History* 97 (2012): 43–69.

———, "Ireland and Irishness in the Political Thought of Bronterre O'Brien," *Irish Historical Studies* 39 (2014): 40–57.

———, "Revolutionary Connection: Maximilian Robespierre and Bronterre O'Brien," *The Historian* 75 (2013): 237–61.

Vogel, Ursula, "The Land Question: A Liberal Theory of Communal Property," *History Workshop* 27 (1989): 106–35.

Wallas, Graham, "O'Brien, James [Bronterre]," *Dictionary of National Biography*, vol. 41, ed. Sidney Lee (London, 1895): 315–16.

Weatherly, U. G., "Babeuf's Place in the History of Socialism," *Publications of the American Economic Association*, 3rd ser., 8 (1907): 113–24.

Weisser, Henry, "Chartism in 1848: Reflections on a Non-Revolution," *Albion* 13 (1981): 12–26.

———, "Chartist Internationalism, 1845–1848," *Historical Journal* 14 (1971): 49–66.

———, review of Ward, *Chartism*, in *American Historical Review* 80 (1975): 643–44.

Whatley, Christopher, "'It Is Said That Burns Was a Radical': Contest, Concession, and the Political Legacy of Robert Burns, c.1796–1859," *Journal of British Studies* 50 (2011): 639–66.

Whatmore, Richard, "The Politics of Political Economy in France from Rousseau to Constant," in Bevir and Trentmann, *Markets in Historical Context*, 46–69.

Whitehead, Andrew, "Dan Chatterton and His 'Atheistic Communistic Scorcher,'" *History Workshop* 25 (1988): 83–99.

———, "The *New World* and the O'Brienite Colony in Kansas," *Bulletin of the Society for the Study of Labour History* 53 (1988): 40–43.

Widdicombe, Richard, "Early Histories of Utopian Thought," *Utopian Studies* 3 (1992): 1–38.

Wiener, Joel, "The Press and the Working Class, 1815–1840," *Victorian Periodicals Newsletter* 4 (1971): 1–4.

———, review of Paul Murphy, *Towards a Working-Class Canon*, in *Albion* 27 (1995): 689–90.

Williamson, Philip, "Baldwin's Reputation: Politics and History, 1937–1967," *Historical Journal*

47 (2004): 127–68.

Wilson, Alexander, "Chartism," in Ward, *Popular Movements*, 116–34.

———, "Chartism in Glasgow," in Briggs, *Chartist Studies*, 249–87.

———, "The Suffrage Movement," in Hollis, *Pressure from Without*, 80–104.

Worrall, David, "Kinship, Generation, and Community: The Transmission of Political Ideology in Radical Plebeian Print Culture," *Studies in Romanticism* 43 (2004): 283–95.

Yelland, Cris, "Speech and Writing in the *Northern Star*," *Labour History Review* 65 (2000): 22–40.

Yeo, Eileen, "Christianity in Chartist Struggle, 1838–1842," *Past and Present* 91 (1981): 109–39.

———, "Some Practices and Problems of Chartist Democracy," in Epstein and Thompson, *Chartist Experience*, 345–80.

Zastoupil, Lynn, "Moral Government: J. S. Mill on Ireland," *Historical Journal* 26 (1983): 707–17.

## Unpublished Addresses, Theses, and Conference Papers

Granath, Andrew, "The Irish in Mid Nineteenth-Century Lancashire, 1830–1881," MA thesis, University of Lancaster, 1975.

Iverson, Robert, "Babouvism and James Bronterre O'Brien: A Study of the Role of Continental Radicalism in the Development of British Socialism," MA thesis, State University of Iowa, 1949.

Jones, T.C., "French Republican Exiles in Britain, 1848–1870," PhD thesis, University of Cambridge, 2010.

Keane, Timothy, "'Ireland's Wrongs as England's Grievance': Representations of Ireland in English Radical Discourse, 1824–1850," PhD thesis, National University of Ireland, Galway, 2010.

Koseki, Takashi, "Chartism and Irish Nationalism, 1839–1848: Bronterre O'Brien, the London Irish, and Attempts at a Chartist-Irish Alliance," MPhil thesis, University of Birmingham, 1988.

Paz, Denis, "Chartist Lecturers and the Culture of Victorian Lecturing," conference paper, Consortium on the Revolutionary Era, Huntsville, Ala., 2008.

Schafer, D. F., "James Bronterre O'Brien: A Working-Class Radical, 1831–1842," MA thesis, University of Oklahoma, 1967.

Stack, David, "A Question of Character: The Reputation of Bronterre O'Brien in the Chartist Movement," paper delivered at Chartism Day, a conference at the University of Sheffield, 16 June 2007, as reported in the *Society for the Study of Labour History Newsletter*, 6 (2007).

Thompson, Dorothy, "The Chartists and Their Legacy," address to the Bristol Radical History Group, 10 April 2010, www.bhr.org.uk/site/events/the-chartists-and-their-legacy.

# Index

## P



## R



## S